Memori
Hundred and

An Indian (

This book narrates the experiences and impression collected by the author during eight years—101 moons—of residence, meetings and travels in India, from 1975 to 1983.

While dwelling on the mystical spell that India has always cast and on the philosophical treasures it enshrines, the book portrays from personal impressions several famous or notable figures, who played significant roles in the country's evolution and influenced the world of today. Indira Gandhi, Rajiv Gandhi, HH The Dalai Lama, Rukmini Devi, Svetoslav Roerich, Dr Karan Singh, Morarji Desai, Atal B. Vajpayee, Satyajit Ray, the Maharana of Udaipur, Gayatri Devi of Jaipur and many others are evoked as well as many historical personalities—sages, kings and queens, saints, warriors, poets and artists—from more ancient times.

The outcome of these recollections is a very personal historic and mythological travelogue harking back to the tradition of the literary journals of previous centuries, when remote lands were being discovered in the course of slow journeys seasoned with observations, conversations, meditations and vivid descriptions, which are altogether the essence of adventure.

By the same author

From India to Infinity

Memories of a Hundred and One Moons

An Indian Odyssey

Côme Carpentier de Gourdon

HAR-ANAND
PUBLICATIONS PVT LTD

To
my parents

Published by Ashok Gosain and Ashish Gosain for:
HAR-ANAND PUBLICATIONS PVT LTD
E-49/3, Okhla Industrial Area, Phase-II, New Delhi-110020
Tel: 41603490 Fax: 011-41708607
E-mail: info@haranandbooks.com/haranand@rediffmail.com
Shop online at: www.haranandbooks.com

Printed in India at Vinayak Offset

Foreword

At the very outset, Côme Carpentier defines his odyssey as "a pilgrimage to the stream and sources of India's perennial soul" as he and his father are "lifted from the mundane to the symbolic." As they converse with leading political, intellectual and media personalities of India in the last quarter of the preceding century, they descend deep into the ocean of the past for that immensity is the foundation of India's present and alone can lead her to supernal heights of what can be achieved today.

As India of the intellect stands in doubt of its roots of thoughts, western mathematicians and quantum physicists speak of the uncanny convergence of world-views emerging from quantum physics with those of Indian sages. Dr G G Joseph of Princeton University speaks of the mathematical correspondence and the doctrine of *shunyata* in his *Non-European Root of Mathematics* (2011). Wholly new realms of abstraction are being sought in the Vedic and Buddhist tradition. Like his iconic predecessors Fritjof Capra, Kaplan, Plofker, Rotman, Dr Côme Carpentier brings to us the message that philosophical antecedents in India's millennial intellectual history have to be seeding of our todays so that we may rise to our highest potential.

Crossing Central Asian lands, the multi-cultural Gandhara, a fleeting passage through Pakistan, glancing at Greek historians, watching Taxila in ruins, father and son come to the cradle of the *Vedas*. This recount overflows with landmarks and ideas connecting centuries. Unexpected memories as that of Guru Nanakdev ji in a Sufi mausoleum in Iraq grip the reader by the evocative expression of the author. The metaphysics of time and the awareness of impermanence in the riotous colours and sounds of India create a pensive ambience in the Indian mind. Accustomed to the bustling chaos of forms, colours, humans, structures and happenings, fail to discern the poetry of our surroundings. Côme lends them a creative dynamism and restores miraculous sensitivity to our metaphysically rooted civilisation.

The coming international yoga day reminds him of Air Marshall Suren Goyal teaching yoga to Soviet pilots flying supersonic jets. His critical observations about "the hypocrisy that seems inherent to 'spiritually semitic' societies in which killing is in principle forbidden though they have arguably caused more bloodshed than others ..." raises issues of contemporary concern. Reading through this book we become acutely aware of the problems of industrial devastation and political extermination. Côme unfolds the galaxy of India's fields of action as **kurukshetras** as well as her universes of transcendence or **dharmakshetras**, like lord Krishna on the battlefield of life and metalife.

The Indo-European dimension, wherein India and European nations have a shared heritage, seeps through the subtle observations of Carpentier. India, as a cradle of mankind, has been the engaging pursuit of the western minds struck by the affinity of their languages with those of Indo-Iranian Asia. The French "dieu" for god, cognate to Samskrit *deva,* is just an orthographic variation. The Greek Latin and other alphabet of Europe are derived from the Phoenician script, which did not have letters for the sounds *ch, j, y, v, sh* that were a must for Indo-European words. The *v* of *deva* became *u* in *Dieu.* The two words, as so many others are transparently identical but have drifted apart due to alphabetic deficiency. Come reminds us that whatever our ethnic, political or geographical differences today, once upon a time we spoke in words that were common when we shared the same languages and beliefs.

The circumflex accent in Côme indicates the dropping of the 's' of cosmos or Greek *kosmos,* which means 'order, world, universe' as well as 'ornament, decorate' whence comes the word 'cosmetic'. His mindscape is a superb display of the universal, cross-cultural cosmetics. I met him when he was fifteen years old and I was nearing fifty. We had the common denominative number 5, which represents the five Buddhas in esoteric Buddhism where the transient and transcendent merge.

Along with his great sage-like father, Côme Carpentier was enthralled by the "India of the Imagination", which is everywhere and yet exists nowhere. The present memoirs record their quest for the frontiers that are everywhere and also in ourselves. To the author India is not just a place, it is also a state of being. He inhabits Homer's world as well as Kalidasa's and gives a voice to Indian inmost feelings that are being lost in the minimalistic trivia imported under the shroud of modernism or post-modernism. This book is a homecoming for Indians, the home being everywhere.

Underlying the hushed tones of mysticism, the Indo-European identity is the unbreakable bond between Côme and India. His words transport us to a faraway cosmology of insights and a vanished world is heaved into view. The eternal Veda is in the heart of awakened man. As the writer uncurtains history, his words leap into life and the winds of the world are our breath. Hierarchical structures, self-enslavement in the denigration of spiritual values, our economic culture and secular totalitarianism melt away in the introspective narrations. They are the redeeming, unspoken.

Like Socrates often found standing and entranced by his students, with orphic mysteries clinging to him to save his critical powers from skeptical sterility, the following pages bequeath to us the fragile balance of intellect and vision. As Socrates offered his affirmative spiritual dimension, he found attentive company in the agora. Côme's quest is for disciplines of illumination that are no longer in speaking terms with the critical intellect. The public realm seeks to muster the transcendent energy, which can balance intellect and vision to meet the spiritual need that has arisen beyond ersatz religion, rituals of totalitarian cults and celebrations of collective power. Carpentier's grand narrative of conversations with Indians of every hue and hierarchy brings to my mind the thought that we will not find what we refuse to seek.

The deeper roots of culture lie in meditation or contemplation whence personality change may spring forth. A forest, a lonely shore, a natural locale or the inner silence are needed for feeling a space free of the burden of overdevelopment. We have to plunge deep into the ocean of consciousness and swim back to the surface with jewels that can be found when we look within. The chapters written by Côme bring us our hared humanity. The stream of consciousness that runs through our minds irrigates other minds as well. Much unites us, much is universal. It is warm tide of likeness flowing within all. The silence that we feel beyond the words in this book gives meaning to everything. He reminds us of Plotinus the philosopher when he said, "There is always a radiance in the soul of man, untroubled, like the light in a lantern in a wild turmoil of wind and tempest."

This delightful book of dialogue with a large number of eminent representatives of India in the last century is a navigational aid to a future. Birds sense infra-sonic waves in their long journeys across the skies; so has modern man to sense his destiny across the earthquakes, depleted water resources, polluted environment from the subtle sub-sensory vibrations of nature's anger.

The overall impact of the following writing calls for a shift in cultural values from independence to interdependences between different nations, between humans and nature, between the secular and the sacred.

Côme Carpentier's dreamlike presentation is where the contemporary and classical knowledge lead us, to a future "becoming". This book is a must read for Indians for it brings home our roots and inspires us to unveil new horizons in keeping with our qualitative headstart provided by a brilliant civilization some 8,000 years ago. To me it has been a "bon voyage" across minds, intellect and time gone for time to come.

Professor Lokesh Chandra
Chairman, Indian Council for Cultural Relations

Introduction

Sri bhagavan uvaca
Bahuni me vyatitani janmani tava carjuna
Tary aham veda sarvani na tvam vettha parantapa

– Bhagavad Gita IV-5

(The Lord said:
Many many births both you and I have passed Arjuna.
I can remember them all but you cannot, O victorious One.)

A travel book is a gallery of landscapes, portraits and still lifes. The writer's eye, as a painter's gaze, is the co-creator of his work. Likewise, memories are impressions of things seen, heard, smelt, thought and then transformed by the mind.

This book does not claim or try to give a precise account of eight years spent roaming across India more than three decades ago; rather, it seeks to evoke the experiences lived in the course of that odyssey across places and times and around personalities that sometimes played important parts in shaping the world then and now.

When still a child I fell under the spell that India has cast along the centuries for people from the West and East. The lure of adventure and discovery and the promise of spiritual blessings and enlightenment compose an irresistible brew for those endowed with imagination and prone to mystical quests. Various illustrious historical figures inspired my teenager's yearning for the remote wonders of Hindustan. Alexander of Macedonia is the first European definitely recorded to have reached the land of Maharajas and yogis and formed personal bonds with both kings and sages. Many followed him Eastwards and closer to us the 18th century administrator and diplomat Joseph Dupleix is perhaps the best known of those Frenchmen, who grew so familiar with India that they became in some way part of it, at least in the eyes of their countrymen.

The figure of Dupleix as a "Firangi Nawab" holding court on the pillared verandah of a palatial bungalow nestled in a tropical jungle on the shore of the Bay of Bengal captivates the French even today. Less famous expatriates such as the eccentric General Raymond who practiced Hinduism and Islam alternatively and was known for that reason as "Moussa Ram" by the locals came to my notice, together with Benoit de Boigne, the talented military commander, adventurer and entrepreneur. For a teenager raised in a family that had both a military tradition and an intellectual heritage, those scholarly warriors held a natural attraction but as I got older, I discovered the peaceful soldiers of the spirit who went to study and discover the invisible treasures of the soul in preference to the glittering gems of the physical world and I realised like the Macedonian that it is better if not easier to follow Diogenes than to emulate Alexander and safer to rise above the vagaries of unpredictable fate than to try to master it by seeking material gams.

I could say that I met members of many of the innumerable classes, communities and linguistic groups found in this vast subcontinent but I must also admit that what is featured in the following chapters is inevitably selective, given the long period it covers and the vast number of locations we visited and people we came across in the course of our periplum.

Making this choice was difficult and I had to omit many figures, humble and privileged, famous and unknown from this portrait gallery. To quite a few of them I remain lastingly grateful for their assistance, advice, wisdom and support. Some readers will say that my recollections are tainted by the rosy hue of wide eyed and earnest adolescence as I have attempted not to superimpose too many judgments and hindsights from the present on initial impressions gathered at the time and the ideals that helped form them. I have however often inserted comments to reflect the historical context and its subsequent evolution as it appears to me in retrospect but I have tried not to tamper with the freshness of discovery, which inevitably reflects the glow of illusions undimmed by the experience and prejudices acquired in later years.

Readers might feel that I have not given much attention to the harsh and often pathetic conditions that affect so many in India and that are so frequently and luridly portrayed in books, magazines, films and other media. Depicting once more the destitution and misfortune of vast numbers of people in this land was neither the goal of our travels nor the intent of this book and I have only in passing mentioned painful scenes that strike anyone who passes through the crowded, poetic, joyous and yet often wretched or tragic Indian landscape. When doing so, I have tried to translate the philosophical reflections that such visions triggered in me, above and beyond the first-degree feelings of pity or revulsion. Circumstances often brought us into rarefied and glittering circles, which were and are also very much a part of the country's reality, and I have therefore related those experiences and not only because images of pageantry, glamour and romance always arouse wide human interest but also because they helped define our overall perspective on multi-faceted India.

Much of this exploration takes place at the conjunction between two realms, the con rete reality of society, geography and history on the one hand and the invisible but very perceptible and essential sphere of myth and mystery that overlays and intersects it on the other. The phenomenon only manifests the *noumenon,* the *pratyaksa* (the direct evidence) hides but also alludes to the *paroksa* (the paradoxical truth behind it) as Samskrit dialecticians teach; the *Alam al khalq* of Arab metaphysicians only exists as a shadow of the *Alam al Ghaib,* the invisible eternal universe of the platonic archetypes that generate the legends. At almost every step of our pilgrimage to the streams and sources of India's perennial soul, we were lifted from the mundane to the symbolic and from the appearance of form to the kernel of the substance that covers the radiant, all-powerful emptiness of the ultimate being.

May this travelogue therefore be useful and interesting to those who wish to find out more about India as it appeared to me in the 1970s and '80s but also about India as it might have been at various periods as far back as traditions and scriptures allow us to peer into the deep ocean of its past.

CÔME CARPENTIER DE GOURDON

Contents

I	Crossroads of Asia	15
II	Cradle of the Vedas	31
III	Sultans and Sages	48
IV	Pradaksina: The Southern Present	72
V	In the Grove of Ancient Knowledge	94
VI	A Spiritual Godmother	115
VII	Exploring Art and Artha	136
VIII	Between Heaven and Earth	155
IX	In the Kingdom of the Wodeyars	169
X	At the Confluence of Legend and Gnosis	179
XI	Indira Gandhi's World	193
XII	The Lake of Snakes and Nelumbos	209
XIII	E Oriente Lux	232
XIV	Echoes of the Holy City	246
XV	Digging into India's Ageless Soul	264
XVI	Kali's Domain	278
XVII	How East and West Meet	296
XVIII	Viceroys, Lamas and Kommissars	315
XIX	Hill Wanderings	335
XX	Meetings and Musings	353
XXI	Exploring Many Paths to the Pathless	373
XXII	Crisscrossing the Centuries	391
XXIII	The Nostalgia of Maharajas	412
XXIV	Gazing at the Hidden Realm	447
XXV	Parting Garlands	462
	Further Readings	479

Preamble: *In March of 1975, after several months of travel by sea and road from Barcelona in Spain, we reached India, the goal of our "Expedition Dharman." I was in my fifteenth year. My father has undertaken the journey partly in response to my adolescent desire to explore the Asia of my dreams. He was a philosopher and an orientalist and wished to reach the source of wisdom that many traditions locate in India. This book tells the story of our Indian odyssey.*

I

Crossroads of Asia

On the Threshold

True to history and physical geography I saw the rugged, canyon-like and dusty Khyber Pass as the gateway of India. So had all the emperors and explorers before us and so does Pakistan remain one of the five Indias evoked by ancient travellers, a part and parcel of greater India, beyond the capricious vagaries of history and despite the contemporary political conventions. When the desolate rocky walls of the Khyber cleft widen towards the valleys of Swat, one feels the quasi-mystical impression of passing from Central Asia to the subcontinent. This feeling strengthened when we stopped at the Torkham border post, where the verdant vegetation and the glistening glow of a spring morning seemed to heighten the spotlessly white shirts of the Pakistani immigration officers. Then the wail of the muezzin rose in the dewy mountain air and its herald must have been very young for the voice was as melodiously pure as that of a choir boy and had a lilting lyrical quality I had not felt anywhere so far in our travels across Muslim lands. Was that an effect of Sufi musicality, the mystical *sama'*, which permeated the local brand of Islam in the land of the Hindus since untold centuries? I was reminded that some of the pioneers of Islamic mysticism hailed from Sind around the lower Indus whence they introduced various elements of yoga and other Indian spiritual and artistic practices to the new faith risen in Arabia.

However, the radiant mysticism of contemplation was rarely apparent in the faces and demeanours I saw around me. We were in Pushtunistan, the untamed region which the British colonial armies had wrestled away from Afghanistan and claimed as their empire's

"North Western Frontier" which they had to defend in a succession of bloody wars. It is a land of free and indomitable fighters and many of the people we saw carried firearms as if to attest that, whether they were Afghans or Pakistani citizens, gunfights were part of life. That situation has not changed, as everyone knows, and violence has grown since terrorism has become endemic and has subverted the ancestral tribal laws.

The primary historical association of that border in a western mind fed on classical literature is with the "Great Game" romanticized by Kipling and well before that, with Alexander's expedition which reached there its most critical and obscure stage as there is no agreement among historians as to whether his troops suffered heavy losses at the hands of local kings or managed to subdue them. I also knew of the illustrious past of Peshawar, the first city we visited in the subcontinent. It was the capital of a vast empire stretching from India's heartland to Central Asia, some 1800 years ago under its sanskrit name of *Purushapura*, the "city of God" and it hosted then many monumental testimonies to its glory, including a magnificently ornate gold and jewel-covered stupa, a pyramidal spired structure which may have been then, with a height of almost six hundred feet, the world's tallest building. It was erected by emperor Kanishka, the greatest monarch of the Kushan dynasty, which had originated in the deserts of Eastern Turkestan, between the Gobi and Takla Makan deserts under the Chinese name of the *Yueh Chih* as the ruling clan of a nomadic confederacy and a description of the wonders of that age and area was penned by the Chinese Buddhist pilgrim Fa Hsien, who visited it three centuries later.

The Kushans are one of the least known and yet most intriguing empire-builders in the ancient world. They appear protean in their tolerance and eclecticism, which enabled them to connect and bring together the many civilizations and religions co-existing within their realm across deserts, mountains and mighty rivers. Kanishka himself, from the few effigies that have survived, appears to have been a mustachioed and bearded horseman, clad in a long coat and Iranian-style loose trousers, wearing tall felt boots with spurs. Contemporary inscriptions allude to him customarily as the Great Saviour and the Son of God. He belonged to the Eastern Persian culture of the age and probably spoke Arian or Bactrian, the Indo-Iranian idiom of what is now Afghanistan and although the coins minted in the early years of his rule bear the effigies of greek gods, they were replaced later by Zoroastrian and Mithraic deities and by various Buddhas, evincing the waning popularity of Hellenic religions and the rise of Buddhism in his empire that was spreading ever deeper into India.

The very uncertainty that remains over the identity of some of the divine names mentioned on those coins shows the fusion that was taking place between the various religions. Is the *Oesho* of Kanishka's mint *Isha*, "the lord", Shiva in Samskrit or Vayu? Is *Metrago Buddo,* the future Buddha of the Mahayana soteriology or the Persian and Vedic Mithra? Was a clear distinction made between those icons of diverse and converging faiths? The emperor had the illustrious Buddhist scholar Asvaghosa, one of the great masters of classical Sanskrit literature and the author of the monumental *Buddhacarita*, as his spiritual mentor but a Greek, Agesilas supervised the construction of the stupas that dotted his realm and a Central Asian Buddhist monk, Lokasena went along with others to Loyang, the Chinese capital to establish a school for the translation of Buddhist texts during the years of Kanishka's rule. At the same time, the city of Mathura on the Yamuna, his winter capital, saw the rise of a school of exquisite figurative art inspired by the Gandharan graeco-bactrian art. What a fascinating cross-pollination was taking place along the thriving Silk Road!

We found however few traces of the pre-Islamic past in Peshawar, outside its museum housed in a Mughal-inspired building erected by the British and predictably called Victoria Hall, where we admired the delicately crafted casket called after that King of Kings, Kanishka who after Ashoka, was the most important early patron and promoter of Buddhist culture in the ancient world. The city is in many ways similar to the many other garrison towns we were to see in Pakistan and India.

It was on the archaeological site of Taxila and at Lahore's National Museum that we could admire the full spectrum of a glorious history about which contemporary Pakistan seems largely ignorant or ambivalent, partly because of a carefully highlighted Islamic identity through which its elites justified separation from mother India.

Yet for many centuries, the Indus valley had been the epicentre, if not the cradle of Indian civilization and to that river, called *Mihran* by the first Arab and Persian visitors perhaps in relation with Mihra or Mitra the vedic and Iranian deity, the subcontinent owed its very name in the Western world.

I keep fleeting memories of our rapid passage through Pakistan, which calls itself the Land of the Pure, out of an increasingly frustrated desire for religious homogeneity over and above its inevitable ethnic diversity. I remember spending a night in a Christian presbytery on the outskirts of Rawalpindi and hearing from the native Pakistani priest that life was difficult and even dangerous for the few Christians left in that unruly area since the breakup of greater India and the mass departure and massacres of non-Muslims in 1947. We had stopped there because one of our fellow travellers, a Goan Indian, had a remote family connection with the priest and regularly sent financial aid to the church. The situation I reflected was in stark contrast with the millennial picture of religious plurality and universal openness which India presents to the world since vedic times, shaping the vision of a perennial philosophy common to all mankind with which I was already so familiar. Religions as motherlodes and expressions of civilizations, are instruments of political and economic power and they often consecrate the mental and material colonization of one people by another.

An apt summary of the self-serving discourse so familiar to kings and politicians of all times is to be found in the statement made by Tamerlan's son, when he decided to conquer India, according to one of his biographers:

> "The Prince Muhammed Sultan said: The whole country of India is full of gold and jewels and in it there are seventeen mines of gold

> and silver, diamonds and rubies, and emeralds and tin and iron and steel and copper and quicksilver and out of the plants which grow there are those fit for making weaving apparel and aromatic plants and the sugarcane and it is a country which is always green and verdant and its whole aspect is pleasant and delightful. Now since the inhabitants are chiefly polytheists and infidels and idolaters and worshippers of the Sun, by the order of God and his Prophet it is right for us to conquer them."

Despite having lost some of its traditional demographic diversity with the departure of most members of the Hindu, Zoroastrian, Jewish, Bahai, Sikh and Christian communities, Peshawar remains a mosaic of peoples and languages as a legacy of its colourful past under successive Vedic, Iranian, Greek, Scythian, Tocharian, Hunnic, Turkic, Mughal, Afghan, Sikh and British rulers and denizens. My readings sketched in my mind the intricate tapestry of the region's history. The vast rounded valley that spread between the Khyber hills and the Indus plains has long been known as Gandhara and was reputed for the musical and artistic proficiency of its inhabitants. The very name is supposed to have alluded to the delicate fragrances that perfumed their glades and with which they made expensive scents. In the hills the *kedars* (junipers or cedars), out of which some of their ritual incense was concocted, still grow and streams in their higher valleys are lined with the golden willows, which I was told years later are the *vetasas* mentioned in the Vedas along with other trees of temperate climates that vanished thousands of years ago when Northern India's climate turned drier and hotter. It was on the bark of birches, the vedic *bhurja*, another tree endemic to these uplands that the earliest Buddhist texts written in Gandhari language and script were to be found and there is reason to believe that in even older times, vedic hymns were consigned to now lost bark sheets.

Gandharans were closely related to the Kurus, who lived further East on the plains of the Ganga and Yamuna but they interacted as well with other nations in the subcontinent to which they were connected by one of the world's oldest highway, the *uttarapatha* later called the *Sadak e Azam* in Persian and Grand Trunk Road by the British East India Company. The wife of the blind Kuru patriarch Dhritarashtra, whose culpable weakness for his sons's unbridled ambition led to the Mahabharata war, was Gandhari.

While we stared at the exquisite statues and icons unearthed from sites dated to the Indo-Greek age, 20 centuries earlier, when Peshawar had reached the peak of its prosperity, I was reminded that the two sovereigns who gave their names to the respective kingdoms of *Pushkalavati* (now the nearby town of Charsadda where the undisputed authority on Sanskrit grammar and etymology Panini flourished) and Taxila were Pushkala and Taksha, both sons of Bharata, the younger half-brother of the God-King Rama, the hero of the *Ramayana,* from the solar dynasty of Kosala in what is now the region of Oudh in the Gangetic plain. They are said to have succeeded an even older line descended from Druhyu, the ancestor of one of the five Indian races mentioned in the Vedas. Bharata's mother, Kaikeyi came from the Gandharan region as her name, evocative of the Kaikaus kings of Persia, shows and her grandsons must have inherited princely claims to the area.

In a much later age, the five Pandava brothers celebrated in the *Mahabharata,* who were from the lunar dynasty, appear to have pushed the Takshak descendent of Bharata back to Gandhara from the forested area near the Yamuna river, which became known as Kurukshetra. The Takshakas may have been of Scythian or proto-Turkic stock but they were associated with the snakes in ancient history, probably because of their specific cults and totems. Their contemporary descendents may be the Tajiks of Central Asia.

Neighbours of the Gandharans, whose name is seemingly related to the mythological *kentauri* or centaurs of the Greeks were the equally warlike, horse riding *Kambojas*, a Scythian confederacy which dwelt in Northern Afghanistan and the adjoining Central Asian plateaux. They periodically rode into the Indian plains and carved out kingdoms all the way from Punjab to the Deccan and Bengal, probably going as far as the Indochinese region of Cambodia to which they gave their name. I also found an echo of their presence in the names of the Achamenid Emperor Cambyses and of his father Cyrus (Kurush) the Great, a relative of the *Kurus* of the Mahabharata, the people linked to the Uttarakurus region to the north of the Himalayas, just as the King of Kings Darius is connected by name to the Kuru prince Duryodhana, son of princess Gandhari, whose uncle and adviser was Sakuni (of the Sakas) known by his wiles and his skill as a gambler.

The variant of Persian spoken in Afghanistan and the Peshawar region is still called Dari.

When Alexander, who is called The Great everywhere save in pre-Islamic India where his battles were indecisive and left relatively few memories, reached the area, his troops were worn down by the formidable resistance he met from the Kambojas, in their various tribes, the Aspasoi (*asvayanas*), Assakenoi (*asvakayanas*) and other fierce dwellers of the Arachosian, Sogdian and Bactrian satrapies. Once he crossed the Khayber Pass, however, he found more hospitable hosts as the local kings, whom the Greeks called hyparchs, probably as a translation of the hindu titles of *narendra, prabhu* or *nrpa*, welcomed him, sometimes in fluent greek. In particular Ambhi, the ruler of Taxila and a descendent of the legendary Bharata, reportedly recognized Alexander's suzerainty, probably in exchange for protection against the bellicose Kambojas who threatened his prosperous state, renowned for its ancient university.

The oldest language of Gandhara has left many vestiges in the *hindko* tongue still spoken by many in Peshawar, alongside the national Urdu, the Punjabi of the Easterners, Dari, Pushtun and the many dialects of the surrounding tribal districts that meet and mix in the legendary Storytellers' Bazaar. In the museum we saw inscriptions in the ancient *kharoshti* alphabet, derived from Achemenid Aramaic, which had been used for centuries as the official script by Parthian, Scythian and Kushan administrators. Kharosthi, initially written from right to left, like most semitic languages owes its name to the *Haroseth*, the metal working and smelting guilds that had the skill to engrave metal plates, according to an immemorial tradition rooted in the proto-historic Indus valley culture and attested by its famous seals. Indus valley wheel-shaped burial mounds may also have inspired the much later Buddhist stupas that were to reach such towering height and size under Kushan patronage.

We beheld a testimony of the more recent past of Peshawar, when we visited the Bazar Kalan, the Bala Hissar which had been the winter residence of the Afghan rulers when the city was within their kingdom and the Sethi mohalla, a cluster of ornate late 18th century mansions, which had belonged to one of the wealthiest families of the city. Those enterprising Hindu merchants had trading offices and warehouses along the silk route in Central Asia, Persia and China and they controlled a substantial part of the business between the British, Russian and Iranian empires until the early 20th century. They poured some of their wealth into the opulent decoration of their homes, which evoke their connections with Samarkand, Isfahan as well as the local style. While we walked through exquisitely carved doors into ornate *balakhanas* and *tehkhanas*, along walls inlaid with geometric mirror work, under polychromous ceilings and paused in the inner courtyards, next to a majestic *Takht Sulaimani*, 'the throne of Solomon' no less, where a fountain elicited my memories of Pushkin's poem about Baksisaray, we felt the melancholy of a bygone era, when India was united and many communities and religions co-existed in the multiracial patchwork of Gandharan culture, the meeting place between the Tocharians and the Indians of all regions.

One character in Peshawar's colourful history could not fail to attract my boyish curiosity. When Punjab was ruled by the Sikh king Ranjit Singh in the first half of the 19th century, he had appointed some Europeans to high positions in his army and civil service, true to the eclectic and tolerant traditions of the culturally composite area. He had wrestled Peshawar from neighbouring Afghanistan and to control that rebellious province he sent a fiery mercenary from Amalfi as his governor. Paolo Avitabile, a former officer of Napoleon's brother in law and king of Naples, Marshall Murat, became famous or notorious, depending upon the side one is on, for his ruthless enforcement of the law against the turbulent and marauding tribes and sundry brigands who held sway around his capital. He had hundreds executed and led bloody but effective campaigns against holdouts; the local legend is that he had criminals thrown from the minaret of the stately 17th century Mahabat Khan Mosque and although he drew condemnation from the self-righteous British for his brutal methods, he was careful to build good relations with them and shortly after his departure, they took over the Sikh Kingdom.

Abu Tabela, as he was known in the local language, left dreaded memories when he retired to his sunny, maritime birthplace with a huge treasure that made him a celebrity and even a legend in the Kingdom of the Two Sicilies. He was indeed the local boy who had become a nabob in the fabulous Orient.

There were few traces of Abu Tabela in Peshawar. His magnificent residence, located in the now bereft area where Kanishka's gigantic stupa had raised its spire to the sky many centuries before, has long been destroyed. We were in some hurry to reach India and had accordingly to renounce the desire of making a detour in the beauteous and untamed Swat valley, the ancient samskrit *Suvastu* where the Macedonian conqueror had fought a hard campaign against the warlike *Assekines* and taken the fortified towns of Massaga and Bazyra. Chroniclers wrote about various other towns and tribes in that region, birthplace of the great sage and magician of Tibet Padmasambhava, which remains, beneath its Islamic cultural veneer a mosaic of races and ancient beliefs that include vestiges of the Greek presence. We did not know where was the town of Nyssa mentioned by Arrian in his Anabasis as having been founded by the god Dionysos or Bacchus during his mythical Indian campaign. We had come across the same toponym in Turkish Cappadocia, possibly also in memory of the same deified hero on his march westward and immortalized by its bishop Gregory of Nyssa, one of my favorite mystic poet-theologians.

It is now known that for thousands of years the vine was grown and grapes were harvested in Gandhara as in Asia Minor. Some ethnic groups of the area have kept their names and recognisable identities such as the *Kathis* (Arrian's Catheans who are possible relatives of the Germanic Chatti) and the *Mallas* (the Malleans), who later came to rule to Nepal as well as the Abhisares, ancestors of the Kashmiris, especially the Hindu ones known as the Pandits. There is an intriguing mystery about Dionysos, the God of mystical ecstasy and wine-making. Was he an Asian hero who conquered Greece as some Hellenic myths record, or was he a Thracian predecessor of Alexander, who claimed to follow his footsteps in the march towards the Orient? The answer to this question is unknown but some Hellenic historians equate him with Manu, the first Vedic monarch and lawgiver and also with Yima-Jamshid the Indo-Persian lord of wine and the netherworld.

ACROSS THE INDUS AFTER MANY CONQUERORS

Cultural boundaries often match tectonic faultlines and we had a vivid instance of that reality in that region located on the Central Asian plate which meets the Indian one in the valley of the mighty Sindhu and causes tremendous earthquakes every now and then as the subcontinent pushes and rubs against the Asian mainland, thereby creating upheavals of which the Himalayan range is the most stupendous result. India is geologically still an island and deserves its legendary Sanskrit name of *Jambudvipa*: the isle of jambu (roseapple) trees. The reputation of the *pentapotamos*, land of the five rivers, both blessed and fateful, led some Greek mythologists to believe it was the other world, accessible only to the departed souls who had crossed the five streams of Hades: Styx, Acheron, Cocytus, Lethe and Phlegeton and indeed the Shiva of the Hindu pantheon shares several traits with Hades, the divine ruler of the Hellenic realm of the dead, who may have been *Adeesh* in samskrit, the first or eldest lord.

Not far from Peshawar, after crossing the Indus, the civilisational artery which was long called the *Nil-Ab* as Graeco-roman geographers thought it to be connected with the homonymous African river (*Nil* is the name for blue in samskrit), at the historic bridge of Attock, another frontier town, we reached the storied ruins of Taxila, one of the wonders of Asia in Antiquity. To us that name evoked also the philosophical dialogue, both Socratic and Upanishadic, of the Buddhist king Menander or Milinda with the sage Nagasena, written around 140 BC, when that venerable academic centre was at its acme. King Ambhi, whom Alexander's followers called Taxiles, was lavish in his hospitality and showered the conqueror with gifts that Alexander returned with even greater liberality. Arrian writes that Alexander found at the crossing a bridge made of boats built by his favorite general Hephestion and no less than two hundred talents of silver – as there were mines of that metal in the mountains and in the desert beyond the Punjab – as well as three thousand oxen, ten thousand sheep and thirty elephants as a tribute from Taxiles.

No such presents expected us but we felt very privileged nevertheless to reach the site of that university where the central and perhaps most comprehensive doctrine of Mahayana Buddhism, the *Prajnaparamita* (highest wisdom) was compiled under the rule of the Kushan monarchs. Although we were broadly familiar with that extraordinarily vast collection of literature which embraces cosmology, philosophy, psychology, semantics, physics, theology, art and aesthetics in thousands of volumes, I would in later years get immersed in that ocean of thought and analysis churned in the fertile land of Gandhara, Abhisara and Sagala (Sialkot, in the Punjab).

As many other legendary ruins we had visited during our periplus so far, Taxila's remains speak more to the imagination than to the senses for relatively little has survived successive waves of plunder and destruction followed by centuries of oblivion. The excavations conducted by Sir John Marshall, the head of the Archaeological Survey of India in the first half of the 20th century yielded many delicate objects on display at various museums in the world. He unearthed the basic layout of the three successive cities, the hindu, reportedly founded by Taksha himself, shortly after the days of the *Ramayana,* the Greek or Graeco-Bactrian one, expanded by the Mauryan sovereigns from Magadha and the Kushan-era settlement.

Most impressive are the rows of cells of the graeco-buddhist monastery of Jaulian which have retained a serene and austere elegance against the background of the Himalayan foothills. One could see in the mind's eye the learned Nagasena elucidate the 82 dilemmas of the nature of reality for the benefit of the philosopher-king Mahendra or picture the illustrious brother monks Asanga and Vasubandhu, both native of Peshawar, expound on the *Vijnaptimatra* ("consciousness as the sole measure") metaphysics.

In even more distant times, according to Hindu tradition the *Mahabharata* epic, then known as *Bharata Samhita*, had been recited there for the first time by Vaisampayana at the court of King Jayamejaya who defeated the *Taksakas* to avenge the death of his father Pariksit. In all regions and times, historical events are eerily but monotonously similar; military or palace coups are carried out, assassinations are performed and popular revolts erupt as if to prove that greed, ambition, violence and treachery spring eternal in the heart of men and women.

We had read some of the available literature on the history of that great city and though the local guide could only recite a few dates and facts on the strength of his visibly elementary knowledge, including the fateful year 185 BC, which saw the murder of Briharatha, the last emperor of the house of Maurya, by his general Pushyamitra Sunga who forthwith usurped the throne, we were privileged a few days later to have a conversation with an erudite Pakistani gentleman in Lahore for whom the Gandharan civilization seemingly held no secrets. Our dialogue, during a sumptuous meal which initiated us to the rich flavours and exotic but heavy delights of Mughal cuisine, ranged across the spectrum of mythology, history and philosophy that are inseparably bound in any chapter of the subcontinent's past. We talked of the relations between the Gandhara of old and the *gandharvas*, the heavenly musicians of Vedic literature whose name is akin to the Gandalf of Norse legends reborn in Tolkien's "Lord of the Rings" trilogy. Our host said that *gandharas* were equestrian nomads from Central Asia who had come to this region of India in remote centuries through Afghanistan where Alexander's soldiers had known them as *Aspasoi*. As for Taxila, he was not aware of the thesis of the 19th century French diplomat and amateur indologist Louis Jacolliot, who saw the *Taksaks*, according to references in the Puranas as a Turkic clan but he held that the etymology of the name is *taksa*: carpenter and taksak a synonym of *Naga*: a supernatural reptilian species or tribe present throughout India mythology.

The Puranas indeed record that the aforesaid king Janamejaya, a grandson of Arjuna, the hero of the *Mahabharata* war, held in Taxila a *sarpamedhayagna* (a sacrifice of snakes). The bellicose *taksakas* were perhaps none other than the *sakas*, known as *Asii* or Scythians by graeco-roman authors.

Many centuries later, the most illustrious political scientist of ancient India, Chanakya, also known as Kautilya, studied and then taught in Taxila where he wrote his famous *Arthashastra*, a compendium of sociology, political economy, statecraft, military science and administrative practices. I had only read a summary of the 6000 stanza work which had captivated me by the depth and breadth of its knowledge and sagacity. Our host was an admirer of the educational philosophy practiced at Taxila during many centuries in the eighteen disciplines that were taught. It was, he said, completely free of cost and informal in a way though rigorous. Knowledge was held to be sacred and could hence not be paid for with money, in keeping with the Brahminical and Buddhist precepts, which forbade educators to ask for fees from students or from society. Teachers were independent and responsible for their pupils whom they could attract only by their reputation and the excellence of their courses. Each scholar had his own independent college, mostly supported through the generosity of patrons such as princes and merchants.

At the end of their studies that lasted up to eight years but were not rewarded by formal degrees, as mastery could not be authenticated by a document, pupils were expected to make a present to their teacher known as *gurudakshina* and, if too poor to afford it, they could ask the local king to underwrite it. Rich students were supposed to be lavish in their gifts. Young men above the age of sixteen came to the famed university from many regions, as far away as Eastern and Central India or Middle Asia after completing their primary education in local schools or *gurukuls*. The latin word "schola" is derived from the samskrit word *kula* as I had learnt in my childhood.

In this first of many conversations we were to have in sundry parts of India about the traditional educational system in place before the British occupation, we reflected on the viability of the informal, personalized, non-bureaucratic character of institutions such as Taxila that were spread around the country and whether that system could ever be revived in the contemporary world, built on the principles of mass, standardized training and information, hierarchical, "cookie-cutter" degrees handed out to reward graded examination results. The increasing inability of this mechanism to provide employment to many of its wards and its mounting economic costs, in spite of its ambition to cater to all people in the world were already becoming all too visible. Relevant warnings had been given by Ivan Ilich and Paulo Freire, but there was no escaping the fact, recognised by innumerable philosophical and paedagogical traditions, that knowledge cannot be sold in a pill or a bottle nor made real by a certificate.

Free education acquired by individual merit, talent and desire through mutual recognition and selection between the teacher and the pupil seems ideal but almost too good to be made widely available; yet it remains obvious that the standard presentation of packaged information is not sufficient to instill an authentic mastery which is, as my father liked to say, understanding above all.

On that afternoon by the time we reached dessert, we had to ask our learned Pakistani friend whether he felt at home in the religious and political post-colonial environment of his country, or whether he yearned for a restoration of the ancestral, composite civilisation common to the greater India of yore. He paused for a moment, a faint smile on his lips before answering that the past could not be brought back to life but that he wished Pakistan could learn from it and forge its identity on that hoary foundation. Alexander's Greeks and others before them had not come as strangers, he pointed out, but despite the customary bloodshed, more like remote relatives restoring immemorial links with a larger family. The Macedonian conqueror had been received with honour by many Indian kings and others he fought according to the chivalrous rules abided by Indo-Aryan warriors under all climes as if he had also been a party to the Mahabharata battle, many centuries earlier. Everywhere he had performed sacrifices to the common deities of Hindus and *Yavanas* (Ionians). The names of the gods might have been different but the rites had remained similar. Alexander had buried his charger, Bucephalus, slain in combat, with the pomp and circumstance with which Indian monarchs practiced the *Asvamedha*, the Vedic horse sacrifice.

"The Greeks and we are descended from the same mythical ancestors," he observed with a hint of solemnity. We did not expect to find such a vivid remembrance of remote origins in a contemporary Punjabi grandee though he quickly conceded that he was an exception in his nation.

"We are nation blind to its past, he went on, many here want to forget what was prior to 1947 and we don't even feel comfortable with memories of the Mughal Empire's heyday because they tell us we were just a part of a greater state whose centre was in today's India. Gandhara is too far back in time for most of us and many in our narrow minded religious and feudal elites hold that it was a pagan and benighted society. Unfortunately, we are too much influenced by the oil-rich Arab states, especially Saudi Arabia with its provincial, bigoted views on Islam and history. In the end, the only era of the past we feel comfortable with is the British Raj and so we are proud of our fluency in English and of our manners copied from our former overlords. Whisky, Cricket, Golf and high tea are not really Muslim cultural features but they are regarded as critical components of the lifestyle of the ruling class here. Is our nation's father not Muhammed Ali Jinnah, barrister in London and WOG par excellence."

This sounded like a fitting conclusion to this thought-provoking discussion and we chose not to raise the probably embarrassing issue of the successive raids and invasions by Arab, Turkic and Persian armies that had reportedly caused so much havoc and misery throughout India during more than seven centuries. Contrary to the Greeks and Tocharians of Antiquity, who broadly respected the social rules of the game and quickly were assimilated into India to whose intricate tapestry they added new colourful strands, the Muhammedan plunderers were admittedly driven by the twin motives of greed and fanaticism. They justified their raids and massacres as showing zeal for the "True Faith" and generally made it a point to humiliate, despoil and enslave the "heretics", if the reports of their own chroniclers are to be believed.

Facing Hindus used to fighting highly regulated conventional battles, which led to settlements among ruling families and payment of tributes by the vanquished, the Muslims often proclaimed their resolve to eradicate the religion of their adversaries and to annihilate their kingdoms for turning all of "Hind and Sind" into a part of the *Dar ul Islam*. It seemed that Pakistan was founded for that very purpose and that its rulers saw India mainly as a land to be conquered anew, in one way or another, even if some enlightened individuals like our amphitryon in Lahore had no such atavistic yearnings.

II

Cradle of the Vedas

Recalling Porus

It turned out that the illustrious and distinguished Pakistanis that my father knew or had introductions for in Lahore were out of the country for various reasons. Zahibzada Yakub Ali Khan was the Ambassador in Paris at the time whereas Iqbal Akhund, another aristocratic diplomat, was abroad as well. The eminent social scientist Mahboob ul Haq had left in 1972 for the United States from where this staunchly liberal economist shunned the entreaties of avowedly socialist Prime minister Zulfiqar Ali Bhutto who wished to induct him into his cabinet.

The doyen of Pakistan's constitutional history Sir Mohammed Zafrullah Khan, the former president of the International Court of Justice, had moved to London, presumably to escape the popular hostility that in Pakistan surrounds the Ahmadiya heterodox sect of Islam to which he owed allegiance. Despite the fact that most members of the affluent and enlightened Ahmadiya community had chosen Pakistan as their country when partition took place and gave it some of its most eminent civil servants, scientists and businessmen, they had been declared non-Muslims and were even made to fear for their lives. They could therefore not bask in the gratitude of their countrymen and Pakistan for various reasons of its own making was deprived of some of its most talented citizens.

Having taken our brief trip into the past at Taxila, it was time to renew our journey eastwards towards our future, leaving behind the Jhelum river, the vedic *Vitasta* known by the Ancients as the *Hydaspes* on whose shores Alexander had fought his last grand battle. His foe was King Porus, a ruler of the Paurava tribe that had founded Peshawar and whose name is rooted in the word *pura*, fortress or city, as if to indicate that they had long been known as urban builders and dwellers as the extant remains of the Harappan civilization abundantly demonstrate. The Greeks had given the name of Hydaspes to one of their titans (the samskrit *daityas*), son of Thauma the ocean as if to remember one of the major natural features of what was perhaps the distant land of their origins.

When the Macedonians reached the river, they caught sight of the troops of the Indian monarch ranged on the opposite bank, and were struck by the large number of elephants deployed at the front. During the night, taking advantage of a violent storm, Alexander managed to take his cavalry and phalanx across the river behind the cover of a wooded island. The battle pitted the war-hardened Greeks against four thousand horsemen, three hundred chariots and two hundred elephants followed by thirty thousand foot soldiers under Porus's direct command. At the end of the fierce contest where the heavily armed western veterans seem to have outmatched the lighter Indian troops, two sons of the Indian king had been slain as well as the provincial governor whom Arrian calls Spitakes.

Alexander and his men were struck by the valiance of Porus who did not flee from the field like the effete Persian King of Kings Darius III, even after he had been wounded and his forces scattered. Eager to make an ally of that brave prince, Alexander sent various envoys, including his new vassal Taxiles and finally had him escorted to his presence by Meroes who may well have been a Hindu as well. Asked how he would like to be dealt with by the victor, Porus in keeping with the chivalrous code of his caste nobly replied that he expected to be treated like a king and, when pressed to express another wish, he refused to ask for any presents. Alexander rewarded his magnanimity with a gift of new lands to add to his dominions and thence found him "faithful in all things."

To those who read Indian history in the Middle Ages and at the time of the British colonisation, Porus's attitude seems typical of the behaviour of Hindu rulers. The Maharajas who, one way or another, were brought under British rule were generally loyal to a fault to their European overlords, to the point of looking quite unpatriotic to the then-virtual Indian nation-state. In a feudal order, the oath of fealty to the liege comes before the claims of ethnic or cultural kinship. Europeans behaved no differently until the advent of the modern concept of political nationality and the values upheld in those not so remote days cannot be judged by more recent standards and conventions.

Porus had an ally in the king of Kashmir, Abhisara but the latter had not been able to send troops in time to join the battle. According to the Greeks historians, Alexander won a hard fought combat in which he lost his beloved steed but the reality was probably somewhat different. There are many indications that the outcome was uncertain and that the "seven foot tall" Porus agreed to make peace with the weary western invaders in exchange for an alliance at very advantageous terms for him. Alexander could go no further as his troops refused to march after reports were received that a host of two hundred thousand infantrymen, eighty thousand cavalry, eight thousand war chariots and the inevitable array of mounted and caparisoned elephants captained by the Nanda royal family was readying to confront them on the *Hydraortes* river. That was more than the heroic son of Zeus and Olympias could handle and from then on the great adventure of the Macedonians turned into a hurried and exhausting retreat that soon became disastrous. The Soviet Marshall Zhukov, in an address to the 1957 class of the Indian Military Academy, compared that *anabasis* to Napoleon's catastrophic exit from Russia in 1813. Alexander's Seleucid successors tried to take back the coveted "Indike" but had to surrender it within a few years to the king of the eastern gangetic state of Magadha, Chandragupta Maurya, whose grandson Ashoka was to spread Buddhism to much of Asia as a result of a philosophical conquest more long lasting and beneficial than military annexations.

Spiritual expansion is largely immune to the cyclical reversals of the political pendulum. The Buddha Sakya Muni had taught how to take refuge in the seemingly unmoving but dynamic axle of the revolving wheel of history.

RAWALPINDI

Pakistan on occasion claims to be the successor of the state of Gandhara and has built its new capital, Islamabad close to its illustrious remains. We however did not go to the small modern town planned by a greek architect but we visited rather rapidly the nearby city of Rawalpindi, one of the country's largest and oldest. It is also located on the foothills of the wooded mountains of Kashmir, that Ptolemy called Kasperia, dotted with hill resorts founded by British officers and settlers. Many, possibly apocryphal traditions about the origins of Christianity remain alive in that beautiful and healthy region and they naturally intrigued me. One of the wise men from the East Kaspar or Gaspard owed his name to the kingdom of Kasperia, according to a legend echoed in John of Hildesheim's medieval *History of the Three Kings* and Jesus himself is supposed to have reached this area during his twenty "hidden years" before beginning his ministry in Palestine. One tradition holds that he returned with his mother after surviving his Crucifixion since Middle Eastern accounts, reflected in the Muslim Holy Book and in the Docetic doctrine, describe him as remaining alive in flesh and blood as the disciples met him.

Near Rawalpindi, a hill town called Murree or Mari is said to have hosted the Mother of the Saviour. It is more likely that Apostle Thomas, who according to some apocryphal Gospels was the twin brother of Jesus, visited the Parthian king of Taxila, Gondophares or Gandapur, whose tribe had conquered the region, and was allegedly put to death by him. Whether or not that happened, it is plausible as Parthians were not always known for religious tolerance but almost two centuries later the last notable Kushan emperor Vasudeva I is reported in the records of the Syriac Patriarchate, to have returned the relics of the Saint to his homeland of Edessa. Vasudeva's son Vazan, allegedly converted, was called Johannes in the syrian chronicles and appears to have been at the origin of the persistent medieval belief in the realm of a Christian Priester John. It would not have been out of character for the eclectic and tolerant Kushan monarchs to patronise Christianity since they had many Nestorians among their subjects and otherwise practiced at various times Hellenic syncretism, Zoroastrianism and Buddhism. Such universalism was politically wise and culturally rewarding.

Most traces of that troubled age have perished along centuries of neglect and plunder. In the fifth century, the invasion of the Hephtalite Huns, those ancestors of the modern Abdali Afghans, was particularly devastating. Rawalpindi's monuments evoke the successive Moghul, Sikh and British periods, apart from the old forts built by a tenacious dynasty of local potentates, the Gokhars, who managed to hold sway for seven hundred years of turbulent history until they were crushed in the mid-18th century by the invading Afghan King Ahmed Shah Abdali, himself a descendent of the Ebodoloi or Hephtalites who carried on the plundering traditions of his forebears.

As in all towns in Pakistan, however, the real primacy belongs to the local Sufi Saint Hazrat Sakhi Shah Char Charagh who lived three centuries ago. Charagh means "light" in Persian and is related to the Arabic *siraj*, whence the French *cierge*: candle. The holy man is the patron of Rawalpindi and his shrine attracts devout crowds whereas his relatives, the Kazmis still hold pride of place as direct heirs to the other great spiritual patron of the area, Hazrat Bari Imam, a cousin of Charagh. The popular religion of the Punjab and of all Muslim communities in India as in Iran, Turkey and many other muslim lands revolves around the tombs of those hallowed masters of wisdom and is inspired by the religious orders or communities they founded. In Punjab, there are four great saints: the *Char Yar*, the *awliya* or companions of the *Qutb*, hidden mystical king of the world, who stand symbolically for the four cardinal points and can be seen as embodiments of the traditional divine monarchs, and of the *Dhyani Buddhas* of the four directions regularly invoked and depicted in Indian iconography.

In the seventies, that ancestral piety had not yet been affected by the rise of an intransigent form of Islam, hostile to the veneration of hallowed local figures and to local syncretistic practices such as chanting (*qawwal*) burning of candles and mystical recitations (*dhikr*). Since then, those sanctuaries of the local faith are under threat; some have been attacked or even destroyed as shrines of idolatrous heresy by the militants of what might be called a Calvinist version of Islam.

Throughout that vast and populous province, whose milling crowds evoked the pithy observation of the Russian traveler Afanasi Nikitin about the many children of the Indians, one could discern the complex warp and weft of its historical tapestry embroidered with the vegetation of the tropics that mingled with trees more familiar to temperate climes. Palm trees raised their green feathers amidst the thick fronds of tamarinds ("Tamar Hind": the Indian dates), the lacework foliage of red blossomed *gul mohurs* and the dark mango groves; planes and poplars still held their own against the sprawling banyans, towering cottonwood trees and swaying bamboos amidst the wheat fields as the Middle East merged with South Asia. Alexander had been only one of many figures in the game of chess or rather *chaupar* played along the millennia from the days when the hymns of the Rig Veda were first intoned to the years of Kipling's Great Game and to our own times.

The interplay had also involved religions, preceding or following conquerors and traders in both directions. All met in that land of the Asian Nile which ancient Greeks believed to be the upper course of its equally crocodile infested African cousin until their navigators discovered the former's delta on the Indian ocean then called the Erythrean Sea at Barbaricum (the land of the Barbarians) where Karachi now stands.

As we pursued our journey across the vast plain that is a palimpsest of almost vanished civilizations, which combined to form the local people and its habitat, I was intrigued by the elusive and yet pervasice *Asii*, those invaders from Central Asia who according to Pliny, had settled in the Punjab not long before his time and ruled from that very town of Bucephalia (now known as Jhelum) where Alexander had given his horse a royal burial and which they called Thocari, indicating that they were Tocharians. They gave their name to the beautiful raw silk known as *tushar* that is a prized fabric until today. The Asii were connected by their very name to horses (*asva* in Sanskrit) and to their short straight swords (*asi* in Sanskrit). The Asian continent seems to owe its name to those people who had long dwelt in its heartland to north of the Oxus river. Some of them were also known as *Arshikas, Rishikas* and *Kambojas* in Vedic literature and nobody could say for sure whether they were ethnically Indo-European or Turkic because they probably were a mixture of both those strains that composed the loosely defined Scythian people as they do the Russian Cossacks their descendents.

Through Afghanistan they descended into India and founded kingdoms in the northern plains. In the oases of the Tarim basin in Turkestan, some tocharian mummies were found and they appear "Northern European" in their features and dress. Long before that discovery, Colonel James Tod, one of the historical mentors in my exploration of India's past had connected them with the Ases of Scandinavia who had founded the legendary city of Asgard. The horizon around the Asii grew even wider when I found out that the people of Magadha were called *Prasi* by the Greeks, the Eastern Asii. Knowing that *Arya* in Samskrt is a honorific term denoting a cultural and moral standard – like "Hellenoi" for the Greeks, – I formed the belief that the hinduized and later Buddhist Asii, Tukharas or Kambojas were among the Aryas sung in the Vedas.

Were the Persians Prasi too, cousins of the Medians and Mitannians "those who carry out the sacrifice" in Samskrit? Was Xerxes (*Kshatra*) not a Kshatriya? Were the Parthians, a branch of the Sarmatian-Persian confederation, not etymologically related to Partha, another name for Arjuna, the main character of the

Mahabharata? Was Alexander (Alaksanda) not named after Skanda, the hindu god of war also known as Karttikeya or Kumara, "the youth"? The Alexander of the Iliad is also called Paris, the king of Purus or *parasu*, the axe-wielding warriors. Then again, was the name of "barbaroi" applied to those who did not share the Hellenic culture, derived from the *Barbara* non-Vedic people of the lower reaches of the Indus valley? The large quarrelsome family of the Aryas, more a linguistic than an ethnic community, appeared to my eyes in its essential unity extending across the Eurasian continent.

Between the Jhelum and the Chenab, towns and villages such as Gujarat and Gujranwala hark back to the Gujjar invaders, who were none others than the Central Asian Guishengs or Gusur, otherwise known as the Kushans, the *kulputras* (noble born ones). They mingled with the successive wave of Hephtalite conquerors to form at least part of the Rajput warrior class of Northwestern India. Those mixed Indo-Iranian and Turkic tribes had ruled a large part of the subcontinent for centuries from their capital of Sagala, now Sialkot and they became assimilated with the local population, embraced the locally prevalent forms of Hinduism and Buddhism although they retained some of their mazdean and shamanistic practices. In later ages, those who had remained in Transoxiana and Afghanistan converted to Islam and kept the old habit of periodically crossing the Khyber Pass to pillage the Punjab plains.

Along a thousand years, under their dynastic clan names, the Ghaznavids, Ghorids, Aibaks, Khiljis, Tughlaqs, Timurids, Mamluks, Lodhis, Mughals, Afshars and Abdalis replaced one another on the coveted throne of Hindustan, renowned for its riches and its polytheism, which made it both a magnet for their greed and fair game for conquest and conversion. The greatest prize in the land of the five streams has long been Lahore which is also the gateway to the Gangetic valley. Genghis Khan's Mongols also turned back in that area after their dreaded overlord was killed by Lahore's king according to a local legend not borne out by history. Those who were not stopped there eventually took over much of India.

LAHORE

Lahore was founded as a fort to control and defend the Punjab, says the tradition by the eldest son of King Rama, Lava who gave it his name. The same chronicle claims that his younger brother Kusa built Kasur, a nearby city. However in the last few hundred years Lahore became an architecturally Muslim metropolis whose mughal character was not much modified by the Sikh Kings who held court there in the first half of the 19th century and it was only partly transformed by the British occupiers. Lahore is still a royal town even though it has not been a capital for some 150 years and had to submit during most of recorded history to Delhi's or Agra's supremacy.

In my childhood, the name of Lahore sounded like a legend, on par with Samarkand's, Baghdad's or Isfahan's. I imagined it as it is evoked in French romantic stories and in Massenet's 1877 Opera *Le Roi de Lahore*: a white and green collection of palaces, mosques, mausoleums and bazaars, crowned with bulbous golden cupulas, garlanded with blood red crenellated walls, spiked with slender minarets and clad in Persian gardens where marble fountains whispered, feathered arrow-like parrots flew and crimson-throated bulbuls warbled at dusk. I hoped to see the galloping horsemen depicted by earlier travelers, clad in chainmail and brocade, their beards dyed blue or vermilion, their turbans rainbow-hued, their earrings glittering, hooded falcons poised on their gloved fists. Such visions alas were soon replaced by the reality of bustling and chaotic road traffic although horses were still to be seen, pulling colourful tongas alongside with even more polychromous lorries and milling bicycles. The prosaic modern world crowded out my exotic illusions borrowed from old lithographs. Even the fabled Shalimar gardens, designed as a haven of delightful repose by Mughal emperors, looked neglected and dusty as it bore the many traces of plebeian picnics around the geometric channels and forlorn flowerbeds and topiary rows.

The famous Lahore museum, one of whose curators was Rudyard Kipling's father and which is often alluded to by the famous novelist, was the first major example of the Indo-Saracenic style I was given to see. It struck it more as an eclectic mix of English neogothic and Mughal elements. It consoled us a little from our disappointment about the city in general as it evoked the image of Kim sitting astride the famous Zamzama cannon still poised in front of the monument, and also by its magnificent collection of Graeco-Buddhist and other Indian sculptural art. Again we marveled at the fusion of Hellenic aesthetics with the ornamental opulence and meditative insight of Indian art. We must have starred for many minutes at the great statue of the fasting Buddha whose ecstatic pathos makes it one of the most memorable masterpieces of all times, comparable in expressiveness to Michaelangelo's Pieta, Nefertiti's head, Sammartini's statues for the mausoleum of the dukes of Sangro in Naples or the great Mahesvara bust in the Elephanta caves outside Bombay.

The fort and the Alamgir mosque, built by Emperor Aurangzeb is, with the tomb of Jahangir his grandfather and the latter's powerful wife Nur Jahan, the most illustrious landmark of the city. The first Muslim empire builder in India Qutubuddin Aibak, who raised the storied 200-foot tall Qutub Minar in Delhi, died in Lahore when he fell from his horse during a polo game, one of the many victims of that dangerous sport of kings which the British embraced with such enthusiasm.

As most towns, Lahore owes its creation to the course of a river, the Ravi whose name evokes the eponymous sanskrit Sun God and which was known as the Airavati, like the Burmese Irrawady on the opposite flank of the subcontinent. Airavata is also the name of the multi-trunked elephant of the vedic thunder God Indra or Sakra. The Ravi was also the river of the elephants; its many arms was symbolized by their trunks and it was known as the Hydraortes by the Greeks who, as usual devised an etymology from a fortuitous homophony. I remember that my father and I concluded from its name that the river flowed through the home of the Aira or Arya and as such runs at the heart of the ancient Aryavarta, the Aryan motherland, designated in the Vedas as "the best country on earth."

Like the other waterways of the Pujab, the Ravi had been a witness to many decisive battles on its shore, from the earliest recorded one evoked in the Rig Veda, which calls the river the Parusni and celebrates the victory of the Tritsu Bharata king from the east Sudasa over ten kings who had to flee to the West. Some of the defeated tribes bore names that became famed in world history. They were the Balhikas, Parthivas, Parsus and Alinas whose descendents ruled at various times over the Middle and Near East as Bactrians, Persians, Parthians, Helleni and Alani. The spread of the Arya civilization towards the Occident may well have been caused by the defeat of some of its clans which migrated towards the territories later known as Bactria, Khorasan and Iran. In this remote chapter of our past, the Vedas and the Avesta provide a surer compass than more recent theories built in the ivory towers of western academia.

IN THE HEARTLAND OF THE GURUS

Our rapid crossing of northern Pakistan prepared me to enter India by feeling its underlying and waxing presence, as an aroma that grows stronger when we approach its source. A few short miles from Lahore in a plain unbroken by any physical boundary India awaited us behind the Wagah border post. I remember watching with delight the swaying eucalyptus, slender poplars, shiny sal trees and crimson draped jacarandas in the warm March sun shining in a flaxen blue sky, while completing the immigration formalities.

It felt as if the soul of the country was revealing itself to me in the tulip-like turbans of the bearded martial Sikhs, in the nimbly scampering squirrels, in the flocks of twittering mainates, in the rhythmic call of the silky black Koel bird and in the mournful lament of peacocks set against the raucous background of ravens' cries. The chattering green Alexandrine parrots shot through the foliage as if to remind me of Attar's *Mantiq ul Tair* in which they are seen as the birds of Prophet Al Khizr, the Biblical Elijah. All birds, teaches the Persian mystical seer, are shadows of the divine *Simurgh*, the symbol of the universal soul and they announced to Gautama under the Boddhi tree his imminent enlightenment by turning a golden colour. The nearby town of Atari had been the home in a very remote past of the illustrious line of rishis, the Atris, credited with the authorship of several vedic hymns and possibly ancestrally connected with the Greek hero Atreus and his descendents. Are the original tribal peoples not called atavikas in the *Mahabharata,* the etymological source of our word "atavism?"

There was a gentleness in the air, though we were still in sturdy, martial Punjab, that was at variance with the fierce tension I had sensed throughout Pakistan. The warlike nomadic fever fostered by Islam had gradually softened into the farmer's bucolic placidity. Was that how India had seduced and domesticated her many invaders, I fleetingly wondered? Trucks were still there in large numbers but the Indian ones were less extravagantly ornate and baroque in their display of the owner's or driver's identity.

The drive towards Delhi through the tree-hedged plain receding into misty horizons dented by the spires of brick kiln chimneys, was uneventful and it was easy to see that advancing armies could not easily be stopped in that flat, prosperous landscape. We soon reached Amritsar, the seat of the holy tabernacle of the Sikh faith, the wondrous Golden Temple, a jewel gasket set on liquid silver tray. It was so close to the border that it still felt as if we were in a suburb of Lahore from which we were now separated by the shadows of a million dead massacred during the partition exodus and by the memories of three wars since fought between the rival siblings India and Pakistan.

The hallowed Harmandir Sahib first built by the fifth spiritual and temporal leader of the Sikhs, Guru Arjun in the late 16th century with the support of Emperor Akbar, was destroyed by marauding Afghans in the 18th and rebuilt by Jassa Singh, the first Raja of Kapurthala whose Francophile and libertine descendent in the early 20th century was to become a celebrity in Europe for his lavish receptions and tiger hunting parties in which he hosted the fine flower of western aristocracy. We were to meet later the living members of that prestigious house. The gold coverings on the inner temple were supplied by the king of Lahore Ranjit Singh who did all things in magnificent style and one catches glimpses of that sumptuous era in the rich dark blue, orange and saffron vestments and turbans of the religious dignitaries who are custodians of this sanctuary.

The visit to that hallowed shrine left me with an impression of noble and martial simplicity and austere piety despite the lavishly ornate polychromous motifs that cover the inner walls of the glittering sanctum. The spotless cleanliness of the vast premises where many thousands of pilgrims pass every day contrasts with the unhygienic neglect that mars many Hindu religious seats and stands witness to the virtues taught by the Sikh masters while the huge dining rooms and kitchens in which untold masses are fed every day and where no one, irrespective of race and religion is denied access and nourishment, demonstrate that the community's priority remains the practice of charity and solidarity. The founder, Guru Nanak, not only prayed at shrines of many different creeds in India, he also journeyed to the Middle East and a Sufi mausoleum in Iraq keeps the memory of his visit. He is also said to have gone on pilgrimage to Mecca and his message emphasizes the essential unity of all spiritual quests.

Around Amritsar there is a district called Chinapati in the first centuries of the common era as it hosted some Chinese princes settled there by Emperor Kanishka. The expatriates were said by the traveller Huan Chwang (or Zuan Xang) to have acclimatized peaches and pears brought from their distant land in the Punjab. One can still notice among some of the local inhabitants the slanted eyes and high cheekbones of the Orient although it is not possible to determine if those are vestiges of the ancient Chinese influx or attest to the much better known and frequent arrivals from Central Asia.

The other towns and villages along the old grand trunk road I found monotonous and uninspiring, keeping few traces of the venerable history of the land. I felt for the first time that history, so treasured in the western world, fades into oblivion or at least benign neglect in civilisations more concerned with eternity, many of whose monuments are allowed to slowly crumble into the dust from which they were built. Only sandy mounds remain of the countless fifty centuries old cities of the Harappan age and excavations have yielded numerous but mostly small and exquisite objects of daily life in those remote times. By far their most precious and enlightening legacy are the peerless Vedic hymns and philosophical treatises that bear witness to the existence of an intellectually and spiritually sophisticated elite dedicated to the contemplation of transcendence and quest for ultimate causes.

Cities of the so-called Harappans or Indus valley people were geometrically laid out, carefully planned, well provided with water and sanitation grids; their citizens were experts in various arts and crafts but they were even more, it seems, concerned with the essential nature of reality and with the exploration of invisible dimensions of being. The Punjab, which may have been, with what is today Afghanistan and Kashmir the cradle of the Vedic culture is since many hundreds of years rather apophatic in the sense that it shuns anthropomorphic representations of divinity, being Muslim in the Pakistani West and partly Sikh in the Indian East. Sikhs worship the universal God whom they call Ram, like many Hindus, but do not they pray to idols and remain faithful to the spirit of the Vedic Rishis, who dwelt on the unknowable supreme self-abiding in the sky, in the fire and in all hearts even when they paid homage to any of its innumerable manifestations and attributes.

One of the first lessons I had learnt about India from a philosopher who had come to our home in Barcelona was that history in the Hindu perspective is a wheel: *Itihas chakra,* which rotates on an unmoving, eternal axis. Its rim revolves across the four seasons of cyclical time like the wheel of Fortune, not just for individual fate but for all creation. If one wants to know and understand the present say western historian, look at history but the Indian metaphysicians go further and point out that history visits us periodically – that is one meaning of the word *itihas* – as we go through successive cycles so that its remote periods are only important for the timeless laws we can learn from them and not for their dates and socio-economic peculiarities or transient personalities that can never be fully recreated as they truly were. If we cannot understand fully the current situation, how can we hope to capture the long past happenings for which we only have some traces and at best, often indirect, necessarily subjective testimonies?

The awareness of impermanence haunted me all the way to Delhi as I beheld the riotous caravan of images, colours, sounds and smells that assault a traveler on Indian roads. There was not much left of the illustrious past of the ancient city of Jalandhar, home of the fabled myrobalan berry supposed to confer immortality and sold in the medieval and Renaissance Europe by traveling healers and quacks. The town, called Prasthala in the *Mahabharata,* was said to have been the farthest reached by Alexander who had built there an outpost named after him. Much later, the 4th Buddhist Council is recorded by various traditions to have been held there. However, if Jalandhar, mispelt as Jullundur by phonetically impaired Britons, is now more than ever a bustling commercial centre, nothing visible is left of the neighbouring Hastinapura, the capital city of the Kuru dynasty that for centuries held sway over much of greater Punjab and Kashmir.

We crossed towns famous for the many battles named after them and which marked decisive watersheds in the fate of the subcontinent. Kurukshetra, Tarain and Panipat bore witness to the epic clashes between the various races and religions of South and Central Asia, related to such heroic or ominous names as Sri Krishna the God King of Vrindavan and Dwaraka, Mahmud of Ghazni, Tamerlane and Babur. At Kurukshetra, the finest knights and soldiers of the land called Bharat, according to the saga of the same name, had laid down their lives in a mighty fratricidal conflict fought over eighteen days more than three thousand years before the Christian Era. The war heralded the advent of the fourth age of Puranic chronology, the dark and unfortunate Kali Yuga and it is perhaps no coincidence that modern accounts of world history trace its beginnings to that very period some fifty centuries ago.

Much closer to us in the last thousand years were the successive waves of Turkic and Afghan invaders, all claimants to Alexander's conquering legacy, who were enabled by their military successes to plant the green banner of Islam on Indian soil. That chapter of the land's history offered the opportunity to draw parallels with Spain's contemporary annals although the grip of Muslim rulers on much of the subcontinent tightened at about the time when their coreligionaries in the Iberian peninsula were losing ground to the Christian crusaders of Castille, Aragon and Portugal. By the time Babur, founder of the Mughal dynasty, consolidated the Sultanate of Delhi, the hapless Boabdil, last Muhammadan ruler on the Spanish soil, had breathed his famous last sigh and repaired to Africa, after being expelled from Granada by the Catholic *Reconquista*. Unlike the Spanish, the Hindus did not form a "sacred union" among themselves to push back the occupiers, perhaps because their ancestral philosophy did not provide a theological justification for a religious war since it proclaimed the unity of all life. That metaphysical vision allows room for political conflicts but not for existential wars of extermination against "unbelievers and pagans."

To the Muslim *ulema* and warriors, Hindus were idol worshippers, followers of false gods, bound for hell unless they embraced monotheism and forsook their heathen past. To Hindus, on the other hand, theirs was the blessed land of *Aryavarta* where divine wisdom had been revealed to their ancestors but all peoples and nations had their own laws and religions, presumably adequate for their needs and adapted to their respective conditions. Dharma and fate are dictated by Karma and all are thus right in their own ways and must endure their lot. One may honour wise and holy men and women from all times and climes and follow their teachings and examples but formally converting to another faith makes no more sense than changing one's lineage or ethnic identity. The deities give power and wealth to whomever they please but these blessings only last for a time. Turks or Persians could take over land and establish kingdoms if that was the decree of fate, their belief system was their own business and at least some of its aspects, such as the gnosis of the Sufis, could even be accepted but the eternal dispensation is not affected by political vicissitudes.

Contrary to the followers of Abrahamic prophets, who are exhorted to make their faith the foundation of society by transforming the latter if need be, Hindus are comfortable with the advice of Jesus: "Give unto Caesar what is Caesar's." While some of the later Puranas and historical texts take a dim view of Islam or at least of its practitioners, many Hindus, and eventually a few eminent Muslims as well, sought to find echoes of Vedic and Vedantic scriptures in the *suras* of the *Holy Quran.*

As we can see, those respective belief systems of monotheists and polytheists have hardly changed until today.

III

Sultans and Sages

Guests of Nizamuddin

Shahjahanabad. The bustling, chaotic, crowded old Delhi of the Mughals gave us a noisy welcome even before we passed the Kashmiri Gate and proceeded, through the collection of faded buildings from the Islamic and British eras mingling with the usual ramshackle structures and incongruous modern edifices that fill and deface most Indian cities, towards the leafy haven of New Delhi. I had seen glimpses in many images and films of the latter's broad avenues, flowery roundabouts and Palladian white bungalows but before we reached them, we drove past the blood red crenellated walls of the Red Fort and the milky onion bulbs of the majestic Jama Masjid, which evoked for me gossamer visions of Indo-Persian romances and Rococo operas. We were tired by a long day on the road after many others and were relieved to arrive in the quaint, picturesque *basti* (walled area) of Nizamuddin, where a waif-like Dutch lady in her seventies called Hayat Bouman received us in her simple but elegant flat.

Nizamuddin, built around the hallowed *mazar* of the famous *Peer* Nizamuddin Auliya, is the Sufi spiritual mecca of Delhi and of much of India where many of the Saint's descendants and disciples still live. Hayat Bouman was a follower of one of the great 20th century mystics of the Nizami Chishtiya *tariqa,* the mystic and musician Khwaja Inayat Khan himself descended from a long line of spiritual teachers and composers who had set up what was perhaps the first Sufi fraternity in the modern West.

The Inayat Khan Sufi Centre was pervaded by the refined and meditative atmosphere of Sufism which the serenely handsome face of Peer Inayat personified by his mesmerizing gaze. The area is a magnet for white-clad, white-capped pilgrims from all over the country and for quite a few westerners who follow the Sufi *tariqa* (path), many of them from the Netherlands where the master built the main meditation and prayer seat of his order in Europe.

I felt a sense of unbroken continuity with the environments I had grown familiar with all the way from Istanbul to Lahore with the ever present *Tekkes, Turbehs* and *Mazars*. Inayat Khan's life was illustrative of the ever constant dialogue between East and West that his teaching reflected in the Hindustani tradition of the *Majma' al Bahrain,* the "merger of the oceans" evoked in the title of a famous treatise written by Dara Shikoh, the 17th century philosopher prince whose spiritual eclecticism had cost him his life before he could ascend the imperial throne to which he was heir.

Dara Shikoh's name means "equal to Darius", and he is one of the most attractive and interesting figures of Mughal Indian history as we discovered when we visited the seat of his personal library, known as the mansion of Ali Mardan Khan in Old Delhi, partly rebuilt by a later British official. He sought to unify Islam and Hinduism as he believed he had found the hidden source of the *Qur'an's* esoteric philosophy in the Upanishads in which he saw the *Kitab al Maknun* alluded to by the Prophet. His research and the enlightenment he derived from it, under the tutorship of his spiritual masters, the Qadiri Darwish Mulla Shah and the Persian mystic Sarmad Kashani, who is buried not far from his royal disciple, might have durably reconciled the Muslim ruling class with the Hindu subjects of the empire and brought about an intellectual fusion even richer than that which had taken place since the days of his great-grandfather Akbar but alas, the emergent Renaissance, a fruit of the syncretistic civilization that evolved out of centuries of Persian influence in India, was snuffed out by the wave of bigotry, which swept the Mughal realm when Dara's power hungry younger brother Aurangzeb seized the Peacock throne of Delhi after defeating and murdering his three siblings and imprisoning his ageing father, despite the entreaties of his sister Jahanara.

Perhaps to atone for his guilt, the fratricidal Padshah remained all his life under the influence of narrow-minded Mullahs and strove to practice a puritanical orthodoxy in his personal life and enforce it over others by oppressing his non-Islamic subjects and destroying as many "heathen" temples as he could manage to, so as to build mosques in their place. That nefarious policy resulted in a series of rebellions, which undermined the state as well as in the wilting of the arts and industries, a decay of the culture and a paralysis of society that made it vulnerable to the rising influence of European traders and mercenaries.

Less than fifty years after Aurangzeb's bitter and lonely death in an army camp in the Deccan in 1707, his feeble and squabbling successors had become petty monarchs used as puppets by sundry regional chiefs and, increasingly by the agents of the British East India Company.

Once again, the attempt to bring back an imaginary magnified Arabian past, so frequent among Muhammedans, stopped in its tracks a healthy and necessary natural evolution, which might have protected India and Muslim lands from Western colonial ambitions.

More than once we debated with Both Muslims and Hindus, who gathered in Hayat Bouman's drawing room about Dara Shikoh's ecumenical endeavour to provide a philosophical and religious foundation for the so-called *Ganga-Yamuni* (Indo-Persian) civilization that had spontaneously formed out of the interaction between the subcontinent's denizens and their various faiths and traditions. The Timurid emperors failed to erase the religious divisions between their subjects, partly because of Aurangzeb's obdurate convictions and one should note that other attempts in the same vein had been aborted centuries earlier in Abbasid Baghdad and in Ummayyad Andalusia by conservative dogmatic reactions. Islam is historically close to the other monotheistic religions born in the West Asian desert and Delhi with its domes and slender spires awoke in me memories of Byzantium.

Dara Shikoh's theosophic universalism, inspired by Akbar's spiritual beliefs, survived however in the music and poetry of Muslim

India after him, in spite of periodic hostile reactions from Wahhabi and Deobandi theologians and Inayat Khan exemplified that syncretistic legacy in his compositions and his writings as did his own scholarly disciples. I still recall one Dr Abdul Wahid Khan, a student of Rene Guenon, one of my father's favourite metaphysicians who coincidentally shared the name that Guenon had been given when he embraced Islam. Our conversations in one of the tiny tea shops of the Nizamuddin neighbourhood on those pleasantly warm March evenings familiarized us with the traditional ambiance of Delhi that had not yet changed much since the early years after independence, while helping me to improve my English speaking skills.

We learnt more about our long departed spiritual host, Hazrat (a honorary title meaning "saintly") Inayat Khan, whose life itself provides rich material for a novel. Born in 1882 in a noble Muslim family related to the Sultan of Mysore, Tipu Saheb, known in France for his alliance with Napoleon against the British East India Company, the Peer was the most celebrated musician at the court of the immensely wealthy Nizam of Hyderabad before he journeyed to the West in the early years of the twentieth century to spread the message of the Chishty Nizami *silsila* (initiatic chain) of *Tasawwuf* (esoteric wisdom) to which he belonged. In the United States he married an American, Ora Ray Baker, and later settled in Suresnes, near Paris in an area that I was familiar with, and had three children. His house there, called *Fazil Manzil* or 'Temple de l'Universel', where he lived during the difficult years of the First World War, still stands as a memorial to his mystical gospel, encapsulated in ten foundational principles that are in harmony with all religions so that his creed is not specifically Islamic but rather reflects the traditional "catholicity" of Indian philosophies.

After falling gravely ill, Inayat Khan left France to return to the land of his birth and chose to die next to the mausoleum of his beloved spiritual master Nizamuddin, where we were given the details of the story. The work of the master was continued by his children, especially the well known Peer Vilayat Khan who headed the

International Sufi Order but also in a very poignant way by his daughter Noor un Nisa ("light amongst women"). That frail looking beautiful young Eurasian, orphaned before she reached thirteen, drafted by the British Government during the Second World War, volunteered to perform the most dangerous function in German-occupied France as a clandestine radio operator for the Resistance, drawing inspiration from the methods of non-violent struggle advocated by Gandhi. Under the code name of Madeleine (coincidentally my mother's own name), she refused to leave her increasingly threatened location in spite of several warnings given to her by colleagues. She was eventually betrayed, arrested by the Gestapo and interrogated for a year. The Germans could not get her to reveal any details about her network and took her to the Dachau Concentration camp where she was shot and cremated. The year was 1944. Her last word is said to have been "Liberté." She was barely thirty at the time and is acknowledged as a martyr of the French struggle for liberation.

I marvelled, like many before me, at the unpredictable succession of lives and events that had led a long line of Persian spiritual teachers settled in India since the 13th century to beget this doe-eyed woman, like a blossoming flower sprung from an ancient exotic tree, fallen in one of the most tragic period of recent European history.

Our temporary immersion in the saga of Inayat Khan and his family gave us a sense of being in intimate communion with his medieval spiritual forebear, the hallowed Nizamuddin and his most famous follower, the polymath and statesman Amir Khusrau, perhaps the only poet born in India whom the supercilious Persians regard on par with their greatest native bards such as Ferdawsi, Saadi, Hafiz and Nizami. The township or *khanqah* of Nazimuddin, built around Nizamuddin's and Amir Khusrau's adjacent graves, basks in their memories and the descendents of the Saint, the Nizamis were traditionally spiritual masters and advisers of the Sultans of Delhi, including the latter Mughals who often visited the shrine to pay respect to the Hazrat and to his community according to the ancient practice of *ziyara*.

Standing before his tomb, an ornate white shrine crowned by a marble cupola modeled on the shape of a lotus, next to a five-domed mosque surrounded by purple walls, like a miniature royal fort in which several emperors and royal princes and princesses are buried near their spiritual master, I more than once evoked this apparently supernatural personality who attracted such veneration and love over the centuries, to the extent that his teacher called him in the attestation issued at the conclusion of his studies *Maqbul al Mashaykh al Akbar*: the beloved greatest of shaykhs, when he was still quite young.

Nizamuddin, as his title indicates, was one of the *Auliya* (friends and representatives) of Allah with whom he achieved intimate communion in those higher states of ecstasy known as *ghousiat* and *farwaniyat* in Sufi terminology. He on various occasions performed the forty day fasting solitary retreats known as *chillahs* which are part of the initiatic steps for those who tread the mystical path since very ancient times in the Middle East. Jesus also is said in the Gospels to have retreated and fasted in the desert for forty days.

Nizamuddin belonged to one of the lines of descendents of Prophet Muhammad through Imam Reza, whose mausoleum we had been to in Mashhad in Eastern Iran. His grandfather had fled Bokhara to escape the Mongol invasion and had settled in Badaun in Northern India not too far from Delhi, where the saint was born. In his childhood, the orphaned boy experienced dire poverty with his mother and often had to do without food. Early in life in Baghdad he met the leading Sufi masters of the day and embraced the Chishty tradition when he became the disciple of the Central Asian mystic Khwaja Qutb Bakhtyar Kaki, whose surname came from his reported gift of miraculously materializing bread like Christ himself and who lived in the ancient site of Mehrauli ("the Light of the Auliya"), one of the early settlements in the area of greater Delhi.

Kaki was a follower of the great saint of Ajmer, Khwaja Moinuddin, founder of the Chishty order of Derwishes, at the origin of innumerable branches of that sprawling spiritual family that encompasses much of the Indian subcontinent. In the *Tasawwuf*, a deserving *murshid* (disciple), one who in the words of Nizamuddin "has knowledge, reason and love," is called *ma'ruf* (the knower of the highest gnosis) and becomes a *khalifa*, an "accredited successor" in the path traced by his peer with whom he has achieved the spiritual intimacy known as *muraqba*. In that way, the spiritual hierarchy of Islam parallels the political one and Nizamuddin was called by various Sultans of Delhi *Sultan al Mashaykh,* implying that he had reached imperial greatness.

I realized, listening to some of our new friends among the practicing Sufis of Delhi, that the Muslim mystical worldview is deeply infused by the awareness of different coexisting realms or dimension among which the most densely material and hence most commonly and directly perceptible or definable one, that rationalism dubs as the real world, is in fact the least important. That disdain for what modern education trains us to regard as the only solid truth goes a long way to account for the relative inefficiency of some eastern social systems and the negligent attitude of many people to material conditions because, for centuries they were given other priorities.

The last Mughal Padshah Bahadur Shah Zafar, who was a renowned poet, expressed this state of mind, so central to India's pre-muslim philosophies as well, in a poignant verse:

"Has this impermanent world ever afforded gain?"

The *'alam al ghaib* or the *batin,* the hidden realm, is much present in the minds of all those who have not been completely divorced from their atavistic cultural background in Asia and in the other "undeveloped" regions of the world. I was told about the constant presence around us of the forty (forty being a symbol for an indefinite number) *Abdal*, the invisible saints who help the spiritual pole or axis (the *Qutb*) to look after material creation and one of Nizamuddin's *khalifas*, Syed Mahmod Kashnakar was said not to have died but to simply have moved into another dimension out of which he manifests every now and then and performs miraculous deeds for the deserving.

According to popular lore, the *abdal* can take the form of the vultures that used to gather around shrines and cemeteries when their numbers were larger in pre-industrial times. In that year 1975, they had already became rare in India's capital due to the noxious spread of certain pharmaceuticals in the food chain but the connection made between enlightened deceased beings with those rather unattractive scavenging birds struck me. It was a powerful allegory hinting at the sacredness of all creatures, including the more repulsive ones by lending them an exalted secret identity and this is how the Indian religions have for millennia protected the ecosystem. Dogs, snakes, pigs, rats and crocodiles are among the many species that have a divine association and there are no impure animals in Hinduism – although the Brahmins have strict criteria of ritual purity – as opposed to the Zoroastrian and Abrahamic faiths, which ostracize those deemed unclean.

As numerous as the vultures that dwelt there, the tombs of hundreds of spiritual teachers and mystics associated with Delhi are still to be found and many are visited by devout pilgrims from all over South Asia. It is as if a crowded invisible city throbbed beyond the borderlines of our conscious perception, within and beneath the bustling metropolis that encompasses at least nine capitals and thousands of years of history, going back to the Indraprastha, the seat of the five Pandava brothers celebrated in the *Mahabharata.* In his 1994 novel *City of Djinns,* the Scottish writer William Dalrymple frequently alludes to this mysterious realm where dim memories merge with fantastic visions.

The supreme patron of the Sufi hagiology of Delhi and throughout the Muslim world is *Al Khizr,* the biblical Prophet Elijah, he who was taken to heaven in a fiery chariot and whose green cloak (*khinqah*) accounts for his surname of "The Green One." Al Khizr is said to have been the hidden teacher of Bakhtyar Kaki in the latter's childhood and the ancient village of Khizrabad near Mehrauli carries his name. The shrines of the masters of *Tasawwuf* are usually painted green as are the embroidered *chadar,* cloths covering their tombstones and I still remember those magical moments, during the invocation ceremony known as *dua roshnai* held before the *maghrib* or evening prayer, when the brocade clad, green turbaned peer of a shrine leads the veneration of the grave, sprinkled with scarlet rose petals, in the waning glow of sunset enhanced by clusters of scented green candles. *Qawwali*, devotional songs in Persian and Urdu are then usually intoned by all present in the tradition of the *sama,* the ecstatic recital whose very name evokes the second Veda which is indeed a collection of hymnic prayers.

Qawwali recitals, known as *mehfils,* comprise various sections, including the *Qulbara*, in a mix of Arabic and Hindavi words, followed by a *talasagar* (an ocean of tunes) and a *rang* (colourful) itself divided in two parts before a conclusion in the form of a *Qaul* (of which *qawwali* is the plural form), a singing recitation of utterances attributed to the Prophets and to Sufi mystics interspersed with *tiranas,* syllabic melodies articulated around the samskrit names of the seven notes of the scale.

In spite of the differences in form and language, it was easy to grasp the continuity of the Indic tradition in that lyrical inflexion of Islam that owes much to Nizamuddin's best known lay devotee Amir Khusrau. He was born of a Turkic nobleman from Central Asia and a Rajput Indian princess and is credited with the creation of medieval and classical North Indian musicology as well as with the development of the Hindavi hybrid language although, like many in that society, he was also proficient in three or four other tongues between which the borders were fluid and variable, including the Gangetic region's medieval vernacular known as *brajbhasa* or *khari boli*.

Khusrau's literary production is so vast that much of it is still untranslated in European languages but the glimpse I got of his monumental *Ijaz I Khusrawi* evinced his ability to vividly describe the myriad professions and trades practiced in the Delhi of his day which he dithyrambically called *Hazrat e Dilli kanaf deen e dar Jannat adan ast ke abaad baad* ("holy Delhi, the haven of faith and mankind, a garden of paradise and so may it flourish").

I could not help finding that praise excessive even if the city of his day may have been more full of charm than the dusty and noisy metropolis we were in but it was pointed out to me that in Amir Khusrau's time much of Asia, including the great capitals of the Middle East such as Baghdad, Damascus, Bokhara, Merw, Nishapur and Herat lay in ruins and turmoil after decades of Turkic, Mongol and other invasions so that northern India was indeed a refuge for much of the spiritual, literary and scientific elite of the disintegrating Muslim Khalifate and it was to remain so until the time of the fateful devastation that was wrought at the end of the 14th century by the hordes of Timur the Lame.

The Persian poetic style was known for its ornate panegyrical excess but Khusrau's encyclopaedic descriptions of daily life in his age was akin to earlier Hindu novels such as Somadeva's 11th century *Brihadsaritsagara,* which enchant the reader with their seemingly endless tales, fables and anecdotes, both realistic and fantastic.

Very near to and yet so different from the crowded and noisy Nizamuddin *basti* whose labyrinthine, dirty alleys brought to mind the *Cour des Miracles* described in Victor Hugo's *Hunchback of Notre Dame* the majestic tomb of Emperor Humayun, second of the Mughal rulers spreads its manicured lawns and thick groves around its geometric red and white, palace-like arcades and domes. That son of Babur, whose ancestors included both Genghis Khan and Timur chose to be buried as near as possible to the dargah of Nizamuddin. He and his widow, Hamida Bano Begum who supervised the construction of that sublime mausoleum, were said to be habitual readers of the *Fawad al Fu'ad,* the Peer's discourses recorded by Amir Hasan Abu Sizji. They must have known, like earlier kings that, in keeping with the instructions of his master Baba Farid Shakarganj: "Do not turn your attention to worldly goods. Do not accept grants of villages or gifts from kings," the *Khwaja* had always refused to meet with the many sultans who succeeded one another on the throne of Delhi during his lifetime but yet, they sought to draw inspiration from his saintly and abstemious life in the midst of the pomp and wealth that surrounded them and they craved the honour to lie next to him in death.

Kings and princes probably meditated on Saadi's verse that was intoned by thousands during the massive funeral procession that took Nizamuddin to his last repose after his *wafa* (extinction) in 1325 when the recently enthroned Sultan Mohammed bin Tughlaq was one of the pallbearers:

As tamasha gah e alam ru e tu
Tu quja bahar namasha mi navi
(O thou who drawest the gaze of the world
On what doth thy gaze linger?")

On reflection, the symbolic equivalence between the hidden otherworldly powers of the *Akhyal* (the sages) and the visible magnificence of sultans and shahs, between the *alim* (he who knows) and the *amir* (he who commands) is a universal feature of theocratic societies. In China, as I had learnt in my childhood, the emperor was to be *nei sheng wai wang* (wise inside, kingly outside) and the accomplished vedic monarch was *rajarishi* similar to Solomon in the Abrahamic traditions. However, in most cases, the two hierarchies were separate and they in fact appeared to be in reverse to each other like the interlocked triangles in the six pointed star.

The spiritual monarch was the poorest and humblest (*faqih*) because his kingdom "is not of this world" so that he stood at the bottom of the political and economic ladder as the servant of all but he was the absolute sovereign of the invisible world where the temporal ruler was but an insignificant subject as "the first will be the last."

This paradox was expressed in the Arab name *malik,* which means master or king but is often borne by slaves. Europe long retained that notion which was illustrated on Carnival when a man of menial rank was parodically crowned as king for a day in the spirit of the Roman saturnalia. In India, kings would prostrate themselves at the feet of the most materially bereft ascetics and both Hindu rajas and Muslim sultans would walk, often barefoot, to the *manzils* of the mystics and bend to the ground before them.

In her autobiographical poem, the aforesaid princess Jahanara, who for years effectively governed the immense Mughal empire on behalf of her sybaritic, art-loving father and called herself a *Faqira*, as she had been initiated to the Tasawwuf, narrates how she went seven times around the grave of Peer Moinuddin *gharib nawaz* ("Providence of the poor") Chishty of Ajmer, "sweeping the ground with her eyelashes and painting her eyes with the dust of the soil." The Invisible was the most important in those royal eyes.

The 12th century Moroccan cartographer of the Normand rulers of Sicily Al Idrissi tells us that when kings died in ancient India, they were paraded around the city lying in a low carriage while their long hair swept the dust behind them, like Hector's mane when Achilles dragged his vanquished foe's corpse behind his chariot circling the walls of Troy. That rite, evocative of Ozymandias's epitaph, was intended to show the humility of all perishable things and the vanity of human glory.

This essential awareness is regarded as nonsensical in our positivist technocratic and capitalist societies when money, as the key to all power, is the indispensable determinant of status so that knowledge is only valued if it provides wealth and the dead are hidden away, not to frighten the living or to cast doubt on the materialist belief system.

Even the most power hungry, greedy and ruthless monarchs of the past had to pay respect to the spiritually realized. We notice that attitude on the part of the monarchs of Judea described in the Bible as we do in India, China and in all other countries in times past. The very same Muhammad Tughlaq, who had taken Nizamuddin to his last abode on his shoulders, was immensely generous and even humble before men of religion, but also cruel and tyrannical to the point of insanity. His historians claim that he submitted himself to the judgment of the *Qadi*, (the Islamic judge) like all his subjects, accepted the verdict and provided the required reparation if convicted. The Moroccan ambassador and scholar Ibn Battuta, who visited him a few years later in his fortified capital, reports that he saw him once surrounded by Hindu yogis who performed levitation in his presence, thus rising up to the ceiling to the diplomat's great amazement.

So shocked was the erudite globe-trotting Ibn Battuta by the uncanny scene that he had to be comforted by the Sultan who assured him that those yogis on whom he lavished his seemingly boundless largesse as he did also on Muslim clerics, could perform even greater miracles.

The annals of Delhi are full of such wondrous tales that never failed to enchant me, especially since I was treading the soil where they had been enacted. In that mystical climate, it is but natural that the rites of power and allegiance on the spiritual level were similar to those enacted in the secular realm. Disciples swore oaths of fidelity, *bayahs* to their masters and were given by them, if deemed deserving, decrees *(khalifatnamas)* affirming their legitimacy as successors in the tradition. Some Sufi Peers ceremonially conferred spiritual knighthood *(futuwwa)* like kings and anointed their elected successors. Every year the spiritual wedding (*Urs*) of the saints is celebrated in a joyous and lavish ceremony highlighted by musical recitals in which participants are invited to symbolically commune in the mystical *sharab al mohabba,* the wine of divine knowledge and love.

Nizamuddin, as many other Sufi masters, evinced his assimilation of widespread Indian spiritual usages by not eating meat and enjoining non-violence amidst the bloodthirsty grandees and soldiers who thronged the capital city. He explicitly acknowledged that many religions and forms of worship were equally valid and respectable in his famous verse: *Har qawm naast radh e deen e wa qibla qaab e,* which led Amir Khusrau to conclude that the real lovers of the Divine make no distinction between heresy and faith, contrary to the affirmations of orthodox Islam. It also shows that many Muslims subscribed to a synthetic creed that transcended formal systems.

The *Khwaja* often visited, on the outskirts of the khanqah, which kept on growing around his hermitage the Qalandari darwish Shamsuddin Ataullah who covered himself in ashes like a Hindu *aghori sadhu*, slept in a grave-like hole in the ground and hid in the bushes when visitors came to see him so that he had been given the surname of Pattey Shah (leaf clad king). Qalandaris were wandering ascetics who walked the trails between Arabia, Iran, Central Asia and India, often practicing the vulcanian craft of ironsmiths inherited from an archaic Indo-Iranian tradition. They were credited with magical powers and wore ankles, ear rings and bracelets made with the metal they forged. Their non-conformist and solitary lifestyles made ordinary people see them as infused with divine madness and it would be vain to regard them as belonging to any particular religion although most were born in the Islamic fold.

THE YOGIC AIR MARSHALL

I recall going one day to a gathering at the house of a recently retired Air Marshall, Suren Goyal who was to become a friend. He was an accomplished yogi who had used some of the mental and physical techniques taught in that wondrous science to perfect his mental and physical performance when flying supersonic Russian jets and he had conducted seminars on yoga for military personnel in the USSR and other countries behind the Iran Curtain. He was now studying *kayakalpa,* the process of age-reversal that, according to the yogic traditions can be mastered. He sometimes told us stories of things he had witnessed in his childhood such as the one when he had killed a bird with a sling and when, much saddened by his unexpected bull's eye shot, a passing *sadhu* had picked the little feathered body slumped on the ground, placed it in his palm, muttered some mysterious words and swung the bird into the air where it flew away in a whirr.

Fresh from my rationalist education at the French Lycée, which the environment at home had only partly mitigated, I could not help being skeptical when I heard such claims. My father commented that the world's sacred scriptures refer time and again to miraculous resurrections, including the most famous one in the Gospels and if Christ himself was said to have brought a few people back from the dead, it would be illogical to assume that all other reports of such prodigies are mendacious or deluded.

At the house of Air Marshall Goyal we met a number of spiritual seekers from various countries. One meeting was addressed by Dr. Homer Jack, an American who was then the General Secretary of the World Conference for Religion and Peace and a scholar on Mahatma Gandhi's life and works. We conversed with him and his wife about India, which fascinated them although they had on it the perspective typical of their nation, separated from ancient Asian cultures by the conceptual chasm that lies between the utilitarian and monetary rationale of its social system and the metaphysically rooted civilizations of times past.

I still remember that Homer Jack expressed some concern when he gathered from our words that we intended to spend long time in India and some years later, as a good academic, he wrote in response to one of our letters that he wished I would go back to the West, reintegrate the educational system and get some degrees that would assure me of a job. "You can't be lecturing all your life," he warned. However, we had already chosen another route, in the words of Robert Frost: "I took the one less traveled by

And that has made all the difference."

Suren Goyal explained that the philosophy of the *Bhagavad Gita* had made present to him both the illusory or rather "relative" nature of reality, including the grim scenes of war, and the obligation one has to perform one's duty in the life path that choice and fate have traced together. As a warrior he internalized Krishna's command to Arjuna to abide by the *kshatradharma*, the code of the fighter for a just cause although there is no absolutely just cause in any conflict and violence inevitably generates a karma that also dooms its perpetrator.

Only ascetic renouncement (*tyaga*) inspired by genuine *vairagya* (detachment from all wordly things) frees one from the chain of cause and effect. The exquisitely complex and paradoxical reasoning of Indian philosophy may appear on the surface ambivalent, amoral or even cynical to someone brought up in the rather Manichean "good and evil" Judeo-Christian dichotomy but it has the infinite merit of accounting for the otherwise intractable contradictions of daily life and thus avoiding the hypocrisy that seems inherent to "spiritually semitic" societies in which killing is in principle forbidden though they have arguably caused more bloodshed of people and animals and developed more powerful weapons of war than the followers of all other religions.

By setting seemingly unachievable ideals, Western civilization often appears to be an exercise in moral self-deception.

India produced Chanakya or Kautilya, her best known political economist and strategic thinker, almost two thousands years before Machiavelli but, unlike the latter, the former's empirical, pragmatic advice was not regarded as an antithesis to mandatory but impractical religious moral tenets. As Christ had said: "Give unto Cesar what is Cesar's and to God what is his."

Hindu and Buddhist scriptures describe all the worlds as being one and make distinctions between three different ways of life, ruled by action, knowledge and devotion respectively. They acknowledge that active life in this conflicted realm carries specific obligations, some of which entail the defence of the extended self, embracing family and community. The way of the sages on the other hand implies *Ahimsa,* imperfectly translated as harmlessness which Mahatma Gandhi sought to apply to political action, though that is not advocated in the Gita from which however he drew much inspiration.

TALKING OF GANDHIS

We had the opportunity to investigate that controversial issue with some Gandhian leaders whom we met then. One was Devendra Kumar Gupta, secretary general of the *Gandhi Smarak Nidhi* (memorial fund) for whom my father had an introduction from an eminent French agronomist and biologist called Professor Keiling, a leading of the Gandhian economist J. C. Kumarappa who had been among the very first champions of sustainable development with his recipe for an economy of permanence. In this area too, India was a pioneer due to the preservation of her ageless traditions. My father shared the conviction of certain conservatives that those who can understand the past are able to see the future, unlike the ordinary men who keep trying to catch up with the fast fleeing present and are thus always left behind.

Gupta received us affably in his Spartan office, not far from Gandhi's serenely minimalistic cenotaph. The almost bare room was dominated by the grinning sepia portrait of the Mahatma, which I still recall spontaneously comparing with other "fathers of the nation" we had grown familiar with in the countries we had visited. The frail, bespectacled, bare torsoed man whom Churchill had contemptuously called a "naked fakir" looked very different from the martial and sartorial Kemal Ataturk, from the uniformed and beribboned Shah of Iran and from other opulent-looking military and civilian rulers we had been exposed to in Pakistan and all over the world. India, despite her millennial tradition of royal and religious pomp and glitter, was definitely at variance with other countries and, as popular wisdom holds, the habit makes the monk.

We spoke of many things with Shri Gupta, from organic agriculture to Nature Cure, Gandhi's own brand of health care rooted in the Indian folk tradition. Of course we could not resolve the riddle that can be worded as "what to do when the doctrine of non-violence is arguably not able to adequately confront aggressors or opponents in all circumstances?"

Gandhi had tried, at least in theory, to push his precepts as far as he could, to the point of excess as when he suggested that the British ought to deal non-violently with Hitler's Germany rather than wage war on him or that Hindus should lay down their lives under the swords of Muslim extremists rather than resist with force. On the other hand, one could point out at least one case when the self-same leader of the independence movement had not objected to the execution by the British government of an Indian freedom fighter guilty of murdering a colonial official and condemned as a terrorist.

Devendra Kumar explained that Gandhi was trained as a barrister and as such he had a deep respect for law and order so that he could not condone its violent breach even when he rejected the authority that imposed that order. He sought to achieve an orderly constitutional transfer of power and opposed some of his colleagues in the National Congress who, like the firebrand Subhash Chandra Bose, saw the need for a war of liberation.

The Mahatma always professed friendship for the British people and even, unlike his intellectual idol Leo Tolstoy, expressed qualified admiration for the achievements of their nation. One consequence of his upbringing and ideology was that he would more willingly admit the exercise of violence by the state than by rebels. In this he reflected the Hindu attitude, not dissimilar to the Chinese one, shaped by innumerable centuries of civilization and regulated by hierarchical religious and political authorities endowed with theocratic legitimacy.

One interrogation has remained in my mind ever since we emerged from that conversation with Gandhian scholars. It has to do with the justification of violence that is always questionable. For example, what if France, the United Kingdom and their allies had managed to come to an understanding with the Third Reich in 1939 in order to avoid war? Would the consequences have really been unthinkable? Much violence was feared in case of acquiescence to Hitler's rising claims but the violence that happened as a result of the declaration of war was unequalled in all previous history and left more than fifty million dead all over the planet. Would "appeasement" of the Nazi state have caused as much death, suffering and destruction? That elementary query is not welcome by the "moral" authorities that rule the world because it challenges the alleged righteousness of their actions.

The same question was asked in the *Bhagavad Gita* five thousand years earlier but in those remote days, war was a highly ritual affair between professional warriors who fought for honour as much as for power and wealth and it mostly spared civilians. It was thus deemed inevitable in some cases but can we say the same of the industrial extermination and ecological devastation implied by war in our age?

The conciliatory proposals suggested by Gandhi were not heeded because they contradicted too many allegedly "common sense" principles or rather ignored many fundamental interests held by all parties in the conflict but might they not have limited the damage and the pain inflicted on so many? Indeed it is far from certain that Britain and France would have declared war on Germany if they had known the shape and extent that the conflict was to assume. The refusal to use violence by at least one of two opposing parties may often reduce the overall amount of killing and destruction but it is not an easy decision to make, either morally or emotionally as it contradicts the primal survival instinct which tells us to either flee or fight.

"Gandhiji reflected every day on the circumstances and on his actions and changed his views and methods accordingly," said Devendra Kumar. "He was conducting a continuous experiment and was not dogmatic or sure of himself about anything, except his intentions. He could err or fail but he willingly accepted that risk and took responsibility. On the day he was killed he was wondering whether he had led India astray since he had not been able to avoid either its partition or the massacres that went with it. He probably was not surprised to die under an assassin's bullets."

One of our first evenings in Delhi, before we had even explored the city's famed ancient landmarks that entomb the memories of so many monarchs of various ages, we spent in the garden of Pundit Nehru's former official residence, a stately white neo-classical mansion which had been turned into a museum dedicated to India's first Prime Minister. It had been built for the British Commander-in-chief of the Imperial Indian Forces, in the so called of Delhi's so-called "Wren-Naissance" style after the great British architect.

I was surprised to learn that the chief planner of the new capital, Sir Edwin Lutyens happened to have also rebuilt the palacio de Liria of the dukes of Alba that I had seen many a time in Madrid. He envisioned Delhi as a new Rome erected to the glory of a Caesarian United Kingdom. Thus the great palace of the viceroys that has become the residence of the President of India in the heart of the imperial capital evokes in its layout both the Versailles of the Sun

King (it is slightly larger) and the Vatican's Saint Peter, erected as a symbol of a far away pontifical King-Emperor.

Amidst the towering domes, spires, boulevards and colonnades of that garden city, Nehru had chosen to reside in a relatively unassuming house laid out in an expansive English garden. We attended the inauguration of the Sound and Light show which portrays his eventful life and his talents as a freedom fighter, man of the world, writer, conversationalist and statesman. It was on that occasion that we first met his daughter Prime Minister Indira Gandhi whose sympathy for the people and culture of France was well known. Her father had been an Anglophile by upbringing and taste in spite of all his differences with Britain's policies but his political heiress, brought up partly in French-speaking Switzerland took a less indulgent view of the former and as a woman, her predilection for France was unsurprising.

The introduction to Mrs Gandhi only led to an exchange of bows and greetings that evening. That is when I discovered that she had a warm and bewitching smile for a reputedly austere person whose usual expression hinged on sternness or melancholy, no doubt because of her exalted position and difficult role in a sphere mostly occupied by men. She said two or three words in impeccable French and moved on. I somehow felt that we would meet her again more than once. One phrase that still hypnotically lingers in my memory out of the lyrical retrospective of her father's saga was one from Robert Frost he quoted in his autobiography:

"For I have promises to keep
And miles to go before I sleep..."

Nehru had died in a first floor room of that very house a dispirited man, in the painful aftermath of India's defeat at the hands of his former friend Mao of China in 1962. Indeed the incursion of the Red Army had exposed India's military weakness and perhaps her leader's idealistic naivete. Less than ten years later, his daughter was to brilliantly win another war, against Pakistan to midwife Bangladesh out of the former. She had restored the reputation of India's armed forces but there were clouds gathering at home when we arrived in the country. Some of her authoritarian socialist policies were meeting with increasing resistance across a wide political spectrum. In 1971, in the wake of that short conflict with Pakistan, she had abruptly cancelled the treaties signed by her father with hundreds of rulers of native states whose largely voluntary accession to the newly independent Republic had enabled India to preserve its political integrity and avoid potentially intractable strife.

The compensation offered to those many monarchs, big and small, for renouncing their powers, incomes and prerogatives consisted in relatively modest "privy purses" designed to maintain their establishments on which many people depended for their living. Yet Mrs Gandhi decided that a poor and socialist state could not afford to maintain such feudal privileges and make those payments. She may have had good economic and ideological reasons but she broke her father's pacts and faith and for many other causes, she now faced several domestic challenges, mounting accusations against her roughshod ways and a precarious financial situation.

A CONTINENTAL MOSAIC

My budding impressions of India confirmed many of the accounts of earlier visitors along the centuries that I had read. The land is an uncanny mosaic of the most diverse geographic and climatic environments and also, seemingly, a collage of all historical periods of civilization. It gathers in close, surreal proximity representatives of our technology-driven age with holdouts of medieval feudalism, personalities holding on to the Victorian era with survivors of the Paleolithic tribal past, Utopian Marxists escaped from Europe's industrial revolution with aristocratic survivors of the so-called western Enlightenment.

In 1975, even more visibly than now the 19th century man of letters Mirza Ghalib met Charles Dickens, William Thackeray and Pierre Loti, Sufi mystics co-existed with whisky drinking, race-horse owning tea planters, MIT-educated nuclear physicists haggled with

Kashmiri carpet merchants, gypsy caravans riding full-wheeled chariots crossed paths with gliding limousines, Sindbad the Sailor met the Beatles, the Dalai Lama blessed Japanese tourists and Jain ascetics walked the same dusty roads which the royal monk Gautama Buddha had trodden or rested under the *peepal*, mango and *neem* trees seemingly planted by Emperor Ashoka 23 hundred years ago.

The calm avenues of verdant New Delhi lulled us into a sense of nostalgic peace that was dispelled by Old Delhi's hectic congestion. Having read reports by wonderstruck visitors of the magnificent capital built by Shah Jahan in the middle of the 17th century, I could not but be sorely disappointed by what I saw. Only the colossal imperial mosque built by Aurangzeb had kept its original majesty intact, rising like a pantheon above the untidy maze of the old city where descendents of the Mongol and Turkish conquerors still dwelt, often in genteel or squalid poverty. The Red Fort, that contemporary of Versailles which in its heyday could favorably compare with any of the world's great palaces, is but a red shadow of its pristine state, when hundreds of delicate, jewel incrusted snowy marble pavilions and fruit-laden gardens seemed to float like a mirage above its bastions.

The Emperor, passionate about architecture, had planned his new capital in keeping with the traditions his ancestors had brought from Samarkand (built for his ancestor Timur partly by Indian stonemasons and craftsmen), and Bukhara but he had also taken into account the basic rules of town-planning enshrined in the Samskrit *Sulba Shastras* and one could compare the result in some ways to Beijing's Forbidden City, whose inner enclave is also surrounded by purple battlements. However, after the great 1857 rebellion, the vengeful British had treated Delhi with exceptional barbarity, massacring all inhabitants who had not fled and destroying many of the buildings while plundering and raping for days in a row. They had blown up many of the structures still standing in the Red Fort and replaced them with hideous barracks for their soldiers.

It is now difficult to imagine what the wide, tree-shaded and canal lined central avenue of Chandni Chowk, surrounded by flowering geometrically laid gardens, fine mosques, elegant bazaars, monumental caravansarais and palaces must have looked like in the middle of today's dense crowds and polluting traffic and only the random decaying arcaded mansion and a few Jain temples, hiding in a warren of narrow lanes, with their exquisitely chiseled inner walls and ceilings covered in gold and jewels, evoke the lavish refinement which characterized much of the city of yore.

Some of the foreign travelers who were received at their court and many later historians have described the Mughal emperors as some of the most accomplished potentates to have ruled anywhere. Such praise surely applies to Akbar, the third among them, whose breadth of vision, military talents, administrative acumen, energy, generosity, mystical insights and artistic judgment are unsurpassed.

Other Padshahs were exceptional in many ways; they had inherited the megalomania, the cruelty and refinement of their dreaded ancestor Timur as well as the mystical sway over men of their other forebear Genghis Khan; Babur was a gifted writer and a keen observer of men and things; Jahangir and Shah Jahan were outstanding builders and aesthetes while Aurangzeb was a powerful strategist apart from his sins, which included deceitfulness and bigotry. Their closest parallels abroad are probably the great tsars Ivan the Dread and Peter the Great, for absolute power, ruthlessness and the talent to govern, organise and create.

Later and lesser Mughals were effete by comparison, generally better known as patrons of culture and the fine arts than as rulers and the dynasty gradually declined as all living things do but altogether they left an immense legacy, which is no mean feat in a land already so crowded with remains of an unfathomable past.

We had a chance to enter two of the rather typical dwellings of well-to-do Delhi traditional families and I was struck in one by the faded but still ornately elegant layout of a 19th century interior in the Mughal style and in another, by the strange but seductive combination of the Liberty design fashionable in the thirties with the lavish and intricate furnishings and artworks of which most South Asians are fond, with religious paintings in the style of Raja Ravi Varma and Tanjore, reproductions of Amrita Sher Gill's master works and original oils by Chughtai, English hippic lithographs, chiseled silver and brass knickknacks, heavily sculpted ebony and teak furniture, ancient Chinese ivories, embroidered velvet Burmese walls hangings, gleaming Tibetan copper Buddhas and voluptuous soapstone and sandalwood deities, Kashmiri silk carpets and polychromous *papier mache* boxes.

The master of that house which evoked for me the old-fashioned charm of the colonial era was an important shop owner and importer and his numerous "joint" family which included a few daughters and daughters-in-law seemed to share that cavernous dwelling. I had to field many questions in my halting English from those young ladies who seemed vastly amused by us and our unusual lifestyle as road travelers from Europe. As usual in those parts, they were keen to know if and when I was planning to get married even though I felt that at my age that prospect was still remote. However, I had to remember that not too long ago people in India were betrothed even before reaching their twelfth year.

For some reason that evening brought to mind the film that has remained perhaps the most famous "Bollywood" production of all, Raj Kapoor's *Awaara,* which partly takes place in a palatial Bombay setting amidst highly "anglicized" characters who dress in smokings and evening gowns but speak only in Hindi.

The mix of East and West is a constantly varying combination, partly determined by economic factors and partly by socio-cultural ones. "It depends upon how much milk is in the tea," one of our hosts explained with a glint in his eye but he added that Marwari multillionaires from Rajasthan were likely to be far less westernized and fluent in English than many middle class Bengalis in Calcutta or even comparatively poor Parsis from Bombay so that the assimilation of the manners and ways of life of the former colonizers is not automatically tied to a higher financial status.

IV

Paradaksina: The Southern Present

A City of Many Mansions

The older royal towns that are part of greater Delhi over the centuries declined to become sleepy villages before being newly surrounded, like Nizamuddin by urban sprawl. In the southern suburb of Mehrauli we visited the site of the first capital of the Turkic sultanate, which was established there by a slave general of the Ghori rulers of Afghanistan on the ruins of an earlier Hindu city made famous by such luminaries as the great astronomer Varahamira.

The royal residence, the fabled Green Palace had stood in the shadow of the ornate Qutub Minar, that needle-like 200 foot high obelisk which may have been used as a giant sundial besides being a symbol of the Pole of the World, the *Khizr* or Elijah and in its shadow we admired the famed iron pillar, a mute rust free witness to the extraordinary metallurgical skills of ancient Indians described by several medieval visitors who called it *haft jush* (seven metals) and who tell us that the best iron was known as Hind, after its land of origin. Scientific investigations determined that this Garuda Stambha that stood for untold centuries in the courtyard of a Hindu temple, similar to the *Djed* pillar of an Egyptian Sun sanctuary, is protected by a layer of misawite (a compound of iron, oxygen and hydrogen) created by the high proportion of phosphorus in the metal obtained through a now lost casting process.

When we saw the scant remain of another former citadel, the *kotla* of Firoz Shah, it brought to mind the memoirs of Tamerlane in which the ruthless conqueror describes inspecting the fortresses of his defeated foe on horseback, distributing gifts to the assembled mullahs, praying at the various mosques and every now and then ordering the slaughter of some unfortunate prisoners or "heathen" local residents of the three cities of Mehrauli, Siri and Jahanpanah that made up the Delhi of his time and that had no less than thirty monumental gates between them.

The Syrian chronicler Al Umari wrote that the capital city was spread over 40 miles and comprised 21 different towns, which contained no less than seventy hospital, two thousand *khanqahs* (sufi gathering places) and a thousand mosques and madarsas. Siri long remained known as "the abode of the khalifate" because it had been allocated by the Sultan to prince Ghaziuddin, a grandson of the Abbasid Commander of the Faithful Al Mustansir who had come from Baghdad in circumstances that are not well known. According to Al Umari, Muhammed Tughlaq had no less than three thousands war elephants and twenty thousand Turkish slaves in his household as well as an army of two hundred thousand while ten thousand eunuchs served in his seraglio. For battles the war elephants' tusks were rubbed with poison in order to deliver mortal wounds to the enemies but Timur caused the feared pachyderms to flee by unleashing on them a drove of camels loaded with burning dry grass that made them run in panic towards the Tughlaq Shah's host, which disbanded under that onslaught.

The conqueror's personal account of his stay in the city in the winter of 1398-99 is enlightening as he was clearly impressed with the grandeur and wealth of that metropolis and made his wives admire the famous one thousand pillared hall (*hazar sutun*) of the palace in Jahanpanah whose stables were full of elephants, horses, camels and rhinoceroses. He almost makes excuses for the woeful massacre and plunder that took place during his occupation which he attributes to an unfortunate incident, claiming that he could not control his "savage Turks" and that the local Hindus "set fire to their houses, burned their wives and children in them, rushed into the fight and were killed." However, he also records without apparent regrets that he decided to have all prisoners slaughtered as they might have caused trouble otherwise and he points out in a lapidary manner that "Maulana Nasiruddin Umar, a counselor and a man of learning who in all his life had never killed a sparrow, now slew with his own hand fifteen idolatrous Hindus who were his captives."

The consolation however was in the booty and he gleefully alludes to the huge amounts of jewels, gold and other precious goods that were plundered. "The spoil was so great, Timur wrote, that each man secured from 50 to 100 prisoners, men, women and children. Excepting the quarters of the syeds (descendants of the Prophet's family), the ulema and the other Mussalmans, the whole city was sacked. Although I was desirous of sparing them, I could not succeed for it was the will of God" is his philosophical conclusion. Yet Timur, one of many tireless warriors who swore they only wanted peace, claims in another passage that he had "been in Delhi fifteen days, which time I had spent in pleasure and enjoyment, holding royal court and giving great feasts."

One might think there is an inconsistency between those two very different stories where perhaps unfortunately there is not as death was never far from the pageantry of royal abodes. According to some visitors, the executioners always stood at the ready with their scimitars at the outer gate of the palace and the bodies of their victims were exposed for three days on a platform in order to instill "salutary" dread in all passers-by as if to remind them that the Capitol is near the Tarpeian Rock, to use a famous analogy.

It now seems hard to believe (but perhaps not so hard) that the rulers and their royal courts indulged in their glittering ceremonies and festive pastimes in close proximity to those gory remains. However they were warriors, proud of shedding blood and they at least had the honesty not to hide the evidence of their cruel deeds or avoid taking responsibility for them, as political leaders are now wont to.

As it appears from the previous pages, Delhi's history, before the British colonial era, has left far more traces of the Islamic presence than of the country's indigenous hindu character.

DHIRENDRA BRAHMACHARI

One of the personalities we came in contact with gave us a glimpse of that strongly defined native civilization that was not so obviously present in that relatively westernized capital marked by its Turkic and Mughal conquerors. His name was Dhirendra Brahmachari and he was a famous yogi, close to Indira Gandhi to whom he taught that discipline and who consulted him on various matters. We had been advised to meet him by our friend the Parisian travel writer and photographer Francis Brunel and we accordingly went to the Yogi's institute where I remember meeting an athletic, long haired and bearded man whose torso was only partly covered by a white silk shawl. He looked rather young and had the powerful gaze and confident calm attitude that was to be expected in someone of his avocation.

We had been told that he had taught advanced yoga techniques to Russian cosmonauts and elite soldiers and that once in the middle of the bitter Moscow winter, he had been spotted walking the streets in such light clothing that amazed Soviet scientists had submitted him to various tests to understand his resistance to cold which was rooted in the practice of Himalayan ascetics known in Tibet as *Tummo*, the art of self-heating by mental concentration and breathing.

By the time we met him, Dhirendra Brahmachari had amassed a considerable fortune and owned a vast ashram on the foothills of Kashmir, near Jammu, featuring a zoological garden and a private airstrip on which he landed the plane that he personally piloted. I remember that he invited us to follow a yoga class that very day with one of the teachers and that did us much good as it always does. We were not to see the enigmatic and laconic Brahmachari again and several years later he died in a crash of his aircraft, doubtlessly taking many secrets, including political ones, to his pyre.

Our short stay in Delhi had come to an end and since we had bid goodbye to our travel companions from Turkey and to the vehicle that they had taken with them to Goa, it was time to embark on the long train ride towards Madras, our ultimate destination in the deep south of the country where the Theosophical Society's Adyar oasis was the goal of our adventurous journey from Spain.

ON THE TRAIN

After almost missing the train and being helped on board the already moving coach with our luggage by a providential young Indian couple that spotted our predicament, we experienced the first of many rail odysseys across the length and breadth of the geographic and human patchwork quilt that is India. I have but dim memories of those many hours paced and racked by the rhythmic staccato breathing, frantic or halting, of locomotives, interrupted by frequent whistles and bellows which provide the background noise for the landscapes running past the car's horizontally barred windows.

Of many passengers met by chance on the trip I have forgotten all but a few glimpses of faces and of words exchanged, including an unexpected conversation on Indian astronomy and astrology practiced in the medieval Buddhist universities of the country such as Nalanda, Pushapavihara and Vikramasila. When I asked our knowledgeable fellow traveler how those expert observers reconciled their sound scientific notions about the planets and stars with the mythology that depicted those astral bodies as gods and goddesses, his reply surprised me: "Depending upon the level at which you look at them, they can appear either as balls of gas or stone or as spiritual beings," he answered. The multidimensionality of Indian thought was expressed in that simple sentence.

We were ever more immersed in the bewildering, teeming mix of people and ages which brought to mind Dante's *Divina Commedia* and the epic and apocalyptic frescoes of painters of the Quattrocento. Rugged canyons, tree framed fields, stern forts built over craggy hills, tightly packed brick towns hugging the rail line and milling with squads of rhesus macaques, mud and straw villages ("wretched dwellings" as seen by the medieval missionary Giovanni di Monte Corvino) nestled amidst pastures and groves, broad rivers lazily meandering in their sandy beds decked in mosaics of brightly colored cloths drying in the sun, next to bathing children and buffaloes, as drawn in the landscapes of William and Thomas Daniell.

All that was a picture which has changed little along millennia. Against that immutable backdrop we could see scattered marks of our encroaching age in the industrial buildings and smoking smokestacks as also in the trucks and tractors plying the roads. As soon as one entered an urban settlement, grinding poverty and overpopulation forced themselves into our awareness still infused with the bucolic serenity of pastoral sceneries.

As everyone who has travelled in India knows, the sight of people in large numbers relieving themselves on both sides of the rail tracks in the early morning hours is an ordeal one always finds painful, no matter how inured one may have become to this unpleasant reality. It reflects persistent habits carried from rural ages which few seemingly have the will to change despite the growing influence of technology and modernity. What a letdown that was for one who remembered the eulogy by the ancient Arab geographer Abdullah Wassaf: "India's ... dust is purer than air and its air purer than purity itself; its delightful plains resemble the garden of paradise and the particles of its earth are like rubies and coral." Despite the obvious exaggeration, more recent visitors such as the future Lady Callcott in the early 19th century wrote similar praise and the soil is indeed ruddy in many areas, as if it were powdered coral.

Aside from the often unappealing urban sights, a journey through India always proves an invaluably exploration of a universe in which so many manage to live in such close proximity with so little. The railway stations themselves, mostly relics of British colonial architecture evince the vigor and diversity of the ecosystem in which men, animals and machines function in chaotic symbiosis involving rats, dogs, cats, flies, crows, pigeons, mynahs, parrots, bats and cows as well as large human families of many castes and regions picnicking, reading, sleeping or playing cards and boardgames on the floor.

In the teeming multitude, everyone, from the deformed and mutilated beggar to the stick wielding, khaki clad, shorts-wearing policeman, from the self-important station master to the humble tea and fried snacks seller, from the newspaper hawker to the skull capped Syriac orthodox Malabar priest, from the bearded Muslim pilgrim to the orange robed Hindu sadhu and from the dark suited businessman to the opulent lady wrapped in a shimmering sari and gleaming with jewels, has a place and a purpose. No one seems to envy the other, as if the subconscious awareness of karma kept everyone convinced that they got their just deserts according to the law of cause and effect applying across generations and reincarnations.

As Pierre Sylvain Filliozat wrote in his anthology of Indian literatures: "Castes and transmigration... The beings that evolve in this world are merely ephemeral passengers, transitional halts in the eternal cycle of rebirths. Everyone participates through his past which has made him what he is, to the whole universe. Everyone will experience, according to the acts he performs, other conditions in another time at another place."

A traveler who has read old descriptions of the places he visits is bound to compare his impressions with those earlier accounts. I often had Megasthenes, Al Biruni, Conti, Bernier, Hodges, Loti and other chroniclers in mind while I looked at the scenery and the people, listened to the conversations of other passengers or sipped the spiced and sweetened tea in discardable clay cups during one of many stopovers. So many have described the India they saw and in spite of so many shared observations the land is so diverse, complex and unusual that each one of them found and reported very different aspects and features.

In common demeanours and gestures I found this permanence of customs and mores described by travelers of centuries past. People drank from copper or silver-plated tumblers or jugs held above their lips, faces upturned, without touching the lid as Marco Polo had reported. They chewed betel and areca nut *paan* for hours and offered it to others as Al Umari had observed. Younger people touched feet with the tips of their fingers to greet their elders as Conti had noticed. Everyone sat on the ground, testifying to the respect, reported by

Marco Polo, in which they held the earth. Some women and children's faces and arms were caked in bright yellow turmeric paste as the Chinese trade inspector Chau Ju Kua had noted, adding that they looked like golden buddhas.

Everywhere, in spite of the demographic density and the obvious scarcity of resources for most people, there was that same impression of security and good natured calm that Conti was impressed with six centuries earlier.

Due to the immense number of regions and communities, it was no wonder that the descriptions of ancient visitors are often contradictory. While some talk of Indians being pleasure loving and sensual, others extol their asceticism and disdain for comfort and self-indulgence. Certain chroniclers saw them as formidable warriors; others discount their military prowess on account of the lightness of their build and weaponry. While not a few credit Indians with unsurpassed proficiency in trade and financial transactions, at least as many emphasize their overriding appreciation of wisdom as opposed to their indifference to opulence and display. The abundance of beggars is manifest according to several accounts but others marveled at the wealth and prosperity they noticed. Al Umari wrote that milk and butter had almost no value whereas people could avail of twenty one different qualities of rice and choose between "sixty five kinds of fruit, drinks and sherbets which are hardly to be found in any other country."

We could confirm with our own eyes that all those accounts were true but as fragmentary as the various perceptions of an elephant by the five groping blind men of the Indian fable.

India remains the least regimented and homogenized nation on the face of the earth. Our train passed emaciated wandering ascetics, turbaned blue-clad Sikh *Nihang* warrior monks and peasants wearing the famed Gandhi cap, which was in fact made better known by Nehru. A Brahmin priest with the occipital tuft of hair which the Manchu rulers imposed on all Chinese, walked on wooden clogs that had not changed in shape since Vedic days and wore on his forehead the vermillion and white trident painted with ash that alludes to Vishnu's mystical footprint, poetically equated to the celestial expanse.

On a country road in Central India, a procession of Jain *Digambar* "space clad" holy men, shaven, barefooted and stark naked, followed by a devout crowd waving peacock-feather fans composed a tableau of Edenic innocence and the peasants' wooden chariots pulled by lyra-horned zebus could have plied the highways of Pharaonic Egypt.

A sundry wedding party, all glitter and shrill fanfare evoked by its caparisoned white horse and gilded flower-decked calash the pageantry of a medieval Italian court while gypsy encampments haunted by copper skinned, wiry men and women of the *Gaudiya Lohar* tribe, clad in brightly hued and sequined garments and heavy silver bangles reminded us of those ancient convoys of jugglers and ironsmiths, *zingaros* and *romas*, experts in the magic and black arts that had slowly made their way to Europe across Asia and the Maghreb for centuries.

Al Idrisi wrote about those ancestors and cousins of the mysterious Eastern looking folks that have been given many misleading names based on their presumed lands of origin, whether Egypt, Bohemia, Hungary, Flanders or Romania. He notes that *chandalas* are singers and that the women are beautiful while *zakyas* specialize in dance and jugglery and the dark-skinned *dumbis* or *doma* – perhaps the origin of *roma* – are virtuoso players of string instruments. According to Al Beruni, they belonged to the lowest social groups in India, in the eight classes of *Antyagas*, and still remain as fiercely attached to their culture and tradition in their motherland as they are in Europe.

Among these many versions of mankind, monkeys, mostly fawn-haired, red faced, dog jawed macaques (the descendents of the *cynocephaloi* described by ancient Greek geographers) behaved like just another tribe. The Russian 15th century merchant Afanasy Nikitin had noticed that they had their own chiefs and exacted a tribute on street vendors who reluctantly tolerated their thievery. He wrote that when those simian armies came into a town, "they pull down houses and beat people." Instead of declaring war on those often annoying and occasionally dangerous intruders, Indians bore with them in the spirit of the truly hindu maxim "live and let live" which Ahimsa sums up in one word.

I was under the impression that macaques owed their impunity to their status as scions of Hanuman the divine ape who became the liege of King Rama and helped him to rescue his wife from her evil abductor but I was corrected by a fellow passenger who pointed out that the less frequently seen, aristocratic, grey-haired, black masked langhurs, related to the Moon deity, are the true descendents of the monkey-God although macaques, very human-like too, are protected as well. Indeed, Hanuman is said to have been a son of Kesari, a lion and of the dusky Anjana and the langhur's face and mane remind one of that mixed ancestry.

"You will see that when a single one appears, all macaques flee, so afraid are they of Hanuman's brood," our informer assured us.

RELIVING LITERATURE

Everywhere the ever changing panorama, studded with villages, temples, churches, funeral monuments and mosques of many styles and milling with toiling, resting or feasting humans brought to mind Conti's observation: "The number of these people and nations exceeds belief."

However to someone who had read some of the collections of magical and picaresque tales that ancient India produced with profusion and that were so widely translated and imitated all over Asia and Europe, this bewildering, kaleidoscopic moving picture was not unfamiliar. I fancied recognizing the shrewd and greedy traders, the wandering adventurers, the indigent landless laborers, the penurious priests, the begging ascetics who might double as spies or tricksters and the coquettish, glitter-enamoured young women described by the mysterious Gunadhya who wrote the original *Brihadkatha* with his own blood in *paisaci,* the demons' tongue.

Naturally the animals, wild and domestic were as present and active as in the famous fables of the *Pancatantra,* which had been copied in so many languages, from Mongolia to France. Only the chivalrous and womanizing princes of the old tales were missing from the tableau as if they had indeed fallen victims to the adoption of democracy.

I rued the absence of the colourful nobles described by Nikitin who "delight in luxury. They are wont to be carried on their silver beds, preceded by some twenty chargers caparisoned in gold and followed by 300 men on horseback and 500 on foot, and by horn men, ten torchbearers and ten musicians." The sultans, the Russian traveler adds, went hunting with trains of thousands, including the inevitable chargers, elephants and hounds as well as trained cheetahs, falcons, monkeys, dancing girls and foreign concubines (*haurikies*) by the dozens. It is interesting that those fantastic numbers are not cited only by Muslim chroniclers who are known for their penchant to inflate all that they saw or heard.

It took two full days and the night in between to cross India from north to south, a short trip if we consider that Al Umari wrote that in his day a similar journey lasted three years. If he was guilty of exaggeration as a travel guide he was closer to truth as an ethnographer and a naturalist since one who goes in a more or less straight line over any territory misses an infinity of things lying at every step of his route and in both directions around it. Reality is a fractal so that every portion of a whole is infinite too and the arrow of Zeno would never reach its target if it paused at every point of its course as the old Greeks realized.

Whatever we knew of the districts we crossed was enough to whisper to our minds names and images of ancient kingdoms. Mathura, the winter capital of the Kushans that we had become acquainted with in Pakistan, had been many centuries earlier the land of the Yadava clan and of their divine king Krishna, the most recent Avatar or incarnation of Vishnu.

In his account of Mahmud of Ghazni's conquests Al Beruni writes, "In the middle of the city there was a temple which can neither be described nor painted. The Sultan was of the opinion that two hundred years would have been required to build it. The idols included five of red gold, each five yards high, with eyes formed of priceless jewels... The Sultan gave orders that all the temple should be burnt with naphtha and fire and leveled with the ground."

I have always felt that, in spite of his professional duty to sing the praise of the ferocious plunderer, Al Beruni could not hide his revulsion at the devastation that was being carried out in the name of religion in order to satisfy the fanatical warrior's boundless greed.

Agra, the seat of the great Moghuls whose Taj Mahal has long been the ubiquitous, almost obsessive image of India in popular perception preceded Jhansi, was one of the strongholds made famous by the 1857 insurrection against British rule. Then came Gwalior, whose cyclopean fort towered on the horizon. In my teenage readings Gwalior was the capital of the Scindia Maharajas in whose service the gifted soldier of fortune from Savoy, Benoit de Boigne had risen to power and pelf. He had inspired many other real life mercenaries to try their luck in that war torn but still very wealthy land and also a plethora of historical novels about European noblemen in 18th century Hindustan, including one I had written when I was ten.

The next big city Bhopal for me evoked the fabulously wealthy begums and their French prime ministers who carried the name of and claimed descent from the royal house of Bourbon. In Malwa, we passed by Indore, another kingdom whose fashionable monarch Yashwantrao Holkar had become, with his glamorous American wife, a society icon in Paris between the World Wars, celebrated for his trend-setting sartorial taste, his collection of opulent limousines and the palaces he had built in the contemporary Liberty style in his remote Indian capital.

Ujjain, one of the seven holy cities, is also the mecca of Indian ancient astronomy, where calendars and ephemerids have been produced since untold antiquity by the *jyotishis* (astrologer-priests) of the temple of Mahakala (the god of cosmic time). It was built along the shore of the sacred Kshipra river, at the spot where the base meridian of Hindu cosmology meets the tropic of Cancer. The names of a few of those scientists who knew that the local universe is heliocentric and who had precisely measured the rate of revolution of the earth around the Sun and many other cosmic phenomena have come down to us as Brahmagupta, whose calculations guided Galileo in his discoveries, and Bhaskara among others.

Ujjain, also known as Aryn in ancient times, was the capital of the hoary kingdom of Avanti, cradle of the nagari script, which has become India's official syllabary and it had been illustrated by the exemplary king Vikramaditya who held his court there, gathering many reputed philosophers, mathematicians, physicists, chemists, astronomers, botanists, grammarians, logicians, poets, artists, architects and novelists, proficient in the sixty-four branches of knowledge listed in Samskrit compendia.

Modern historians have not been able to identify Vikramaditya after whom the Vikrama era, – starting in 56 BC and widely used throughout the Hindu world – is named because traditional chronologies are confusing. He was a contemporary of the Scythian invasions from the North West and is celebrated for repelling the aggressors known in India since the age of the Mahabharata as Sakas. He has also been credited with innumerable feats and conquests so that he may be compared with Charlemagne in the European *chansons de geste.* His royal virtues are sung in the *Narasimha Dvatrimsika,* a long poem which was translated in many languages and as far away as Mongolia during the medieval period.

I had first met the noble and chivalrous Vikramaditya in Sir Richard Burton's 'Tales of the Vampire', which is a translation of Somadeva's *Vetalapancavimsatika* of which he is the hero but much of India's medieval ancient and legendary literature revolves around Ujjain, from the days of the illustrious Kalidasa and his *Sakuntala*, so beloved of romantic European poets, to the fantastic adventures of the fictional princess Vasavadatta, daughter of a king of Ujjain and mother of the seventh universal emperor (*cakravartin*) Navahasanadatta, not to forget the historic prince Sudraka, the gifted author of that wonderful play called *Mrcchakatika* or 'the clay chariot', whose various characters speak in no less than seven different languages, which characterize their respective social ranks while remaining understandable to each other and to the audience because all those prakrit tongues are related within the wider samskritic family.

With the possible exception of Valmiki, the legendary composer of the original *Ramayana,* no author perhaps got greater acclaim in the whole of Asia and even in Europe than Kalidasa whose poetic abilities and dramatic talents have rightly been equaled with Shakespeare's. His epic *Meghadutam* in particular betrays his familiarity with Ujjain and the region around the holy Narmada river which, true to the conventions of Indian literature, he lyrically describes not without inserting many mythical and fantastic features as if to highlight the inseparability of the visible and invisible planes so that observation, vision and imagination are seamlessly interwoven. Ujjain is also one of the settings of Dandin's great thirteen hundred years old novel the *Dasakumaracarita,* a seminal work for the genre of poetic supernatural novel that flourished in Europe from the 16th century onwards thanks to the talent of authors like Ariosto and Tasso.

Nicolo Conti in the 15th century thought that the Vikrama era was another name of the Augustinian one (both words mean exalted or mighty) and that the name Aditya was a version of Octavian, the first name of Augustus although this may only be a reflection of western ethno-centrism. The fact that an acclaimed and glorious monarch left scant material traces of his existence, other than the praise of literati evinces the elusive complexity of India's past. Mahakala devours everything and no great care is taken to hoard vestiges of the innumerable kings and conquerors passing through the endless galleries of time. Indian civilization does not display the historical fetishism that has long been a feature of western societies although it has also long been practiced in China.

THE DECCAN

We pursued our itinerary through India's heartland, which still carries the name of Gondwana, from one of the major tribes that inhabits it. The Austrian geologist Suess used it to designate the austral mega-continent of the Pleistocene that until some 180 million years ago included South Asia, Australia, Antarctica, Africa and South America in a single landmass and whose mineral vestiges he detected in that venerable South Asia plateau.

Passing Daulatabad, whose castle on top of a sheer hill could only be reached by climbing a leather ladder in the past, I was reminded of the descriptions given by Al Umari of the vast bazaar located at the foot of that citadel, Deogiri for the hindus, where one could see thousands of dancing girls and ladies of pleasure coquettishly lying on benches or ornate bedlike *jhoolas* (swings), rocked by attendants, waiting for patrons and buyers. My teenager's imagination could not but be stirred by the image of so many young women, some of whom were reportedly proficient not only in music and dance but also in poetry, calligraphy and even in various philosophies "able to recite the *Qur'an* by heart and playing chess and backgammon." Al Umari reports that some slave girls could sell for as much as 20,000 gold *tankas* or as little as 8 if they were uneducated maidens only good to perform domestic chores. However, if they were "fit for conjugal purposes" the price could rise to 15 *tankas.*

Even if as usual Al Umari's figures should be viewed with caution, Conti less prone to exaggeration testifies that in the Deccan "public women are everywhere ... residing in particular houses ... who attract men by secret perfumes and ointments, by their blandishments, beauty and youth." "The Indians are much given to licentiousness," he adds, "but unnatural crimes are unknown to them."

Visitors of various origins seemed to agree on one thing. They were not disappointed by the women of India. The garrulous Al Umari reports that "... the pretty Indian girls are superior as regards beauty to those of the Turks and Qipchaks, besides their good breeding, manifold accomplishments and attainments; most of them are of golden colour, some are of brilliant whiteness mixed with red." He notes that women of many nations (including "byzantines") were available in those cities but that the Indians were unequalled in beauty, grace and sweetness and "in other things which words cannot describe." It therefore appears that those alluring creatures had not forgotten the lessons of the *kamasutra* and other classics of the abundant local erotic literature.

Watching the crowd on the platforms of the railway stations or on city streets, I thought of what Al Umari and many other visitors had described in times not so remote but yet so exotic in our view. The age when a large part of humankind was publicly and legally traded amongst a smaller and more opulent section has long ended, except in a few regions of the planet but the reality of general poverty and want is still overpowering. India became a socialist republic after gaining independence from colonial rule but the vast majority of its teeming population is still subsisting hand to mouth. The poorest only have their bodies and their wits and skills if any to survive. Although the idea of human bondage is now abhorrent and the institution thankfully banned, has there indeed been such a transformation in society and are the destitute today happier than those who sought to be purchased by a good master?

Even more troubling is the thought that slavery might come back one day under the pressure of economic need and greed that can easily bring about new changes of the common mindset. Are the very poor not always at the mercy of the rich and powerful and do we not, in one way or another, sell or at least lease ourselves to an individual, company or government to make a living and gain material security?

A few decades ago, many girls in India were still wedded before reaching puberty and in some cases to already married men, who were decades older than them and although that now seems little short of monstrous, we cannot regard the people of those times as inhuman barbarians, given the fact that they were inheritors of ancient and refined civilizations. Conversely, the celebrated founding fathers of the American Republic owned slaves and gave little thought to freeing them, much less to regarding them as equals, despite their many statements and writings about freedom, justice and democracy. Their equally "enlightened" successors did not hesitate much to despoil and massacre the native tribes whose territories they coveted.

Our criteria for morality and decency or even humanity are highly subjective and prone to frequent changes and one can therefore understand, though not approve, the otherwise decent persons who for many centuries saw nothing wrong in the institution of slavery in all its forms or in the existence of untouchability, which appears indeed more forgivable than the former since it is a predictable effect of extreme social stratification.

Those rather somber thoughts visited me on occasion while my eyes reveled on the constant, joyous or pastoral moving feast that flowed past the rail track.

Botany and topography reflect history and culture for knowing eyes. The fields, forests and hills we beheld spoke of so many stories buried in my literary memory, succeeding and blurring one another like remote stars in the mirror of a telescope. I read the lines of a pastoral poem of Amir Khusrau from a book we had bought in Delhi:

"The fields burst with the flowers of mustard
Mango buds blossom and the trees are aflame
On every branch the cuckoo cries
As the beauty smears kohl to her eyes
Maidens bring in flowers clustered
And the fields burst with the flowers of mustard."

The repetition of the first verse at the end of the stanza is a poetic device found in some Vedic hymns and it has perdured in European poetry in forms such as the ballad as well as in the Malay *pantoums* (*panchams* in sanskrit).

The broad-leafed *sal* forests that succeeded the thorny *babul* thickets endemic around Delhi brought to mind the birth of the Buddha, who had come into this world while his mother grasped the overhanging branches of one such tree in the Lumbini grove; as we advanced southward, they were replaced by the illustrious teak forests that had made India a prized ship-building country on account of their excellent timber; the *ashokas*, with their laurel-shaped leaves clustered on branches radiating around a straight trunk struck me as memorials to the great Buddhist Emperor whose name ("he who removes pain": *a – shok* whence comes the English word "shock") they share. Peepals evoked the Sakya Muni's enlightenment at the term of many days of meditation under the sacred ficus of Gaya.

Hirsute, sprawling banyans spread their pending tentacles and stalactites as if they were Vedic rishis who had been covered in bark and taken root after centuries of ascetic penance. Indeed, the name of one of the seven cosmic rishis enshrined in the constellation of the Great Bear, Pulastya, means "The hairy One."

The green pennants of banana trees reminded us that Mohammedan travelers had called their golden crescent-shaped fruit Adam's apples, in the belief that they adorned paradise. The gloriously crimson or orange starbursts of towering *palash* trunks rose high in azure skies, like the dyed nails of Radha, the eternal lover of Krishna sung by Jayadeva. The flowers were flashy and ephemeral like desire but the timber that they grew on was used for burning in vedic fire sacrifices. The sun glowing on their fiery petals was blocked from reaching the soil wherever thick groves of mango trees, blossoming in that season, covered it in permanent dusk.

Flocks of birds of many sorts flew, hopped and twittered everywhere and the occasional peacock perched over a wall or a low branch made me think of the fabulous *semenda* bird described by Conti who never saw one but relied on local tales that had certainly inspired the Persian legend of the *Simurgh.* Like the Greek Phoenix, that divine winged creature was said to be reborn from his ashes after burning himself on a nest-like pyre. The symbolic equation between birth and death is obvious in this allegory, which aptly symbolizes reincarnation out of the fire of the soul and Hindu ascetics and widows would in the past surrender their lives to the flames in order to rise to a higher realm.

What a contrast between that willingness to surrender the mortal shell like dead wood to the elements and the general concern of semitic religions to somehow preserve the physical envelope of human beings through burial in a box – as a robe in a drawer – or even mummification in the hope of a future return in the flesh!

On the sheer limbs, festooned by dark pods, of a towering gulmohar, bereft of foliage at that time of the year, I glanced at a murder of crows perched not far from a bevy of twittering parrots and I was reminded by that crest of *sable and sinople* – Saturn and Venus – of the famous medieval tale *Sukasaptati* in which a merchant gifts to his wayward son a raven and a parrot, knowing that those exceedingly clever birds will bring the debauched youth back to the path of dharma by example and discourse respectively.

The magical ambience of the story was still to be found in that scene, which brought to mind the uncanny sagacity of both avian species and a few of the sixty-nine fables with which the parrot of the story enlightens the inexperienced but lascivious bride of the young Madanavinoda during the latter's long absence about the wiles that women display to cheat on their lords and masters without being caught. The parrot protects his master's honor by keeping the lady so entranced by in his narrations that she never ventures out and one wonders how many parrots in reality managed to dissuade their lonely wards from surrendering to adulterous temptation. Sultan Timur, whose cruelty paradoxically was matched by his refined appreciation for beauty and romance, records that he was gifted two white parrots while in India and that he could not tire of admiring them and listening to their chatter. I had not seen indigenous white parrots in India and in fact never have since but I suppose there must be albinos, just as there are white elephants that have been for untold centuries symbols of kingship in Asia. Many centuries ago, the monk Jordanus of Severac in his travel annals described multicolored parrots but only the green ones now seem to remain in numbers in this region of the world.

Until Independence, the court of the Maharajas of Baroda was known for its team of trained parakeets, which performed all sorts of games and tricks for the benefit of the royal family and their guests. I had read in a traveller's account from the mid-thirties that the colourful birds amazed spectators by riding toy bicycles, driving one another on small carriages, loading and firing tiny silver cannons, taking pictures after loading a camera, shooting arrows with miniature bows and even dancing to the tune that one of them played on a piano. They demonstrated the truly "human" cleverness of their species, which also has the gift of imitating our language apart from speaking their own, which seems to subtly differ from place to place and from flock to flock.

In that thickly forested region every time our train made one of those long and unexplained halts in open country, between stations, I expected we might have to continue the journey on an elephant, like Jules Verne's Phileas Fogg, the hero of "Around the World in 80 Days." Indeed India was not a country I saw only through scholarly chronicles since I had vivid memories of novels that had fed my imagination .

Feathery crests of graceful palmettos rose like green fireworks as if to proclaim their eminent role in the literature of India which for thousands of years used their dried leaves to inscribe texts while their fermented sap made an intoxicating drink. Millions of these *tuz* or *tari* tree manuscripts – scholars say some thirty million in fact – are still scattered across the subcontinent and abroad, although many more perished due to the humid climate, neglect, disasters of all kinds and frequent social turmoil.

We passed Nagpur, the seat of the snakes, ever present Nagas of tribal India, which lies near the geometric centre of the country and for that reason perhaps had served as capital of the Maratha dynasty in the 18th century and later was chosen by both Mahatma Gandhi and by the RSS Hindu Nationalists as a headquarters. We had by then entered the Deccan, whose landscape is strewn with fantastic rock formations. They look like they have been left over by playing titans. That land had for centuries been dominated by Turkic dynasties, which brought Persian culture in that heartland, where local aborigines are still numerous.

Hinduism in its many forms has grown organically from Paleolithic pantheons, which it has assimilated and instilled with a philosophical depth that underlies what Al Umari called "the forty two sects of Indians"; it is a forest of gods, sanctuaries, scriptures, festivals and rites in which every human being can suit himself, find his path and improvise his own creed as in Indian music by composing a variation on one of the common threads, thus adding his voice or the sound of his chosen instrument to the cosmic symphony of Sanathana Dharma, the universal cosmic law.

India, south of the Vindhya mountain range, lived for very long not in separation but in autonomy from the northern regions because thick forests, extensive wetlands and rugged mountains raise a daunting barrier that only wandering hermits, expert traders and determined conquerors could cross. Many were drawn there by the fabulous gem deposits of that region, which I keenly remembered when we stopped at the station of Hyderabad, the capital of the Nizams, reputed in the early 20th century the richest monarchs in the world. We could not get a glimpse of Golkonda, their old citadel that had been the diamond emporium for hundreds of years because of the flawless and large precious stones extracted from its mines but I remembered the stories about that mysterious and inaccessible mountain described by Conti as being littered with those invaluable crystalline teadrops for which kings were willing to go to war and men wont to kill and forsake their eternal souls.

That seemingly inexhaustible fount of wealth had dried out more than two hundred years earlier, strangely about the time when a new diamond Eldorado was discovered by the Portuguese in Brazil.

When the invaders from Afghanistan and Turkestan rolled into the Indo-gangetic plains, the Deccan was under the sway of powerful Hindu and Jain native kings who held the Central Asians at bay for another century or two and the last of them, the emperors of Vijayanagar, were decisively defeated by a coalition of Sultans only in 1565, almost half a century after Babur founded the Mughal empire in the North. However, Muslim rule never prevailed over the entire peninsula and even before the last of those Sultans at Bijapur and Golkonda had surrendered to the Emperors of Delhi the Hindu reconquista began, spearheaded by the great Shivaji.

It was about the same time that a Hindu prince, the Nayak of Chandragiri ceded to the East India company in 1639, not long after the thirty years war in Europe, the sandy shores of what was to become Madras, the first major foothold of the future British overlords. Within a century the latter reduced the Mughal Padshahs to insignificance but it took them another hundred years to seize the imperial crown and proclaim their supremacy over the entire subcontinent. History has few examples of such slow and gradual conquest.

Our train finally brought us to Madras, named either after the Portuguese Madre Deus or the Arabic Madrasa depending upon which scholar you believe, in a balmy tropical evening whose coral glow heightened the faded pink Indo-Gothic arcades of the station and the crimson rags of emaciated and raucous, turbaned luggage carriers.

V

In the Grove of Ancient Knowledge

ADYAR

I keep a memory of Madras filing past like a parade of red Indo-Saracenic buildings in a blaze of twilight as a backdrop to the seafront boulevard along which we drove in a rickety taxi, past coal black statues of Tamil heroes and politicians, to the lush refuge of the Theosophical Society's domain in Adyar.

We entered a mysterious tropical forest in the twittering dusk of innumerable coconut palms and landed at the threshold of the Headquarters building, white, columnated and solemn like the Victorian interpretation of a greek temple. It was the hundredth anniversary, almost to the day, of the foundation of the Theosophical Society on 3 April 1875.

When I stepped in the cavernous empty hall, whose walls are decorated with white stucco *bas reliefs* of some of the great spiritual teachers of mankind, Krishna, Buddha, Zarathustra, Moses, Jesus, despite the tiredness of the journey I felt a thrill of elation that was quickly replaced by the sense of enigmatic nostalgia that pervaded the place as in an engraving by Albrecht Durer. I knew that Madame Blavatsky had lived in that building and allegedly interacted with her supernatural spiritual guides from the Himalayas, who appeared once in a while or simply dropped letters – from the astral plane – around her. Although our attitude to that aspect of her strange life had always been healthily skeptical, I could not fail to experience the eerily serene and meditative atmosphere of that mausoleum-like edifice.

We were eventually able to find the Recording Secretary of the Theosophical Society, the ever smiling Dr Jean Raymond, a lady to whom our letters of introduction from Spain were addressed, and whom we learnt later was from Australia although she had been born in Singapore. From the moment we saw her, we knew we had a friend and she was indeed both gracious and helpful, making sure that we were properly accommodated in a guest house called the *bhojanasala,* huddled beneath the palms and bougainvillea blossoms in the sprawling park that we were yet to explore.

Our arrival in the ground floor room we had been given disturbed a huge bandicoot rat which unhurriedly clambered out before our startled eyes. After recovering from this unusual welcome we began to settle down in what was to be our residence for several months. The Bhojanasala was built in the typical South Indian style as a square surrounding an inner courtyard framed by a pillared elevated verandah roofed with Mangalore tiles like the rooms that lined it on three sides. We could see from our barred windows, across the road that ran along the length of the park, amidst the foliage the dining room which however we neglected for most of our stay as we found the South Indian fare too spicy. We took relief in the "western style" Leadbeater Chambers, which dispensed simple and healthy European food three times a day. Our room was monastically bare and its four-postered beds carried the compulsory mosquito nets. Many months of travel in variable conditions had made me used to minimal comfort so that I was neither surprised by nor dissatisfied with that arrangement. All around us was the magnificent expanse of trees, grass and flowers of Adyar, which enraptured us with the varied songs and cries of its birds and animals and the sense of peace was striking after the almost perpetual motion we had experienced since leaving Barcelona.

In the following days we met many of the people, from India and from several other lands who inhabited this languid tropical Eden lying on the shore of the Bay of Bengal and fell into a routine. In the early morning we would invariably walk across the park and along the mangrove clad shores of the Adyar river, honeycombed by the warrens of legions of large crabs, up to the little gate in a fence under the casuarinas that opened onto a vast expanse of beach eternally caressed or whipped by a glittering grey and warm sea, where we beheld fishermen returning from pre-dawn forays and hauling their net-laden rope-sewn barks back on the sand.

Yoga, walking on the beach and swimming inasmuch as the nearly constant waves allowed, occupied the first hour of the day. Then we would have breakfast and read or write in the room until the time when I would walk to the historic Adyar library, a great repository of old and new books, magazines and journals on many subjects that were of particular interest to me. The librarian told me that it contained a quarter million printed volumes and more than twenty thousand ancient palm leaf manuscripts. Esoteric traditions of all climes, history, philosophy, occult teaching, frontier science and psychology filled the shelves and drew me in for countless hours.

When I plunged in that ocean of knowledge and belief, I was reminded of my earlier bath in the liquid sea, which shivered and foamed a few hundred steps away and I evoked the images of those young men of Indian and Arab legends, such as the ten princes of Dandin's tale who were instructed in all sciences and arts and "took all knowledge as their province." In Renaissance France, Rabelais had illustrated the same ideal in the education he credited to his imaginary hero Pantagruel.

On weekends, afternoons were lazier and often we went to the poetic wind caressed bungalow of the Shastris. Norma, a dynamic, blue eyed white haired American lady, always clad in snowy cotton sarees and her shy and wiry Brahmin husband, whose brother had been a president of the Society, had lived there for decades and they played classical music records in their spacious, light-filled first floor drawing room looking out to the sea. I remember enchanting moments on the high ceilinged columnated verandah while some hallowed score by Mozart, Chopin, Schubert or Rachmaninoff soared from the vinyl, drowning the soft whisper of the breeze in the swaying palms outside.

On some days the hushed thud of the waves could be heard wafting from the eastern horizon as it slowly went dark under the pall of twilight. Often I picked up a book among those that were lined in shelves on the walls and I spent hours reading and gazing entranced at mannerist pre-Raphaelite illustrations of the collected works of Shakespeare. It is there that I truly discovered the magical world of the Bard whom I had only read in French translations until then.

There were some long-term foreign visitors in Adyar and other more ephemeral guests from many parts of the world, South American spiritualists, Italian artists and English poets as well as travelers in search of exoticism. We met around the long dining table of Leadbeater Chambers, at the afternoon music sessions or at functions arranged by the Theosophical Society on certain festive or commemorative occasions. The President had not been in India when we arrived as he travelled often around the world, visiting the many lodges spread far and wide, but he returned a few weeks later and we met him soon after. He was a towering, friendly and ruddy faced Scottish septuagenarian called John Coats. He had inherited a rather large personal fortune and could therefore dedicate himself to the preservation and promotion of theosophy.

Many of the administrators and visitors, including us, were photographed together beneath the historic Banyan tree that had become a forest by itself, on the occasion of the centenary celebrations. That photo was eventually published in an article dedicated to the Society in the leading magazine, the *Illustrated Weekly of India* and I still keep a copy of that image now filled with the lights and shadows of childhood memories. Those recollections include the graceful figure of a girl, always clad in white, with long black hair and doe eyes who lived with her family in a bungalow situated across the road from us. We used to stare at each other across our respective windows and wave several times a day. Once I managed to approach her just outside her house when she came back from school and we exchanged names. She fought her shyness to tell me that she was called Radha, like the beauteous beloved of the god Krishna at Vrindavan and to know that she dwelt so near us made me dreamily happily. I realized since then that such innocent love affairs are among the most beautiful presents that life offers us because they embody all our ideals unalloyed with the humdrum prose of reality.

MADAME BLAVATSKY'S SAGA

Among my readings at that time I naturally included several works dealing with theosophical knowledge as taught by its founders, Blavatsky, Olcott, Leadbeater and Annie Besant among others. I had known relatively little of that voluminous literature until then and my first impressions came from the accounts given by Pierre Loti, my favourite exotic travelogue writer and by Count Hermann Keyserling, who had visited the TS in the early decades after its establishment in Adyar in 1886. I was also aware of the sternly condemnatory critique of the theosophical doctrine leveled by René Guenon.

While the romantic Loti was much impressed by Annie Besant and her teachings and makes his readers believe that he had actually become a theosophist, Keyserling, with his deeply analytical and sophisticated German intellect, was far more skeptical. He raised numerous objections to what he saw as a rather naïvely materialistic interpretation of Indian metaphysics in theosophy and was quite critical of the Society's attempt to build a new religion out of elements borrowed from all others. He reserved judgment on the claims of Theosophical leaders to have extrasensory perception and to be guided by nearly eternal spiritual masters or "Mahatmas" dwelling in the Himalayas but he deplored the extreme importance they accorded to supernatural powers and occult rituals.

As he saw it, in his "Diary of a Philosopher": "... In the hands of the theosophist, the Indian doctrine of the essential independence of the individual, which is heightened from stage to stage, has retreated so considerably ... that the theosophic religious community, in spite of all assertions to the contrary, is being crystallized more and more into a kind of catholic church within which faith in authority, readiness to serve and obedience are the cardinal virtues."

Keyserling had a sharp, nearly clairvoyant perception of human nature and spiritual matters and he realized that the theosophical doctrine taught by Madame Blavatsky reflected the Victorian *zeitgeist* and its interest in parallel realities, fostered by the need to escape from the technocratic worldview of imperial liberalism. He predicted that it would soon become outdated and that its founders would fail in their endeavour to build a new world religion. My own readings of parts of the monumental *Secret Doctrine* written by Blavatsky made me feel that, in spite of her striking intuitions and of genuine references to a very ancient gnosis, it was a construction too systematic and dogmatic to be widely accepted, given also that its author made multiple references to the scientific knowledge of her day which has since become outdated. It was rather dauntingly complex for my young mind but at same time I was fascinated by its intricate yarn which reminded me of certain esoteric mystery novels.

I was used to reading rather convoluted stories about the unknown ancient history of mankind by authors as diverse and controversial as Fabre d'Olivet, Bulwer Lytton, Erich von Daniken, Eliphas Levi, Churchward and Lobsang Rampa.

The genesis of the *Secret Doctrine* is a fascinating enigma, like many circumstances surrounding the author's life. Madame Blavatsky is supposed to have been inspired to compile it when she inspected, in her astral body, a collection of long lost texts called the *Stanzas of Dzyan* in an unknown library of Tibet but she leads her readers to believe that those texts, written in a forgotten sacred language called Senzar which she defines as the "root of samskrit" and the *brahmabhasya* (tongue of the gods or of the Creator himself) as well as the original devanagari, may only exist in a parallel etheric reality.

When she wrote her major books in the last years of her life, partly with the help of her friend and disciple Countess Wachtmeister, Madame Blavatsky had accumulated an extraordinary store of experiences and knowledge from forty years of travels across Russia, the Americas, Western and Southern Europe, Asia, Egypt and the Levant. Her aristocratic and scholarly family had helped her, financially and otherwise, during most of her odyssey in which she seems to have symbolically recapitulated the lives of her ancestry which included Russian saints and princes, German generals and French noblemen. She had an encyclopaedic grasp of philosophy, history, symbology and metaphysics and was also a virtuoso pianist and a gifted painter.

From a very young age this exceptional personality had acquired the conviction that she was guided by a great spiritual power that had imparted her with a mission of transcendent importance for the world and she claimed to have met her Teacher, a "Master of the Ancient Wisdom" for the first time in London's Hyde Park in 1851 on her twentieth birthday. In the following year she went to India and spent two years there. She returned in 1856 and, like her compatriot Prince Soltykoff, witnessed the great rebellion that the British dismissively called the "Sepoy Mutiny." Again, in 1868, she travelled in the land she regarded as her spiritual home and appears to have studied for many months in Tibet at the Tashilhumpo monastic palace of the 8th Panchen Lama to whom she reportedly became close. One last time she arrived in Mumbai in 1879, with her American friend and supporter Colonel Henry Olcott and after spending some time in the island then known as Ceylon, they came to Madras where in 1882 they acquired the land on which to build the world centre of the Theosophical Society.

Madame Blavatsky was to spend barely three years in that mystical location of her choice. Unlike Olcott who stayed on as president of the Society until his death in 1907, she left India never to return in 1885, dogged by accusations of spiritual fraud that often attach to students of the occult but which were never finally proven.

It was later revealed that many of the allegations were motivated by personal grudges and fostered by Scottish missionary clergymen, who were understandably quite unsympathetic to Theosophy's "universal wisdom-religion" of truth. While they were fighting their church's battle against the "heathen" creeds of India, the mysterious Russian woman occultist and polymath proclaimed the universal hidden gnosis that was at the core of all ancient traditions and especially the Hindu and Buddhist ones. She was therefore an enemy to be discredited by all possible means.

It appeared, as I became more familiar with her voluminous and abstruse writings that Madame Blavatsky had also been a victim of many of her followers who had interpreted theosophy too literally as a ritual belief system and liturgy, as people are wont to in all times and ages for figures and ideas that they respect. She herself had accused some of her fellow theosophists of that fault and as time passes, many of the theses she expounded are found to have indeed come from some little known but genuine ancient sources such as the Hindu Puranas, the Vedas, the Tibetan *dGyud Dte or Tantras* and possibly some other, hitherto hidden documents. Her complex and sometimes controversial life journey evokes many analogies with the similarly adventurous and puzzling existence of George Gurdjieff, another very influential esoteric master strongly connected with Russia and the Caucasus region whose ideas I had tried to understand first in the writings of his disciple Ouspensky.

Helena Blavatsky also anticipated the later lady explorer of Tibet, Alexandra David-Neél, with many of whose books I was acquainted. The former however was particularly disliked by Orientalist scholars of the "orthodox" variety beginning with Max Mueller but that in itself may rather speak in her favour as she was quite the opposite of a literal translator of old manuscripts.

Mueller, in spite of the acclaim he deserves for his monumental contribution to Indology and orientalist scholarship, was not exempt of pettiness and Eurocentric narrow-mindedness, as when he asserted, sincerely or not, that his main goal in studying the Hindu scriptures was to facilitate their followers's conversion to Christianity. His claim that the Buddha's message is purely exoteric and does not contain any of the esoteric features that the Russian occultist alludes to reflects poorly on his own understanding of Buddhism, which indeed contains elaborate metaphysical notions reserved for the initiates, although it is not possible to say what was part of the founder's original teachings and what was added later.

I had learnt in my parent's library in Spain that western churches and academics had long sought to isolate Buddhism from its Hindu roots by claiming that it is an "atheistic" psychological theory that rejects speculations about gods, the afterlife and parallel worlds. Such an interpretation is only possible if one restricts oneself to a narrow range of Buddhist texts from the Pali Theravada canon and ignores all the passages, even in those admittedly exoteric documents, which refer to many of the deities of India and to a "higher" set of teachings only accessible through symbols.

Even if one does not agree with Madame Blavatsky's at times "Victorian" perspective on mysticism and spirituality that she inevitably applies to Sakya Muni's message, one must acknowledge her familiarity with some of the most abstruse notions of Tibetan Tantric Buddhism as was pointed out by one of the Panchen Lamas himself.

THE MAHATMAS OF THE HIMALAYAS

A young romantic mind such as mine could not fail to be utterly captivated by the romance and the mystery of Helena Petrovna's life. Her many references and allusions to her masters of wisdom whom she defines as real men at a very high degree of initiation but still bound by the laws that apply to physical existence, made me want to know as much as I could about those beings, in particular the two that she was personally in touch with, Koot Humi and Morya. She said that they mostly live in the High Himalayan regions beyond Ladakh where she had visited them. The portraits that have come to us show two bearded, long haired, regally handsome Christ-like figures who evoke some of the Sikh and Rajput warriors and religious teachers one meets even today in India.

Indeed, some have speculated that one of the two paintings may be an idealized image of the then Maharaja of Kashmir, Ranbir Singh who was regarded as a high initiate by Helena Blavatsky.

Many letters, allegedly handwritten by the two masters were received by Blavatsky and by some of her friends and followers over the years from 1880 onwards, without anybody being able to trace their point of origins and methods of delivery as they appeared to have been "precipitated" in the immediate surroundings of their recipients. They are written in fluent English and in a rather calligraphic style. Repeated attempts were made to discover the actual identity of those enigmatic characters who were said by Blavatsky herself to have several names and to have lived in many parts of the world during the countless centuries of their presence on earth. Koot Humi (also known as KH) is cited in one of the Puranas and he refers in one of his letters to his stay at the University of Leipzig some years earlier. Someone actually tried to find traces of him there and found out from a professor cited in KH's letter that he had indeed had an Indian student named Nis Kanta Chattopadhyaya. However, that name reveals said student to have been a Bengali (unless he used a false name) whereas master KH was described by Helena Blavatsky as a Kashmiri Brahmin.

According to explanations contained in some of them and also provided by Blavatsky, the letters were rarely if at all penned by the Masters themselves. They were said to be mentally dictated to certain *chelas* or disciples, who wrote them down under some sort of remote control. Automatic writing and mediumnity were quite fashionable in those days so that many people, including eminent intellectuals, were willing to believe in that account of the letter's origins. The Mahatmas themselves say that they travel across Tibet and India, often on horseback and telepathically convey their messages to their physically distant amanuensis.

There remains a technical mystery about the way in which the writing was committed to paper but, whether or not there was a supernatural process behind their composition and delivery, they contain much interesting information. I was intrigued by the statement in one of the earlier missives that: "the adept does not create anything new but merely utilizes and manipulates materials which nature has in store around him" and also by the assertion that "man is constantly projecting his current state in space with a world of his own." Such statements have been echoed many times in texts pertaining to the New Age philosophy but they faithfully reflect ancient wisdom teachings of many traditions.

The Mahatmas also argue in favour of a scientific interpretation of the eternal knowledge, noting that "the era of blind faith is gone; that of inquiry is here" and calling for a "needed universal religious philosophy." The advances of science in the last few decades are providing abundant confirmation of those statements and vindicate the Mahatmas, or at least Blavatsky's prophetic awareness of civilisation's future evolution, irrespective of whether or not one believes in the supernatural context of these revelations.

All the mystery and vagueness about the circumstances surrounding her Masters have convinced many naturally skeptical or scientifically trained minds that the reports given by Blavatsky are pure fiction. However, a researcher more familiar with Indian philosophical culture and history would rather tend to believe that there may be a basis of truth for those stories, even though they may have been enlivened and transformed by her romantic imagination and her artistic propensities.

Asia and Europe were being visited, even before her lifetime by Indian students and spiritual seekers who often disguised their true identities by assuming convenient aliases or posing as Muslim pilgrims or *Faqirs* when they travelled in the Middle East and beyond. It is quite possible that Helena Petrovna came in contact with some of them because it seems difficult to account otherwise for the many messages that they sent to her and several other people, even though various attempts have been made to prove that she wrote them herself.

Even more fantastic than the descriptions of Koot Humi and Morya, who as reincarnated masters had been reborn on earth under many identities since untold antiquity, was the description of the Great White Brotherhood or occult hierarchy to which they were said to belong. That order of high initiates is headed by the Sanat Kumara, the "eternal teenager" who is regarded as the king of the world. The word *sanath* means eternal in Samskrit and is related to the greek "thanatos" which is the name of the Hellenic god of death. The Sanath Kumara lives, according to that account, in an astral city suspended high in the sky above the Gobi desert in Central Asia; he originally came from Venus with other beings similar to him called The Lords of the Flame in theosophical lore.

In me that legend struck an essential chord as I knew since I was ten in Spain about the extraordinary testimonies of George Adamski of his many meetings and contacts with youthful looking beings who came from a very superior en enlightened civilization originating on Venus. It was quite possible that Adamski had read theosophical literature which had a vast influence across the world. Lord Desmond Leslie, a student of Blavatsky's doctrine in the second half of the twentieth century, was a close friend of Adamski and he connected the two accounts of alien visitors from parallel worlds or other planets.

Indeed, aside from her likely influence on Leo Tolstoy, to whom she had personally presented her books, Madame Blavatsky and her fellow writers inspired scientists like Flammarion, the first "modern" astronomer to have expounded an infinite cosmology and envisioned the existence of an untold number of galaxies when his contemporaries were still convinced that the universe was limited to the Milky Way.

Apart from the fact that she reportedly was wounded while fighting at Garibaldi's side in the battle of Mentana, she had also made friends and admirers like Thomas Edison and her cousin Count Witte, though not a theosophist, when he become the Tzar's Prime Minister undertook to reform the Russian Empire in order to prevent a revolution that he foresaw. It appears that the intellectual current generated by the gifted Russian noblewoman became a force that shaped the world of the next century when it was espoused by some of the members of the British elite that spread it throughout their empire.

In the 20th century, some of the most renowned writers of fantastic fiction, such as Frank Baum, the author of "The Wizard of Oz" and James Hilton who penned "Lost Horizon," not to mention the prophetic H P Lovecraft, read Blavatsky's works and evinced a debt to her in their novels.

Soon after we came to Adyar, we were told that a tradition kept alive for alive for many decades affirmed that a new lease of life would come to theosophy exactly one century after its creation. The fact that we had reached it, without intending to, at that very date encouraged me to think that there was a higher design behind our spontaneous initiative. Blavatsky would surely have thought so since all her life took place under the apparently quixotic and inscrutable guidance of a higher will.

There was an uncanny correspondence between the results of her action and contemporary events that had reshaped her age. Queen Victoria was proclaimed Empress of India at the Darbar of 1877, two years after the foundation of the Theosophical Society, by a Viceroy who dabbled in occultism, he being the son of the famous esoteric novelist Lord Bulwer Lytton. On the other hand, the Indian National Congress, which was to lead the country to independence, was co-founded in 1885 by a high-ranking British civil servant who was also Blavatsky's disciple, Allan Octavian Hume, shortly after the Theosophical Society came to India.

In Ceylon, Olcott and Blavatsky gave a powerful impetus for the rebirth of Theravada or Southern Buddhism as an international religion and Olcott designed the flag that still symbolizes it officially and unites all the countries that follow it. Like Hinduism, Buddhism gained renewed global attention due to the action of those two western visitors who were able to promote the inter-connected venerable traditions more easily than any local scholar or teacher could have, given the tributary status of Asian nations vis-á-vis the hegemonic Western powers.

A British theosophist, Ferdinand Brooks was a tutor to a boy from a wealthy family in Allahabad, where A. P. Sinnett, the main recipient of the Mahatma letters, was the editor of the Pioneer newspaper. At thirteen, in 1902 Brooks's pupil was himself initiated into the Theosophical Society by Annie Besant and then grew to be the leader sworn in as independent India's first prime minister in 1947. His name was Jawaharlal Nehru.

In 1911, the year of the imperial Durbar that crowned Edward VII in Delhi Theosophical leaders founded the Order of the Star in the East, meant to pave the way for the proclamation of the "world teacher" who was to save mankind and usher in a new age of spiritual enlightenment. It had the support of many eminent personalities and gave an impression that it was intended to give the British global commonwealth a universal religion, destined to replace the Christian creed Constantine had proclaimed in his empire.

One could either believe that theosophy was fated to play a critical role in the world in that period of momentous changes or conclude that a grand "conspiracy" of powerful people at the heart of the British Empire used the doctrine and the Society to guide an evolutionary process that they had planned.

THE SUPERNATURAL IN NATURE

My readings of the theosophical classics led me to renew and deepen my earlier acquaintance gained in Spain, with the voluminous literature connected to mysterious flying vehicles and the super-human or non-human beings reported to operate them by numerous witnesses since many centuries in various regions of the earth. There is a comprehensive collection of books on UFOs at the Adyar library and I had the opportunity of devouring some of the most rigorous and hard-headed studies authored by military and scientific experts, such as Major Donald Keyhoe, Captain Edward Ruppelt, Professor J Allan Hynek, Dr Jacques Vallee, Aime Michel and several others.

Even the most skeptical and prejudiced reader would have had to recognize, after becoming acquainted with only a few of those books, that there is considerable, undeniable and scientifically verified evidence for the existence of a phenomenon which bridges the gap between "hard factual measurable reality" and what we call "the supernatural" for lack of a better understanding of it. At the same time, a technology much more advanced than the ones we currently master is bound to appear miraculous or incredible, depending upon whether we are open-minded or dogmatic, as much as our electronic gadgetry would seem to a man of the Paleolithic age.

It is a mark of human conceit that we have so much trouble accepting that others may be far above us, even though our ancestors were still existing in the era of animal traction and wind power only a few generations ago. Of course at every period of its history, the human species has thought that it was at the highest point of knowledge and power that could be reached.

I was mesmerized by the many connections and correspondences I noted between accounts given by esoteric documents and realities experienced by witnesses of "UFO sightings and encounters." Was there a clear distinction between those we usually assume to be "extraterrestrials" and the many adepts or initiates and denizens of parallel worlds described by Theosophists and, much earlier by the metaphysical traditions of the East?

I interspersed my investigations in those "borderline" areas with readings of scientific philosophy and history and I remember discovering in those days Raymond Ruyer's "The Gnosis of Princeton," Fritjof Capra's "Tao of Physics," Ernest Mach's "Knowledge and Error," Carlos Castaneda's "The Teachings of Don Juan," George Sudarshan's "Doubt and Certainty," Isaac Asimov's "Foundation Trilogy" and Arthur Clarke's "Rendezvous with Rama," all of which gripped my mind. I also began to write a book on the connections I perceived between the accounts of divine visions reported in all religious traditions and the phenomena recorded by so many diverse witnesses and investigators in the context of UFO sightings. That work eventually amounted to a voluminous manuscript, which I never tried to put in a publishable form. I saw it more as a compendium designed to facilitate my own understanding of the subject matter.

The richness of tropical nature around us provided an idyllic counterpart to the vastness of the intellectual horizons I was exploring. Meadows surrounded by thick groves gave a sense of the peace one finds in many of the mystical treatises of Silesius and Eckhart while religious teachings were symbolized in the park of Adyar by the small sanctuaries of the world's main religions that dotted the compound. Gulmohurs, champas, kusums and other trees offered to the sky their crimson and white offerings like the sacrifices prescribed by many creeds and the precious mahogany and teak trunks rose as the columns supporting the higher realms.

The banyans were embodiments of the Vedic Aswattha, the cosmic rhizome-like arborescence of creation. The sultry heat of the day was stirred by the frantic call of the cuckoo and when rain approached, it was heralded by a rythmic cascade of cooing sounds in the lush canopy, punctuated once in a while by the dull thuds of cocoanuts falling on the ground. Amidst the leaves and blossoms I occasionally spied the tiny azure flash of a diminutive fluttering bee eater. The brief and shimmering sunsets brought out the stealthy fleet of black kite-like fruitbats before the night blanketed the park in the whispering rythmic bass of insects, against which at times rose the jackals's howls.

Much as I was seduced by Blavatsky's exploration of hidden archives of the various races and kinds that had occupied the earth, I found the writings of Charles Leadbeater, the former Anglican clergyman who had become theosophy's most prolific exponent, too literal or too imaginative, as the case may be, for acceptance. His attempts to map and describe all levels and sections of the "occult reality" had attracted the criticism of Keyserling and of many other thinkers reticent to embrace his colourful mythology and it was one of the features of the doctrine that had led many to break away from it, especially as Leadbeater was supported unconditionally by Annie Besant, the charismatic Irish former trade unionist and feminist who succeeded Olcott as president after the latter's death.

Keyserling noted about him: "He is hardly intellectually equal to his material. Nevertheless, again and again I meet with assertions on his part which on the one hand are probable and, on the other, correspond to philosophical truths. He will, therefore, in all probability, have seen something which really exists."

Contrary to her American predecessor Olcott who promoted a rather "protestant" version of Buddhism to which he had converted in

Ceylon, Annie Besant, who shared with most theosophists a Masonic affiliation, was attached to the theatrical pomp and mystery of the Catholic liturgy. After toying with Marxism and Fabian socialism, this friend of Bernard Shaw who shared the playwright's vegetarian convictions, had turned into a stalwart of the struggle for Indian home rule and even became President of the Indian National Congress in 1917. She also founded the Indian National University in Madras and the World Hindu College in Benares, which became part of the new Benares Hindu University so that her contribution to India's emancipation was extraordinary but she was more of an orator and organizer than a researcher and scholarly writer although I found her introduction to Hinduism most useful because of its clarity and accurate appreciation of the tradition's inner meaning.

Her ability to inspire great people in their own right is also notable and William B Yeats, probably the greatest English speaking poet of his age who introduced Tagore's *oeuvre* to the West, owed a lot to her teachings about esotericism.

Keyserling, who is an apt judge of character, wrote about her: "This woman controls her being from a centre which, to my knowledge, very few men have ever attained to.... Mrs Besant controls herself – her powers, her thoughts, her feelings, her volitions-so perfectly that she seems to be capable of greater achievements than men of greater gifts. She owes this to yoga."

The seminal and often decisive role that Theosophy had played in the final years of the 19th century and in the first half of the 20th was however not widely remembered by the time we reached Adyar and I wrote about that impression of decline in some articles I penned, including one that was published in the French theosophical journal, *Le Lotus Bleu* whose title enchanted me as it evoked the adventures of Tintin, one of my childhood's heroes. We discussed the present situation of the Society with various office holders, such as Jean Raymond, John Coats and the delightful old Brahmin archivist Swami, whose knowledge of Hindu philosophy and theosophical history was encyclopaedic.

We also gathered valuable insights from an octogenarian

Englishman, who had more than half a century of practicing theosophy behind him and had known Leadbeater and Besant. His name was Captain Russell Balfour Clarke and he occupied an apartment on the ground floor of the stately Olcott Bungalow, named after its original resident. The first floor of that colonial mansion overlooking the sea at the eastern extremity of the Society's grounds was the traditional residence of the President. Captain Balfour Clarke loved to evoke old memories when we went to see him after dinner and sat together on the verandah that surrounded the house, cradled in dense vegetation. He recalled his travels in the Middle East, for what we assumed to have been missions on His Britannic Majesty's more or less secret service, and the many theosophists he had met in all walks of life. "Do you know, he said, that one of them was Armine Woodhouse who was a poet and a brother of PJ Woodhouse?."

My mostly Franco-Spanish education had not familiarised me with the famous humorist whose *Jeeves* series I discovered later with delight but the old Captain spoke of other personalities whose names told me more. He recalled Lady Emily Lutyens, the wife of New Delhi's famous architect, and pointed out that she perhaps owed her esoteric penchant to her father, the first Earl of Lytton who had written allegorical poetry under the pen name of Owen Meredith and had been a Viceroy of India.

THE STAR OF THE EAST

"Lady Lutyens was an early member of the order of the Star in the East," our host added, "and a devout follower of Jiddu Krishnamurti when Annie Besant proclaimed him the new World Teacher, the Messiah Maitreya. Her daughter Mary later wrote this book about him" and he lent us his copy of the biography of Krishamurti authored by Mary Lutyens, which I was to read in the following days. "Contrary to their husband and father who was convinced of the innate superiority of the British over Indians and their civilisation, Emily and Mary Lutyens put all their faith in a Hindu Mahatma."

I realized how much hope and anticipation had been aroused in many people around the world by the promised saviour although Besant's and Leadbeater's decision to pick a local South Indian Brahmin boy for such a divine mission, in conformity with ancient prophecies about the identity of future Buddha Maitreya, had been quite controversial and had further divided the Theosophical Society into rival groups.

By then, the doctrine had been adapted and modified by various national sections and, while William Judge, one of the three founders, had built up a more idiosyncratically American theosophical federation, Rudolf Steiner had developed a culturally Germanic strand of it under the name of anthroposophy, proving once more that no school of thought remains for long untouched by local cultures and power politics. Theosophy could not remain supra-national any more than Socialism would retain its universalistic character.

Krishnamurti himself had dismayed his pygmalions and mentors when, in 1929 he decided to renounce his appointed role as an Avatar of the Wisdom-Religion and to reject the theosophical doctrine altogether, stating that no one religion or philosophy could express the truth. Although he remained personally close to Annie Besant, his abdication of the divine mission that had been cast upon him as a child dealt to theosophy a blow from which it never recovered.

"This was the great disappointment of Annie Besant's life," Balfour Clarke said ruefully. "She saw herself as the bringer of the light for future humanity... Remember that she had been a Fabian and then some sort of a Marxist. She had a belief in changing the world and she put motherly love as well as her own formidable energy in the service of her adopted child."

"Do you believe that he betrayed her?" my father inquired.

"She did not think so. Leadbeater did and was bitter about it but she kept all her love for Krishna. She probably realized that the boy had been groomed for something too big for which he had never given his consent and was not ready. Then there was a bitter fight between the Theosophists and his real father who did not want his son to be cut off from his Hindu roots and made into a westernized prophet.

Annie Besant won the protracted case but Krishna, whose mother had died when he was a small child must have been very affected by that famous legal battle in which he was a powerless pawn."

He paused for an instant before adding: "Leadbeater visited Krishna's *Akashic* records of his past lives and taught him about what he said were the boy's previous incarnations. He published all those stories as part of the theosophical literature. I think that Leadbeater was sincere but it was a lot for a teenager to absorb and Krishnamurti did not have a normal childhood. He was treated like something between a prince and a god. At some point he got fed up with the mythology and the personality cult being built around him and he sought to escape. Man proposes and God disposes," the old man concluded softly.

Knowing that Balfour Clarke was a product of one of the elite public schools of his country I could not bring myself to question him on an issue which was rather delicately addressed by Mary Lutyens in her book when she mentioned that Leadbeater had faced accusations of paedophilia years before Krishnamurti was discovered by Annie Besant in Adyar. He had defended himself by claiming that he had merely advocated masturbation for teenagers under his supervision but that very admission raised a scandal and the defrocked Anglican priest was exiled in semi-disgrace to Australia for a few years before being exonerated of the graver charge. Had his interest for the handsome young Krishnamurti been impure? That question remains unanswered and English society is known to be rather tolerant of such vices as long as they remain hidden. I however wondered if an unhealed wound in the young Indian's psyche had led to his rejection of theosophy and his quest for another path to self-realisation for himself and for others.

Keyserling had this to say when he stayed at Adyar two or three years before the great war of 1914: "What fascinates me in the atmosphere of Adyar is its expectation of the Messiah. Among the residents here, there is a young Indian of whom it is said that the Holy Ghost will one day use him as his vessel… He is to be the savior for the coming age. I have accepted this belief for a few days … and I confess that I was sorry to surrender it, because it is a joy to live under such a supposition." He concluded presciently that "unless something happened to him," the boy would become the founder of a religion. Indeed something did happen to Krishnamurti which changed his life but he did found some sort of an intellectual cult around himself, howbeit devoid of ritual and theology, which still has thousands of followers, years after he passed away.

VI

A Spiritual Godmother

Rukmini Devi

"You should meet Rukmini Devi," Jean Raymond told us soon after our arrival. "She is one of those still with us who belonged to the inner group of founders. She knew all of them except Blavatsky and Olcott."

The name of Rukmini Arundale was legendary in theosophical circles and we had heard it pronounced with reverence among our friends in the Circle of Friends of India in Barcelona. At sixteen, that beautiful daughter of an eminent Brahmin scholar had married George Arundale, an Englishman more than twenty years older, who was a favourite of Annie Besant's and a talented educator. He was related to the Duke of Norfolk, the head of Britain's black Catholic nobility and the first peer of England. George's aunt, Francesca Arundale had been a friend and a supporter of Helena Blavatsky and an important and wealthy promoter of theosophy.

Under her husband's tutorship, the young Rukmini had travelled in many countries and had been inspired by Anna Pavlova, after attending her recital in Bombay, to study and revive the ancient traditions of sacred Indian dance, which had fallen in disrepute under the puritanical influence of English rule. She then studied with Cleo Nordi, Pavlova's choreographer. In those years exotic icons such as Mata Hari and innovative dancers, beginning with Ruth St Denis and Uday Shankar, had made Hindu mythological themes famous in the art world. Rukmini was groomed in a cosmopolitan atmosphere and learnt acting in both western plays and Indian lyrical productions of

Tagore and other contemporary and ancient authors. In some she personified divine or legendary figures like Queen Guinevere and Kwan Yin, the Chinese goddess of universal compassion, and created a stage version of Edwin Arnold's epic on the Buddha's life, *Light of Asia.*

In 1928, when she was only twenty four years old, a movement had started to proclaim Rukmini the "world mother" as a reincarnation for the age of the eternal Virgin adored in many religions. Since then she had dedicated her life to the fine arts academy or *gurukul* that she had founded with her husband near Adyar in conformity with the vedic traditions of education.

One evening we went to see Rukmini in her charmingly simple house, set in a garden haunted by ancient granite statues of deities who were adorned with jasmine, hibiscus, *samandi* flowers and marigolds every morning. Although age had wrapped its folds around the statuesque body of her youth, she had retained the erect regal bearing of a temple dancer and deep dark eyes that cast smiling or brooding gazes in tune with her mood. She was quiet and soft spoken but exuded a natural power and confidence. She received us gracefully, with Shankara Menon, a tall, willowy and elegant white-haired scholar who had shared her life for many years since George Arundale had died, at her side. We talked about our travels and about our philosophical interests. She kept a parrot, a green *kili* flying freely around the living room. It sometimes perched on her shoulders or ours, nibbling at my earlobe or ruffling my hair and reminded me of Shuka, the divine parakeet which sits on the right shoulder of Raja Shyamala, the goddess of music and dance, and is said to teach her those heavenly skills.

"If you wish to discover India and her spirit, you should not study only philosophy in books," she said, looking at me intently. "You should also practice her arts. How would you like to study at my school at Kalakshetra?"

The question came as a surprise. I knew of Kalakshtra mainly as a dance academy and had never thought to learn Bharata Natyam, even though I had spoken about the philosophy and history behind it in Spain at the Friends of India Association, some time before our departure for India.

I don't recollect how the conversation ended but in the days that followed, the decision was reached between all concerned that I would enter Kalakshetra at the start of the new academic year and that we would move to the campus.

The days flowed fast and only once or twice a week did we venture outside the serene enclave of Adyar into the noisy and colourful suburb that lay outside its gates. On a few occasions we went to downtown Madras that we found both provincial and teeming, as is true of most Indian cities and repaired for lunch, with Jean Raymond and a few other guests of the TS at the old-fashioned and stately Connemara Hotel, which preserved in part the spirit of the bygone British Raj. We visited some of the historic monuments and spent an entire day in the wonderful though somewhat neglected Government museum, enraptured by its splendid Dravidian bronzes and stone sculptures, its extensive mineralogical and archeological collections and the paintings of many different styles featured in the National Art Gallery.

STORIES FROM OLD MADRAS

I could not fail to be impressed by the sheer grandeur of Madras's neo-Gothic public buildings that seemed rather out of place in the tropical glare but stood as witnesses of Britain's imperial pride, from the days when the city had been one of the important commercial hubs of its far flung colonial network. In Fort Saint George, a relic of the early years of the Madras trading post, I learnt the history of Elihu Yale, its 17th century governor whose bewigged portrait stared down in majesty from a wall of the Art Gallery. Yale, born in Boston, had ruled a large part of the Carnatic, married in the fort's church that still stands, and accumulated a vast fortune until charges of corruptions led the East India company to dismiss him. He traded in spices, slaves and opium like most English merchants of his day and was buried many years later at his English seat where his gravestone displays an inscription beginning with the following lines:

"Born in America, in Europe bred
in Africa travell'd and in Asia wed
Where long he liv'd and thriv'd, in London dead."

Madras in his day was still an outpost surrounded by other European enclaves, including a Portuguese town at Sao Thome of Mylapore, around St Thomas mount where the doubting Apostle was supposed to have been martyred, according to a contested tradition, and a Dutch trading factory at Pulicat in the North. The French were not far to the South at Pondicherry and the Danes were to plant their flag as well on that sandy stretch of the Coromandel coast.

While Yale was Governor, our old acquaintance Aurangzeb took over the Sultanate of Golkonda and required the British of Madras to declare their allegiance to the Mughal empire in exchange for a guarantee that they would be allowed to retain their colony. The pragmatic Yale promptly did so as he was threatened by French privateers. In his native America, the former Governor was to endow the college that named itself after him and grew to become one of the world's leading universities.

Among the eminent denizens of the city we eventually met the State Governor, KK Shah and Ranee Meena Muthiah of Chettinad, the heiress of one of the principal financial dynasties of South India who dwelt in a sprawling 19th century Walter Scottian palace we could behold on the opposite shore of the mangrove fringed Adyar estuary. Her adoptive daughter, Kumari Preetham, a tall and handsome girl, did perform her *Arangetram* (initial dance recital) at the Kalakshetra theatre where she had just finished her training and which we visited for the first time on that occasion. Her mother invited us for tea at the palace in the following days. We also met on another occasion His Highness Ghulam Muhammed Abdul Khader, Prince of Arcot who dwelt in the imposing Amir Mahal in Royapettah, one of Madras's boroughs.

Through one of the anomalies of history of which India is an infinite repository, this descendent of the second Khalif of Islam, Hazrat Omar and of a governor of the Carnatic appointed by Aurangzeb after he had submitted the region, was the only Indian prince still recognized as such by the Government of India since the abolition of all other royal titles and he was still paid the privy purse granted to him by the former British overlords. He recalled that one of his ancestors, Nawab Anwaruddin Khan had been killed in battle by French forces from Pondicherry in 1749. He showed no resentment however and pointed out that the Nawabs of the Carnatic had generally been allied with the British while the French had been granted their foothold on the coast by the Sultans of Bijapur in 1674, in order to block further expansion by the aggressive Dutch colonists backed by the rival Sultans of Golkonda. Foreigners in India had once again played on the rivalries between neighbouring kingdoms to further their own interests.

The Nawab explained that his forbears had dwelt in an ever larger estate, known as the Chepauk palace that we often had seen from outside, before the British took it over in the late 19th century and gave his family his present residence in compensation. One of the most noted English architects, Robert Chisholm had reconfigured the building to make it a suitable state residence for the Arcot dynasty.

I was struck by the composite picture that formed out of these exotic elements. A British built "saracenic" mansion amidst cocoanut trees under tropical skies still hosted, in independent republican India, a stateless Arab monarch who owed his title to a long-vanished Central Asian turco-persian dynasty in an old Hindu land, next to a Christian place of pilgrimage that had fallen under the sway at one time or another of almost every nation in Western Europe before being bombed by a German cruiser during the first world war. History everywhere had left bewildering mosaics on India's soil.

We gradually ventured further away than Madras, its bustling Mount Road, its white cathedral whose crypt allegedly held the bones of Thomas, the "twin" of Jesus and the historic Higginbothams book store.

We also visited the ancient Armenian church and befriended its caretaker, a rather grouchy old member of that once thriving community which had contributed much to India's trade and industry during untold centuries. Like most of his countrymen, he needed no pretext to express his bitter resentment at the Turks who had massacred so many members of his nation in the early years of the century. He was a sad man also since most Armenians had left Madras and India to resettle in America, Europe or Australia. He told us how until a few decades earlier, prosperous Armenian communities had formed a network extending from the Mediterranean and the Persian Gulf to the South China Sea.

"They were far flung and had existed in many of those cities since antiquity, he said but they all kept their identity and religion. The Armenians did business with all and had no conflict with any other people but they remained Christian and continued to speak their language and marry other Armenians. That is why we endured, even though we were not many. In Madras and Calcutta, we were what the Parsis were in Bombay, the life blood of the economy," he noted with a glimmer of old pride in his melancholic dark eyes.

TEMPLES OF THE CARNATIC

As we ventured farther away from our base, one of our firs destinations had to be the legendary seven pagodas of Mahabalipuram, which had for many centuries provided a beacon to passing ships. That abandoned cluster of granite hewn spires and caves strewn on the ocean shore inspired many visiting writers and artists and it exudes exotic romance like few places can in that part of the world.

I realized, while admiring the many tiered tower whose foundations are licked by the waves, that such pyramids of receding stories had inspired the Chinese to build their characteristic corbelled, multitiered temples which the first Europeans also called pagodas, perhaps from the Sanskrit b*hagavat* or from the Sinhalese *dagoba,* the local name for Buddhist stupas. The sanctuary that still stands in rugged isolation at Mahabalipuram is the last of six, after the five others were devoured by the rising sea. An entire temple enclave, an *agraharam*, was thus buried beneath the bay of Bengal and its fate reminds us that Southern India has gradually shrunk in size and lost much of its early past to the ocean that surrounds it and gnaws at its sandy shores.

The Pallavas who built Mahabalipuram ruled the region for almost seven centuries and many were great warriors and builders. Like most Indian monarchs, they patronized Hinduism as well as Buddhism and even Jainism at various times. They extended their sway to much of South East Asia where some of their dynastic offshoots ruled several kingdoms in lands now known as Sri Lanka, Malaysia, Cambodia and Southern Vietnam.

The name of Mahabalipuram has been linked both with the legendary Asura Bali and with the island of the same name, although its Dravidian name was Mamallapuram but even if we discount unproven legends, it is well known that the literature, art and architecture patronised by those Southern Indian kings of kings, who claimed descent from the god Brahma and from the Rishi Aswatthama, shaped the great civilizations of Indonesia and Indo-china, which built the stupendous monuments of Angkor, Prambanan and Borobudur among others.

Chroniclers of the time tell us that Mahabalipuram, a major port city of the Pallava kingdom of Kanchi, was full of ships riding at anchor and loaded with the treasures of Asia and Africa. "Nine kinds of gems and big-tusked elephants." Vessels must indeed have been large if they could load pachyderms on board. In that era, the Tamil country was a land of plenty and many remains have been found of the thriving business that linked it with Arabia, Egypt and the Roman Empire as with the Far East.

Despite the deliberate tendency sported by many contemporary scholars to emphasize the differences between Dravidian and Northern "Aryan" Indian forms and traditions, I was struck in Mahabalipuram as in the great temple of Tanjore that we visited soon afterwards by the palpable unity of that civilization from one end to the other of the subcontinent, notwithstanding the considerable diversity inherent to such a vast area. The languages, Sankrit and Prakrits, the underlying metaphysics of the culture and its modes of expression kept Hindusthan together, more than Christianity could assemble Europe's diverse peoples through a common faith. The Pallavas sacrificed horses like the northern emperors; they used the title "Malla" shared by the warrior-princes of the Himalayas; they used the symbols of Ganga-Yamuna on their banners and seals and their sculptures, poems and theatrical plays were inspired by the *Mahabharata* though the latter had taken place 1500 miles to the North untold centuries earlier. As so many other kings, they also claimed descent from the Nagas, the serpent race of the archaic age.

Before the gigantic stone frieze of Mahabalipuram depicting the descent of the Ganges to the earth, to which the Pallavas compared their own origins, and at the foot of the honey-coloured vimana of Brihadesvara, tall as the spire of a gothic cathedral but much more massive and elaborate, I beheld the colossal ambition of Hinduism to allegorically represent the universe and all its indwellers in a flawless fusion of complex geometry, ornamental profusion and visionary symbolism.

One glance at the rigorously orthogonal ground plan of the temple and a moment of contemplation of its soaring mole showed that Keyserling, influenced by the prejudices of his western contemporaries misread the religious architecture of South India as "totally unintellectualised." He saw the great sanctuary of Madurai, not far from Tanjore as similar to "a primitive organism...without plan, without self-control, following every impulse blindly...The mastery of the Hindu in detail as opposed to his insufficiency in great structural concepts, is here given its deepest explanation and reason."

How wrong was the Baltic aristocrat in not noticing the elaborate mathematically ordered layout of sacred monuments in India! Possibly, despite his admiration for Brahmanical civilization, he was drawn to the facile Nietszchean antonymy between Apollo and

Dionysos, not realizing that Indian traditional aesthetics integrates both in its profuse but orderly extravagance.

When it was brightly painted in a myriad colours, as all temples were originally, Brihadesvara's shrine must have been a dazzling sight, evocative of the cosmic Mount Meru which rises at the centre of the universe and hosts all the gods on its slopes. Now it only retains the russet gold of its substance. The tower of Babel must have been similar in shape when it stood amidst the palm groves of Sinear's flat plains, but unlike Babel the pagoda of Tanjore has been completed up to its massive monolithic crowning stone shaped as a myrobalan fruit or a lotus bud. The Hindu Gods are not afraid of men, unlike the biblical Elohim and they do not want to keep them ignorant and divided by thwarting ambitious endeavours, as long as the natural law, the Dharma is abided. Temple builders in India may have wanted to reach the skies, but not to protect themselves from the lord of thunder and rain; rather they sought to come closer to Him in adoration.

The great tower of Tanjore is indeed an object of endless meditation as it offers to the Sun the mountain-like fifteen layered honeycomb of rhythmically narrowing stories, called *talas* like the patterns of a musical composition or poetic metre. Its intricate outer facades, which might have been the template for the spirit of 18th century Rococco in the colonizing west, contrast with the polished, smooth dark simplicity of its great linga, standing as a singular lodestone, or a boundary marker, in the centre of the cavernous sanctum, evocative of the Biblical Bethel and of Arthur Clarke's *Space Odissey* monolith. The intricately sculpted outer roof also covers the inner, missile like inner vault which truly made me think of a Soyuz or Apollo rocket and reminded me in a very graphic way that *vimana* also means a flying man-made or divine vehicle in Sanskrit. As most Dravidian temples, it is crowned by the monolithic sikhara itself surmounted by the gold ball and spike of the *stupa* and symbolizes the polar Meru peak surrounded by rising rows of hills and outcroppings. The sanctuary is hidden in its core as a cave in a mountain or as the pharaoh's funeral shrine within a pyramid.

The secular pendant of this sacred wonder is to be found in the grandiose palace of the Nayak kings of Tanjore, to my eyes a strange blend of Hindu, Gothic and Saracenic styles which hosts a great collection of valuable ancient manuscripts and art works. I was reminded of Italy where even provincial towns are graced by regal monuments on a scale that can only be found in national capitals elsewhere.

The paintings and sculptures of the Tanjore temple, that masterwork of the Chola dynasty which 800 years ago ruled much of the immense Insulindian archipelago and traded with China, brought me back to Kalakshetra as many of those artworks were inspired by the arts of dance and music, *sangeet natak*, as codified in the *Natya Shastra* of the great Bharata many centuries ago. The hundred and eight dance *karanas* or postures codified in that classic compendium are represented by separate statues, which exemplify the inseparability of the arts in the perspective of the Indian tradition.

IMBIBING SAMSKRIT WISDOM

In the Upanishads, there is a story about someone who wishes to study a particular art and is taught by his *guru* that in order to know it in depth he must study the other arts as well. Music is linked with poetry and with dance, which is reflected in sculpture, in turn related to painting and architecture and so on. The Indian and generally universal traditional view of all things is holistic and organic so that specialisation is only possible when the widest context of any discipline is comprehended and assimilated. The part and the whole reflect each other mutually just as an individual life *karma* enshrines and partakes of the larger karma of our many previous stages of existence and of the area, time and world we live in.

This is the vision I was imparted with when I went through the initiation ceremony before joining the classes at Kalakshetra by praying for Shiva's blessing. Shiva, the master of the Tanjore temple, the lord of the cosmic dance embodies the three fires of the pyre, the Sun and the moon and has both a terrifying and a gentle appearance.

He is a wandering contemplative ascetic and as such he is also the supreme artist since the creation of beauty requires detachment from wealth and power. His dance creates, sustains and eventually annihilates the universe only to create it anew but all forms exist only in his dreaming mind and vanish when he awakes.

He teaches the sixty-four arts – *chatushashti kalas* – taught and developed in traditional India, of which I saw the nomenclature in one of the books I was reading at the time. There are as many secret arts (*abhyantara kalas*) that are a part of erotic science but the exoteric or practical (*bahyakala*) disciplines are according to most recensions:

1. Singing, 2. Instrumental music, 3. Dancing, 4. Painting, 5. Forehead adornments, 6. Making decorative floral and grain designs on the floor, 7. Home and temple flower arranging, 8. Personal grooming, 9. Mosaic tiling, 10. Bedroom arrangements, 11. Creating music with water, 12. Splashing and squirting with water, 13. Secret mantras, 14. Making flower garlands, 15. Head adornments, 16. Dressing, 17. Costume decorations, 18. Perfumery, 19. Jewellery making, 20. Magic and illusions, 21. Ointments for charm and virility, 22. Manual dexterity, 23. Skills of cooking, eating and drinking, 24. Beverage and dessert preparation, 25. Sewing (making and mending garments) 26. Embroidery, 27. Playing veena and drums, 28 Riddles and rhymes, 29. Poetry and games, 30. Tongue-twisters and difficult recitations, 31. Literary recitation, 32. Drama and story telling, 33. Verse composition game, 34. Furniture caning, 35. Sexual arts, 36. Crafting wooden furniture, 37. Architecture and house construction, 38. Distinguishing between ordinary and precious stones and metals, 39. Metal-working, 40. Gems and mining, 41. Gardening and horticulture, 42. Games involving animals, 43. Training parrots and mynas to speak, 44. Hair dressing, 45. Coding messages, 46. Speaking in code, 47. Knowledge of foreign languages and dialects, 48. Making flower carriages, 49. Spells, charms and omens, 50. Making simple mechanical

devices, 51. Memory training, 52. Game of reciting verses from hearing, 53. Decoding messages, 54. Meaning of words, 55. Dictionary studies, 56. Prosody and rhetoric, 57. Impersonation, 58. Artful dressing, 59. Games of dice, 60. The game of 'akarsha' (a dice game played on a board), 61. Making dolls and toys for children, 62. Personal etiquette and animal training, 63. Knowledge of dharmic warfare and victory, 64. Physical culture.

However, the six principal or major sciences, in an order similar to the western medieval *Trivium* and *Quadrivium,* consist of *vedangas* (arms of the Vedas) that are *shiksha* (phonetics), *chandas* (metrics or prosody), *vyakarana* (grammar), *jyotisha* (astronomy which also includes mathematics and geometry) and *kalpa* (ritual and seasonal ceremonies marking the passage of time). I would not be taught those as Vedic students were but merely given a basic understanding of them in order to facilitate my initiation into the sanskrit language which, as its name indicates is the very expression of Indian or rather Indic culture.

From Shiva Nataraja, king of the dance we were to learn the highly codified gestures and expressions that structure classical choreography and play acting. All human action, including artistic expression is understood as a *yagna*, a sacrifice of the self to the highest entity that moves the universe, shines in the Sun and sits in our hearts. I wrote an article in French around that time which dealt with that theme and was entitled *Agnihotra and Eucharist, the myth of Sacrifice*.

As I read later in an article by Professor Usha Choudhuri: "The sacrifice is the navel of the world, says the *Asyavansya* hymn of the Rig Veda.All this, whatever exists, is made to participate in the sacrifice...Even a standing tree is symbolic of life and is participating in the cosmic sacrifice...The basic principle is that the word and the act are united by the force of the mind. Speech is another form of sacrifice."

THE QUEEN OF THE HELLENES

Sometime before we settled on the bucolic Kalakshetra compound, we paid a visit to one of the renowned scholars of Indian philosophy, Professor TMP Mahadevan, who was by then retired from the University of Madras but still taught in his simple home in a suburb of the city where, as Brahmins are wont to, he kept cows and buffaloes in the stable that surrounded the courtyard. He received us with soft-spoken affability and invited us to attend his bi-weekly lecture which we did fairly regularly for several months. His most illustrious disciple was Frederika of Brunswick Luneburg, princess of Hanover, Great Britain and Ireland and former Queen of Greece, apart from being the mother of Queen Sofia of Spain whom we had met in Barcelona and Madrid on various occasions.

I knew little of the Greek Queen's previous life, except that her staunch anti-communism and her adolescence as a member of Hitler's Youth had made her unpopular in many circles. My father told me that she had also been known for a rather uninhibited temperament which might have reflected her Germanic roots as well as the carefree ease of blue blood. Her past, both colourful and dramatic, made our meeting in such plain though unusual circumstances rather strange. The grand-daughter of Kaiser Wilhelm II and descendent of Queen Victoria looked imposing and haughty but was rather cordial. She wore rich jewelry and flowery silk that looked even brighter in the Spartan surroundings of Mahadevan's study, but then had she not been princess of Sparta before ascending the throne? Her natural hauteur contrasted with the reverence she showed to the elderly Tamil professor before whom she prostrated herself, forehead to the floor, before and after attending his discourses.

We talked of many things on this and on following occasions and she seemed to take pleasure in conversing with Europeans as she must have felt a bit isolated during the few months of the year she spent in Madras. I remember what a staunch Vedantin she claimed to be and how many times she advised me to follow the path of Advaita wisdom: the knowledge of the Unknowable One without a second. She had passed on her convictions to her two daughters—the Queen of Spain and Princess Irene. The latter often accompanied her in India and we met on various occasions. In compliance with the Hindu injunctions, she had set up a foundation dedicated to saving cows from slaughter in Spain.

Her Majesty could be prolix and she liked to evoke memories. Her interest in Indian wisdom had been awakened by the great German physicist and Nobel prize winner Werner Heisenberg who had been a guest at the royal Tatoi estate outside Athens. She had come to know him through Field Marshall Jan Smuts, the famous South African statesman who had hosted there the exiled Greek royal family during the second World War. Smuts, himself a scholar of no mean repute had been influenced by Heisenberg's realization that Hindu and Buddhist philosophies held the key to the understanding of the puzzling nature of the universe revealed by quantum mechanics. The Afrikaner statesman had developed since his young age a theory of holism that proved to be ahead of his time and influenced Einstein among others.

The Queen admired the Boer leader as most of those who had met him did, in spite of his controversial political and military activities—first as a foe and then a champion of British power and empire and an often ruthless warrior and conservative statesman—which often seem inconsistent with his philosophical thoughts, so contradictory is human nature, depending upon whether its pursues personal interests and ambitions or speculates on larger metaphysical questions. Frederika's own authoritarian penchant had probably been strengthened by Smut's faith in the righteousness of western supremacy but she had also noticed his own doubts about Christianity. From Heisenberg, whose father had been a Hellenistic scholar, she had gathered the sense that physics was groping its way towards a spiritual understanding of reality and that, as he had put it: "The first gulp from the glass of natural sciences will turn you into an atheist but at the bottom of the glass God is waiting for you."

"That is the parabrahman of the nirvikalpa samadhi," Mahadevan suggested in his soft, thoughtful voice.

There was also in Heisenberg's life and work the contradictions that seem to haunt great men. On the one hand, as a religious thinker and a humanist he had opened many eyes to the spiritual significance of scientific investigations, as demonstrated by his colleague Schrödinger and by his disciple CF von Weizsacker, but on the other hand he had been part of the earliest group set up by the Nazi regime to develop technological and military applications of nuclear physics, the German *Uranverein*; he had also taught students such as Edward Teller and Isidore Rabbi who later became key-members and apologists of the American atomic weapons programme.

I remember that we alluded to those historical paradoxes that Chinese philosophy explains by saying that there cannot be a face without a obverse side and that no light can exist without creating a shadow. The only way to avoid that contradiction according to all spiritual traditions is to choose a life of renunciation or Taoist "actionless action," which is however only accessible to some.

The non-dualism of Sankaracharya offers a solution to the conundrum of wave-particle ambivalence and predicts the uncertainty principle formulated by Heisenberg inherent to all attempts at a quantified description of material phenomena. Although she had no scientific training or disposition, the apparent convergence of spirituality and advanced research certainly comforted Frederika's Germanic love of clarity while vindicating the mysticism intrinsic to passionate temperaments.

There is in one of Sankara's sutras an allusion to the vedic concept of the *rajarishi*, the superior being who is both a ruler and a seer, like Plato's philosopher king and the Taoist equivalent. We talked about that with the Queen and Professor Mahadevan after one of his teaching sessions and I could not help feeling that the royal student must have pondered her own, reputedly unwise exercise of her past monarchical function. Her son Constantine, exiled king of the Hellenes, could not lay claim to being a *rajarishi*. Her son-in-law, who was to become about that time the sovereign of Spain might have, perhaps under his austere wife's influence, come closer in some ways to that ideal but his personality and upbringing would not allow him to achieve it.

KALAKSHETRA

The daily schedule at Kalakshetra was meanwhile becoming habitual. We had moved to a simple guest house located at the edge of a casuarinas grove that separated the school campus from the wide Coromandel beach. After the light South Indian breakfast of *iddlis, puris* and *uttapams* eaten with tea or filter coffee from the blue mountains I went to the morning assembly under a banyan tree where prayers of various faiths were recited, beginning with the auspicious Gayatri mantra in Samskrit, followed by the Buddha's invocation in Pali and then by short Jain, Sikh, Zoroastrian and Christian texts. Sankara Menon, who usually led that ceremony, spoke a few inspirational words commenting on one of the Indian epics or spiritual classics and then students dispersed to attend their respective classes.

I, like most of them, took a three-hour practical and theoretical lesson in Bharata Natyam which, in the tropical spring, was rather strenuous since it took place in thatched mud-walled classrooms, modeled on the huts of the local villages, that had fans but no air-conditioning. Fortunately the sea breeze often blew in through the many windows and brought fragrances of the flowering bushes and creepers that pervaded the surroundings.

Sometimes, however, the smell of roasted flesh drifted in on lazy afternoons from a nearby funeral pyre and we knew that a humble dweller in one of the fishermen's hamlets had left his mortal form. Others, especially those raised in a western contemporary environment would have found that pungent reminder of human mortality horrifying but in such a pastoral setting, it did not disrupt the peaceful atmosphere and provided a sobering but still serene context to the vision of youthful beauty that the mostly female dance students blessed me with constantly.

There were dozens of girls in their late teens and early twenties, colourfully dressed in sarees or in the tight-fitting dance ensembles they wore for classes, often garrulous and giggly; their long dark tresses were braided with jasmine, hibiscus and *champa* flowers and they sported glittering ear and small nose rings. On their foreheads the red *bindi* evoked the third eye of Shiva and the pineal gland that connects the mind to the cosmic self. Most of these young ladies were Indians but a few came from families long settled overseas while four or five hailed from Bangla Desh, Indochina and the Malay archipelago. There was even a lanky blond girl from Gelong in Australia with whom I developed a natural complicity. I soon made friends with several and despite the inevitable erotic attractions and romantic playacting of that age in life, we made a small band in which I was the only boy. The few Indian male students of Kalakshetra were perhaps a bit too intimidated by those alluring but self-confident young women to seek their company outside the classes and so I had that "escadron volant," to paraphrase the metaphor applied to Queen Catherine of Medici's female inner circle, to myself.

Inevitably, joking comparisons by a few were made to Krishna and his gopis, the cowherdesses of Brindavan. I did nonetheless unselfconciously delight in my lovely cluster of honeybees which displayed the diversity of attractions and spells that the female gender has in store. Those girls were all apprentice dancers and musicians so that they had physical and mental graces of those predisposed towards art and the combination of shyness, coquetry, wiles, innocence and dreaminess that characterizes most of the fairer sex was to me an endless source of learning, amusement and surprise.

I also got to know in those days Leela Samson, the daughter of an Indian admiral, a former pupil who taught at Kalakshetra on occasion and was already an accomplished dancer destined to become famous. I always admired her refined beauty and her unfailing gentleness and poise although I saw that she was quite able to maintain discipline among her students. The rainbow hued female flock was ministered to and supervised by two venerable ladies, always clad in sarees as white as their hair, who looked as refined and aristocratic as the lotuses after which they were named. Padma and Kamala, both known as "Padma teacher" and "Kamala teacher," had the aloof and delicate distinction of Brahmin *rishipatnis* but their metaphorical velvet gloves could, when need warranted it reveal an iron hand.

The joyful and flirtatious atmosphere that pervaded part of my day was suffused by the long hours of reading and learning I dedicated to the various aspects of Indian philosophy. Sankara Menon taught a course on the *Upanishads* and the *Bhagavad Gita* twice a week in the courtyard of the small administrative building of Kalakshetra and apart from the Samskrit classes I took everyday, I read various introductory classics, including books by Heinrich Zimmer, Sri Aurobindo, S. Radhakrishnan, S. N. Dasgupta, T. R. V. Murti and I also acquainted myself with important sacred and secular texts such as Patanjali's *Yoga Sutras*, Jayadeva's *Gita Govinda*, the *Srimad Bhagavatam*, Chanakya's *Arthasastra* and the Buddhist *Nikayas, Dhammapada* and *Saddharmapundarika*. I would be lying if I denied eagerly perusing the famous *Kamasutra* of Vatsyayana after discovering an English translation of it I know not where. I soon found out that it is a fairly prosaic catalogue of practices and techniques for love making, particularly among those who do it professionally but I made many discoveries in that exotic domain although I missed in that classic the thrill of romance and mystery that is the best part of *ars amandi*.

THE LANGUAGE OF THE GODS

The subtle, complex and precise mechanics of Sanskrit is an object of wonder for all and I could not fail, despite the difficulty of learning its alphasyllabary and grammar to fall under its spell. I was especially fascinated by the polymorphic flexibility of its vocabulary whose roots could take so many verbal forms and borrow so many meanings, depending upon the context in which they were set.

Al Beruni, who must have had only a superficial acquaintance with the language, described that feature as a weakness: "Sanskrit, he wrote, calls one and the same thing by various names, both original and derived, and uses one and the same word for a variety of subjects, which...must be distinguished from each other by various qualifying epithets, for nobody could distinguish between the various meanings of a word unless he understands the context in which it occurs and its relations both to the following and the preceding parts of the sentence." However, is that not a feature of thought and language once it reaches a certain degree of sophistication?

Everything assumes a number of possible meanings, depending upon how it is intended, literally or at various levels of metaphor or antinomy and objects or facts are merely results of or stages in the evolution of a particular action or a set of actions...

My Sanskrit teacher, backed by the beginner's manual *Samskritabaladarsha* and the venerable *Bhandarkar* would not indulge in such semantic reflections which I heard from Sankara Menon in the course of his lucid explanations of the Upanishads and Yogasutras. I found out that he was a cousin of the late Foreign Minister of India, Krishna Menon but, contrary to his feisty relative who was a Communist, Shankara was a phlegmatic traditional philosopher who certainly qualified as a conservative, just as Rukmini Devi, known for her friendship with the late Rajagopalachari, founder of the right wing liberal Swatantra party.

What a delight the *Upanishads* are to the inquiring mind and what peace they give the soul! It is no wonder that Schopenhauer expressed such admiration for those wonderful scriptures whose luminous simplicity touches the heart while striking the mind. In comparison with their elegant and psychologically sound pedagogy, which makes us feel that it confirms what we may have intuitively sensed, almost all western philosophy, produced by "professional" intellectuals for their own kind, is weighed by theological prejudices or taboos and encumbered by a historical baggage that turn out to be superfluous when we enter the enchanted realm of those discourses and dialogues between wise teachers of both sexes and their students.

I was naturally captivated by the stories of those boys who go through the various stages of superficial and real knowledge under the attentive supervision of their gurus. The *Chandogya Upanishad's* Satyakama's selfless devotion and earnestness enabled him to win liberation despite his humble background and lack of formal education; a counter example in the same Upanishad is provided by Svetaketu who was so proud of his intellectual excellence that he thought he knew everything until his father and guru Aruni asked him whether he knew that by which all knowledge is known. When the supercilious student fell silent, the paternal student made him dissolve some salt into water and bade him drink a sip before telling him that the divine essence pervades the universe as salt gives its taste to the water.

Queen Frederika once compared me to Svetaketu because she saw me as too self-assured and advised me to follow his example.

Another memorable youthful figure appears in the *Katha Upanishad,* another of the ten major ones, out of the hundreds originally composed, of which most are now lost. Nachiketa is one of those child prodigies whose faculties were awoken early by the rigorous discipline of the vedic *gurukulas*. He wishes to fathom the secret of immortality from Yama, the god of death and the beyond (known in ancient Iran as Yima or Jamshed) who is also, in all logic, the first mortal man. The inscrutable lord tries to deflect him from his goal by offering him all kinds of treasures and pleasures but the boy is unmoved. He compels the king of the underworld to finally reveal to him the supreme knowledge which was then passed through the corpus of Hindu, Jain and Buddhist scriptures until it reached Tibet centuries later.

We found an unexpected researcher in that field in the person of Peter Hoffman, whose father was Paul Hoffman, the late architect and administrator of the Marshall Plan and president of the Ford Foundation. His son, a theosophist and admirer of Rukmini Devi, had married the lovely Tamil dancer Sarada, her pupil and they lived in Kalakshetra where Sarada taught, with their two children a few years younger than I who became friends. Peter, a tall and white haired Germanic American with smiling blue eyes and a sunny disposition dwelt in a typical South Indian villa surrounded by a lush little garden and one of his passions was "thanatology" (the study of death for the layman) which had led him from the *Upanishads* to the writings of a kashmiri Brahmin yogi called Gopi Krishna, whom we were to meet later on. I recall a chat or two on this rather solemn subject over sweet cardamom perfumed tea in his book filled living room.

Seeing him in those simple surroundings, devoid of a television and of many of the other modern amenities that most of his countrymen regard as essential, I realized how abstemious our life was since we had effortlessly distanced ourselves from most of the technological additions that fill western life. We did not have a telephone at home and made infrequent calls from a set located near the dining room of the school for the use of the students and staff. Neither of course did we have a radio, a cassette player, tape recorder, washing machine, refrigerator or even an air conditioner. Yet, none of that seemed to matter as readings, exercise and swimming, conversations and visits to places of interest filled the time not taken up by my classes.

VII

Exploring Art and Artha

The World and the Self

On 25th June of that year, a national state of emergency was declared all over India and we got to know it through someone or another but was it so important to see a daily news report? We read the local newspapers two or three times a week, especially the venerable *Hindu,* but I at least did not regret the innumerable distractions with which modern society tries to occupy itself.

Since we were no longer staying in Adyar, we met fewer westerners excepting the occasional visitor to Kalakshetra. However, we were introduced to a French neighbour who lived in bohemian style in a bungalow on the beach outside the nearby village of Thiruvanmiyur. Jean Deloche was a researcher with the Ecole francaise d'Extrême Orient and he devoted his studies to the history of science and technology in medieval India and to the reports of French travelers in past centuries. He had published an account of the visit to Bengal by a Count of Modave in the 18th century. He, his wife and young son reminded me of some of the flower children we had met on our way from Europe and he explained to us that as a couple, they had come on foot from France in 1961, well before the anti-establishment youth wave rose in 1968. "We were among the earliest Dharma bums in Europe" he said with a wry smile.

Back to the *Upanishads,* another appealing aspect of those wonderful treatises, as I have already hinted, is the natural and conceptually equal recognition it gives to both genders in the pursuit of wisdom without indulging in any superfluous argument about enforced equality, despite the well-established reputation of Hinduism in the West as a male dominated religion. Thus, the great rishi Yajnavalkya has two wives who are both philosophers as well and he also learns from them in deep discussions although one seems more theoretically inclined while the others appears more concerned with practical duties and the story anticipates in some way on the famous evangelic parable about Martha and Mary around Jesus.

All those who have read anything about Indian philosophy know that its core teaching, essentially common to all "vedic" traditions, is *Aham, brahmasmi* (I am the supreme reality) and *Tat twam asi* (that thou art). An equally famous aphorism is *Ekam Sat vipra bahudha vadanti,* which broadly means that the truth is one but that sages express it in different ways. This should not be interpreted as a bland affirmation that all belief systems are equally valid, which would lead to relativistic indifference or nihilism but is merely a recognition of the inexpressibility of the ultimate essence that is sought to be conveyed in many different languages and metaphors to the limited human intellect. Indian philosophy is a gnostic wisdom in the sense that it reveals a transcendent and immanent knowledge of divine and cosmic origin and character.

In contrast with the solar warmth of the Vedic scriptures that always shine with the reflected glow of the *agnihotra*, the fire sacrifice that represents the universal process of birth, expansion and death, the *Astadhyayi* of Panini is a miracle of lapidary semantic condensation meant to convey the largest amount of syntactic and grammatical information in the shortest format. Although I was only given a brief introduction to it, it struck me with its nearly algebraic concision which I also found in the *yogasutras* of Patanjali, another great master of the Sanskrit language and the first known systematic exponent of yoga in all its forms.

Side by side, ancient India had developed the highly symbolic, sensory and poetic imagery of the cosmological rituals and the abstract intellectual expositions of complex concepts intended for silent meditation or sapiential dialogue. By studying that age-old lore, in its arts and in its scholarly records, I realized the shallowness of the concept of progress which assumes that people of each generation must be more intelligent, accomplished and learned than their predecessors when in fact neither art nor philosophy have made any essential advance in thousands of years—indeed they have decayed time and again in certain respects—and only in industrial technology have we moved far ahead, with ever more visible negative consequences which may soon cancel out the material gains and benefits of which we are so proud.

Whereas the masterworks of painters and sculptors of the last few centuries cannot be demonstrated to have reached a higher aesthetic level than those that survived from antiquity, both in East and West, the description of the human identity in its many dimensions within its cosmic home is far more intellectually and emotionally fulfilling and sophisticated than what the "modern" sciences of psychology and anthropology were able to grasp until recently. The *Taittriya Upanishad* explains the five *koshas* or sheaths that make up being, from the chemically organic "grosser" body, the only one normally seen and physically felt, to the increasingly subtle and radiant but usually invisible ones made respectively of breath, mind, consciousness and pure bliss or light.

Sankara Menon commented, during one of his lectures, that current scientific research might soon come to validate that ancient physiological description. He would now, almost four decades later, feel vindicated by the recognition of the inseparability of matter and life from information networks which use the bioelectromagnetic force and light to operate. In the perspective of the "new biology," physical bodies are indeed manifestations or projections of energy patterns that may well be rooted in consciousness.

In both dance and music as I studied them, one found the application and illustration of the lessons that the Hindu *sarvajnana* or *brahmavidya* (divine omniscience) enshrines. The choreography of Bharata Natyam is the articulation of a series of sculptural poses animated by the *prana*, the breath of life and as such it is a ritual, both *mysterium* (in the sense of sacred theater) and *mimus* (imitation) as Ananda Coomaraswamy described it. Music provides the rhythm, pitch and mode for the dance and as such it is the wind that pervades and moves the earthly fire of the dancer's body.

In both the Northern or Hindustani school of music and the Carnatic or southern style, which was taught at Kalakshetra, the fundamental unit is the *raga*, the "colour" or mode, of which seventy-two fundamental ones (*malakanta*), are known in the Southern tradition. Each raga is a melodic cluster of five, six or seven *swaras* (tones) although all malakanta *ragas* have seven, in both ascending and descending scales. These seventy two "parent ragas" have spun off a large number of *janya* or secondary or derived ragas. The complexity of Indian thought in this as in most other matters is such that it is almost impossible for someone who has not been familiarized from childhood with all the nuances of this classification to tell all ragas apart from each other, especially as they are also to be distinguished according to the pitch (*sruti*) being used and the *bhava* (feeling) with which they are sung and the *rasa* (aesthetic impression) that they produce.

All in all, Indian music is less rigid in its categories, more improvisational and more individual—though not individualistic—than its western classical equivalent which relies heavily on annotated scores and requires great fidelity to an original composition.

Before the invention of acoustic amplification, an Indian musical performance was meant for more intimate settings and limited audiences. The Flamenco of the Spanish gypsies has retained certain distinctive features from its South Asian origins although it is obviously closer to folklore than to academic or religious Hindu musicology.

WHAT IS THE SOUL OF INDIAN MUSIC AND DANCE?

Carnatic music is almost entirely devotional as it mostly consists of *kritis* or *kirtans,* which are invocations of the divine in its many forms. Rukmini Devi undertook early in her career to compose and represent

Indian epics and classical literature in dramatic musical plays inspired by the traditional *harikathas* (dramatic musical recitations). Her major work is the enactment of the entire Ramayana of Valmiki in a series of six plays, traditionally staged on as many successive evenings. She thus harnessed Bharata Natyam, which was hitherto predominantly performed by single dancers, to enact operatic ballets with stages, costumes and some modest special effects.

I was brought back to the perspicacious Count Keyserling's impression of Indian dance which he witnessed in the very city of Tanjore whose colossal sanctuary had filled us with wonder. He had this to say: "... In the presence of these girls (the "Nautch" dancers) I lost all consciousness of time, and found happiness. The idea underlying these dances has little in common with that which underlies ours... The movements never signify more than a transient ripple on smooth water ... and if by chance a perfect arabesque is achieved, it disappears so rapidly that it only attracts momentary attention and does not lead to continued tension."

The distinguished visiting philosopher captured what is perhaps the essence of Bharata's choreography and also of the corresponding music, in the following few lines: "this dance possesses no accelerating motive; for this reason one can watch it ceaselessly. Our dance means a definite, finite formation, which begins and ends in time; the onlooker enters into its play of lines and ... when the design is completed, sinks back into himself wearily because no one can live outside himself for long. In the case of the Nautch it is different. Their contemplation does not take the onlooker beyond himself ... it allows him, on the contrary, to be conscious of his own life ... and no one tires of this. Every rapid movement sinks back as soon as it has been shown, into the *bathos* of the calmly flowing stream of life, and that gives us a direct experience of its flow."

The theatrical productions conceived by Rukmini Devi with the help of some of the best remaining musicians and dancers of her time were inspired by the spirit and rules of the Sanskrit dramatic school, probably the world's most technically sophisticated and abundantly documented. To understand its principles and concepts, one must acquire at least a cursory knowledge of the great exponents Bharata and Abhinavagupta, as I had strived to, despite limited access to source in Spain. Readings in the Kalakshetra library and the classes I took familiarized me with the complex theory of India's performance art which is regarded as a total, all encompassing aesthetic experience, similar in spirit to Richard Wagner's concept of opera.

Indeed, trained as I was in French classical theatrical literature of the 17th and 18th centuries, I found myself instantly familiar with the notions and techniques described by the ancient Hindu masters and often had the uncanny feeling that the great French tragedians Corneille and Racine and our most illustrious comedian Moliere had been close to the sanskrit concepts. Going beyond the graeco-roman traditions revived in post-Renaissance Europe, one had to recognize the wider common Indo-European legacy that pervaded the Indian, Latin and Germanic civilizations.

The plays of the famous dramatic authors—Bhasa, Kalidasa, Bhavabhuti—often feature characters who speak different languages, from Sanskrit to sundry Prakrits reflecting their respective social stations—although certain Brahmins, including court buffoons for example do not speak Sanskrit unlike kings who do—and then there are those surprisingly "modern" details, such as the device of the "play within the play," as in Strauss's *Iphigenie*, or the description of an ancestors' portrait gallery in the palace of Rama in Bhasa's *Pratimanataka,* which is believed to have been written early in the Christian era or the subtle interplay of dream and reality in *Svapnavasavadatta* by the same author who preceded Calderon de la Barca's *La Vida es un Sueño* by one millennium.

Any cursory investigation of Indian literature reveals the debt that the rest of the world owes it, in the works of authors as diverse as Shakespeare, Carlo Gozzi, Goethe, Theophile Gautier, Baudelaire, the French Parnassians, Mallarmé and the other Symbolists who did not always acknowledge their sources of inspiration. Many westerners seem to have felt that like India itself in their days, its intellectual production was an anonymous and remote lode that could be mined freely.

The construction of a play as prescribed by Bharata is partly recognizable in the architecture of both Shakespeare's dramas and French classical tragedies and comedies. The four media used to represent a character or a personality are the soul, the body, language and costume. There is a distinction between a heroic play (which is the greek tragedy), the character play (or comedy), the monologue and the farce. The plot must evolve over five or more acts, like Greek, Latin and most European classical theater, which respectively depict the "seed" (*bindu*) of the action and its initial unfoldment, its subsequent development, a secondary plot, the *prakari* or "catastrophy" that creates the suspense by coming in the way of the expected result and the *dénouement* that brings about the fulfillment of the initial endeavour.

Those "limbs" of the story are respectively set in motion by specific happenings that connect with them through the conjunction known as *samdhi* through which the tale acquires and maintains its dynamism and its logic. The play was written by a *kavi*, a composer or poet and its performance directed by a *Sutradhar*, "he who held the thread of meaning." As an impresario, a conductor and often a lead actor one can say that Moliere in France was a sutradhar apart from writing his own plays.

In the broad framework he lays out, Bharata lists sixty-four different elements of a plot among which the playwright may choose to diversify his story. In a way, those sixty-four options are like the squares of a chessboard amongst which there is an astronomical number of possible moves and combinations. Indian culture was fond of computing all components of an essentially unlimited or unpredictable process in order to organize randomness as nature apparently does.

However, a play is also a religious ceremony. It begins with the invocation to a deity and an explanatory prologue and ends with a blessing to the patron of the performance and to the audience.

The classification of all characters of the play is equally systematic and both Greek and Italian theaters are familiar with the prototypes described in Sanskrit drama. There are for instance four types of male heroes (noble minded, recklessly brave, courtly and sagely serene), four kinds of lover (faithful, gallant, cheeky and deceitful) but eight different sorts of beloved.

As much as the Kalakshetra ballets enchanted us, my father and I had greater difficulty appreciating Carnatic music which requires educating the ear in order to be enjoyed as it is in so many ways alien to western notions of music. Gradually, however, I fell under the spell of the *nadesvaram*, the reed flute soaring as a tropical birdsong, paced by the thrumming of the *mridangam*, the Carnatic drums which sound like a monsoon rainfall. They combine with the voices of the singers who intone the epic or lyrical verses while the violin's high pitched drone evokes the flight of a swarm of honey gathering bees.

With time I began to feel the dreamy emotion and the meditative pleasure generated by those sounds and in comparison much of western chamber music, especially the romantic one lost some of its prestige as I realized its rather dry academism, not to speak of the squarely uninspiring and unpleasant sounds produced by dodecaphonal, serial and other "modern" compositions that often seem to be gratuitous technical exercises divorced from any interest in aesthetics or enjoyment.

I remain a passionate admirer of much of the western classical repertoire, created between the 16th and early 20th century, by which time it seems to have lost its way under the influence of the industrial and pragmatic materialism of Euro-American civilization. No one can fail to admire and revel in the extraordinary creations of Vivaldi, Bach, Haendel, Haydn, Mozart, Beethoven, Chopin, Liszt, Verdi and many, many others but the secularization of the West gradually tore it from its metaphysical roots and the reliance on the precise rendering of a written set of symbols took away some of the spontaneous inspiration. It gained in accuracy and reliability but one sometimes feels, when the interpreters are not above average, that it sacrificed some of its soul. Baroque sacred music however preserves the essence of the blissful contemplative, self-transcending tropism which one might vainly seek in the scores of many more recent composers, even among the very talented ones.

The reason for the academic nature and feeling of meaninglessness produced by much of the concert music composed since the beginning of the 20th century must be found in the neglect of the notion of *rasa* or flavor that all true art must create, according to Indian theories but which lies in the spectator or listener, not as such in the work itself that is intended to evoke it. In that metaphysical optics, *rasa* is a mystical feeling, comparable to the union of the soul with the divine, and it is partly aroused by the recollection of old, hazy memories (*vasanas*). The *saudade* of Portuguese lyricism and the famous cupcake of Proust are European equivalents of at least one manner of *rasa;* Indian artists know of nine kinds covering the gamut of human emotions but all of them can perhaps be encapsulated in the delectation (or delight as in de-light) that French 17th century painter Nicolas Poussin defined as the goal and secret of any artwork.

Nature, physical and psychological is the fount from which all art springs and draws images, metaphors, euphemisms and impressions. Living in the verdant landscape of Kalakshetra, cradled in the sky and sea I could easily relive the sensations described in the poetry I read, the *bhavas* or emotions aroused by plastic or performing arts through the alchemy of external stimuli and internal states.

There are a few stable emotions (*sthayibhavas*) and thirty-three flighty or momentary ones (*vyabhicaribhavas*), which are conveyed by voluntary and spontaneous gestures, facial expressions and patterns of behavior. All these trigger *rasa* in both the artists and the spectator, together with environmental factors or impressions (*vibhavas*), such as the shimmer of the moon, the sight of a starry sky or landscape or a scent whereas other *vibhavas* are staged, like the tears and swoon of the heroine or the ire or melancholy of the hero.

Total art therefore addresses all the senses and choreography expresses that concept by codifying and using bodily positions and gestures as well as the language of the hands and fingers, facial and eye expressions coordinated with instrumental music and singing.

One could not fail to notice the strangely abstract, symbolic nature of a dance form that seems to purposely avoid any overt sensual gesture, unlike most Western or Middle Eastern choreographies. The demure costume of the dancers does not provide in its modesty an invitation to carnal desires. Gestures are gracefully geometric and always take the spectator into a disincarnated world of form and essence. The rhythm is pressing and inflexible, controlling all movements and the entire exercise is an offering to the presiding deity and only accessorily to the audience. The performance takes place in the sphere of myth and allegory, inviting adoration not lust. As in all things essentially Indian, meditation is the intended state of mind. The "show" is to be contemplated, not merely watched and the performers appear as both embodiments of divine beings and their worshippers. They are hypostases of a spiritual reality, not luscious bodies offered for enjoyment. There is a hieratic austerity even in seemingly seductive poses and glances. The profane is wrapped into the sacred.

THE SACRED TOWN OF MYLAPORE

The beach was the arena where to temporarily escape from and yet assimilate the teachings received in the school. We saw there the fishermen, dark as Africans and naked but for a textile fig leaf, hauling their cocoanut rope-sewn primitive catamarans towards the water or back on the sand and we sometimes helped them in that burdensome task and watched them unload flat round baskets brimming with fish or prawns which the scrawny women carried away on their heads.

Noticing how all smelt of fish I easily grasped the origin of the practice of untouchability in the aversion of a vegetarian population, concerned about ritual purity towards those hardworking children of the ocean. However I also knew that the legendary compiler or organizer of the Vedas and Mahabharata, Krishna Vedavyasa was said to have been born to a fisherwoman and was surnamed Dvaipayana, which means "islander."

Our strolls along the shore of the bay of Bengal at dusk regaled us with the celestial magnificence of tropical twilights that I strived to describe in floridly allegorical French but we also made a few unusual acquaintances. One evening we were hailed by a rather young bespetacled man walking on the sand with his wife. Our conversation revealed that he was a reader in philosophy at the renowned university of Madras whose vice-chancellor Malcolm Adisheshiah we had met after a ballet performance at Kalakshetra. Dr A Raman invited us to have dinner at his home and soon became a friend. He lived in an old typical Brahmin's house around the 7th century Mylapore temple, in an area of Madras that is full of history as it was known to the Graeco-Roman geographer Ptolemy, visited by Marco Polo and occupied by the Portuguese before being taken by the Dutch and then the inevitable English.

Our host was descended from the original *Smarta* ("those who remember") caste of Brahmins who had come to the area many centuries ago. That community traditionally worships five main deities, Visnu, Shiva, Mahadevi, or "the great goddess," Surya the Sun and Ganesha, the elephant headed son of Shiva so that they may be regarded as "catholic" in comparison with the more specifically sectarian *sampradayas* which are devoted to one main *Deva*. I was surprised to discover that a nearby suburb called Luz (Light), like my birthplace in the remote Canary island, stands as a reminder of the long Lusitanian presence.

The French had taken over the Dutch fort there in 1662, well before they settled in Pondicherry and fought the British of Fort Saint George until capitulating to them in 1687. Despite its cosmopolitan past, Mylapore is a typical bustling Dravidian town where one feels the pulse of Hinduism beating strongly in its many temples as it is also the birthplace of the most illustrious saintly poet of Tamil literature Thiruvalluvar. More than once we went there to the haven of calm of the Ramakrishna Mission and to the milky white neogothic basilica of Saint Thomas built on the spot where a Syriac Christian church was said to have risen over the remains of the doubting apostle before his body was repatriated to Edessa in Syria, near his land of origin.

The great shrine that dominates Mylapore, Kapaleesvara is dedicated to Shiva, "the lord of the skull," and to his wife Meenakshi, whom the ascetic god is said to have courted in the form of a peacock. The bird gave its name to the spot, which means "the land of the peacock's call" in tamil. The peacock, as well as the rooster is also the symbol of Shiva's eldest son, the warlike Subramanyam otherwise known as Kartikeya, who is a very ancient Tamil deity.

We had soon learned after arriving in Madras that the regional government led by the head of the DMK pan-dravidian Party, Karunanidhi was known for its anti-brahminical and even anti-Hindu ideology which had caused an exodus of the traditionally dominant Tamil Brahmins. The DMK had even openly championed secession from India for Tamil Nadu until a few years earlier and was still suspected of harbouring dreams of regional independence. For that reason, Rukmini Devi and Kalakshetra did not enjoy the favour of the local authorities who regarded the school as a holdout of high caste sanskrit culture. However, despite the political climate, Brahmins like Raman were still dominant in the intellectual and cultural professions and the innate Indian sense of compromise helped people who should have been sworn enemies to tolerate each other.

In the event, Dr Raman invited us to give a lecture at the university and we accepted with pleasure. In view of my father's limited knowledge of English and of my own research work in Hindu philosophy, we decided to speak on the relations between Taoism, Hinduism, Buddhism, a topic that had long attracted our interest, given the many traces of centuries of interaction between those great traditions which may in par explain the similarities in their respective messages. It has long been held in China that Lao Tzu went to India and taught the ageless wisdom to its inhabitants, thus giving rise to Buddhism which indeed was born at the foot of the Himalayas.

The Tao can be compared with the vedic *Rita*, the natural law or rhythm of the universe. In a later period, the Shangqing and Ling Bao schools of Taoism acknowledged their Mahayana Buddhist sources. That was the basis for our talk, which was well received. Sankara

Menon attended it and it was the first of various seminars that we held in the city subsequently.

ANOTHER IDEA OF INDIA

The monsoon season had by then been upon us with its diluvial rainstorms that left behind a semi-aquatic landscape, smothered at dusk in the drone of a hoarse batracian choir. Even the stars shone with a wet radiance in cloudy skies and the call of the rainbirds rose obsessively in the moist air.

One late afternoon we found in the casuarinas grove that spread behind the house, a small group of men gathered to listen to one of them and perform certain exercises that seemed to be a cross between a military drill and a religious rite. We were intrigued by the unusual discipline they displayed and when we saw that they seemed about to disperse, we greeted them. Their apparent leader came forward affably and introduced himself by the name of Srinivasan. His gentle and rather priestly attitude contrasted with the resolute, almost martial demeanour of his companions. A moment of conversation disclosed that he was the head of the local branch of the Rashtriya Swayamsevak Sngh or RSS (the "league of volunteer servants of the nation"), an all-India militant organization that had been banned by Indira Gandhi's government when emergency had been declared a few weeks earlier. The RSS is deeply distrusted and disliked by much of India's political and academic establishment as it is accused of cultivating an ultra-national ideology verging on fascism which champions a religiously hindu form of government and rejects the western inspired secularism adopted in India's Constitution. Dr Srinivasan lent us some of the literature produced by the founders, K B Hedgewar and M S Golwalkar in the years before and soon after Independence.

I saw in those writings, "We, or Our Nation Defined" and "Bunch of Thought" that the organization was born, from an offshoot of the Congress Party in the rugged Deccan region where Shivaji had risen against the Mughal empire in the 17th century and that it carried his legacy of warlike patriotism.

After defeating the Muslim rulers of India, Shivaji's successors came close to uniting the subcontinent under their rule when the British East India Company managed, in alliance with a number of local monarchs, to curb their power in a series of hard-fought battles in which the two Wellesley brothers rose to fame and eminence well before one of them, Sir Arthur, crushed Napoleon's army and was made Duke of Wellington.

In a land as vast and diverse as India, it was no wonder that the particular and homogenous Maratha political culture of the RSS found little favour in other regions that have very different religious and social traditions. The Marathas had been seen as invaders by other Indians in the north of the country and the old royal dynasties resented those rural upstarts who had attacked Islamic power even though they had never shown opposition to the Muslim faith but only the resolve to cast off the yoke of the Turkic and Persian invaders.

We had several opportunities to discuss the philosophy of the RSS which had borrowed from various ideological sources, including the messages of Lokamanya Tilak, the great intellectual and Congress leader from Pune, Sri Aurobindo, the "prophet of Pondicherry" and Swami Vivekandanda. In fact *guruji* Golwalkar had studied under Swami Akhandananda, a direct disciple of Sri Ramakrishna, the saint of Dakshineshvar but like his mentor Dr Hedgewar he had been much affected by the impact of the *khilafat* movement, which had led the Muslims to agitate violently, with the support of Gandhi and other Congress leaders, against Ataturk's decision to abolish the supreme Islamic institution. The turmoil which resulted in bloody riots between Muslims and Hindus in some parts of India convinced the RSS founders that followers of Islam owed their primary loyalty to an extraterritorial hierarchy and did not regard Hindustan as their motherland but only as a conquered territory which they had ruled for centuries with the support of foreign armies.

This conclusion, combined with resentment against British occupation, led Hedgewar to define a religious form of nationalism that stood squarely against the secular multi- or non-denominational model favoured by Gandhi and Nehru. When he died in 1940 however there was as yet no split between the Congress and the RSS which concerned itself primarily with education and social work. Vallabhbhai Patel, India's first home minister was known to sympathize with the RSS and Gandhi visited some of the local branches of the organization. The British however became alarmed when Golwalkar, who had succeeded Hedgewar as the head of the Sangh expressed support and admiration for the German Third Reich in his 1938 book, although he also condemned Hitler's persecution of the Jews which he described as a constant Christian feature. It must be added though that some members of the Congress party initially sympathized with the Fuhrer's policies and that even Gandhi advocated India's neutrality in the looming conflict while he advised the United Kingdom not to resist Hitler's assault.

Golwalkar took notice of the Nazi policy to expel Semites from the territory of the Reich and to encourage their transfer to a land of their own, which is how the German strategy on this issue was generally perceived at the time. He felt that a similar measure might have to be adopted in India towards the Muslims that did not want to pledge their loyalty to the nation above their faith and community. At the time of independence, his concerns were vindicated as the majority of India's Muhamedans, under the leadership of the Muslim League, opted to set up a separate state. That Gandhi resigned himself to that catastrophic and bloody partition was deeply resented by the nationalist bodies that had grown around the RSS ideology.

In early 1948, the Mahatma was shot dead by a former member of the RSS, Nathuram Godse, and shortly thereafter the organization, whose leaders unequivocally condemned the murder, was banned for the first time but only for a few months. Golwalkar remained its leader until his death in 1973 and less than two years later, Mrs Gandhi, in the wake of the imposition of Emergency outlawed the organization once again.

It struck both my father and me that, as a result of their resolve to build a united national consciousness in a country that did not have much of it, the RSS fathers had borrowed aspects of western religious and linguistic nationalism that seemed ill adapted to India's history and conditions. They were far from being isolated in that endeavour since Vivekananda as well as Subhash Chandra Bose and Patel among others had also championed a patriotic "refoundation" of the country but their definition of an indigenous cultural and political identity set them against a number of minorities and more particularly the Muslims who had been used to ruling much of India during centuries and were not prepared to subsume themselves into a larger identity characterised by what they regarded as polytheism. They had constantly brought in soldiers, theologians, poets and administrators from Persia, Turkestan and Arabia to help them govern the country and had little doubt that India was a part of the worldwide *Umma*. The ideology of the RSS appeared radical and dangerous to them as it did to the many Hindus who saw the risk of further civil wars and breakups of the country if the Hindu nationalists were allowed to come to power.

The RSS ideologues had perhaps been the first to challenge the theory of an Aryan invasion of India sponsored by the British rulers. They held most Indians to be sons of the soil and saw no ethnic gap between the brahminical upper castes and the rest of the population and accused the Europeans of fostering division in the subcontinent by propagating that hypothesis as if it had been a proven fact. Unfortunately, their alternative history of India came wrapped in their ideology and was hence frowned upon, irrespective of its intrinsic merits, by all those who opposed it politically. However, the more I looked into this vexed question, the more I found that, on purely scholarly ground, Hedgewar and his followers might well be right, if only because they relied on traditional accounts of India's history instead of adopting the supposedly "scientific" discoveries of European linguists and archeologists.

In the following years, we were to find many more reasons to believe in the primarily indigenous origin of Vedic culture. Quite a few of the romantic notions introduced by German and British scholars in the colonial age have been disproven, beginning with the biblical myth that humanity arose in the Middle East a few thousand years before the birth of Christ from the offspring of one primeval couple. The almost equally farfetched view that some horse-riding invaders from an undetermined location had taken over India three thousand five hundred years ago, bringing with them Sanskrit and the Vedas is gradually been discarded. The Vedas are geographically rooted in the Punjab region of India and frequently refer to fortified cities, seafaring and agriculture which would have been foreign to Central Asian nomads. Furthermore, Indian literature contains innumerable references to very ancient times and events that clearly predate the 1500 BC dateline hypothetically assigned for the "Aryan invasion." The "Indus valley" settlements discovered in the nineteen thirties go back thousands of years before the assumed invasion and seem to have been both autochthonous and culturally vedic although their writing system has not been deciphered yet.

Aryas are described as a spiritual and cultural elite in Sanskrit speech, not an alien invading race. All in all, it is easy to detect a naïve pan-Germanic hubris in the western concept of the Indo-Aryan *ürvolk* that provided a legendary ancestry to triumphantly imperial northern Europeans.

Srinivasan was ancestrally associated with Mylapore's Sri Srinivasar koil, founded by an illustrious Vedantin saint who belonged to Madhvacharya's *visistadvaitin* ("nuanced monism") school of Vedanta. His own family tradition was thus highly metaphysical, unlike the political and activist brand of Hinduism promoted by the Sangh but he clarified that the latter did not attempt in any way to modify or homogenize the forms of worship of its members but rather strived to build a common ground between all Hindu traditions through social service.

"The Sangh is non-sectarian, he pointed out, and it has been at the forefront of the action to eradicate castes as they are major factors of division within our people. We are a reformist body and we welcome modernity when it is beneficial to the nation and suitable to our true culture. In fact many Hindus don't like our doctrine because we want all children of Bharat to feel equal."

As Srinivasan's younger and energetic colleague S Gurumoorthy argued, the warnings given by Hedgewar about the role of Muslims in independent India had been prescient even though they had been interpreted as threats and aspersions motivated by his hostility to the descendents of invaders. "In fact, he said neither Doctorji (Hedgewar) nor Guruji hated them...They merely wanted India to be protected from civil strife and subversion by a fifth column. They did not dislike Jews at all and if you read their words, you'll see that they actually admired them and supported the creation of the state of Israel. They however felt that Germans might have had reasons to reject a minority that they saw as behaving against the national interest in pursuit of their own goals."

I had been made aware well before coming to India that for a few years after Hitler's rise to power, the first Zionists of Palestine and the Nazis had behaved as objective allies since they all supported the exodus of the Jews to their promised land. Reality is usually more complex than accounts given by politically motivated history. Yet, we were not convinced that the RSS could encompass the teeming, virtually limitless, ever-evolving diversity of India within its paramilitary framework which seemed inspired by the Boy Scout movement and the Spanish Phalangist ideology. After all, it had been built in the inter-war years when regimented social systems were arising in many countries and the world had been transformed since then.

We once pointed out to our RSS friends that as our familiar mentor Keyserling had observed in his day: "There is no Indian nation... No Indian faith... On the other hand, how marvelously rich and well adjusted is India's humanity! How wonderfully each type is defined!." Did Hedgewar's endeavour to forge a single type of Indian *swayamsevak* through a course of rigorous physical and mental training not run counter to that natural and flexible diversity? In his urge to build one nation would the RSS not wipe out the innumerable delicate peculiarities and apparent disconnections in the subcontinent's human tapestry? To that Gurumoorthy replied that the Sangh was only meant to serve as a framework to keep the country together without erasing its pluralistic fabric. "Without that, he concluded, the nation will fall apart again and break up into many warring fiefdoms which will inevitably come under the influence of foreign forces."

One aspect of the Hindu nationalist nebula we found particularly valuable. We first heard of Deendayal Upadhyaya's Integral Humanism which struck us by its synthetic combination of western social thought and Indian metaphysical insights that also adopted "Gandhi's socialism" and its precepts for a decentralized government and a self-reliant economy. It became clear to me that Upadhyaya and his followers had remained more faithful to the ideas of the Father of the Nation than the Congress Party with its Nehruvian focus on heavy industry and mixed economy loosely based on European models, both Marxist and Liberal. In that perspective, the bitter hostility of the ruling party for Upadhyaya's RSS inspired political movement, the *Jan Sangh* (people's league) seemed more a matter of political rivalry than ideological aversion.

The will for power is what guides professional statesmen, not love for social ideals and Mrs. Gandhi was a full-fledged politician in the tradition of Chanakya and Machiavelli, who had attained almost absolute power at that time and would brook no challenger.

VIII

Between Heaven and Earth

THE SANKARACHARYA OF KANCHI

As I was becoming more familiar with the contemporary articulation of Hindu thought in the political sphere, we were recalled of one of its most venerable and transcendent aspects when Rukmini Devi gathered the Kalakshetra staff and students to welcome a visit to the area by one of the great spiritual leaders of Hinduism, His Holiness Chandrasekharendra Saraswati the fifth, sixty-ninth Sankaracharya of Kanchi Kamakothi Peetham, known as Paramacharya Mahaswami.

I had first read about the "Sage of Kanchi" in Paul Brunton's *Search in Secret India* in which he describes his meeting with that spiritual successor of the great Hindu reformist philosopher Sankara, the founder of Advaita Vedanta, the school of absolute non-duality. The very Deendayal Upadhyaya, who grounded his unitarian and organic social philosophy on Advaitin psychology, had written his biography. Both Professor TMP Mahadevan and Queen Frederika were his devotees as well as many intellectual luminaries from India and abroad. I learnt that this keeper of the spiritual tradition had studied in an American Mission School although he had been born in a high class Kannada *Smarta* Brahmin clan. He was an octogenarian at the time of his visit but continued to perform apostolic missions. In his younger years, he had walked all the way to Varanasi from the Southern tip of India, followed and greeted by vast crowds on his path.

As could be expected many legends surrounded the founding and history of the Kanchi Math—*matha* is a seat of leaning in India and the root of the word is at the source of *mathematica*, or science in Greek—which he headed since the age of thirteen. Tradition affirmed it had been established by the first Sankara when he was not yet thirty in 483 BC, about the time when the historic Buddha also flourished.

Sankara is recorded to have left his body at the young age of thirty-two in 477 BC or 2593 of Kali Yuga but western scholarship rejects that chronology and assigns to the first master of Advaita much more recent dates in the 8th century of the common era. Naturally, the Hindu record keepers have not adopted the "modern" estimates and hold on to their rather precise annals which keep the names and signal deeds of the sixty seven acharyas who successively occupied the holy seat of Kanchi, beginning with Suresvara, one of Sankara's five chief disciples. Kanchi itself is regarded as one of the *panchabhutasthalas* (the nodes of the five elements) in the Tamil world and stands for the earth. It is also called *Sarvagna Matha*, or the supreme see among the five that perpetuate the Advaitin tradition in as many holy cities of India.

I had often peered into the amazing complexity of the hindu religious geography, composed of multiple networks of sanctuaries, pilgrimage sites, hallowed ashrams and sacred spots for the innumerable sects and lineages of the Dharma and I realized that an entire life would not suffice to map it out.

It is nonetheless a typically western misconception to assume that there are deep divisions and conflicts between the followers of the myriad branches of the Hindu tree. Sankaracharya himself is regarded as an Avatar of Shiva and his name alludes to the crescent moon that adorns the divine yogi's hairlocks but he composed poems in honour of Vishnu in his Krishna form and throughout history there are multiple cross references and dialogues not only between the properly Vedic confessions but also with the Jains and Buddhists who remain so prominent in the cultural landscape until the age of the Muslim conquests. In the South, for example, one of the greatest literary works in Tamil is the *Manimegalai* written by a Buddhist in the early centuries of the common era, primarily in order to affirm the moral and metaphysical superiority of Buddhism. Kanchipuram had been a famous seat of Buddhist studies and the legendary Bodhidharma who spread Dhyana or *Ch'an* (Zen) in China in the 6th century of the common era came from there as well as the brahmin Bharadwaj who in the 8th century taught a Sanskrit-based alphabet in Japan and is still revered there as Baramon.

I was also intrigued by the perhaps wholly anodyne connection between the "crescent" of Sankara, the teacher of "pure non-duality" and Islam's choice of that celestial form as its universal symbol, given that it is the religion of *Tauhid*: divine indivisible unity.

A persistent and irritating feature of the western mind is evinced in its overwhelming concern to assign "correct" and precise dates to all events and people in history. If their place in the chronology is not deemed valid or accurate, their very existence is doubted or denied. Western civilization is based on dates. They are signpost and benchmarks that lend reality to everything. On the contrary in India they are often contradictory, vague or appear implausible because time is cyclical and all things and figures, rishis, kings, Buddhas and Sankaracharyas keep returning and reappearing. I still wonder whether more than one "Sankara" flourished and whether the period ascribed to the founder of the line by western scholars does not in fact apply to a later eponymous pontiff in the nomenclature.

Again, I found most Indians' view of this matter encapsulated by Keyserling in one sentence: "they accept what is likely just as they accept what is improbable, and they do not take anything specially seriously simply because it is historically true."

The traditional chroniclers of the Vedantin succession have been accused by modern historians of pushing back the dates of the founder to make him a contemporary of the Buddha and of Mahavira, the "prophet" of Jainism but all three figures whose names double as titles seem to be divinized, somewhat impersonal archetypes in the Indian tradition in which myth engulfs the past and the Hindu culturally lives in myth, not in history. Is the basic tenet of Advaita Vedanta not *Brahma satyam, jagan mithya, jivo brahmaiva naparaha,* or "Only Brahman is real, the world is a myth (not ultimately real) and the individual life or soul is no other than Brahman"?

Whether he lived twelve or twenty-five centuries ago, the saintly reformer of Vedanta opposed his interpretation of the Upanishadic legacy to Buddha's approach. He rejected Sakya Muni's emphasis on emptiness and suffering to proclaim the supremacy of Being (*Sat*), Consciousness (*Chit*) and Bliss (*Ananda*) and he reaffirmed the imperishable nature of the self in its transcendent, infinite dimensions after discarding the Buddhist view that there is no such thing as a constant being. Sankara's message resonated with the Indian spirit which probably found the Tathagatha's teaching too dryly abstract.

Though he is famous mainly for his vast allegorical poem *Naisadhiya* on the love story of Nala and Damayanti, which prefigures the Russian *byline* of the Firebird, the brilliant polygraph Sriharsha for example also wrote a treatise to expound Advaita philosophy, the *khandanakhandakhadya* which demonstrates that the world, according to Sankara's analysis cannot be said to be either real or unreal but rather lies beyond both notions as it reflects the eternal cosmic self. The *Naisadhiya* provides mythological illustrations of that state of being and portrays the psychological situations created by the coexistence of multiple personalities in one body which the Buddhists describe as *samskaras*.

One could easily admit the claim that the the First (Adi) Sankara came soon after Siddharta Buddha and undertook to refute his doctrine but after all, is it really important to settle that controversy?

It seems that people become obsessed with technical details when they miss the essential contents of a story. That is why ritual survives meaninglessly long after its significance has been forgotten.

We left in joyously hushed procession after nightfall and walked on a road that led out of Thiruvanmiyur into open country. We were surrounded by rows of palm trees whispering in the breeze and dimly shiny paddy fields. More and more people poured in from all sides and by the time it became dark lights blossomed along the path and we caught sight of a long procession coming towards us.

I had read about the multitudes that had greeted the Sankaracharya on his visit to various cities in decades past and on the oriental pomp deployed to welcome him, when caravans of elephants, camels and golden chariots pulled by milk white oxen preceded and followed hundreds of musicians, priests and ascetics around his silver palanquin carried on the shoulders of devotees. However before us was a man walking on foot, shod in wooden sandals and holding the tall staff of Hindu sadhus. He wore the orange saffron robes of his order, one of whose edges hooded his patriarchally bearded face. The wide forehead shone with the white ash of Shiva's three horizontal lines. I had a vision of the first figure of the *I Ch'ing* whose three unbroken strokes stand for *Qian*: heaven, the father and the head and also represent the patriarchal virtues of protection and solace. Was that hoary sign a legacy of primordial connections between the two largest nations on earth?

The scene exuded a timeless and pastoral innocence and made me realize how much western societies have moved away from the simplicity of the Eastern world in the days of Jesus whereas India still retains in many places the original spirit of the ages of prophecy. I still treasure the mental image of that walk in moist and scented penumbra, in the footsteps of a venerable ascetic, clad as Christ and the Biblical prophets must have been, surrounded by his humble flock, beneath the palms amidst the murmur of mantras and the joyous devotional cries *Jagadguru jai* : victory to the world teacher.

A SIGN IN THE SKY

Reality however consists of many superimposed diachronic layers and one night that we were on the beach after dinner, admiring the panoply of stars in a cloudless sky that invisibly merged into darkly shimmering seas, we noticed two bright points of light above us that flickered and pulsated in an unusual way as they travelled towards the east. Very few people were on the seaside at that hour. We could as usual dimly see the outlines of occasional fishermen carrying on their shoulders along the shore the wineskins loaded with the potent and smelly toddy liquor fermented from the juice of the palmyra tree. The two lights grew in size and their rhythmic crawl made us feel that they were not planes or artificial satellites. They moved in a straight line until one went low over the ocean while it waxed in size and luminosity, with a reddish, twinkling sparkle. The other remained higher over the horizon and seemed to move from side to side or in a circular pattern until the first one disappeared in a fiery burst after seemingly reaching sea level.

For a few more minutes, the other light kept hovering above before drifting farther and farther and vanishing in the distance. We were left puzzled by that spectacle but with a feeling that gradually grew later that we had seen UFOs, in the sense that they were not man-made aircraft. We were brought back to our memories of Spain's many cases and witnesses and my recent readings at the Adyar library acquired a concrete presence in my mind. Some weeks earlier, we had attended a reception at Kalakshetra for Rukmini Devi's long-time friend Muriel Lady Dowding, the widow of Air Marshall 1st Baron Dowding, the Scottish Commander in the Battle of Britain. Like her late husband, the effusive and cheerful Lady Dowding was a well known campaigner for spiritualism, vegetarianism, theosophy and animal welfare; she had founded *Beauty without Cruelty,* an international organization dedicated to the eradication of animal testing in the cosmetics industry and she shared the Air Marshall's convictions about paranormal phenomena and UFOs which he had expounded in several public talks and books. Lord Dowding had spent six years in India as a young officer at the beginning of the century and he had later witnessed mysterious spacecraft during his sorties in the course of the war. He was convinced that they belonged either to supernatural beings originating in higher dimensions or to visitors from other planets.

Next morning, it turned out that one or two other persons in the area had seen the two celestial lights and noticed their unusual motion. Two days later, which was a Sunday, we went swimming in the ocean in the late afternoon as we often did and I ran along the shore to a nearby small temple being built at the edge of the expanding suburb that was gradually filling the open coastal plain between Adyar and Thiruvanmiyur. We had watched the construction of that lavishly ornate shrine since its inception and admired the precision and speed with which it was taking shape. As I walked nearer, I noticed, seated on the steps that rose up to the sanctuary's door, a lady wearing wide sunglasses and draped in a luminous azure and mauve chiffon saree. She waved and I recognized Queen Frederika, who had come to gaze at the sea in that quiet place where she attracted the curious glances of strolling families.

She visibly enjoyed the attention of the small bright eyed children who stared at her as if she were some strange exotic creature emerging from a western film. I was obviously in my bathing trunks and felt a bit self conscious but she put me at ease by jovially asking me one or two questions and we began a conversation. Not long before I had briefly met her grand-children Paul and Nicolas, the two boys of King Constantine who had come to see her in her Indian refuge and we talked about them. At one point I mentioned that we had watched two mysterious flying objects near the very spot where I had found her and she asked me casually if I thought they were UFOs. I answered with a cautious affirmation, hinting that I had read and heard a lot on that subject and therefore believed in their existence.

She remained silent for a moment, smiling quizzically at the horizon and then she quietly said: "In America I was told that the Government knows about beings from other planets and has seen and talked to them."

I was thrilled by that statement which later on took additional significance when I learnt about her relations with President Kennedy, his family and the so-called Camelot team and especially her rumoured affair with Allen Dulles, the CIA's infamous head. I wanted to explore this topic further but, used as she was to the royal prerogative of controlling the dialogue she returned to her favourite topic, Hindu philosophy and its potential to bring the west back to the path of reason and truth. I knew that she was quite skeptical about the benefits of modern civilization and took a dim view of the future.

"Don't waste your life by joining the race for money and social success, she said with Prussian decisiveness, take care of your soul first and last. That is the only way to happiness." For a second I got the impression of listening to her grand father the Kaiser of Germany when he preached to his family and friends as he liked to sometimes, except of course that he was not a Vedantin but a staunch Lutheran.

ILLUSTRIOUS VISITORS

Kalakshetra was a shrine of tradition, whereas it had also been conceived by the Arundales as a place for innovation and creation in line with that tradition. Maharaja Jayachamaraja Wodeyar of Mysore, a reputed protector of yoga and the arts had been its chief patron until his demise in the year prior to our arrival. His successor as patron was Maharani Sethu Parvati of Travancore, the other great kingdom of South India, whose matriarchal ruling family sported such an intricate genealogy, in keeping with all things Indian, that I had to read quite a few pages to understand her place in the dynasty in which the line of succession was assured by the eldest sister of the ruling monarch whose son became the ruler after his uncle.

Perhaps also in tribute to those aristocratic associations, many crowned heads came to visit the school, apart from other famous figures such as the American astronauts Armstrong and Collins, who had been there during their visit to India after the first moon landing. I still remember the passage of the imposing Queen of Tonga and also of the King of Bhutan with a small retenue. I was seeing the handsome citizens of that legendary Himalayan state for the first time. The men's plaid skirts, long wool stocking, patent leather shoes and colourful jackets looked exotic in a tropical setting and evoked the Highlanders of Scotland in my mind and it is probable that the first sovereign of the mountain kingdom's ruling dynasty was influenced in his choice for a national dress by some visitors from British Calcutta in the early twentieth century. However, the most exalted visitor was the elected "empress" of India, Indira Gandhi herself who came during that winter in the early months of 1976 with her son Rajiv, Italian daughter-in-law Sonia and grandchildren.

My father had recently written to her, to recall our meeting in Delhi and to suggest some ways to reconnect the country's polity with its philosophical and socio-political legacy. It was therefore a fortunate occasion to meet her again.

Shortly after, two or three gleaming American cars followed by a small motorcade of official Ambassador vehicles glided into the sandy and shaded haven of Kalakshetra, Mrs Gandhi, holding by the hand her grandson Rahul and granddaughter Priyanka, just a few years of age, walked into some of the classrooms, including one where I was attending the dance lesson and stayed for few minutes. She smiled briefly at the teacher and students and I had a feeling that she had recognized me. Indeed she was reputed to have an amazing memory of faces, always an asset for politicians. Rajiv who followed her appeared to me a kindly, courteous and rather shy man and he shared the latter feature with his wife who avoided calling attention to herself.

The school's students and staff all gathered at the theater before the end of the visit for a brief dance and music performance preceded by a short welcome speech by Rukmini to the illustrious visitors. Sankara Menon acted as the master of ceremonies. As Mrs Gandhi rose to leave with her relatives, on my father's earlier request, Rukmini summoned us forward so that we might have a chance to greet the Prime Minister. As we came close, I noticed the heavy metallic, very unfeminine chronometer she wore on her thin wrist as a ponderous reminder of a tight and exigent official timetable. My father referred to his letter to her and said a few words in French on his action for a reappraisal and revival of the hoary notion of Dharma for both India and the world. She listened carefully and replied also in French that if we came to Delhi she would meet us and put us in touch with some personalities concerned with that general subject matter.

I was impressed with her receptiveness with regard to a rather abstruse subject that in most other countries, statesmen would have regarded as being outside their bailiwick. However, this was India and I remembered her father Nehru's philosophical discussions with André Malraux. Indira took pride in having been a student of Rabindranath Tagore's school at Shantiniketan and could hence relate to metaphysical issues as most of her countrymen do.

After bows and another smile which I took to be also addressed to me, Mrs Gandhi and her party departed. I remember that we shook hands with Rajiv, who had seemed less familiar with the topic of that brief exchange than his mother. Rahul and Priyanka were quiet and decorous for children of their age and it looked as if both their parents and their famous grandmother had taught them discipline and discretion.

That two minute conversation had a role in our future activities as my father saw that eventually we would have to return to the capital of India for a longer period than our initial visit as there would be much to do and many people to meet. On the other hand, neither he nor I wished to interrupt my first year of study at Kalakshetra and we agreed that the time had not yet come to take a long journey.

INDO-EUROPEAN LITERARY PARALLELS

My forays into the Sanskrit language and literature absorbed much of my time and I found the realm of classical literature as thick and flowery as an Indian monsoon forest, compared to the tame and predictable fields and woods of Europe. From the terse and axiomatic aphorisms of philosophical literature and its lyrically epic illustration in the *Bhagavad Gita* I ventured into the floridly metaphorical realm of medieval drama which bridges the gap between the heroic *gestae* of antiquity and the technically sophisticated and erudite poetry of court minstrels and mystical devotees.

I located there the roots of the late medieval and early Renaissance craft of the *rhetoriqueurs* in France and of the precious British Euphuists and Spanish Gongorists. The most complex creations in samskrit belong to the didactical category of *shastrakavyas* where grammatical acrobatics and alliterative tours de force are conjugated with extraordinary allegorical depth so that the same sentence may hide several superimposed meanings and allude to different levels of interpretation, from the literal to the philosophical through the mathematical and the magical. One of the most brilliant examples of that virtuoso style is the *Bhattikavya,* structured as a poetic illustration of Panini's grammatical abstract and another is Bharavi's *Kiratarjuniya.* In both of them as in the other three classics that are taught in traditional schools one finds many verbal plays, tricks and feats such as shlokas featuring only one consonant, rebus or verses that can be read meaningfully in either direction, some of which appear in European literatures only centuries later, like Greek boustrophedons and the calligrammatic stanzas that Guillaume Apollinaire made famous in some of his poems in the early 20th century or the monosyllabic or single word rhymed lines that a young Victor Hugo composed in his *Odes et Ballades*.

I could not even dream of reading those enormous texts *in extenso* as they deploy thousands of verses ordered in dozens of cantos or chapters. I felt like the proverbial Einstein's child playing with pebbles on the shore of the ocean.

In Bana's much admired poetic novel *Kadambari,* I recognized the form of the "roman en abyme," the story that enshrines other stories told by its narrators, one within the other like the proverbial Russian dolls, as in the 19th century *Zaragoza Manuscript* by Count Potocki and in its endless but elegantly constructed agglomerative words containing the equivalent of several English phrases (which I could only decipher with the help of translations obviously) I found the ancestry of Marcel Proust's multipage sentences.

The frequent recalls of the illusory or dream-like nature of reality in Indian literature find later echoes in some of the western classics, such as Cervantes and Lope de Vega. Modernity, I thought, has no meaning in the context of an old and sophisticated civilization. What looks new is merely what has long been forgotten.

CONVERSING WITH THE DALAI LAMA

In the midst of that very enlightening period, we learnt that the Dalai Lama of Tibet was coming to Madras from his remote abode in the Himalayan hills to attend a function. He knew Rukmini Devi well and when we got in touch with his staff and mentioned that we were her guests at Kalashetra, we were promptly given an audience at the Chola Hotel where His Holiness was staying.

I had read much since my childhood about the legendary saga of the living Buddhas on the roof of the world who had fascinated so many curious minds and inspired so many authors, from Csöma de Koros to Ossendowski, Hergé, the demiurgic creator of Tintin and Alexandra David Néel. I remembered devouring a gripping account of the Dalai Lama's flight from Lhasa across the high mountains in 1959 and his arrival in India on the back of a mule, with a long caravan of ministers, followers and porters loaded with treasures. When we were received by his secretary Tenzin Geyche in a suite of the hotel and made to sit down and wait I felt my heart pounding as it probably had not in front of any other famous figures. After a few minutes the door opened and the slightly bent, bare armed, bespectacled religious potentate of Tibet entered with his usual, cheerful smile. We began to bend deeply before him but he would not let us and gently bade us sit down as he settled on an armchair and peered at us with the relaxed and eager expression that I had noticed on some of his photographs. I think that our first statement was to the effect that I had been born on the day when the great uprising had begun against the Chinese garrison in Lhasa and led to his own flight from the capital. He seemed intrigued by that coincidence and asked us more about our activities in India. That was the first time I heard his bass voice and his somewhat halting delivery in English.

When my father told him about our interest in promoting Dharma in order to bring Indian civilization back to its source and enlighten the world he nodded in earnest assent. "In Tibet we say *Cho* for Dharma, he pointed and we think it means religion.... But it is not religion in western sense. For us Buddhists it is the law of Buddha but it is in fact natural law, human and universal law. Hindus and Buddhists are not very different on that" and he went on to state a point that he always likes to emphasize, Buddhism is an offshoot of Hinduism and Tibet is a son of India which kept many scriptures and secrets lost in the motherland.

In the half an hour we spent with the fourteenth reincarnation of the great reformer Tsong Kha Pa, we broached many fascinating subjects of which details are now fuzzy in my memory but I recall how he laughingly dismissed Lobsang Rampa as someone who knew more about Tibet than he himself did "but a lot is in his imagination" he quipped. Then he added with a characteristic merry guffaw: "Good for us Tibetans. So many people interested in our culture because of Rampa."

Another topic we raised was the alleged visit of Christ to the Roof of the World and his stay in a western Tibetan monastery either during the twenty "lost" years of his life or after his Crucifixion. His Holiness was grave but non-committal on that point. "Possible, he said but I have not seen proof. However, for Buddhism the two fishes are an auspicious symbol and Jesus multiplied two fishes to feed people. The fish is his symbol and a great tantric master is also called Fish Lord: *Matsyendra*. Perhaps same person!."

His telegraphic English was endearing. Sometimes he whispered a few words in Tibetan when he was not sure of the translation and looked to Tenzin Geyche for assistance. During the entire meeting, a bodyguard stood by the door of the suite with his hand on the knob. The Dalai Lama called for tea after asking us if we would have some and we talked about the present and the future of his country.

"Chinese brought some good things, he said nodding. We were too far back. Feudalism, slavery, much poverty and almost all land belonged to monasteries and great lords. We were bringing in reforms but I told Chinese: "Go slow, Otherwise people will revolt." They did not listen to me because they believed Buddhism was bad and had to be destroyed. They did not even want to admit that they were foreigners. They said Tibetans had always been Chinese subjects. Yet everything between us and them is different: language, food, religion, way of life, idea of government."

While listening respectfully I thought that there were great similarities also between the Chinese and the Tibetans, if only because they had interacted for many centuries. Both languages belong to the wider so-called Sino-Tibetan family, Tibetan Lamaism had many followers in China and had been a state religion there as well and anyone who has seen Tibetan textiles, dress, metalwork, architecture, furniture and carpets would recognize the Chinese influence. However, the Tibetan syllabary is a faithful transcription of the Indian Brahmi and almost all the ecclesiastical, scientific and literary culture of Tibet was derived from India.

"All Central Asia has mainly Indian heritage," the Dalai Lama said, shaking his head. "You go to Mongolia and South Siberia and you find same indo-Tibetan culture, books, gods, rituals."

To a question about the multiple and constant references to parallel planes or realms of being that Tibetan scriptures refer to and on which the theosophical doctrine also dwells he answered gravely after marking a brief reflective pause: "Buddhism like Hinduism and most religions teaches the existence of those other levels or worlds... They are invisible to most people but they are accessible only in non-physical body, through mind travel, although," he added, "some great yogis are able to modify their bodies for the journey. It is as when a good swimmer trains to dive underwater, holding his breath for a long time. It is difficult but it can be done."

When asked about the possible future of Tibet, he was non committal but expressed the hope that China would leave Maoism behind and go back to Buddhism, thereby healing many wounds between his people and their conquerors. At that time the "Great Helmsman" was still in power and China was regarded as India's major enemy after Pakistan so that the prediction sounded wishful but it was clear that His Holiness looked at human affairs from a higher, long-term perspective. What are mere centuries in regard to the astronomical time scales of Mahayana cosmology?

Towards the end of the conversation, the Gyalpo Rimpoche (his Tibetan title) suggested that we should come to Dharamshala and visit the Institute of Tibetan Medicine. In Spain we had met two of the most important practitioners of that venerable science, Dr Yeshe Dhonden and Dr Wangyal Barshi and my father had told him of his professional interest in that field, which is related to both the Indian and Chinese therapeutic traditions.

"India and Tibet together can heal the world," the Dalai Lama concluded with the youthful candor that was so seductive in him. We took that as his blessing for our journey through many spheres of experience and being.

IX

In the Kingdom of the Wodeyars

Rishi Valley and Bangalore

In the early summer of 1976, it was decided, in agreement with our hosts at Kalakshetra that we would take refuge from the damp heat of the season in the cool Eastern Ghats and from there would travel to some of the places we had planned to visit for quite some time.

We were invited, on Rukmini Devi's suggestion, by the Rishi Valley School of the J Krishnamurti Foundation in Chittoor district, not far from the holy temple town of Thirupathi. The school is famed for the beauty of its natural surroundings and the quality of its curriculum and staff. It is nestled in a verdant valley circled by rocky hills a few hundred meters above sea level and we immediately enjoyed the setting and the kindness of the welcome extended by the director and his charming wife. We arrived there in the final period of vacations when the campus was almost empty but the students returned a few days later and filled it with the youthful activity typical of boarding schools.

We gave some talks to various classes and were elated to find the acute interest of some of the teenagers in the topics we evoked. In the secluded environment of Rishi Valley, the pupils had plenty of time to think and few distractions so that, coming as most of them did, from privileged families, they were relatively cultured and eager to learn. The school has a well supplied library and offers various extra-curricular activities, including film shows on certain evenings and other cultural programmes. In those blessed days, there was no television outside cities and no one had heard of personal computers, videos, cell phones and other invasively disruptive electronic devices.

When I think of the peace and serenity that prevailed when conversations, books and magazines were the only distractions, along with walks in the tranquil sylvan surroundings, I rue the day when new means were invented to fill our lives with needless noise, images and allurements.

We soon came to the end of the few weeks spent in that haven which reminded me of the landlocked hidden wonderlands imagined by Thomas Mayne Reid in his robinsonian novels that had enchanted my childhood, after inspiring earlier generations of readers. We went to Bangalore, still a mid-sized garden city where we first stayed at the small "Nature Cure" Centre that perpetuated the healing practices popularized by Mahatma Gandhi.

Bangalore was a hybrid product of two legacies, the ancient culture of the kingdom of Mysore, an heir to the medieval Vijayanagar empire and the colonial way of life of the British administrators and soldiers who had made it their favourite base in South India because of the town's central position in the Deccan and cool salubrious climate. We took an instant liking to its luscious parks, quiet roads and quaint bungalows that evoked visions of Rudyard Kipling and the young Winston Churchill who had spent several months there. Some articles about us in the local newspapers made us known in the area and one gentleman came to see us one day and invited us to stay at his institute, located in the area of Basavangudi. As we had many common interests and found him a knowledgeable and original thinker, we accepted his offer a few days later after holding various conversations and learning about his own projects and activities, often while strolling in the nearby Cubbon park.

Our new host, named Prabhakar Yadav, was an urban planner and designer who had developed a passion for the science of Ekistics, created by the Greek architect Constantinos Doxiadis. I had never heard of it before but found the concepts and underlying philosophy of ekistics, expounded in the abundant literature available in Yadav's library most interesting and could not but agree that India would have been better served if it had chosen Doxiadis, instead of the cold and drab modernist Le Corbusier, to plan the city and main buildings of the new city of Chandigarh in the Punjab.

Doxiadis, inspired by classic Hellenic theories of life and art, had built Pakistan's capital Islamabad, regarded as one of the world's most attractive new cities and he had conceived a global strategy to organize and improve human habitat that was both visionary and elegant. Yadav thought that Bangalore, which was already growing fast and was expected to become a metropolis, ought to be planned on the principles dictated by ekistics but he realized how difficult it would be to get his forward looking ideas adopted by the innumerable political, bureaucratic and corporate decision makers involved in so vast and long-drawn a process. He also had strong medical interests, which is why he had been intrigued by the newspaper reports that had mentioned my father's activities in the field of Chinese and Japanese traditional therapeutics and dietetics.

As we moved around in the small Bangalore social and cultural circles, we were invited to lecture in various colleges and intellectual fora and got to know some of the interesting personalities of that pleasant city, thanks to a young and dynamic couple of lawyers, Mr and Mrs Jayaram, who were friends and former protégés of Rukmini Devi and supporters of Kalakshetra. We also became friends with a retired High Court judge who was a theosophist and had keen literary interests. He introduced us to some of the poets and writers of the city, including the elderly Masti Venkatesha Iyengar who had been president of the PEN Club and who was the leading and most prolific author in the kannada tongue.

Not many authors can claim to have revived a language and contributed most of its modern literature but Masti, though born in a Tamil-speaking family and initially writing in English, was one of those and produced well over one hundred and twenty books of original works and translations in the local tongue in the course of his very long life as a novelist, poet, critic and historian. He was the first to popularize many long forgotten periods and events of the region's ancient past and his intellectual fecundity was in keeping with India's tradition of prolific compositions and encyclopaedic outputs.

MYSORE ROYALS

The city had grown around a small historic nucleus, which includes the remaining building from the palace of Tipu, the last Sultan of Mysore, well known in France because of his alliance with Napoleon and his ambitious attempt to overthrow the British East India company from South India. Despite his imperial pretensions, Tipu, the son of a military commander who had usurped power from the local maharaja, is a rather minor figure in the immense tapestry of Indian history and would have remained little known abroad had it not been for his highly publicized battles and final defeat and death in 1799 when English forces, allied with the Marathas and the rival Nizam of Hyderabad overran the Sultan of Mysore's fortress at Srirangapatnam, located on an island of the Kaveri river.

Despite being often cruel, Tipu had enjoyed great popularity among the French as he had invited soldiers and engineers from that country, then in the throes of the Revolution, and even allowed them to open a Jacobine Club and plant a Tree of Liberty in his capital. Many of his republican guests must have noticed the incongruity of that symbol of democratic equality at the court of a despot who kept hundreds of slaves and concubines and on various occasions massacred thousands of prisoners, whose sole crime was often to be born Hindus. Soon after Tipu's fall in battle, the victorious Britons restored the Maharajas of the Wodeyar line and the largest estate in Bangalore, which was their secondary headquarters, was the royal palace whose walled park encompassed hundreds of acres.

We were fortunate to be introduced to one of the sisters of the late twenty-fifth Maharaja, deceased in 1974, as I have earlier noted. Princess Vijaya Devi was, like him an accomplished pianist and had studied at Juilliard in New York. She lived in a villa adjoining the palace grounds and received us for tea on two or three occasions as she was a friend of Rukmini Devi who was a patron of the International Music and Arts Society she presided. It was a delight to speak with that pretty and elegant woman, whose wide culture reflected a family tradition. She did not speak much about her royal brother although she clearly admired him as all those who had known him, for his many talents.

Jayachamarajendra Wodeyar was educated like princes of ancient India had been for centuries and shared their polyfacetic talents. He was an expert practitioner and connoisseur of Western music, had been the chief patron of the London Philharmonia and had even enabled the orchestra through his largesse to hire young Herbert Von Karajan as conductor. The Maharaja was an authority on Beethoven's life work and he promoted a number of contemporary European composers whose scores were published at his costs while on the other hand he hosted some of the eminent South Indian musicians as he himself was deeply versed in the indigenous lyrical art and played the *veena* expertly. He had authored almost a hundred *kritis* or songs in the Carnatic style. While he had one of the world's largest collections of western classical music recordings, he also patronized painters, sculptors, philosophers, poets and scientists, both Indian and foreign. His forebears had supported Swami Vivekananda's work for the renaissance of national culture and provided funding for Rabindranath Tagore's school at Shantiniketan. The dynasty had made Mysore a Mecca for both native and western culture in the subcontinent. Jayachamarajendra was an early supporter of the independence movement, despite being aware of the fact that he would probably lose his throne as a result of the unification of the country.

The accomplishments and interests of that true philosopher-king would take volumes to retrace. He himself wrote several books on diverse topics and yet found the time to develop his capital of Mysore into a model city, inspired by ancient Indian architectural treatises as well as by some of the contemporary urban trends coming from Europe. With his fellow maharajas of Baroda, Dhrangadhra, Bikaner, Travancore, Cochin, Tripura and Jubbal he was a member of a small club of enlightened and scholarly princes who exchanged ideas between them on the best reforms that they could bring to their respective states.

"My brother was a devout Hindu," Vijaya Devi said proudly. "He was a Vedantin and a devotee of the Sankaracharya of Sringeri. He even authored a monograph on the founder of that *math*, Suresvaracharya, the direct disciple of Sri Adi Sankara. Here are some of the other books he wrote on various aspects of our philosophy. He was the founder president of the *Vishwa Hindu Parishad*, the World Hindu League, yet he had a Muslim Prime Minister, Mirza Ismail and the Catholic cathedral of St Philomena was built near our family's palace, with the help and support of successive maharahajas."

We glanced at some of the titles of the late monarch's works. They covered a wide range of topics and showed both his immersion in tradition and his interests in modern problems. "The Quest for Peace: an Indian Approach" was one of them; "The Geeta and Indian Culture" was another, intended to educate a general readership about the continuity of India's heritage while "Dattatreya, the Way and the Goal" appeared more esoteric, revealing his own advanced initiation. He had also authored surprisingly *An African Survey* and had also been an early advocate of ecological causes and nature conservation by focusing on the protection of the magnificent natural landscapes and biological systems found within his realm.

Princess Vijaya Devi urged us to visit the sites that bore the legacy of her family, which Mahatma Gandhi had praised, despite his reservations about the monarchic principalities that British rule had preserved. The Mahatma had even quipped that if all of India were ruled like Mysore under its Maharaja, there would be no need for a social revolution. This showed Gandhi's lack of prejudice, which set him apart from many revolutionaries who would destroy even an efficient and successful system not in keeping with their own political doctrines.

THE VIRTUOUS CITY

Accordingly, we set out to see Mysore, a few miles away from Bangalore, and we instantly fell under the charm of that well laid out and harmoniously designed capital, located at the foot of the sacred Chamundi hills. The main palace is a fifty meter high Indo-Saracenic wedding cake, built in the early part of the 20th century after the old one, mostly built of wood, burned down. To prevent another fire, the frame of the palace was made of cast iron according to a then innovative technology, but its facades and interiors were decorated with the exuberant imagination of traditional Indian art and its symphony of colours, sculptures and designs is bewitching. In various places one could see the royal crest featuring the *gandabheruda*, the two-headed mythical bird of Hindu mythology that is probably the earliest image of the imperial aquiline emblem that was adopted by the Byzantine Basileus before being also claimed by the German and Austrian Kaisers and Russian Czars. It is however related to the twin birds and also to the "dark blue and golden fowl with flaming eyes" all described in the Svetasvatara Upanishad.

The Wodeyar dynasty traces its ancestry back to the *Mahabharata* as it claims descent from the Lunar line of Yadavas, the kinsmen of the divine King Krishna but historically it ruled Mysore since the year 1399 of the Christian era and always had sported that symbol and worshipped the main deity of the Chamundesvari temple, the goddess who vanquished the buffalo headed giant *Mashishasura,* the original name that the British had interpreted as "Mysore." Yet, while cultivating the legend of those mythical origins, the Wodeyars acknowledged their roots in a humble potter community and displayed its tools among their insignia. Like all Indian aristocratic clans, they thus kept their heads in heaven but held their feet to the ground.

The private Darbar hall is a kaleidoscope of colours dominated by sky blue and gold while the huge public audience hall is almost byzantine in style and has the emerald green hue of a fairy tale submarine cavern. The Swan Hall is a huge pillared space opening up to the immense perspective of the ceremonial courtyard bounded on the far horizon by the neo-hellenic domed Lalitha Mahal, the palace built for illustrious guests. The hall's arcaded walls are decorated with paintings on copper and produce the effect of an endless perspective through the mirrors that line one side and reflect the intricately sculpted and painted rows of columns.

Standing in the glittering splendor of that house of glass, inspired by the famous palace of mirrors described in the *Mahabharata,* I was reminded of the poem by Shabestari in his *Rose Garden of Mysteries*:

"Know that the whole world is a mirror
In each atom are a hundred flaming Suns
If thou splittest the heart of a single water drop
One hundred pure oceans flow out
If thou gazest at every speck of dust
A thousand Adams can be seen...
A universe hides in a millet seed;
All is gathered in a point of the present.
In every point of this circle
Millions of shapes emerge
Each point in its revolution
Is sometimes a circle and sometimes a rotating orb."

This exotic dwelling so full of symbols in its layout and decoration inspires comparisons with other royal constructions that evoke ethnic or Oriental fairy tales, such as the Brighton extravaganza of George the IV in England, the Castelho de Peña in Sintra or Neuschwanstein in Bavaria. I was struck, however, by the colours and semi-abstract geometric patterns of the tiled floors in some of the room. They were similar to the ones I had so often stated at in the house of my maternal grandparents near Paris. Many years later, I was to encounter similar designs in the Royal Palace of Pnomh Penh in Cambodia. All three structures had been built around the same period and testified to the style of the time.

The sprawling palace, still inhabited by members of the royal family, exudes the atmosphere of tradition married with western influence to which the Maharajas and their subjects were clearly receptive. A confident and proud culture does not fear alien inputs and South India has hosted many foreign visitors from both the Far East and the remote West since time immemorial.

The bastion of the local religious faith is the Chamundesvari temple to which we repaired on a late afternoon. The white and russet ancient temple with its seven-storied sculpted tower is surprisingly charming despite the baleful appearance of its patron deity, the fierce Chamundi Durga. The temple is one of the eight *mahashakti peethas*, the most holy places of the mother goddess's tantric cult and stands on the spot where the hair of the sacrificed goddess fell to the ground. There are no less than 1008 steps to climb if one wants to go up the hill in the traditional, hard way and at about two thirds of the ascent one beholds the magnificent black stone bull of Lord Shiva, placidly seated on a pedestal which it dominates from its height of almost 17 feet.

Once the top is painfully reached, the view on the surrounding plains and on the city, dotted with palaces, lakes, temples and gardens is breathtaking and one envies the royal family that spent time in that exalted spot in the nearby Rajendra Vilas palace that looks as attractive as the many other mansions erected by the splendid and art-loving rulers of that fortunate state.

The body of Sati ("reality" or "truth"), the first Shakti-was torn into fifty-two (or sixty four, depending upon the version one reads) pieces after her wedding to Shiva Virabhadra (the terrifying one) and the inconsolable groom, while carrying the mangled body let the fragments fall on as many places of India. A hallowed sanctuary stands on each one of those spots where a ritual daily commemorates the cosmic tragedy since the remote past. There can hardly be a more striking symbol of the physical and mystical unity of the subcontinent than this network of sacred locations, each of which corresponds to one letter of the Samskrit alphasyllabary. It irresistibly brings to mind the ancient story of Osiris being dismembered into sixteen pieces by his brother Seth (Sati?) who scattered the fragments across Egypt. Is it a coincidence that the spelling of Osiris in old Coptic was Aser or Isvar, which is another name of Shiva, "The Lord"? All those traditions carry the echo of one original divine mystery, spread across space and time.

Another excursion that we had been advised to undertake led us to the old river-bound capital of Srirangapatna, still full of the memories of Tipu Sultan who had been killed there. Tipu was a fierce fighter who wanted to acquire the most modern technology for war and peace, like his contemporary the royal prince of Iran Abbas Mirza. However, he fell to formidable enemies, as the 50 000 strong Indo-British army that overwhelmed his forces included among its commanders no less a man than Arthur Wellesley, whose elder brother was then the Governor General of India. The victorious Britons behaved like average plunderers after killing their most resolute foe; they destroyed the Sultan's palace, ransacked the city and carried away to England all the loot they could get their hands on although they offered "hospitality" in Calcutta to the ruler's surviving relatives.

Tipu, who had been after his father the *Dalvai* or commander of Mysore's armies before proclaiming himself grandly Badshah Bahadur, had taken over this old capital in an island sacred to Vishnu Ranganath and crowded with temples, amidst which he built a large mosque. In that enclave protected by the river and powerful walls, he held his exotic and cosmopolitan court and collected precious jewels, fine muskets and pistols, rare wild animals and an array of automata and mechanical toys which evinced his taste for curiosities of all kinds. We visited the spot in which the ambitious warrior met his death, at the "water gate" of the fort.

Near that mausoleum of military history, we found solace in the vast and monumental Brindavan gardens, laid out by another Maharaja of Mysore as a sort of tropical park of Versailles and even went a few miles away to admire the majestic Shivanasamudram falls that completed our tour of that beautiful stretch of the Kaveri river, flowing along grand sanctuaries all dedicated to Vishnu.

Some days later, we had a chance to talk about our impressions to the Mysore princess who had advised us for this tour and we told her the powerful impression that her family's tutelary goddess Chamundi had made on us.

"She is the great yogini in one of her many forms," she pointed out in response; "she sits in a pose such that her right heel presses against the *muladhara chakra*, at the base of the spine where the *kundalini* is coiled and rises when awakened through breathing and concentration."

The subject came up again in a different place soon after when we evoked the relation of Shakti, the embodiment of cosmic energy, with other feminine images of ancient lore.

X

At the Confluence of Legend and Gnosis

A Russian Icon

The man we were talking to looked a bit like a Siberian sage. His high cheekboned, lightly pink face crowned by a vast brow above limpid eyes was prolonged by a carefully trimmed white beard. He wore a dark, well cut Indian suit and had a faintly ceremonial manner. He was clearly familiar with the mythology of the mother goddess in various traditions.

"The Hindu and Buddhist Shaktis under their many names are nearly identical," he said in a low, cultivated voice. "They are all hypostases, as the greek orthodox would say, of the *Dakshini* or *Dakini*, the goddess of the South or Earth. They embody the energy of nature which lies dormant until aroused by the Lord of cosmic consciousness, like Sleeping Beauty of our tales who waits in the enchanted forest for the kiss of the prince of spring. In Russia, a folk variant of the mythos is the *skazda* or fairy tale of *Snegurochka*, the Snow Maiden whose dissolution into nature ensues her discovery of absolute love. Thereby she puts an end to the deep freeze and brings forth Spring. For me this analogy came naturally. My father designed the setting for a famous New York production of Rimsky Korsakoff's opera on this theme."

That brought to my mind the fact that in the famous fairy tale of Sleeping Beauty, the princess falls into deep sleep when she pricks her finger with her mother's spinning needle, a very discreet hint of the bloody dismemberment of Sati in the archaic myth of the Puranas. Like her, she is the victim of a curse from the one deity who has not been called for the ceremony. The Vedic Scriptures time and again insist that all otherworldly powers, even the frightening ones, must be invited to the sacrifice if it is to fulfill its purpose. One could of course read a reference to the advent of puberty in a woman's life, initiating a stage that lasts until her virginity is taken away but, as always, there are many levels of interpretation in those universal allegoric yarns.

Our host was the renowned painter Svetoslav Roerich and we were in his tasteful drawing room, faintly reminiscent of a *dacha*, decorated with antique icons and some of his own paintings and mementos collected from all over Asia, in his sprawling *Tataguni* estate, in Bangalore. His father, the even more famous Nicholas Roerich had been a living legend and an acclaimed painter. Descended from a line that went all the way back to prince Rurik, the Scandinavian founder of the first Russian state, Nicholas had travelled across continents and met many of the influential men and women of his day. He had worked with Maxim Gorki, Benois, Diaghilev and Prokofiev for whom he had designed the stage sets for the first production of the *Rite of Spring*. Accompanied by his family, he had carried out two major expeditions across Central Asia and Tibet while pursuing his quest for the esoteric realm of Agartha before settling down above a village of the Western Himalayas, in the ancient principality of Kullu with his wife and two sons, George and Svetoslav.

Later Svetoslav, who inherited his parents' passion for Mahayana Buddhism and Tibetan mysticism, had married the most famous Indian actress of the time, Devika Rani, a grandniece of Rabindranath Tagore, whom we met on one of our visits to the estate, and settled in Bangalore but kept close relations with the Soviet Union's Intelligentsia and its rulers who professed great respect for his father in spite of the artist's spiritual convictions and his rejection of materialistic modernity.

We enjoyed some delightful conversations with Svetoslav who displayed the imaginative intelligence and mental openness that are frequent features of the Slav soul. His mother Helena, was as distinguished and talented as her husband. Related to the Princes Putyatin, Counts Kutuzoff and to the composer Mussorsky she was a polymath and a theosophist who translated some of Blavatsky's Secret Doctrine into Russian as well as the famous *Mahatma letters*. The Roerich couple had founded the Agni Yoga Centres and, many years later the *Urusvati* Himalayan Research Institute in Naggar. Their sons had been raised in an atmosphere of oriental gnosis and in the expectation that a new civilization of peace and wisdom would flourish on the roof of the world, at the confines of the Tibetan, Chinese and Russian lands.

George, the elder brother, had died in Russia in 1960. He was a pioneering Tibetologist who translated many classics from that language and even helped restitute lost sanskrit texts from extant Tibetan translations. I had been amazed by his extraordinary gift for languages, hearing that he was fluent in Russian, English, French, Bulgarian, Chinese, various Tibetan and Himalayan dialects as well as Pali and Greek. The combination of aristocratic grandeur, encyclopaedic scholarship and martial bravery that the Roerichs had displayed, sometimes in trying and dangerous circumstances, seemed almost superhuman. At any rate it was a vestige of a bygone age.

Looking at the portly old gentleman sitting across us on a cashmere draped sofa, I could hardly believe that he had been born in Saint Petersburg and had lived in Imperial Russia until his early teenage years. With his family he had endured the hardships of the 1917 Revolution. In 1923, at nineteen, he had come with his parents and siblings to India which had been his home since. On a corner table, there were yellowed photos of his parents, Nicholas Roerich looking every inch like the venerable Saint Nicholas of Myra and Bari, the beloved protector of Russia or like a Taoist version of Father Frost and Helena, his wife, a white haired embodiment of female nobility, and Svetoslav himself together with Prime Minister Nehru, Indira Gandhi and several other personalities. I later found out that when Soviet Premier Kosygin came to India on an official visit he made it a point to come to Bangalore and call on Svetoslav, so great was the prestige of that mystical family among the atheistic members of the Presidium.

We were eager to find out more from him about his family's dream for the future of mankind.

"My mother had been told by the mahatmas who guide the human race that a new age would arise and spread from the ancient lands of Central Asia, the cradle of the continent of Mu and the seat of Agartha-Shambhala," Svetoslav explained as quietly as if he had been talking about the weather.

"That was the mission of the Urusvati institute: to pave the way for that syncretistic civilization rooted in timeless divine wisdom... We were constantly exposed to Eastern traditional philosophies and arts. In Russia our family estate was called *Isvara*. We are originally Livonians from Riga on my father's side and as such we are Balts, rooted in an Aryan civilization very close to the Sanskrit past of India. Long lost relatives of Russians live in the Himalayas. They are the Tibetans, Bhutanese and Tokharians who moved across Asia during many centuries. My late brother showed that our graphic arts and our folklore and legends are similar. Much of orthodox Slav mysticism is akin to the esoteric philosophy of Mahayana. Do you know that George helped Prince Peter of Greece and Professor Sanskrtyayana translate the *Pramanavarttika* from Tibetan back into the lost original Samskrit?"

Indeed, Peter of Greece and Denmark, a cousin of "our" Queen Frederika's husband, had spent time on various occasions in South India and had even married his Russian wife in Madras. He had also lived near Bangalore amongst the Toda tribesmen of the Blue Mountains. He was a well-known Tibetologist who was still alive then.

I gazed at the icily lucid panoramas of craggy mountains and snowy horizons painted by Nicholas Roerich and at the enigmatic Tibetan ascetics who stood against some of those Empyrean landscapes. They reflected the universe of the Roerichs and the soul of mysterious Eurasia, the common home of Mongols, Turks and Slavs according to Lev Gumilev.

"How did you think that this new age would come?" my father inquired.

Roerich closed briefly his deep, dreamy eyes and his handsome face became ever more confucian. "My parents believed the messages from the masters that a new world teacher would come from this region and display miraculous powers to enlighten mankind and assert his authority," he recollected.

"As a theosophist, my mother long believed he was Krishnamurti. We were all convinced that his first task would be to bring Soviet Russia back to the path of spirituality, in unison with East and South Asia. Such visions were widely shared in those days. Even General Baron Ungern von Sternberg who had ruled Mongolia not long before my parents went on a mission there had that dream. Now of course, we know things were not meant to be such but the Lord works in mysterious ways.

I teach Agni Yoga and Vedanta to Soviet intellectual and military leaders and am a frequent visitor to Bulgaria where president Todor Zhivkov and his daughter support my work. I think that after some years the USSR will change drastically and reconnect with its atavistic genius."

How could we know at that time when Mao Tze Tung was still alive and when Leonid Brezhnev held the Soviet Empire in his weakening but still steely grip that the prediction would at least partly come to pass shortly before our host's demise in 1993?

We also wished to know about the interactions of the Roerichs with the Nehru family, given our own previous meetings with Indira Gandhi. Svetoslav recalled the then Prime Minister and his daughter with warmth and respect. He saw Nehru as a somewhat conflicted man who strived, with variable success, to reconcile the skepticism instilled by his western education with his own national culture that he beheld as an outsider looking into an ancestral house. Indira, on the other hand, because of her feminine intuition was more receptive to and less questioning of India's ancient worldview.

"Both the father and his daughter always seemed fascinated by my parents and their vision," he concluded.

"They may have thought they were impractical artists survivors of a vanished age, but they acknowledged that they had access to higher sources of knowledge than what rational education and experience could impart. Nehru shared our reverence for Ramakrishna, Vivekananda and Tagore and Indira had faith in the mystical powers of the great seers of all times and places. If you talk to her about India's spiritual mission to build a new civilisation, you will find her very receptive."

CELESTIAL MYSTERIES

This assertion led us to raise another issue, which fascinated us. Had he or his parents witnessed some of the prodigies and supernatural apparitions commonly associated with Tibetan religion? Where most westerners would have smiled with a modicum of irony, our Russian host's serene impassivity was unaltered.

"My father had studied many texts about the famous underground realms of Agartha, mentioned by Ossendowsky among others and also knew of the golden flying citadels that glide in the sky, as in the story of King Sudarsoma," Roerich replied.

"I believed he may have sighted some of them during the expeditions in the Gobi desert and on the Tibetan plateau. You may want to find out more about the *vimanas*, the aircraft mentioned so often in Hindu and Buddhist texts, some thousands of years old. After all this is the area where one of the main documents was rediscovered. The *Vaimanika Shastras* aroused a lot of interest in the beginning of the century when Pandit Subbaraya Shastri brought them back to light in Mysore. Russian space scientists were also interested as there are many Soviet engineers and researchers who readily believe that certain vanished or declining ancient civilizations had access in the past to very advanced discoveries."

Svetoslav further said that a certain judge of the Mysore High Court, B Subbana had helped spread information about the long-lost aeronautic technology of India. He seemed to have no further details to give us but we thought we could find out more through our friend, the retired judge and we soon had an opportunity to seek his help in the matter during a dinner in the spacious bungalow-like Bangalore

Gymkhana Club, seemingly untouched since the days of the British Raj. He indeed had known his senior colleague and remembered that for several years a magazine called *Bhautik Kala Nidhi* (the abode of Earth Arts) dedicated to the subject matter of the *Vimana Shastra* had been published by one professor B. S. Rao, on the basis of documents furnished and translated by Pandit Subbaraya Shastri, who held them from his guru Yogi Bhaskarananda.

There were some reports about an experiment that had been conducted in Bombay before the First World War to build and fly a craft based on the instructions contained in the Shastras. The sponsor of that seemingly aborted or suppressed attempt was a Dr Talphade who ran a journal called *Arya Dharma*. The rumour was that the British colonial authorities had stopped the work on the *vimana*, suspecting it of being a subversive indigenous enterprise that might be used against them.

Subbaraya Shastri, who had become a lecturer at a college of Mysore State in 1902, had written his autobiography which was published in 1972, many years after his death.

We were able to gather more information in the following weeks although it was not easy as the enigmatic documents were dismissed as frauds by most "serious" intellectuals. It would not be the first time that ancient lore would be dubbed charlatanism on the basis of prejudice about the assumed ignorance of our remote forebears. However, the available data were most intriguing and defied attempts to define them as the mere imaginative rants of religious dreamers.

In 1952, various major Indian newspapers had broken the story of the mysterious ancient documents following a release from the Press Trust of India.

It turned out that late judge Subbana had written the preface to a book published in 1932 by Subbaraya Shastri and called *Prasthanatrayee* (the Triple Foundation or treatise). That book contained a section entitled *Yantravimana shastra* (collection on machines and mechanical vehicles). The original author of the compendium was given as the legendary Rishi Bharadhwaj, from one of the hoary Vedic seer lineages but the Prasthanatrayee is actually a compilation of much older texts, dated to the 12th century of the Christian era and attributed to a certain Madhusudhan who may have been a scholar of the court of King Bhoja of Dhara and refers to no less than 42 earlier treatises, many of which are not known to have survived.

The sixth chapter of the Prasthana is based on the lost *Amsubodhini* by Bharadhwaja and is titled *Yantra Saraswa.* It enumerates 339 different types of vehicles for land transportation and as many as 782 craft that move on and underwater. It also lists 101 kinds of air and space ships that are divided into three broad categories, those moved by formulas (*mantras*), those moved by designs or mechanisms (*tantras*) and the *kulakas,* which require specific materials or fluids. Along with that interminable nomenclature, there are brief descriptions of many other technologies and contraptions that seem to cover all aspects of energy generation (dense and subtle), radio, telephony, phonography, radar, film, photography, electronics, sonar, robotics and others that are not quite understandable in the present state of our knowledge.

Eight main types of aerial vehicles are alluded to, distinguished by their respective systems of propulsion. The seventh kind, the *Bhamani* for instance, harnesses the power of thirteen different *manis* (stones or gems), some of which are naturally found and some man made and of a liquid kind of fuel which remains unidentified. The eighth kind or *marutsakha,* which some enterprising Indians had attempted to rebuild in Bombay either in 1895 or in the first decade of the 20th century, used a mercury filled battery powered by the Sun and a mysterious fluid called *naksharasa*.

It is worthy of note that another type of *vimana* mentioned in the same work, the *dhoom varga* is powered by smoke or steam whereas the *taramukha varga* operates on the energy drawn from "stones from the stars," presumably extraterrestrial materials.

What to make of this extraordinary and enigmatic report? If it was all invented, it would be a unique case of an ancient, allegedly primitive society going to great lengths, at a time when writing resources were precious and few, to compile many pages of purely fictitious and useless, technically precise but esoteric data, unrelated to anything that people experienced in their daily lives. If it was all created to pander to the imagination of readers, why take the trouble to record so many boring and abstruse facts in a catalogue format? Shastras were meant for study by the intellectual elite for practical reasons, not for the entertainment of the idle classes of society. They are not *itihasas* (historical epics), *kathas* (tales) or *kavyas* (poems). The latter consistently refer to the prodigious air ships and weapons displayed and utilized by gods and heroes but provide few details about their components and manufacturing, unlike the compendium that had come to our attention.

Our friend Yadav, whom we involved in our quest, pointed out that King Bhoja had taken great interest in ancient scientific and technical works which were probably being forgotten in his day. He had a lot of them copied, compiled and commented on and the *Vaimanika shastras* were probably one of the results of his efforts at collection and conservation. There was no doubt that for many centuries, Indian traditional scholars had taken all the lore related to vimanas and *yantras* seriously, as part of the knowledge inherited from a remote past, many of whose secrets had been lost.

It also was clear to all of us that the late Maharaja of Mysore, after his own predecessors, had seen himself as the continuator and heir to the tradition of preserving documents that had survived a turbulent history and an often unforgiving natural environment. As crown prince he apparently supported the work of Subbaraya Shastri for translating the occult scientific literature. We learnt from our magistrate friend that the Maharaja had been initiated to the *Sri Vidya* by his personal guru Sri Siddalingaswamy and that hint led us to find out more about that mysterious path of learning.

Siddalingaswamy was a *shilpi*, an architect and sculptor trained according to the ancient Hindu techniques laid out in the vedic *Sulba Shastras.* He had built and decorated the three temples erected by his royal *upasaka* (disciple) in Mysore, all dedicated to different aspects of the supreme goddess. Sri Vidya is the secret knowledge associated with Shakti, the mother energy of the universe who according to

Shaiva Tantra doctrine is above all deities and is often called *Tripurasundari*: the beautiful mistress of the three cities of heaven, earth and the underworld, like the Greek Hekate.

The cult of Shakti under her thousand names celebrated in the *Lalitasahasranama* and in many other texts has an esoteric component symbolized by various *mantras* and *yantras.* The higher level of initiation is verbally manifested by the 16 syllable *shodakshari mantra* and results from the contemplation of the *Sri Yantra,* a pattern of 9 interlocking equilateral triangles. In three dimensions, it becomes the *Sri Meru Chakra* that represents the cosmic mountain. Traditionally, that stepped pyramid is made in an alloy of silver, antimony, copper, zinc and pewter coated in gold. At its apex or centre is the *bindu*: the seed of all things which is equated with the *Linga,* the sign of infinite consciousness that expands into geometric shapes to manifest as matter and energy.

A look at the Meru Chakra makes an open-minded observer feel that it is indeed what a yantra is supposed to be: a diagram but also a machine. This quest for the boundless energy matrix of the cosmos that the Sri Vidya stands for may have led the ancient adepts of that wisdom to discover the technologies repertoried in so many shastras. As students of these spiritual disciplines, many Maharajas, such as Bhoja of Dhara were aware of the treasure of power and knowledge hidden in the scriptures and the late king of Mysore, initiated under the spiritual name of *Chitprabhananda* (Bliss of the Light of Consciousness) was an heir of that glorious tradition, perhaps the last one in his lineage.

It was not easy to go any further in this investigation without seeking a living master of the Sri Vidya, who might reveal more about the scientific knowledge connected to this esoteric lore. Many other pursuits took us away from the quest for the elusive *vimanas,* which we were however to resume later.

THE BUDDHIST GNOSTIC

We had been advised to meet a renowned Buddhist monk, Buddharakhita Thero, who headed the local Mahabodhi Society. We had been in touch earlier with members of the Theravada Sangha from Sri Lanka and South East Asia who had seemed more familiar with prayers and ceremonial than with the inner meaning of the Buddha's teachings. We were thus delighted to find in the Venerable Buddharakhita a man of great intellect, cosmopolitan culture and warm disposition who obliged our interest in his tradition by providing rare insights into its origins and context. Unlike many Buddhist ecclesiastics he unreservedly acknowledged both the debt of the Buddha Dharma to its Hindu fountainhead and the essential relation between the two living faiths.

"Buddha represents the *Ksatriya*, lay aspect of the Indian spiritual heritage," he pointed out.

"In the Vedas and other scriptures there are references to *Brahmarishis* and *Rajarishis*. Buddha arose from the tradition of kingly sages, or as the Chinese put it: sagely within, kingly without. Indeed, our texts say that he roared like a lion. At the foothills of the Himalayas and the Hindu Kush, there were warrior clans that had a strong desire to access the ageless wisdom on their own and not merely to watch the Brahmins performing rituals and discussing metaphysics in Sanskrit, a language that others did not understand. Prince Siddharta spoke a local variant of Prakrit and that is the language in which he taught his contemporaries. He laid out the essential features of the human condition: suffering, ignorance, the ability to perceive the material world as relative and impermanent and the aptitude to achieve detachment from it and hence freedom and bliss...He said that although preparation for this liberation can take several lifetimes, awakening occurs suddenly like a bolt of lightning."

We recallled that in the Western world, Buddhism is often represented as a sort of Indian Reformation, a democratic revolt against stratified, abstruse and polytheistic Hinduism.

He smiled wryly, "The West often sees itself wherever it looks," he quipped. "The Buddha was not a South Asian Luther. He was the highest enlightened being in the immemorial tradition. He himself says in the *Nikayas* that he is like the pilgrim who rediscovers a lost, ancient city buried in the forest, similar to Angkor and so many other abandoned ruins that dot the map of Asia. He brings back to light the original message of the sages which had been forgotten due to the excessive emphasis on elaborate sacrifices and mechanical recitations of old hymns. That is why he did not want his followers to learn the Vedas. They were not accessible to non-Brahmins in his day and they were in their versified form too complicated and esoteric anyway. To make it easier to know the teachings, Buddhists relied on writing more than the Hindus who preferred to commit everything to memory. However, Buddhism accepts and reveres the gods of India whom it acclimatized abroad just as it did accept the deities of all the nations where it spread.

See how symbolic it is that Sakya Muni was born to a father called Suddhodana, "the pure upward going breath" that rises along the *susumnanadi*, the mystical and energetic spine of the body in yoga. Prince Siddharta's mother was Maya, the ocean of phenomenal existence or the world of appearance and she died as soon as he was born because enlightenment makes the relative world vanish from the mind. Her child was educated by his aunt Prajapati, the "lord or lady of creatures" Purusha, which is also the night name of God Rudra-Shiva. Thus, he was raised by the Creator. The Tathagatha is a man but he is also an allegory."

Buddha himself is not really concerned with forms of devotion and worship. What he teaches is a therapy for the human condition, a medicine for all of us, irrespective of our religion. Likewise in society he did not prevent brahmins, warriors and traders or agriculturists from carrying out their traditional tasks. Monks in the *Sangha* are like sadhus—the righteous ones—in many other spiritual orders or *paramparas*, notably the Jain *munis*. They spread the good work, preach by example and live off public charity. The priest and the wandering teacher are two different beings. One takes care of the social order, the other helps and guides the individuals who want to go beyond the mere fulfillment of their material chores."

We eventually came to ask him about the most famous disagreement between Hinduism and Buddhism: the existence of a self or soul, affirmed by the former and denied by the latter.

"They are two different methods of dealing with that problem," Buddharakhita responded,

"Hindus look at the ultimate essence or Being which they call Brahman or Atman and they say that the sole reality in man and in the world is that Brahman. In Buddhism, we hold the view that this ultimate reality is in fact Non-being, Nirvana or rather that it is neither being nor non-being. As such it is not Atman but *nairatmya*. Many hindus also profess that Brahman is *Nirguna*, which means that it has no characteristics whatsoever and can therefore be equated with our Nirvana. In that light arguing whether there is an ultimate cosmic self or not can be seen as a rather futile debate. It is a matter of perspective.

Buddha described all things as processes rather than objects. In physics light is made up either of waves or particles depending upon how you observe it. Is it not the same problem? To see something you must objectify it but you should not forget that it is a transitory phase of something that is indescribable. Japanese Buddhist like to say that if you want to picture a closed hand you must draw a fist, yet you must realize that the fist is only the result of a gesture and ceases to be seen once the hand opens up."

This conversation and one or two other similar ones took place in the small garden that surrounded the Mahabodhi society or in the venerable monk's office. It gave us some additional perspectives on the boundless horizons of India's thought as it evolved and yet remains itself across so many centuries and latitudes. It made me think of the Sun, golden in the morning, searingly white at noon and blood red at dusk, changing size and colour but shining its light over all creation.

Green Forests and Blue Mountains

Time had come to go back to Delhi and we prepared ourselves, with some regret, to leave Bangalore and its leisurely lifestyle. However we decided to experience briefly the lush and pristine environment of a nearby national park which had been the private hunting reserve of the Maharajas before becoming a nature sanctuary only a couple of years earlier. We accordingly went to Bandipur, on the way to the storied "hill station" of Ootacamund, beloved by the British administrators of yore and admired the forests, valleys and streams where tigers and many other wild animals still roamed. We were not fortunate enough to get a glimpse of the king of the jungle but herds of huge *gaurs*, the Indian bison and of nimble footed, artistically antlered *chitals* and the ubiquitous avuncular elephants consoled us of that disappointment. My readings of various illustrated volumes on the Indian wildlife I had found at Kalakshetra served me well to recognize the various types of herbivores and birds we admired in that magnificent landscape. I was intrigued by the endogenous wild dogs known as *dholes,* which combine features of the jackals, wolves and foxes and are probably the ancestors of many of the domesticated breeds in the subcontinent and in other regions since Indic societies are believed to have been the first to adopt and breed canines.

The four-horned *munjak* deer were mentioned in the Vedas as a symbol of Agni, the fire god and they, as well as the large and powerful *sambhar* antelope, were another pleasant sight in that lush environment of hilly forests of *champas*—which in the west are known as sandalwood trees—teak, rosewood and bamboo mixed with many other vegetal species.

Bandipur, whose altitude above sea level varies between 1500 and 4500 feet, enjoys an ideal climate in the dry season under those latitudes and the landscape is a feast for the senses at every step. In the Southern Ghats called by them the Blue Mountains, the British aristocracy could feel close to home in the cottages and manses they built and surrounded with lush gardens sparkling with the colourful blossoms of temperate climates such as honeysuckle, chickpeas, hollyhock and forget-me-nots as well as their beloved English roses. They laid out neatly clipped tea and coffee plantations and grew cardamom and cinnamon surrounded by eucalyptus groves. In the vales and dales they went fox hunting, *par force* riding to the hounds in pink coats as if they had been in the Scottish highlands or in Devonshire. Some of the Indian nobility took a liking to that culture and adopted it with relish. Power breeds respect and imitation is both the highest form of flattery and the natural effect of envy. That colonial way of life however was gradually fading when we visited the area.

XI

Indira Gandhi's World

Meeting the Prime Minister and Her Circle

Our trip from the hospitable and gentle environment of Bangalore was uneventful and we rediscovered the more politically charged and the harsher, dustier atmosphere of Delhi with some wariness. However, we soon found comfort in the welcome that we were given by some of the personalities that we had introductions for. Within a few days we were granted an appointment with the Prime Minister and were instructed to come to her home at 1, Akbar Road. Ushered in the meeting room where she used to receive visitors in her residential compound, we found Mrs. Gandhi as graceful and welcoming as on previous occasions. I was struck by the simplicity of the precincts in which she lived and worked. Though it was not humbly austere in Mahatma Gandhi's way, it was functional and minimalistic, in marked contrast with the grandly opulent premises of other statesmen we had visited in Europe and Asia.

To my father's reminder of his suggestion for a code of duties to be adopted in India, the Prime Minister readily replied that, as we already knew, the project was already being implemented as part of the 42nd amendment, introduced in the Lok Sabha on September 18th of that year, which proclaimed the primacy of directive principles of state policy over fundamental rights. That was controversial but necessary in her government's view as reforms could otherwise be easily be paralysed through legal obstructions raised by vested interests. She expected the passage of the amendment by year end. On another subject she advised us to meet Dr Karan Singh, who was then the Minister of Health when the issue of Sino-Japanese traditional medicine and macrobiotics was brought up. "India is interested in all forms of traditional and particularly traditional Asian medicine, she assured us and there could be fruitful collaboration with Japan and other countries in this chapter."

Another matter of interest was the opportunity of interacting with Indian academic institutions and spreading my father's notion of Dharma in its timeless significance as a fundamental concept for the modern age. The Prime Minister showed once again her receptiveness to the idea and told us that she would ask her personal assistant to set up a meeting with the Director of the Indian Council for Cultural Relations.

Her keenness on the ideal of dharma was surprising, at least to other people we met in the following days, as Mrs. Gandhi had banned the RSS and other organizations connected with a Hindu Dharmic political agenda and was a stalwart for secularism, which she had made, with socialism, a fundamental constitutional principle in keeping with her leftist social and ideological agenda; however, we came to think that above and beyond her public political positions, Nehru's daughter was a Hindu at heart and a devotee of the renowned female saint Ma Anandayee so that she could not help subscribing to Dharma as a rule of life, provided it was not used as a political weapon to reject or accuse other religions and communities.

On the political front, the wily stateswoman she was may also have seen the wisdom of supporting a universalistic vision of Dharma as seen by non-Hindus against the often overly parochial definition of it given by some of her foes.

Mrs Gandhi as a leader commanded prompt obedience and brooked no procrastination in the implementation of her instructions. We were forthwith signified that we were expected at the ICCR by Mrs Kochchar, the Director, an elegant, well travelled woman who welcomed us and entrusted us to the care of two of her executives. We were told that we would be given a grant to travel and lecture in various universities of the country and that introductory letters would be written to vice-chancellors and department heads to prepare for our visit.

Another appointment was arranged with Dr Karan Singh, who was a long-standing friend of Rukmini Devi as well as a devoted follower of Sri Aurobindo and a scholar on the latter's works. We knew Karan Singh by reputation as a prolific writer and gifted speaker and also as the son and heir of the last Maharaja of Jammu and Kashmir who had acted as regent and then governor of his family's kingdom for several years before joining the Union cabinet in Delhi. He received us as if we had been long time friends with the gracious cordiality that is his trademark. His first words in French were to inform us that he had been born in the Hotel Martinez in Cannes where his parents were holidaying at the time. We went on to talk about many things, including people we knew from various parts of the world. Since his childhood he had met a bewildering array of statesmen, spiritual leaders, scientists and intellectuals and remembered with proud enjoyment his conversations with the likes of De Gaulle, Malraux, Premier Zhu En Lai, President Sukarno of Indonesia, the Mikado of Japan, the King of Spain, Prince Charles, Leonid Brezhnev, the Shah and Shahbano of Iran and Emperor Haile Selassie of Ethiopia.

We found his curiosity and genuine pleasure in meeting and exchanging ideas with people in all stations and regions of the world stimulating. He was as fluent in Sanskrit as in French and had travelled in most continents. He instantly evoked in my mind the image of those aristocratic scholarly globetrotters of earlier eras who also found the time to be statesmen and intellectuals, although I suspected that he must have found the bureaucratic work and cumbersome procedures associated with contemporary politics and administration unsavoury. He was better fitted, in my father's opinion, as we exchanged our impressions subsequent to that first meeting, to play the role of a monarch in the old sense, as an inspirer, adviser and guide to a nation, able to instill his own philosophical and artistic talent and discrimination in his countrymen, rather than competing in the drab electoral contests that weave the fabric of democratic institutions.

Karan Singh was interested in Chinese medicine whose parallels and connections with Ayurvedic science had not escaped him. He also saw the desirability of reinvigorating the essential notions of the Indic civilizational heritage in the nation's policy and told us that Mrs Gandhi had broached the subject with him and with other members of the government. With regard to our upcoming tour of India he predictably advised us to begin with Kashmir. "You can still enjoy the beautiful autumn weather and the golden foliage of the forests before the cold sets in," he said. "Go now and stay on a houseboat on the lake. That is how you will best enjoy the Kashmir valley, the land of the gods which is surely one of the most spectacular places on this earth. Being from there, I may be expected to say this but after visiting so many famous mountain havens, in the Alps, the Rocky Mountains and the Andes, I can affirm that nothing really matches the harmony of nature and art in Kashmir."

Given this introduction, we could hardly miss the opportunity of experiencing by ourselves the wonders we had been promised but there was more to be done before we could leave as the Council for Cultural Relations had set up an appointment with the Director of the India International Centre, Delhi's premier cultural circle, bordering on the superb Lodi gardens; we were informed that it had been founded under Prime Minister Nehru's patronage, partly funded by John Rockefeller III and inaugurated by the then crown prince of Japan in 1964. Dr Karan Singh was one of the life trustees and so were a few of the most eminent personalities in the country. The Director, John Lall, a punctiliously formal veteran of the elite Indian Civil Service received us with old-fashioned British courtesy and after a few minutes of small talk proceeded to schedule a lecture for us. He suggested that we meet one of the most renowned scholars of Indological scholarship, Dr Lokesh Chandra, a member of the upper House of Parliament and the president of the International Academy of Indian Culture located not far from the Centre in the Saraswati Mahal, an unpretentious red-brick building in the suburb of Hauz Khas.

ASIAN TREASURY

Lokesh Chandra was already a legend in the field of scholarship although less than 50 years of age. Educated under the supervision of his father, the formidable orientalist savant Raghu Vira he could read and write in two dozen languages, ranging from Sanskrit and Pali to Russian, Mongolian, Tibetan, old Javanese and other even less known ancient idioms and alphabet. I was struck by his glance, at once ageless and witty, his Buddha-like ears and his delphic composure. His office was like the whole building, which is in fact a library crammed with books, papers and manuscripts of many times and styles, including numerous silk wrapped Tibetan rectangular wood-block printed volumes.

Like his late father who boasted of knowing every major Indian language and who had coined some 150,000 new scientific and technical words based on sanskrit etymologies for the Hindi national vocabulary, Dr Chandra's working capacity seemed limitless and yet when he received us, he appeared to have all the time in the world and showed kind and flattering interest not only in my father's ideas but also in my own budding erudition, which must have appeared inconsequential in comparison with his extraordinary mastery of much of Asia's literary and religious history. He showed the fondness for France shared by many intellectuals and recalled that he had attended the 29th international conference of Orientalists in Paris just a few years earlier.

After readily agreeing to chair the lecture that the IIC had scheduled and discussing at some length the matter of dharma in the form of duty as a prospective addition to the National Constitution, he suggested that we visit Nepal and promised us an introduction to the Kingdom's Prime Minister Tulsi Giri who was a friend of his. He then proceeded to give us a glimpse of the work he was pursuing at the time. The library of the institute enshrined many priceless and venerable manuscripts from all regions of the continent "from Lake Baikal to Bali and from the Fuji Yama to the Caucasus" as he put it and it evinced the far-flung, lasting influence of India's thought and culture across this vast expanse of land and ocean. "Neither high mountain chains nor treacherous tropical seas stopped our monks, scholars, princes and traders" our host proudly mused.

"Here for instance is the great Mongol *Kangyur* in 108 tomes, a collection of one thousand one hundred and sixty one sutras translated from the original Sanskrit. Many of the originals are lost since the great looting and destruction of libraries carried out by Turkic invaders in the Middle Age, but the texts in Tibetan, Mongol and Chinese have been preserved to this day in huge xylographed volumes kept in many regions of Northern Asia and the Far East.

There is the *Bu-ston* in 28 volumes, the reference work on the history of Tibetan Buddhism and civilization, and here are the 15th century *Blue Annals* of Lotsava, first translated by George Roerich; this is *Sudhana's Way to Enlightenment*, a 12th century Chinese version of an exposition on the huge *Avatamsaka sutra*, about a pilgrim's visit to 52 spiritual masters of diverse schools all over India which I published last year. It is the earliest illustrated text on the *Gandavyuha*. The original which has perished was known all over Asia as early as the 9th century when its stories were depicted in stone on the gigantic temple of Borobudur in Java."

In a rush, memories of the *Avatamsaka* cosmology came to my mind, with its evocation of trillions of enlightened beings reflecting each other in as many monadic atoms like the infinite reflections of the one and only supreme Buddha.

Professor Chandra then told us about his current work. He was publishing many of the sanskrit documents found in the Chinese Imperial library in Beijing. One was the four language encyclopaedia of *dharani sutras* (in Manchu, Chinese, Mongolian and Tibetan) authored by the Hutuqtu Rolpahi Dorje, a Mongolian reincarnated Lama who was the spiritual confidant of the Ch'ing "Son of heaven" Ch'ien Lung in the 18th century, and like him a student of the imperial preceptor Lalitaraja.

"Few people realize the influence of India through Buddhism on the Chinese emperors right until the 1911 revolution," Lokesh

Chandra commented. "Ch'ien Lung, the mighty emperor who received successive European embassies seeking to trade with China was initiated into the *cakrasamvara* by the Hutuqtu who also wrote a major compendium of Buddhist philosophical systems, mainly inspired by our *vijnanavada* (theory of consciousness) school.

All those intellectual disciplines were either created in or inspired by Indian *acaryas* in our great medieval universities. That is why India was called the western paradise and the land of wisdom in China as in Japan and Korea. In Mongolia there are some 6 000 surviving Indian classics in all areas of literature, from cosmetology to theater and from astronomy to philology or botany."

He went on, "For instance, see here the *Vajravali* which is the seminal text for all Buddhist symbolic iconography and religious painting techniques, the mandalas. It was written in the twelth century in the Bengali *mahavihara* of Vikramasila by a scholar called Abhayakaragupta, under the reign of the Eastern Indian Pala kings. Then you have that huge collection of texts not included either in the Kangyur or Tanjur, over seventeen thousands that were assembled mostly in the mid-19th century, in part by Akhi Sherab Gyalpo as *Materials for a history of Tibetan Literature*. Most are Indian or based on Indian sources. Do you know that the *Mula Tantra* which is now lost, had 300 000 granthas or chapters? Only a few thousands of them have survived in Tibetan or Mongolian and I have been able to retrieve fifty five ancient sanskrit manuscripts from Japan in our old *siddham* script.

He paused thoughtfully for a moment and added: "In another area, the *Lankavatara Sutra*, that I am also working on, contains the teachings of Bodhidharma who, coming from Kanchipuram, founded *Ch'an* in China, later to become Zen Buddhism in Japan. As you know he also built the great *Shao Lin* monastery, popularized by Bruce Lee nowadays, where *Kung Fu*, derived from Indian yoga and martial arts is still practiced. The intellectual and spiritual commonwealth built by India was the largest in the world. It encompasses even today all of South, East and much of Central and even West Asia and managed to survive a few centuries of European colonial occupation but will it shrug off the invading American globalised pop culture and its materialistic, hedonistic creed?"

There was no ready answer to that loaded question. The density of the information provided by Lokesh Chandra was overwhelming and the vastness of his collection of manuscripts made it graphically obvious that the ancient literature of India is by far the most extensive in the world. Many thousands of teachers and commentators working during millennia accumulated millions of texts, many of which lay dormant on dusty shelves or locked trunks and had not been seen or read by anyone in living memory. His father was said to have brought back three hundred wooden cases full of them from his 1956 mission to China alone. Premier Zhu En lai, aware of the danger that those archives might be destroyed by his Communist colleagues, had allowed him to take them away to safety.

"It is not only the great number of often dead or dying languages that makes many of those works accessible to only a few, Lokesh Chandra pointed out. There is also the problem of many writing systems that have fallen into disuse. For example, look at this treatise. It is written in Soyombo, an alphasyllabary created in the sixteen hundreds of the common era by the Jetsum Dampo of the Mongols on the basis of Devanagari. New scripts were often invented on the pattern of the sanskrit "mother" *varnamala.* The Tibetans, the Mongols, the Manchus, the Koreans and the Japanese did it on various occasions and so did the various nations of Indochina and Indonesia. Now the challenge is to access those archives and transcribe or translate them so that more people can get acquainted with them."

"I am merely scratching the surface of a gold mine, he concluded thoughtfully. The intellectual treasure hoarded for so long in Asia is inexhaustible and that is why the West was fascinated for so long by the secrets of India and Tibet. What I do with my limited resources should be undertaken by thousands working under the auspices of various government-aided foundations all over the world but our country is too busy with day-to-day survival matters for the poor and with further wealth acquisition for the rich. How much of what still exists will have disappeared in a few decades?"

This melancholy question sounded like another echo of the eternal reflection about the frailty of all created things. It marked the end of what was to be the first of many conversations with this fascinating mind. Lokesh Chandra is a poet and a philosopher and his endless poring over austere hermetic manuscripts has not dried out his sources of lyrical inspiration nor wilted the wings of his childlike imagination.

THE INDIA INTERNATIONAL CENACLE

In the same period of time we were introduced to one the *grandes dames,* who had become famous even before independence for a fearless championing of many noble causes at a time when few women were allowed a role outside the walls of their homes. Kamaladevi Chattopadhyaya had precociously broken the fetters of tradition to take a leading role, when she was hardly more than a child in the struggle for national freedom.

Born in a privileged and erudite Southern family and married to one of the famous Chattopadhyaya siblings, a brother of an early associate of Sri Aurobindo in the freedom struggle who had become a Communist leader in pre-War Germany and Russia and had been executed in the 1937 purge ordered by Stalin, Kamala had become the president of the Youth League of the Congress in her early twenties but by then she was also an artist and a writer who had studied and even acted in sanskrit dramas and their film adaptations. In her various capacities she had met, worked with and often befriended most great names of that heroic period, from Annie Besant and Mahatma Gandhi to Rabindranath Tagore and from Subhash Chandra Bose to Jinnah and Nehru. Later on, she had come to know many of the celebrities of the century and she had often surprised and charmed them by her frank and challenging questions. One of her sisters-in-law, the noted poetess Sarojini Naidu, had become the first woman governor of an Indian state and several other relatives had occupied eminent positions in various fields.

When we met her she was in her seventies but had kept the sharp sense of observation, the strong temper and quick wit of her earlier years. She spoke fondly of Rukmini Devi whom she knew well but made no effort to hide her loathing of the Emergency rule then in force. She had turned against the Prime Minister despite knowing her since childhood.

We avoided politics and talked instead about the cultural heritage which she had done so much to preserve, through the creation of various craft and art organizations. "If India knew how to use traditional skills and the very abundant manpower we have, we could find indigenous substitutes for many consumer products and employ many more people to make them" she argued.

I recall my father asking her if she felt that the ruling party's industrial policies had gone against her precepts which were quite faithful to Gandhi's own recipes.

"I am no politician or economist, she said, but I think much more could have been done to promote small scale industry, with very little capital ... Pandit Nehru did not really understand this, although he generally supported my work. He felt however that India had no choice but to combine the Soviet model with the American one, instead of creating its own."

Like Rukmini Devi, Indira Gandhi and other eminent women we were to meet subsequently Kamala Devi, the "lotus goddess" struck me by the feminine strength she displayed beneath the soft appearance of elegant and understated womanhood. The name steel magnolia would have suited them more if magnolia had been a native plant; I preferred as a local variant the image of a diamond sharp *palasa* flower.

Our lecture at the IIC took place a few days later and was quite successful as it attracted a distinguished cast of scholars from India and also from other countries, partly on account of Dr Lokesh Chandra's presence. On that occasion we met a young British biologist in the audience, who was studying Vedanta and Yoga. Many years later, I was to see him again in the USA after he had become famous and we thus struck a friendship. His name is Rupert Sheldrake and he has proposed some revolutionary theories in the natural sciences that validate teachings found in ancient Indian scriptures.

The theme of the lecture was "Duality and Dualism in Indian philosophies" and in it I sought to distinguish the recognition of polar duality in all things created from the artificial dualistic interpretations derived from the Cartesian description of reality as something made of two separate worlds: matter and mind. After the talk, a gentleman came forward, engaged us in a brief conversation and invited us to have tea with him on the following day. His name was JC Kapur; he was a well known industrialist, an engineer strongly committed to alternative economic theories and to the development of renewable energy as well as a friend of the Prime Minister and of several other national leaders. He had recently given a talk and published a paper on the subject of India in the year 2000, which had had a wide impact as he advocated an ecologically sound form of sustainable development within a "mixed economy" system for his country.

In the following days and years, we had many interesting conversations with Kapur and some members of his circle of friends, including Lokesh Chandra, Prem Kirpal, a retired educationist, who had held a high position in UNESCO and other equally eminent intellectuals.

Kapur at the time resided at the India International Centre where he and his wife Urmilla occupied a suite that overlooked the manicured lawns of the Centre and the dense foliage of the Lodi garden. The conversations were as wide-ranging and profound as I could have wished. Our amphitryon had studied at Cornell University and his intellectual formation was mainly western and scientific in character but he had, later in life, developed a keen interest in philosophy and rediscovered the spirit of his native land through the writings of Coomaraswamy, Gandhi, Tagore and Aurobindo although the metaphysical spark in him had been kindled by the works of the French Jesuit paleontologist and theologian Teilhard de Chardin.

I remember Kapur debating with my father about Teilhard's attempt to reconcile contemporary discoveries in biology with Christian theology, drawing ideas in the process from Oriental cosmological systems. My father felt that the Jesuit's vision of the "Omega Point" symbolized his wish to give a modern, non-denominational character to the Christian notion of Redemption while Kapur saw it as a western interpretation of the Hindu goal of *Moksha* or liberation, predictably dismissed by most scientists and theologians in Teihard's day as a speculation that was neither scientifically supported nor religiously orthodox. Lokesh Chandra drew the semantic analogy between omega in the Greek alphabet and the second component of the *Aum* in the *Upanishads,* the 'U' sound taken as the initial of the sanskrit verb meaning "to elevate" which follows the initial A that Greeks called alpha.

All of us were familiar with recent works in scientific philosophy by, among others Jacques Monod, Raymond Ruyer and Fritjof Capra and Kapur knew the latter personally. He made us aware of another friend of his, Amaury de Riencourt, whom we discovered as a profound and original thinker on many issues related to the present world and the future and who became a friend much later.

UNVEILING ARCHETYPES

The many facets of Indian traditional civilization shone through our discussions and we were drawn to Hindu and Buddhist thought as by a magnet. Lokesh Chandra displayed his peerless ability to retrieve hidden gems from that vast ocean to illustrate suggestions offered to our reflection.

"Think of all the passages of the Upanishads which anticipate expression found in the Christian Gospels, he said. When Nachiketas in the *Katha* goes to the realm of Yama, he waits during three days before the Lord of death returns.There you have the three days in the Underworld before the Resurrection. Also, Yama is the god of death because he was the first man and thus the first to die but in the Scriptures, death is the third birth and within it is immortality, the first birth being conception and the second the emergence from the womb. In ancient Mesopotamia, Yam is the Sea...."

"And Moses, my father continued, led his people across the Red Sea, *Yam Suph*, which also means the Sea of reeds which means the passage through death before rebirth. On the way there is exile, wandering in the desert to reach the Promised Land."

"Think of how Shiva is called, *Pasupati*, the lord of animals, Lokesh then pointed out. The thracian Zagreus Dionysos is also the lord of animals and so is Orpheus but Pasupati is another form of Pusan, the good shepherd or cowherd, depending upon the cultural context, like Jesus and he rides a bull; so does Mithra who however kills the bull in the Persian myth. In vedic India bulls were sacrificed, as in ancient Greece but gradually blood offerings were replaced by vegetal ones and the *yagna* became symbolic. The earth *bhu* is depicted as a cow. From *bhu* you have the latin *bos*, the ox. Civilisation grows more abstract as it develops."

"The contrast between the two types of sacrifice is present in Genesis, I noted, Abel's holocaust is preferred by Adonai to Kain's plant cremation. Probably because Adonai was the chief god of a nomadic pastoral people that disdained agriculture. Indeed, there are other versions of the story which depict Kain as the hero and Abel as the outcast."

"It is all a matter of perspective, Kapur remarked. In India we have kept that in mind in all our legends. Almost no one is completely virtuous and right and all have a karma they must fulfill or atone for. In the *Mahabharata* the Pandavas are held to have truth on their side but they are guilty of many faults and the Kauravas are the victims of their past misdeed in previous life and individually they also display certain virtues. There are still tribes in India that honour and even worship Duryodhana and his many brothers."

"That is why Indians are held to be morally ambiguous and often unprincipled or unreliable," Prem Kirpal asserted. "We can find justifications at some level for almost any action. We are the ultimate realists despite our fantastic mythology. One can always argue that he is conditioned by his karma and fulfilling his Dharma, even if it seems wrong from another point of view."

"This cannot be said in truth," Kapur objected. "The fact is that all of us have to act according to our circumstances. I cannot divorce myself from my country and my family and therefore I have to abide by certain rules, whether or not they are ultimately valid. Talking of abstract universal good is almost never a useful standard to decide on our actions in specific circumstances. We never know all the facts and cannot judge everything, therefore we have to do the best we can on the basis of our beliefs and obligations."

"This is a subject of many years of my work," my father explained.

"Duty is the rule according to which we must exercise our responsibilities and in the feudal sense of it, which all Indian epics highlight, our conduct is dictated by the commitments we have made and faith we have pledged to those who are closer to us. That is what you call Dharma in Sanskrit. It implies a hierarchy of values, as Confucius taught. In fulfilling your duties you might harm someone because you can never see the entire picture but better that duty loyally accomplished than a flight from responsibility or uncertainty that would end in inaction and cynicism. The only way to escape the dense net of liabilities and constraints in which we are enmeshed is to embrace the anchoritic, ascetic life and leave the social matrix, as your *sadhus* do since time immemorial."

The evocation of the feudal past common to much of the old word led us to consider some archetypes of chivalry in East and West, such as the Pandava brothers and the knights of the heroic *gestae* in medieval Europe.

"I am intrigued by the image of Sahadeva, the fifth son of Kunti," I said.

"He was in fact the son of the Ashwins, the divine horse riding and seafaring twins, together with his own twin Nakula but he was the only one to follow the advice of his human father Pandu to eat his brain after his death in order to inherit his knowledge. As a result of such cyberophagy, Sahadeva knew everything about the past, present and future but he could not reveal things to come under pain of his brain splitting so that he had to live through all the events that he foresaw without uttering a word, unlike Troy's Laocoon who indeed was killed by the gods for revealing his insights to his fellow citizens. Like the greek Pollux or Polydeuces, Sahadeva's name means a thousand or multiple gods.

Sahadeva's chariot carried a silver swan as its banner. He is the Swan Knight, like Lohengrin who also has divine knowledge. An enduring Indo-European archetype. Lohengrin has a brother Kerdeiz, like Sahadeva has a twin Nakula, and his father Parzival, the white knight had a brother too, as King Pandu of the *Mahabharata* whose name means 'white", or 'pale'. Parzival like Pandu is raised by his widowed mother and while Pandu was begotten by the sage Vyasa, the organizer of the Vedas, his mother's brother-in-law, Parzival is the nephew of the king of the Grail. Pandu and Parzival are both under a curse and they die when their sons are still young. Sahadeva and Nakula on the one hand and Lohengrin and Kerdeiz on the other grow up as orphans and the Swan Knight Lohengrin is also called Helias, like the Sun Helios while Sahadeva is a grandson of the Sun *Vivaswan*.

Wolfram von Eschenbach who wrote the Parzifal romance claimed some of his sources were oriental. One wonders if the underlying legendary material came from Asia through Arab story tellers. According to another tradition the Germanic Swan Knight is a son of King Orient, the East personified."

My father pursued:

"Lohengrin is a figure of the Grail legendary cycle and there is in the Upanishads a reference to a golden cup that hides the face of the truth as well as many verses alluding to the holy water of light that is the *amrita*, the nectar of immortality. It is the *dhruva* or polar goblet of the vedic *Agnistoma* or fire sacrifice, guarded by a royal prince, indeed a knight of the Graal which is a solar emblem. There is also a clear reference to what we call baptism in Christianity, in its two forms; by water and by the fire of the holy spirit. It seems as if both John the Divine and Jesus were aware of those Vedic rites in some form."

'There is no end to the analogies that can be drawn between the Indian and western graeco-roman Germanic and even semitic names and symbols remarked Lokesh Chandra. In Samskrit *gati* means path and it has become the gate in English. Our *hotr* became the latin *hostis, the hostle* and both are offerings to the fire, actual or spiritual. We call the sun *Rohit*, from the Sanskrit root *Rah*:fire; in Hebrew *Ruach* and in

Arabic *Ruh* is the spirit, the fiery breath. Agni, our fire god is often described as a tawny or golden calf in the Veda. Shiva is known as Hara, the catcher or ravisher and is shown holding a noose or a net which is often called Indra's net, *indrajala* and in your Gospels, Jesus tells his future apostles to cast their net and send them to fish for men's souls. The net is an emblem of both imprisonment and freedom.

Some concepts and words migrated from East to west and others went the other way. There is a dialogue since many millennia and we cannot trace its beginning. There may be an ancient Indo-European theme behind the swan that brings Lohengrin to Elsa and the golden swan messenger of king Nala to princess Damayanti in our epics but the relation between the Samskrit Ashwins, the Greek Dioskouri and the German Alcis, all connected to the sea, hippic sports and cattle is stronger. Like Nakula and Sahadeva, Castor and Pollux look after horses and cows."

"Even so-called biblical scriptures are studded with images and analogies found in the vedic scriptures," I noted. "When Moses comes in the presence of God on Mount Sinai he beholds smoke, flashes of light, strong winds and lightings before Elohim passes unseen and the same phenomena are cited in the yoga sutras to describe the signs that the practitioner experiences as he reaches enlightenment and Rudra-Shiva is the lord of the mountain, like the God of Abraham, Isaac and Jakob, *El Shaddai*."

Soon after this foray into the boundless forest of mythology, we left for Kashmir, this other garden of the gods.

XII

The Lake of Snakes and Nelumbos

The Garden in the Mountains

While our bus was climbing the increasingly steep and sere mountain range that separates the hilly plain of Jammu from the vale of Kashmir, my mind was already absorbed in the reflections that prior readings on that legendary realm had sown. I was constantly distracted by the wild and stark panorama of precipitous slopes amidst which the road spun an infinity of hairpin curves. Every now and then our vehicle had to stop on a kerb to let interminable convoys of Ashok Leyland olive green military trucks pass on their way to or from our destination. Every three or four hours, the bus made a brief halt to enable the passengers to sip a cup of hot *chai*, munch on snacks and stretch their legs. More than once, we gazed in shocked silence at the carcasses of cars and buses that had rolled far below us to the bottom of the deep gorges edging our narrow ledge of a road, hurling their passengers towards a crashing death. I was both concerned for and amazed by our driver, who relentlessly negotiated the perilous twists and turns with utter phlegm and seemed none the worse for the wear upon our arrival after ten exhausting hours on that trail during which he consumed very little food or drink.

Faced with the craggy bleakness of the landscape, I imagined the verdant bliss of the Srinagar vale, sparkling with lakes on whose shores so many great saints and scholars had come to study and write. According to the myths, it had been an inland sea, called *Satisaras* in Samskrit, after the goddess Sati or Parvati, the lady of the mountains, haunted by an *asura* or demon called Jalodbhava and by the ubiquitous *nagas* and *pisachas*, ghostly beings mentioned in the Vedas.

However the great Rishi Kasyapa, the solar husband of the goddess Aditi, the boundless celestial mother and father of many of the gods, heroes and fabulous creatures of mythology, including the nagas ordered his son Ananta—"the endless one"—to drain the lake, just as it had churned dry the primeval sea of milk in the Puranas. The demon fled and the vestiges of the former inland sea are the lakes that are strewn around the valley like a broken string of pearls.

On the shore of the best known one, the Dal lake, the town of Anantnag stands in memory of the founding reptilians and the connected Nagin lake also owes its name to them. The drained and now fertile land became *Kasyapamira* or Kashmir.

The story is picturesque but there is more below the surface of the names and figures that they designate. Kasyapa, the turtle, is an archetype of Asian civilization whose origins are sunken in remote antiquity. He is one of the seven *rishis* of Vedic lore and his name is connected to the Caspian Sea, known as *kasyapasagara* in India, which is called after the tribe of the Kaspi. In that tribe, according to Buddhist hagiology was born the Buddha Kasyapa, who preceded the historic Siddharta-Gautama by several thousand (or million) years and attained *nirvana* in Varanasi after living successively in three palaces, the last of which is called Sirinanda, often believed to be the future Srinagar of Kashmir.

I wondered, and still do, if Kasyapa was not the divine ruler of one of the many clans that moved across Central Asia, between the Caucasus and the Hindu Kush which the Greeks knew as the Indian Caucasus and in which Herodotus and Hecateus of Abdera located the Kaspapyri tribes, around modern Peshawar.

The seeds of what was to become Buddhism seem to have been planted well before the latest Enlightened One, the Sakya Muni was born in the Himalayan foothills and Kashmir might have hosted his predecessor who gave it his name and seems to have won a wide renown outside the subcontinent. Is that why the valley was to play such a great role in the evolution and dissemination of the noble doctrine of the Eightfold Path?

The name survived in Greek mythology although it was feminized into Cassiopea, but it carried some faint remnants of the archetype as queen Cassiopea of Ethiopia, a land often equated with India by ancient Hellens had to rescue her kingdom from a flood by offering her daughter to a sea monster. The princess Andromeda was saved by Perseus, who killed the monster and married the damsel. Both their names indicate a connection with Persians and Medes and confirm the Eastern origin of the legend which still involves fighting a demon to drain a flooded country.

The history of that mountain kingdom is better recorded than in other parts of India because it was collected by a remarkable scholar, Kalhana in the *Rajatarangini*—the flowing river of kings—a chronicle which was continued by subsequent historians right up to the end of the 16th century when Kashmir fell to the Mughal Emperor Akbar. Until then, it had had a long succession of Hindu, Buddhist and Muslim monarchs who had generally preserved the rich composite culture of the country as a blend of North Indian, Iranian, Turkic and Tibetan influences. Many of the greatest Hindu and Buddhist thinkers and literateurs were from Kashmir or came to seek knowledge in that hospitable cradle of art and philosophy. From there they traveled to the remotest parts of India, Turkestan and China.

The Tibetan King Songtsen Gampo, a great patron of Buddhism in the 7th century of the common era, sent to Kashmir the erudite Thon Mi Sambhota to learn the Brahmi alphabet in use there. Thon Mi went back to Lhasa and retreated in the nearby hermitage of Pabonko, a dependency of the Sera monastery, where he created the Tibetan script, closely patterned after the Kashmiri model but adapted to the exigencies of the non-Indic local language. Also in Kashmir the princely monk Kumarajiva translated hundreds of important religious and philosophical texts into Chinese to help spread the Dharma in the Celestial Empire. Thus, the fame of the land of Kasyapa spread far and wide, all the way to Mongolia, Siberia and Japan.

As the day began to set, we reached what seemed like the steepest climb in this daunting journey and were suddenly engulfed in the darkness of the Pir Panjal tunnel. After what seemed to be a very long time, we emerged in the golden glow of the evening and beheld a vision of quiet and beckoning beauty comparable to that which greeted the characters of Conrad Hilton's "Lost Horizons." Inside a circle of distant reddish and purple mountains crested with milk, a green plain spread at our feet, dotted with the lofty plumes of poplars and the rounded boughs of chinars and further away a lake glittered with the pale hues of silver and opals. The tiny dots of houses spread on that silky carpet heightened the resemblance of that immense picture to a polychromous Tibetan *thangka* horizontally rolled out ahead of us.

The last hour of the drive, on a straight road fringed with solemn poplars, was oddly effortless after the breathless climb of the day. Before we had even reached the city, we saw groups of men of all ages waiting by the road, waving and trying to attract our attention. By the time we got to the bus station, we realized they were vying to promote the merits of hotels and other lodgings to the passengers. I knew that the tourist season had ended and that visitors were few, especially in that time of National Emergency and economic crisis. The locals seemed desperate to get patrons but then I was soon to learn of the pressing and insinuating character of the Kashmiris and of their unwillingness in business to ever take or say no for an answer. In this regard they may be compared with Egyptian shop keepers and tour guides.

Surrounded by a noisy and enthusiastic crowd of agents and touts who described with superlative enthusiasm the peerless beauty of their respective premises and facilities, we settled for the offer of a young man who behaved more discreetly and seemed trustworthy. He told us that his family owned a houseboat on Dal called *Alzira* and that he would take us presently there. The rate was reasonable and we rode a tonga to the shore where we were escorted to the creaking but cozily carpeted and hazelnut paneled embarkation that was to be our home for a few days.

Exhausted by the journey, we settled with relief in our immobile ship. Next morning when we awoke, we were dazzled by the liquid gold that the Sun poured on the still watery surface, in places clogged with clusters of nelumbos. Around the edge of the lake, hundreds of boats like ours were placidly moored and on the shimmering mirror, slender, crescent-shaped shikaras flitted like lazy dragonflies.

I was struck by the Central Asian atmosphere that brought me back to the oases of Afghanistan and Turkestan. I could feel the influence that for centuries had penetrated this tiny haven through its Gandharan, Hunnic and Iranian monarchs. They had not taken the uphill treacherous route that had brought us into the valley as there was a much easier and more open highway to the West from the Punjab plains of what is now Pakistan. Thus, it was not so difficult, for invaders to sweep into Kashmir and I wondered if the greatest local Hindu dynasty, that of Karkota in the Middle Age, had not taken its name from or given it to the fabulous ancient city of Karakhota in Mongolia, which Churchward describes as the capital of the prehistoric Uyghur empire.

The Mughal potentates had inherited that migratory tradition and they regularly came to the blessed vale from Delhi through Lahore, along the grand trunk road, followed by a retinue of tens of thousands of people. Those descendents of Central Asian nomads were used to living in moveable tent cities and they led much of the population of their winter capital in this precisely choreographed exodus. Upon arrival they all settled in the flowery glades that still wrap the lakes in a lush garland. For the natives, this invasion must have meant a massive disruption of their tranquil lifestyles but it also brought much income as the imperial court was wealthy and generally paid its bills.

IN THE FOOTSTEPS OF HISTORY

We had various tasks to fulfill, including a visit to the University where we gave a lecture as part of our mandate from ICCR. The heavy military and police presence found an echo in the perceptible tension that we felt among the students and faculty and even in our meeting with the Vice-Chancellor and the administrators. However while exploring the maze of the old city huddled around the brown waters of the Jhelum and its green mosques and mausoleums, painted like silk carpets, we were also treading on the footsteps of some of the spiritual luminaries who had dwelt in this holy and tormented land. We could not fail to visit the old maharaja's palace, the *Sher Garhi* or Lion's Abode in its faded glory, particularly visible in the lovely polychromous and flowery *papier mâché* panellings of the former Darbar Hall which has since burnt to the ground unfortunately.

A young scholar from the university who volunteered to accompany us in our tour of the region took us to the legendary Sun Temple at Martand, a few miles away from Anantnag. The ruins of that sanctuary set on a commanding height testify to the grandeur of the monument which synthesized the various styles of the wider region, including Gandharan, Gupta and Central Asian elements. The temple was dedicated to the worship of the Sun God Aditya also known as Martand, which probably meant also the shell or sphere of death since everything under the Sun shall change and perish.

There are speculations about the "Scythian" origin of the Vedic Sun God, who is often shown wearing the boots of Central Asian horsemen but rides a chariot driven by seven horses which stand for the seven rays of the prism. One can also speculate on his historical kinship with the latin god Mars whose name is at the root of both the spring-ushering month of March and martial pursuits that began at that time.

"The Hindu kings of Kashmir were especially devoted to the Sun," our cicerone pointed out, "and the main builder, Lalitaditya carried the solar god's name, but most variants of Hinduism and Buddhism were practiced and encouraged. Lalitadiya invited many scholars from all parts of India, including the ancestor of our greatest Kashmiri scholar Abhinavagupta and perhaps also the first Sankara from the Far South who gave his name to the hill that crowns Srinagar. The city is said to have been founded by the Buddhist Emperor Ashoka but Buddhism which took over Ladakh and Tibet did not survive the arrival of Islam although we preserved Kashmira Saivaism. It is here on the Pradyumna or Shankaracarya hill that the Bible of yoga was written, the *Moksopaya* which was expanded into the 32,000 verses of the *Yoga Vasishta,* later summarized into the *6000 slokas* of the *Laghu Yoga Vasishta* by another Kashmiri, Abhinanda."

We knew that our learned guide was a Kashmiri Brahmin and we were hence not surprised to hear him evoke with melancholy the destruction of the Martand Temple in the early 15th century by a Muslim ruler who, according to the contemporary chronicler Ferishta took one whole year to demolish the cyclopean structure.

"Islam has in itself a seed of intransigent conformism which does not easily accept otherness," the young man reflected ruefully.

"Despite the fact that there are many tolerant and peaceful Muslims, fundamentalist Islam even destroys the artistic and intellectual achievements of its own more talented followers. There is an otherworldly self assurance that ignores any other insight or perspective. Even though our earliest recorded kings were related to the other royal clans of India as far back as the Vedas and the Mahabharata and one of our rulers converted to Islam only in the fourteenth century of the common era, mainly for political convenience it seems, most Kashmiri Muslims still feel they are not Indian and define themselves by their religion and their links with Turkestan and Iran. They'd rather forget the original identity of the land which they regard as pagan."

I was reminded of that perceptive passage by Keyserling about Muslims in which he condensed impressions gleaned during his travels: "Why has this religion alone understood how to substitute national feeling by something wider?... Radical monotheism, he concludes, point men absolutely to themselves."

The natural beauty of the ever-changing panorama enchanted us at every corner of the road and at every hour of the day and night, whether we glided on the glistening lakes edged by the misty shapes of towering trees at dusk, wandered in the geometrically laid out alleys of the moghul gardens, amidst the flowerbeds and whispering fountains and canals or paused for tea on the emerald lawns of the Maharaja's white summer palace turned into a luxury hotel, beneath the russet and gold canopy of the chinars. It is an oasis of Parnassian peace huddled between a forested hill and the Dale Lake that shimmers in the distance, haunted by skiffs that look like scimitars. I tried to imagine what it would be like to be raised in such edenic surroundings as crown prince Karan Singh had been.

From the top of the Sankara hill, which is locally known also as the throne of Solomon, we gazed far below at the puzzle of green and red roofed toy houses, sinuous waterways cluttered with houseboats that looked vaguely like ornate wooden pagodas and calm expanses of iridescent water. On the horizon the formidable Hari Parbat Fort crowned a hill near the centre of the old town. It was from that eyrie that successive rulers, including Karan Singh's father, had watched and dominated the often restless populace. On the other side, Sankara had come to teach what is perhaps the most abstract version of Hindu philosophy. In his honour the fourth, southern gate of the hilltop temple had been opened to symbolize the fact that Kashmir welcomed wisdom from the four direction. There the great master from Kerala in the deep south established the *Sharada* or *Sarvajna Peeth* and the former name makes a connection with the traditional kashmiri *Sharada* script.

In contrast to the poetic charm of partly wooden stuccoed old mosques that reflect a peculiar mixture of Persian and Chinese influences, we could not but be disappointed by the cold white domed new sanctuary at Hazratbal, which seemed out of place in that panorama. It was being built to house the hair of Prophet Muhammad, a relic that reached the valley many centuries earlier.

THE SHAIVISM OF KASHMIR

The Kashmir valley is not only a geographical feature or the abode of a picturesque poly-ethnic, multireligious society, it is also a many layered spiritual phenomenon and a fountain of intellectual creativity which irrigated all of India and there was no greater example of that rich and subtle tradition that the Shaivite philosophy that took its name from the land.

We had been given some information on the living masters of that *parampara* and in particular Lakshman Joo and his disciple Sharika Devi.

Abhinavagupta, who lived a thousand years ago in what was then a haven of relative peace, was the son of a scholar at the court of the local king, descended from the lineage of the Vedic Rishi Atri of Northern India. He was reportedly "yoga born" from deeply spiritual parents steeped in the cult of Bhairava, the fierce form of Shiva and, in that capacity he acquired spontaneous knowledge of all disciplines taught in his age. Surrounded by a loving family that fully shared his mental disposition, he could dedicate his celibate life to study, meditation and writing. He is said to have had fifteen masters, including Utpaladeva and Sambhunatha. The latter was probably the most important as he taught him the *ardha triyambaka* doctrine while his own wife initiated the precocious disciple in the *kaula* or esoteric "left hand' practices of tantric shaivism by acting as a *duti* or conduit for illumination. In some Indian traditions, one can remain chaste while channeling sexual energy devoid of carnal desire towards spiritual awakening.

With this comprehensive and advanced training, Abhinavagupta displayed a mix of prodigious erudition and understanding in many areas, from poetry and aesthetics to metaphysics, grammar, logic, semantics and literary critique. Among the thirty-five works he is credited with, many of which have not been translated in any western languages while others are probably lost, the *Tantraloka* is the most massive and important as he exposes in it the vast range of tantric philosophy and praxis.

The fundamental doctrine that Abhinavagupta was raised in is called the *Trika* due to its recursive triadic structure and it is expounded in the *Malinivijayattatatantra*. The first triad consists in the three levels of being of the supreme goddess, *para* (absolute), *parapara* (at once transcendent and immanent) and *apara* (relative and immanent). The three shaktis or powers in creation are *iccha* (will in pure consciousness), *jnana* (wisdom in the intellect) and *kriya* (action, in the physical world). In turn knowledge consists of three parts, the subject, its variable modalities and its object. Whoever can unify in his perception the three aspects achieves omniscience because the nature of all reality is revealed to him. That universal understanding corresponds to the fourth state of the mind, the *turiya* described in the shortest of the Upanishads.

To reach that hallowed stage, there are three ways. The path shown by Shiva is abrupt and short, similar to the Zen *Satori* which was being propounded around the same time in China and Japan. The path of *Shakti* consists in acquiring the mastery of all emotions, thoughts and sensorial reflexes through a complex succession of meditational practices and finally the "human" or intellectual path relies on study and exercises to train and master the intellect (*buddhi*) and the physical body (*deha*), involving yoga, the use of mantras, mandalas and yantras.

Those three methods reflect the three fundamental units acknowledged by Kashmir shaivism: Shiva or the undefinable source of all manifestation and Shakti, the intermediary energy that connects the former to *Anu* or *Nara*, the individual being or man. They also respectively relate to the three levels of speech identified in the Upanishads: *pasyanti*, the subtle mental intention or vision, *madhyama*, discursive but unvoiced thinking and *vaikhari*, articulated, sonorous language.

Like most other great philosophers and seers of his lineage, Abhinavagupta mastered the three schools of the Trika, namely the "non dual" one or *Abheda*, the subjectively dualistic one (*bhedabheda*) and the *bheda* which is the scholarly doctrine found in the "theistic" shaiva *agamas*.

In that late stage of the twentieth century, there were very few teachers of that tradition but we were directed to Lal Sahib, the popular surname given to Lakshman Joo Raina, a kashmiri pandit who had a great reputation for saintliness and who resided in a village called Ishber with a few followers who formed a small community.

We found the place near the walled Mughal garden of Nishat Bagh. It was a typical Kashmiri house, partly built of timber surrounded by an orchard, which exuded the serenity of pastoral contemplation. We had not telephoned as we did not have a phone line in our houseboat and we were sorry to find out that the master of the premises was away on a teaching tour. We were however admitted in the presence of his chief follower, Sharika Devi, who was also regarded as a realized saint. She must have been in her sixties at the time and we were blessed by a few moments in her presence. She graciously asked one of the disciples of Lakshman to spend some more time with us and enlighten us further on the doctrine practiced in the Ashram.

We spent almost two hours with the old gentleman who was from Punjab but had come to spend the remainder of his life at the feet of his master. He was both a devotee and an avid student of Kashmira Shaivaism so that he was able to give accurate and thoughtful responses to our queries while we drank the peach-blossom coloured *poshrang* local tea.

At the outset, he pointed out that the surrounding village, named after Ishwar or God, was a sacred place as the great Abhinavagupta himself had stayed there during much of his adult life and then he told us about some of the European followers and admirers of Lal Sahib, including a Frenchman called André Padoux and a German scholar of Sanskrit, Bettina Bauemer. He then proceeded to explain briefly how Kashmira Shaivaism had developed in contradistinction with the rival teachings of the *Sarvastivada* school of Buddhism and of Sankara's Advaita Vedanta.

"Arguments between Indian traditions have often been misinterpreted as violent conflicts," he clarified, "perhaps because Europeans were used to religious wars within both Christian and Muslim denominations and they wanted to find parallels in India. Debate here was a universal practice at the philosophical level but ritual and devotional freedom was left to the individual or to his tribe or family. Each one could choose his own path to reach liberation. According to the *Shaiva* teachings we follow here, there are four envelopes or shells that encompass all things at different levels."

Our host described the four *andas* or "eggs", which do not include Shiva, the supreme who remains outside of all and yet pervades everything. The *Shakti Anda* is the seat of the primeval dual and yet undivided power that initiates creation; the *Maya Anda* is the realm of fluid and changing phenomenal existence in its boundless diversity that appears real to us because of five intrinsic limits or *kancukas* attached to all sentient beings; at a denser stage is the *Prakriti Anda* that is the seemingly solid material realm of nature and within it the *Prithvi Anda*, the local universe which enshrines the *Kundalini Shakti* or seminal energy locked at the basis of the spine. At the other end of the bodily axis, on the top of the skull is the cranial fissure which is called *Ananda*—"the boundless," the very name for bliss as it is the orifice through which the atman leaves the corporeal shell. The highest joy is indeed tied to the infinite and also to the immortal soul's hatching from the egg of the self.

We recognized in those *andas*, and in the *tattwas* or features that they contain, the *Sankhya* system of classification of all components of reality attributed to Rishi Kapila in early days of the Vedic culture. The continuity of fundamental notions through the length and breadth of Indic philosophies reflected an immanent unity despite many more or less superficial variations.

My father asked our temporary mentor in what way the *Shaiva* doctrine contradicted Sankara's advaita Vedanta.

"Our emphasis and our analysis of the process of enlightenment are different," he responded. "Sankara was also a devotee of Shiva to whom he dedicated many hymns of his composition but in his abstract writings, he emphasizes the ultimate unreality of the individual self. We see that self as *pasu*, an animal that is bound to the notion of material existence by the *pasa* or noose that consists of three *malas* or impurities.... Notice the root of your latin word *Malus*: evil," he noted in passing. They are the *anavamala,* which stems from the individual sense of a separate identity, the *mayamala* arising from the surrounding maya: relative, ever changing appearances and the *karmamala* which consists in believing that actions are actually performed by us as material, free beings.

Once we cleanse ourselves of those parasites which cloud our perception, we can behold the Lord: *Pati,* who releases us of the bond and the *pasu* which is the *jivatma* (living soul) can achieve liberation from its conditioning as *Pasupati*, another name for Shiva. It is then a matter of different opinions if it remains separate or merges with the absolute. Even *Shaiva* schools disagree between them on this point on which absolute knowledge is impossible since we can only approach the truth but never seize it fully.

The cooling temperature brought to our mind the arrival of dusk and we took our leave after spending a few moments of silent recollection before a small altar in that abode of prayer and study. We were given a polycopied version of Lakshman Joo's recent translation of the *Sivastotravali* of Utpaladeva, a classic commentary on the Shaiva doctrine.

Yet it is as always in poetry that the human soul communes with a revelation and Kashmiri Shaivaism found its widest echo in mystic verse. It was the humble medieval woman mystic Lallesvari who came upon the most poignant expressions to translate the otherwise ineffable experience of oceanic awareness in her collection of songs. How we enjoyed reading them, albeit in an English rendering, in our floating refuge while we watched the unceasing, colourful flow of life on water and land!:

"Playfully you hid from me
All day I looked.
Then I discovered
I was you,
And the celebration
Of That began."

And again:

"And the longing in me became so strong
And then I saw that I was gazing
from within the Presence.
In that wait and in giving up all trying
Only then did Lalla flow out
From where I knelt."

Despite the inevitable loss of the lyrical essence of the original language I heard as in an otherworldly choir the songs of John of the Cross, William Blake, Ibn Arabi, Rumi and so many others, in all traditions and languages in Lalla's voice.

THE KUNDALINI YOGI

We had heightened our familiarity with that particular form of Tantric philosophy but had yet to meet a living experiencer of the

Holy Grail of that quest, the famed arousal of the Kundalini which reportedly opens the door to the illumination of consciousness. We had however kept the name and coordinates of Pandit Gopi Krishna that we had been given by Peter Hoffman in Madras. We called the Pandit and he invited us to join him at his house in the old city in the evening of the following day. With great expectations we reached the unassuming dwelling on a particularly chilly evening and while we waited for him in an unheated living room we could hardly repress shivers. The gentleman who entered and greeted us with a quiet "Namaste" and a warm smile seemed to cast away the icy gloom with his solar presence. Bespectacled and wearing the white "Gandhi cap" that was ubiquitous in those days in India, he exuded friendliness in his voice. Inquiring in fluent English if we were cold, which must have been apparent from our expressions, he promptly called for hot *kawa,* the Kashmiri festive tea deliciously flavored with cinnamon, cardamom and crushed almonds and had a typical brasero placed at our feet as well as ample woolen shawls brought in which we wrapped ourselves with relief.

We had expected to meet an ascetic and laconic saintly figure unfamiliar with western culture but instead we found an urbane, unassuming and articulate householder who freely shared his experience in chaste English. He described the sudden flow of light that he had felt flooded with one day during a meditation when he was thirty four years of age. His life had been changed by that transcendent experience which had made him realize that he was a boundless sea of radiant consciousness and not a mere physically limited and material body. The arousal of the kundalini he compared to a radiant roaring cataract rushing into his being from the top of his head and making him rock as if a slow continuous earthquake was taking place in and around him. "It should have been a terrifying sensation" he commented "but there was such joy and exaltation that there was no room for any other feeling."

Listening to this, we were inevitably led to draw comparisons with an orgasmic rapture, a parallel so often found in tantric literature and the Pandit readily agreed although he emphasized that his experience had been far more ecstatic and full of awareness than the sensations achieved in a sexual union.

"I never did such intense *sadhanas* as some of our ascetics practice all their lives in the hope of reaching enlightenment and yet I was blessed almost without trying...One can explain it in one of two was. Either I inherited a karmic legacy that brought me this gift or I was granted a boon by Lord Shiva and the Shakti smiled on me."

We were eager to know the effects of this awakening on his mindset and behavior since then. With his usual spontaneity he responded without pausing as if telling an evident truth.

"There is an overwhelming peacefulness and a sense of security, an awareness of the world around you as you never saw it before...It is very simple and yet invaluable because it has nothing to do with the material gains that we associate with success from an outer viewpoint. Such gains or losses are seen for what they are, so transient and immaterial that we don't feel the need for the former or fear of the latter even though we can still understand why others are conditioned by their sensorial experiences to seek and dread only that."

"However, he continued, during the intermediate state, which for me lasted twelve years, there are also very difficult moments because at times I lost the glorious illumination that kept me in a blissful state and instead I felt great pain and anguish as if I were burning. I was extremely dejected and forlorn on those occasions. I believe that this is all part of the process of adaptation to the new state of consciousness which requires great changes in one's mental and physiological being. When you lose attachment to the material goals of action you occasionally succumb to doubt about the reality of the ecstasy that tore you away and wonder if it will come back."

To anyone who has read the recollections and impressions penned by great mystics , the state of mind described by Gopi Krishna sounds very familiar. The sincerity of his tone made it clear that he was not quoting Saint John of the Cross, Jakob Boehme or Jelaluddin Rumi although he might have read them.

As the conversation continued, we gleaned revealing facts about his past. His powerful build kept traces of his youthful profession as a free style wrestler and his former career as a government servant might have given him the skills he used in many years of work for women's upliftment. He had early on felt the urge to get involved in social reform and had been a pioneer in this field even before India's independence.

"I felt the pain of widows in the poorer strata of our society" the Pandit commented in his unassuming tone. "The death of a husband was almost a death warrant for the wife. Although *sati* (self immolation) was almost never carried out anymore by then, the widows were, and still are, often doomed to a miserable life of neglect and solitude as they could never marry again and were often expected to take refuge in a charitable institution. You cannot put an end to such abuses by trying to change the society or the religion from outside. You have to convince people to abolish such customs by reflecting on the real meaning of their tradition and on the sacred nature of all human beings."

The most important part of Gopi Krishna's message was however steeped in the conviction that the kundalini energy, which had tapped in him unsuspected gifts and resources, usually locked away in a "secret" cell of the brain, the *brahmarandra*, is at work to transform consciousness and gradually awaken all human beings to their boundless divine potential. In his words, cosmic humanity was on its way and that was the theme of some of his writings.

At the end of our lengthy visit, our host gave us a copy of his most famous book, aptly entitled "Kundalini" and we left hoping to meet him again. Unfortunately we never did.

A GRAVE'S ENIGMA

We had been intensely exposed to the various shades of the Hindu spiritual heritage of the magic valley in the last few days but we could not forget the fascinating enigma of Jesus's hidden life and death, associated with Kashmir for many since the publication of a popular book on the subject by Faber Keyser in that very year 1976.

We knew that the story had first been publicized widely through the writings of Mirza Ghulam Ahmed, an aristocrat of the Punjab who in the late 19th century had proclaimed himself the new prophet of a reformed Islam and had declared that the Galilean Messiah was buried in Srinagar. Long-standing legends about Jesus traveling around India and Tibet, either during the "hidden years" of his youth, before initiating his ministry or after his presumed death on the Cross thus gained a wider audience. They were related to his mother's rumored stay in the eponymous mountain village of Murree, now on the Pakistani side of Kashmir.

Ghulam Ahmed founded the heterodox Ahmadiya faith which was condemned and declared an apostasy by Sunni theologians. Thus his claims about Jesus's tomb were also rejected and at the end of the 1965 Indo-Pakistani war, some fanatics had actually destroyed the mysterious grave. Rozabal, as it is called, has however been rebuilt more or less identically and we were able to see it from outside although we could not gain access to the padlocked interior. The humble rectangular, green roofed structure crowned by a central octagonal turret still holds its secret. The original name of the saintly person who lies under the gravestone is Yuzasaf, who is also the hero of the well known Manichean and Eastern Christian tale of Barlaam (or Balauhar) and Josafat or Yuzasaf. The latter originally was no other than the historic Buddha as the Sanskrit designation Bodhisatta was mistranscribed in Arabic and Persian as Yudasaf.

Buddhist tradition situates the passing away of Gautama Buddha at Kusinagara in the Gangetic plain so that if a great Buddhist figure is buried at Rozabal, it cannot be the historic founder of the tradition.

We had seen photographs of the tomb which showed two footprints carved in the stone. That seemed to denote a Buddhist origin as the early followers of Sakya Muni represented him only through images of his soles on an empty throne.

Was Yuzasaf then a hallowed Buddhist monk, one of the many who travelled across the valley on their way to or from Ladakh, Bactria and Turkestan or was he a later day Muslim Peer or even possibly a respected Jewish Rabbi? History is silent on this and myth has taken over, seeking some support in apocryphal Christian writings such as the *Acts of Thomas* which describes the physical twin or image of Jesus, Judas Thauma Didymus visiting this region of India.

There can be no doubt that an important propagator of the Gospels came to or near Srinagar in the second or third century because he founded several churches and appointed bishops in that vast area of northwestern India. Could he be the one buried on this quiet shore of Dal lake? Traditions about "that Jesus" having gone to Tibet persist although the claims of the 19th century Russian adventurer Notovich of having located documents related to his passage in the Hemis monastery of Ladakh have long been exposed as fraudulent. Nevertheless one of the luminaries of the Ramakrishna order, Swami Abhedananda did visit the monastery many years later and confirmed that it kept records of "Saint Issa" whom he also took to be Jesus. That testimony was accepted by many and supported by the great Parsi mystical leader Mehr Baba.

Indeed there may well have been more than one Jesus since the name was common in his time. The *Qur'an* declares that Issa bin Maryam was not crucified because God saved him and took him away with his mother to a secret location and Docetic Christians held the same belief but since many centuries Christians and Muslims affirm that he did not leave a mortal body for burial so that the story of the Rozabal Jesus is regarded as a heresy.

Like many other mysterious supernatural personalities in the subcontinent, the Yuzasaf of Rozabal is claimed by more than one religion and his undefined status perhaps makes him a fitting symbol of the complex and ambiguous cultural identity of Kashmir, poised at the crossroads of Hinduism, Buddhism and Islam. I wondered whether the origins of Christianity might not be shrouded in Buddhism, whether or not Jesus the Nazarean, *Yeshue Nazrani* had come to India himself.

There were Buddhist missionaries in the Levant and Egypt around that time and they must have spread their doctrines. We also know that there were heterodox and syncretistic groups such as the Essenes living in Palestine, Syria and Egypt. Would it be surprising if some of them had absorbed the tenets taught by the oriental messengers who centuries later inspired the Persian founder of manicheism? At any rate, Christianity eventually influenced Mahayana Buddhism in its iconography and in its clerical structure so that a two way communication is likely.

ECHOES OF ANCIENT LOVE LORE

While we sat at dusk on the cushioned upper deck of our houseboat, watching the muffled ballet of the *shikaras* on the purple, moss festooned water, I realized how different from the Indian plains Kashmir felt and looked. The flowers that fill its meadows and decorate the local handicraft are not the tropical blossoms of Hindu mythology, they are the four favourites of the Ottomans: roses, tulips, prune blossoms and peonias.

Centuries of Islamic presence and Central Asian influence had made the valley more evocative of Saadi's *Gulistan* than of Amaru's amorous glade, even though the latter's erotic lyrics had been written here. The sensuous power of his verses had often troubled me. It is said that, like Solomon's *Song of Songs*, they can be given a mystical significance in spite of their voluptuous and graphic descriptions. The complexity of classical Sanskrit syntax makes a literal translation awkward and almost meaningless so that an interpretative recomposition is needed to give foreign readers a notion of the very dense and subtle content of those stanzas, packed with multiple references to literary conventions and allusions.

For instance, one of the first verses in the *Amarushataka* (hundred strophes of Amaru) has been rendered as:

"The countenance of the slender one
During the love act in reverse
With fluttering. dishevelled locks of hair
The swaying ear pendents, the tilak(forehead mark)
Blurred by fine beads of sweat, eyes languid at the end of love play
May that countenance preserve thee..."

and it goes on to suggest that there is no need for any of the gods when one has had this experience, a curious but not so unusual hint of atheism, by western standards.

And another one, even more troubling:

"'Pity', she says,
With bruised breasts and legs still trembling.
'Enough' she says in a choked voice...
And now her silence grows lasting.
Is she dead or sleeping?
Is she meditating in delight
On what has happened?
Or thinking of another?"

The strict meter and multiple alliterations and polysemic plays of the poems add several dimensions to the highly charged meaning and while many stanzas highlight the latent cruelty and the tragic potential of passion, others are delightfully humorous without falling into ribaldry. Some even hint at the freedom enjoyed by many women such as the one by that other outstanding Kashmiri love minstrel, Bilhana when he has his unnamed heroine say to her departing beau: "After you are gone you may hear what I see fit to do with my love life."

My favourite story from the anthology of Sanskrit erotic verse, attributed to the same Bilhana, was, in my teenage years the couplet in which an indiscreet parrot repeats to the parents of a young couple the words he overheard during their lovemaking. That fills the young bride with shame and to punish him she feeds the indecent bird a ruby of her earring as if it were a pomegranate seed, thereby reducing him to eternal silence. However I was even more delighted when I discovered another quatrain that describes the lover chancing upon his lady asleep in her mother's home and when he touches her, she turns away whispering *"Mother, he disturbs me even in my dreams"* as if to make room for him on the couch.

There seems to be no emotion, game or device in the sphere of Eros left unexplored by those experienced chroniclers of the "ars amatoria" who went further than Ovid and Tibullius in their explorations, so true it is that the Indian spirit always pushes deeper and higher than others in the undivided realm of the mind and body.

However Kashmir is more redolent with the poetic atmosphere of the Mughal court civilization; it exudes its perfumes, its melodies and its Persian distychs. In the copper shaded woods and on the silken meadows laid like prayer rugs against incandescent peaks one can still imagine the pleasure loving Padshah Jehangir smelling an autumn rose while watching sunset in the company of some of the beauties of his harem or his son Shah Jahan playing a game of polo with princes and court ladies. It must have felt like paradise, as "a veil of the most delicate beauty hung above severe reality" as Keyserling aptly noticed.

The Mughal, half-Rajput emperors and princes were as ardent and refined in the pursuit of pleasure as their ancient Hindu predecessors and they adopted many of the allegoric conventions enshrined in the *raga-ragini* painting albums which depict the atmospheric and seasonal settings for the many stages of romance.

We had made it a habit by then to engage in varied and rambling conversations with the head of the family that owned our temporary floating home and we answered his questions about the outside world, huddled around the tall copper samovar perched above the ornate ceramic stove which tried its insufficient best to heat our fragile wooden home. We all wore the traditional *phelan*, a kind of ample and thick caftan on our other clothes.

Our "boatlord" had had many foreign guests but had not been away from Kashmir, except for some short trips to Delhi. Like most Indians he was very interested in knowing if I had wedding plans and suggested once that I should take a Kashmiri bride as I was approaching the right age. When we pointed out half seriously that the local religion might not look favourably upon a local girl marrying a non-Muslim foreigner he claimed that not everyone cared so much about this and that many Kashmiris liked and wanted to live abroad. "Most of us only go to India" he added innocently.

The way he said it made it clear that he, like many in his stubbornly tight-knit community, saw the valley as a separate country. We pointed out to him, in a spirit of loyalty to the nation that hosted us, that Kashmir had been for many centuries a privileged region of Hindustan and that its gifted population had given it some of its brightest lights. He seemed unconvinced and replied: "*Kashmiriyat* is our culture and as you must have seen, if you came from there, it is very different from the mainland's...Our music, our carpets, our food are more Iranian."

We saw there was not much point in arguing further. Kashmiris like him reminded me of people who live in islands and who can never feel fully part of anything larger. My parents had experienced the same attitude from the Canarians in the island of my birth. However in Kashmir religion had created an additional barrier even though the local Muslims have never ceased to travel and live in all regions of India where they display their famed artistic talent and their business savvy. In fact they are conspicuously devoid of the militaristic, somewhat rigid character that Keyserling noticed in many Muhammadans although they have the unspeculative, concrete earthiness that he rightly detects in the faithful of that creed. Their rather big noses and often blue or green eyes too assimilate them to Afghans and Iranians although many could also be mistaken for oriental Jews. The latter resemblance may be more than fortuitous, given the records of Israelite traders coming to the region at least since the days of the Achaemenid empire along the silk route.

One late afternoon we took the skiff tied to our houseboat and paddled away on the lake in search of adventure. Intrigued by the shadowy channels that opened up beneath tall rows of trees, we entered one which led to another and after more than an hour of navigating this watery labyrinth we realized that we were lost. By then the night was falling and darkness made our surroundings ghostly. We tried methodically to find our way back to the main lake but we were in a network of waterways that led my father to say, by way of a pun, that Dal in fact must have meant *Dedale* (Daedalus in French). We were relieved to see the dark mass of a large boat sailing towards us under the arboreal canopy, carrying with it the echo of songs, conversation and laughter. Our calls were heard and the passengers told us that rather than trying to give us directions in their halting English, they would take us on board and pull along our bark as they were going towards the mooring area of the *Alzira*, our houseboat which of course they knew of, since Kashmiris are privy to everything about their fellow denizens.

Once on deck, we realized that we had joined a floating wedding party for the family and friends of the groom. The all male crowd on board was sedately joyous and food, tea and soft drinks were passed around constantly. We sat down amidst the group on the rugs that covered the planks and comfortably whiled away the two or three hours that it took for the nocturnal cruise to rejoin our boat's neck of the woods. On the way we could dimly see the houses and gardens which lined the sinuous channels and arms of the river and hid on thickly forested islets that sprung up here and there. The landscape was surreally mysterious and could have been painted by Caspar David Friedrich. On occasion we moored briefly against a rickety wooden pier to allow some more people to join the party. Some guests smoked *hookahs* also called hubbly bubblies while others munched kebabs and sweets. An effeminate young man with heavily painted eyes and a colourful scarf draped around his head and shoulders danced to the tune of popular local songs. In the Islamic local culture a woman dancer would not have been a decent choice and her role was played by a transvestite. I must say that I found him ugly and that his mincing gestures and high pitched voice made me uneasy but I remembered that until quite late in history all women's roles in European theater were played by men for the same reasons.

No society seems to have been able to establish a strong distinction between the actress and the prostitute and performing professions have almost inevitably attracted the suspicion and condemnation of mainstream society.

We were grateful for the simple and hearty welcome of our fortuitous hosts who once more illustrated the generosity that characterizes much of the East. They left us a few yards away from our floating house to which we repaired with relief as it was close to midnight and we were quite tired by our expedition. Two days later we were on the perilous and exhausting return road journey to the Indian lowlands and to New Delhi.

XIII

E Oriente Lux

Delhi Politics

In Delhi on our return from the timeless haven of Kashmir we fell into the simmering cauldron of politics as tensions temporarily repressed by the state of emergency were again erupting. Leading figures who had won fame in the struggle for independence, led by Jayaprakash Narayan, an illustrious social reformer, campaigned against the government despite the curbs on public expression. Many were under arrest but managed to make themselves heard. Indira Gandhi was under attack from many sides, at home and abroad as we accused of aiming for personal dictatorship on the advice of her ambitious and perhaps reckless son Sanjay. When we met her again, about the time when the 42nd amendment to the Constitution which included the charter of ten fundamental duties, was passed by the Lok Sabha on December 2nd, the stress and fatigue were visible in her demeanous. The rising hostility to the highhandedness and widespread abuses of the Emergency regime was taking a heavy toll on her. She had been brought up in a tradition of parliamentary democracy, even though her father had enjoyed several years of unchallenged power and she could not take lightly the accusations of tyranny levelled against her. As for all Indians of her generations, the image of Gandhi in his popular struggle against an arbitrary state was always present and she carried his name and regarded herself as one of his spiritual children.

We could feel the malaise in many of our conversations with people from various walks of life. Even members of her close entourage were rumoured to be turning against the Prime Minister. The roles of the great powers were discussed in closed circles and in somewhat hushed tones. The USSR was seen as fully backing the "leftward" turn taken by India which was perhaps the greatest ally of the Soviet giant at the time while the USA had become Mrs Gandhi's bête noire and was accused of plotting to overthrow her rule and supporting her political adversaries. India's politics thus reflected the global cold war and it was said that the Prime Minister suspected the CIA of wanting to assassinate her. She relied on the advice of an inner circle of confidants and advisers, some of them members of her fairly pro-Soviet Congress Forum for Social Action. The group included her principal secretary PN Dhar and a few other of her Kashmiri "countrymen," her personal assistant R. K. Dhawan, her private secretary P. N. Haksar, an eminent left wing intellectual and administrator, V. C. Shukla one of her favourite ministers, I. K. Gujral who had just been appointed India's ambassador to Moscow and J. C. Kapur, Gujral's childhood friend, among others. Under their influence Nehru's daughter was inclined to steer the country away from the global financial and corporate influence of western powers and to seek an alternative, autarkic form of socialism. Her leanings had long set her against the once powerful "syndicate" which had controlled the Congress party after Nehru's demise and which was sympathetic to Washington DC. Unsurprisingly some of her main opponents, who were either in jail or under house arrest were members of that syndicate, such as Morarji Desai, a former Deputy Prime Minister and Finance Minister. However even in her family there was dissent. Sanjay was seen as rather hostile to leftist ideology and attracted to the American business and pop culture like most members of his generation. He was becoming the visible face of a younger faction in the government that balked at the cumbersome bureaucratic regulations of socialism and wanted change. His power over his mother who naturally idolized him made him a key factor in the evolution of the country and there was a widespread opinion that he wished to turn India into a presidential dictatorship of sorts, on the model of economically prosperous East Asian nations such as South Korea, Thailand and Taiwan. Nethertheless Mrs Gandhi's fear and resentment of the Americans prevented her from following that course and the head of the KGB Station at the Soviet Embassy, Leonid Shebarshin had both her ear and Chairman Brezhnev's trust so that there was an intense and confidential communication between the two governments.

To compensate for an increasing dependence on the USSR's support abroad, Mrs Gandhi cultivated her links with France and West Germany which had been damaged but not interrupted by the Emergency and she gave a high priority to the vast but inchoate Non Aligned Movement in which India played a predominant role.

We discussed the fast evolving situation with Indian politicians and public figures as well as with some foreign diplomats, such as the Count of Santovenia who was the Spanish Ambassador. An amiable gentleman of the old school who enjoyed his hunting trips in the wilds of India with blue blooded friends, he privately took a rather dim view of the leftist lurch of the country and predicted that the excesses of Emergency would bring about a rapid end to Congress rule. He was to be proved correct in January 1977 when Mrs Gandhi announced general elections and relaxed restrictions on her opponents in order to allow them to campaign. Reportedly she had been told that she would win with a large majority and thereby gain a new legitimacy for her economic policies. It is not known if her son Sanjay shared this optimistic and misinformed assessment, allegedly made by some of her close advisers, the Indian Left and even the Russian experts on India but at any rate, Indira had rejected the suggestions to change the regime on authoritarian lines.

We were exposed to many of the members of the exiguous ruling circle through our frequent presence at the India International Centre and the dinners we attended. We thus met some of the noted old Delhi families, the Bharat Rams, Charat Rams and Bansi Dars and we soon realized the permanence of the westernized educated elite at the centre of power, revolving around the Nehru dynasty. Despite his democratic credentials and the simplicity of his lifestyle Pandit Nehru was very much an heir of the culture of the British Raj and he felt most at home among his Indian and European peers. He also displayed a very atavistic degree of nepotism as he appointed several members of his immediate family to top positions in the Government and the diplomatic corps. In the fifties and sixties, India was ruled by an elected monarch and Indira Gandhi had been anointed as the crown princess according to her father's implicit will. She had kept the habit of entrusting key responsibilities to her relatives but found that some had turned against her, especially her father's favourite sister Vijayalakshmi Pandit. One eminent figure on the intellectual scene pointed out to us sarcastically how the Nehru kin occupied the top rungs of the power pyramid while the descendents and relatives of other stalwarts of the Independence struggle such as Gandhi, Subhash Chandra Bose, Patel and Rajgopalachari had been reduced to comparative insignificance.

During that period of social engagements we were granted an audience by the President of India and on the appointed day we drove up the steep Raisina hill to the imposing Rashtrapati Bhawan where, after passing the ornate wrought iron gates guarded by gurkha sentries, we alighted in one of the courtyards of the presidential palace. The architect, Lutyens had ambitioned to forge a new imperial Indian style by combining elements of early Buddhist architecture and mughal aesthetics although he claimed to despise most of India's artistic creations. His own taste for austere grandeur led him to design a peculiar hybrid of the Spanish Escorial and a Turkic royal mausoleum which now rises broodingly above the central Delhi skyline. Led by a gold braided ADC through the succession of vaulted corridors and stately halls that still resonated with dim echoes of the British Raj's pageants, we were ushered into the yellow drawing room where the president, clad in white and wearing the Gandhi cap greeted us with the courteous and impassive dignity that often distinguishes the Muslim nobility.

He was from a notable family of Assam in the North East of the country and we were aware that his religious and geographical background, coupled with a long career in government, had been a key factor in his selection. Mrs Gandhi trusted that old Cambridge-educated colleague of her father in the Independence struggle who had practiced law at the Inner Temple Bar and he had indeed supported her by promptly signing the decree proclaiming the emergency.

In the ensuing conversation he told us that he regarded himself as a product of India's composite culture as his mother hailed from the border of Punjab and Rajasthan. We learnt later that she was a daughter of a ruling prince descended from Afghan warlords. Thus, like many aristocrats, the president had a mixed ancestry and spoke various languages. On his father's side there was a distant Persian origin as well although his forebears had mingled their blood with the local population.

While we drank tea in exquisite porcelain cups my father told him about our expedition to India by road and explained our campaign for the revaluation of the dharma, in its universal, trans-religious significance. The president was intrigued by our long stays in Turkey, Iran and Afghanistan and asked us a few questions on our impressions about the situation of those states. He was more reserved on the issue of Dharma which he probably did not wish to comment upon. It was not the first time that we noticed the feeling among Muslims that Dharma is a Hindu religious notion tied to a specific pre-islamic heritage that they had been taught to regard as pagan. However Fakhruddin Ahmed acknowledged that Sufis had often bridged the gap that separated their faith from the other traditions of the country.

He wished us well in our travels when we took leave and looking at him one last time I noticed that he seemed frail. He had a heart condition which brought about his untimely death less than four months later. Although he was regarded as a pliable president and disliked by many for his role during the Emergency, I remember him as a gentleman whose manners and demeanour denoted the qualities of an old world that was rapidly fading away.

We spent the Christmas and New Year eves at the houses of foreign diplomats. We became good friends of Isabel Alvarez, the secretary of the Spanish Embassy and her husband Nizar El Kadi, a former Ambassador of Iraq who gave beautiful parties in their home in Sujan Singh Park, attended by sundry maharajas, cabinet ministers, foreign envoys and other distinguished representatives of

Delhi society. Another diplomat posted in Delhi's Embassy of Spain was Mariluz Jardiel, the somewhat bohemian daughter of the famous writer Jardiel Poncela. In January 1977 we went to the University of Kurukshetra not far from Delhi where we had been invited by the head of the department of philosophy, Professor Sinha.

LAND OF THE MAHABHARATA

Kurukshetra is a hallowed place in India and can compare with holy cities such as Jerusalem or Bodh Gaya in terms of its spiritual importance for a very large section of mankind. The atmosphere of the town is steeped in sacredness since the mighty eighteen day Mahabharata battle was fought between the armies of most Indian kingdoms more than five thousand years ago, according to traditional chronology. One is quickly taken by the peaceful, semi-pastoral atmosphere of the countryside which was known for innumerable centuries as *dharmakshetra,* the field of the divine law and as *vara a prithvya,* the best place on earth or *nabhaprithvi,* the earth's navel. In the Vedic era it was irrigated by one of the affluents of the mighty, long dried out Saraswati river, the Apaya where the Arya tribes celebrated their main oblations to the fire. Although modern historians still subscribe to the 19th century theory of an Aryan invasion from Afghanistan in antiquity, Max Muller could not help notice even then that the Rig Veda retraces an expansion of the Aryas towards the West from that heartland also known as *Ila.* When we went there archaeological research was being carried out around Kurukshetra while the erstwhile courses of the Saraswati and its lost affluents, the Apaya, the Drisadvati and the Hakra were being plotted.

The ancient battlefield and the modern town are named after the clan of the Kurus to which the leaders of the two camps in the war belonged. It was a fratricidal struggle within the most prominent royal tribe in Northern India. According to the oldest annals, the Kurus came from the mountains in the North (*kuru* means mountain and has become *gora* in slav languages and *oros* in greek) and married by tradition women from the kingdoms of Madra and Gandhara, both now in Pakistan. They had apparently mingled their blood with the ancient Puru and Pancala tribes, indigenous to the Saraswati region while retaining the memory of their origins in the northern land of the blessed in Uttarakuru, beyond the Hindu Kush in Central Asia where the Kura river has perhaps kept their name. They may have been "Indo-Aryan" Tokharians from the area which is now populated by various Turkic tribes, between the Pamir plateau, today's Kazakh plains and the Tien Shan range, a region that Roman geographers including Pliny call *Ottorokorai.*

The Rig Veda sings the victorious campaign of King Mandhata who conquered the "four great islands" in the North and returned with a large following of Uttarakurus long before the era of the two great epics. It seems that those were the ancestors of the Kauravas who struck an alliance with their victors and eventually succeeded them. The part of Jambudvipa or India where they settled became known as Kururastra and it may not be a coincidence that the Sumerians said they came from Kura Aratta, a highland lying behind seven mountain ranges to the North East, either in the Punjab or in the valley of the Kura and Araxes in Central Asia.

The *Mahabharata* is not the only text which indicates that in that area of Bactria and Transoxiana also lived a tribe made up or at least ruled by warrior women. The *Strirajya* (women's kingdom) appears to be the cradle of the Amazons who rode into Asia Minor and the Hellenic peninsula centuries later and were, according to the Greeks an Indo-Iranian speaking people. Their queen when they conquered Athens was called Panthesilea which may be a greek spelling for *Panchashila,* the "five principles" that regulated the conduct of various Central Asian and Himalayan peoples even before the advent of Buddhism which adopted them.

According to those diverse but generally convergent stories, the Kurus were a vedic matrilineal polygamous and polyandric clan related to the neighbouring Bahlikas, Kambojas, Daradas and Rishikas and descended from Prajapati Karddama and his son Ila. The Ili river in the region of the Uighur still keeps the trace of that name, as do the "Iranian" Alani, and the peaks of the Pamir may have been the Meru of Vedic mythology. However even before some moved to India, the Tocharian Kurus, probably related to the so-called Andronovo culture, appear to have been kinsmen of the Puru-Bharatas and other *pancha janas* of India and were therefore not invading Aryans. Indeed had they not created in their Central Asian home a colony of the original *Ilavarta* as many Indian traditional scholars affirm?

In modern archaeology that "Outer Indo-Aryan land" is called the Bactria-Margiana Archeological Complex or BMAC. Another branch of that federation went south west and gave their name to Khurasan (kurasthana) and Iran (Aryana) where one of their descendents Kurush or Cyrus founded the first Persian empire.

Most 19th century European indologists, steeped in biblical lore would not seriously consider the possibility that human history might be older than the dates assigned in Genesis to the creation of the earth. They tried to fit the Vedas and the Indian epics in the fifteen hundred years which in their assumptions separated the arrival of the conquering Aryans into India from the dawn of the Christian era. For that purpose, they discarded traditional native chronologies as our scholarly host, professor Sinha pointed out and assumed that the great battle of the *Mahabharata* could not have taken place many centuries before Alexander's invasion. They cited as proof the pervasive presence of horse drawn chariots and iron (*shyamayas* or dark metal) in the epic and assumed that only a primitive culture could have existed in the ages before the nomadic warring Aryans brought a higher civilization from Central Asia.

Many data stand in contradiction to that "official" interpretation of the past. The discovery of long abandoned urban settlements that are more than four or five millennia old has evinced the presence of a sophisticated and well organized society and the very ancient use of copper and bronze long before iron was cast and steel was invented. Although horses seem to have been introduced later since their remains or representations have not been found in those protohistoric cities the Vedas celebrate them with great frequency and there is reason to believe that ancient Indians domesticated the native wild ass or onager locally known as *gur* that still survives in the wild in

Gujarat and whose name in my view is still echoed in the castilian name for the animal: burro.

The *Mahabharata* says that horses come from Sindh, which can mean either the western province of that name or the ocean (sindhu) with which the animal is symbolically associated in India as in Greece. Therefore the battle could have taken place as early as the third or fourth millennium before the common era in a region that was already densely populated and civilized although the story was gradually enlarged during centuries until it became the gigantic saga that has come to us with its eighteen sections and hundred thousand stanzas.

It must have been a defining battle even if millions of soldiers from all over India and Asia did not participate and die in it as the poem alleges. It is said to have brought about immense destruction and devastated Northern Indian civilization, ushering in the beginning of the fourth and darkest age of history, the Kali Yuga.

It is significant that from about 1900 BC according to the findings of the last several decades, the cities of the Saraswati and Indus valley abruptly decayed and were abandoned, partly as a result of environmental changes including earthquakes and the drying out of rivers but also perhaps because of a great war that depleted the population. India's collective memory kept a vivid record of that disaster and seems to have developed as a result the aversion to violence and the quest for otherworldly truth so marked in later Hinduism, Buddhism and Jainism. It is hence impossible not to view the Kurukshetra war as a historical event comparable in its significance and effects to the first and second world wars for our modern world and nowhere does the battlefield evoke this titanic struggle between rival factions of the ruling clans of the heroic age better than in the spot where Sri Krishna, the divine and royal adviser of the Pandavas taught his divine song, the *Bhagavad Gita* to his friend and protégé Arjuna.

We spent some thoughtful and inspiring moments in the shadow of the sacred tree that stands over the space consecrated by tradition. Faith lends a greater reality to what one sees than mere material certainty. The Gita is a stupendous document, which seems to combine the styles and contents of the Iliad, Plato's Dialogues and the *Visio Johannis.* It summarises the Dharma in its three dimensions as action, devotion and wisdom that it unifies in yoga. Sri Krishna who is at once the king of the Yadavas, the incarnation of Vishnu and the charioteer and adviser of Arjuna gave to India on this blood drenched field a Gospel which has defined its permanent identity and shaped its civilization ever since, despite innumerable invasions, religious and political turmoil, economic changes and cultural evolution.

If the *Mahabharata* seems to encompass all the legends and myths known to mankind at one time or another and to provide an exhaustive description of Indian civilization as it unfolded and transformed over several centuries, the *Bhagavad Gita* as its crown jewel directs our gaze upwards towards the transcendent and the eternal even when it tells us to continue the daily fight for existence which is both a game and a play since it is ultimately a figment of the cosmic imagination. Krishna's message is a Gospel to the epic's Old Testament. It acknowledges the feudal and traditional conventions that the larger work illustrates and prescribes but surpasses them by disclosing the invisible essence that lies beneath the veil of existence and thereby dispensing the only real freedom, the inner spiritual one of which the political and social symbols are only empty forms.

The following is perhaps the most important and simplest message it addresses to all in all times and places:

> "Who is contented with whatever he gets
> without having sought it, free from negativity and envy,
> balanced in success and failure,
> even though he is acting, is not bound by his actions."

Another feature of the Gita that I find deeply appealing to our western "indo-european" sensibilities, especially for one familiar with the poetic traditions of romance languages is that it is written, like much of Sanskrit sacred literature in the *anustubh shloka* format resuscitated in the Italian and French octosyllabic quatrain. If the *jagati* verse's twelve syllables found in other poems have their equivalent in the French alexandrine, some of the more vehement passages of Krishna's Song follow the vedic *tristubh* structure, a forerunner of the Spanish hendecasyllabic four verse stanza. In another register, the two tercets of the romance octosyllabic sonnet have a metric form similar to the *gayatri* verse which gives its name to the most important mantra of the Vedic creed. The persistence of those rhythmic patterns indicates their organic connection to the deep structure of classical languages from the Ganges to the Tiber. If the Malaysian pantom, itself of Sanskrit origin, was adopted by the European Romantics, could the troubadours and their successors in the *dolce stil nuovo* not have borrowed centuries earlier some poetic conventions from the East?

LOST SECRETS OF THE PAST

Apart from the metaphysical dimension which enables the spiritually inclined reader to see in the *Mahabharata* an allegory of the cosmic cycle of life and death, there are many factual and technical descriptions which surprise our contemporaries by their apparent anachronism. Even if we accept that the original story was modified and added to as late as in the medieval age, the multiple references to what can only be called modern or science fiction weaponry seem strangely out of place in a society that did not know gunpowder or firearms. The scale of the death and destruction wrought by the opposing armies is also stunning, even if one allows for the Indian tendency to exaggerate everything in works of imagination. How could a supposedly pastoral culture made up of small kingdoms even conceive of conflicts on such a scale, involving vast armies from as far away as Southern India and today's Turkestan?

We had an occasion to discuss this subject with some of the faculty of the university, a few of whom were erudite and enthusiastic researchers on the national epic.

"Our grandparents and even traditionally educated Hindus today have no problem accepting the story as more or less literal truth" one of the professors pointed out. "In Indian thought, there are three fields of reality, the human one which deals with the here and now, the divine sphere that encompasses eternal conditions and the realm of the *pitris* or ancestors to which history pertains. It is the world of the dead and we believe that what exists now or will in the future also existed many times before because of the timelessness of being or nature."

"In vedic civilisation, people lived not only in the material visible field" another scholar stated. "They were trained to see the astral and spiritual aspects of life so that events to them had many more dimensions than those we are scientifically and consciously aware of."

The word "astral" naturally brought us to the Sanskrit *astra* which meant weapon and gave the word "astrum" in latin that alludes to all celestial bodies. The astra of the *Mahabharata* are described as airborne arms or mentally triggered phenomena endowed with enormous destructive capacity. Some, like the *agneya,* the *indravajra* and the *brahmastra* look like modern ICBMs and other missiles carrying huge explosive charges or like high power laser-shooting guns. Others such as the *varunavastra* and the *vayavastra* would qualify today as weather or climate modifying weapons while the *asurastra,* the *sammohana* and the *nagastra* meet the definition of chemical and biological armaments. Finally the *bhaumastra* is an earth digging and tunneling device which anticipates recent achievements in the technology of burrowing tunnels at high speed by the US military industrial complex.

Many of those super-weapons are said to remain under the control of their masters until they reach their targets and others are described as having an intelligence of their own, similar to the most advanced computerized missiles while others still are guided by sound towards targets that have made themselves invisible. The concept of stealth technology at least was explored by the contemporaries of that ancient war.

When I recall this conversation now, I realize that in that year 1977, artificial intelligence and cybernetics were far from what has now been achieved in those areas. As we develop technically, the descriptions provided by the Indian texts are becoming less mysterious and more understandable, at least in a literal sense.

Victorian age indologist could be forgiven for concluding that ancient Indian poets were writing under the effect of hallucinogenic drugs in view of the, to them utterly incredible performances of the machines they depicted.

My father however saw the obvious contradiction between the alleged existence of that space age arsenal and the continued use of traditional hand held arms which the knights of Europe continued to wield until the 17th century. "The double edged battle axe, the mace, the javelin, the straight and curved sword and the bow and arrow were the essential tools in battle for the *Mahabharata* soldiers as they were many centuries later in medieval wars across Europe and West Asia" he recalled. "Yet their use would not have been possible had terrifying weapons of mass destruction been in the hands of the leaders of those armies. They did not survive long the appearance of firearms in the West. In France they are still called "white arms" (armes blanches) as they were known to the chivalrous caste of yore that distinguished them from the dark creations of the gunsmiths, long seen as practitioners of the Devil's craft."

"We still say 'forgery" in English to qualify a counterfeit work" noted someone in the group. "In India as always we see both sides. The smiths and metalworkers are not all bad, some are devas like Visvakarma or Tvastir and others, Maya for instance are asuras and there is still a tribe of ironsmiths in India called the Asurs. It all depends what use is made of those inventions. Many divine weapons are said to be only usable for upholding Dharma and they don't perform when summoned for an unrighteous purpose. However it is also intriguing that the effects of certain weapons on living beings and the environment are described as if they had resulted from a nuclear explosion or from the use of a biological weapon. How did Vyasa or whoever wrote this know of such results which are far from obvious and could not easily be imagined without having witnessed their impact?"

"Notice the case of the *Narayanastra,* the huge "bomb" of Vishnu which supposedly releases five million projectiles on its target, as if it were a multi-headed missile or MIRV. The only defence against it is total submission. If an army drops its weapons and lies on the ground, the astra is harmless. Is this not a striking allegory of the power of non-violent resistance? I think mahatma Gandhi was inspired by the image." This thoughtful comment was made by Professor Sinha and we were struck by his insightfulness.

The enigma of India's epic literature was not to be demystified in our debate. There is a tradition pertaining to the use of an advanced and powerful military technology which pervades Vyasa's colossal poem, whether it was inherited from older texts and integrated with the story of ancient war fought with more primitive means or whether it was added later to the core story by narrators who had witnessed or read about secret devices that are frequently alluded to in Hindu, Buddhist and Jain literature throughout many centuries. Orthodox scholars continue to assume that the astras, yantras and vimanas are imaginary objects inspired by natural phenomena but that explanation is not entirely convincing and was crafted ad hoc by rationalistic western historians and linguists unfamiliar with technology and prejudiced against the "fantastic claims of the Hindoos."

Skepticism is commonly misused. It should reflect a critical ability of the mind to assess the merit of an information or opinion and not amount to a rejection of what one is not in a position to understand for lack of background and context.

After delivering a few lectures that were inevitably inspired by the hallowed resonance of the Lord's Song, we returned to Delhi carrying the memory of the tree lined swaying wheat, mustard and safflower fields in that plain, drenched in the blood of so many mythical heroes, which a hymn of the Rig Veda celebrates thus, many centuries before Jehovah told Moses about "streams flowing with milk and honey":

Sarasvati sarayuh sindhururmibhirmaho mahiravasa yantu vaksanih

Devirupo natarah sudayitno ghrtavat payo madhuman no Arcata (RV, X-66-9)

"May the very great rivers Sarasvati, Sarayu, Sindhu come with their waves. For our protection may the divine maternal animating streams grant us their water mixed with butter and honey."

XIV

Echoes of the Holy City

SUNRISE ON THE GANGES

A purple dawn surrounded us when we alighted from a rickshaw in the premises of the Theosophical Society in Benares. The copper disk of the sky, Etasa the vedic stallion rose above the river, turning its dull bronze into rippling silver as the last stars flickered away in the fading gloom of the celestial vault: the Sanskrit parama vyoman.

Still drowsy from a night journey on the train I dimly felt why the Vedas call the atmosphere rajas, reddish darkness and why the solar god is Pusan, the good shepherd and hiranyahamsa, the golden swan or goose which is also the heart in us and as matarisvan brings down to earth the heavenly fire. Indeed the Sun seemed to be reborn in the river as it shimmered and I had a fleeting illustration of the hoary symbol of apam napat (fire as an offspring of water). A long standing dream finally rubbed off the clouds of sluggishness from my mind as I beheld the Ganges in its full glory: yasas, a word still sounding in the greek greeting and in the name of a forgotten celtic deity echoed in the original name of Jesus, Ieshue.

Above the silent flow the bridge built by the British government in the previous century despite widespread local outrage, rose in steely defiance of the sacred water. The mighty stream had calmly ignored that sacrilegious structure, so powerless are the works of men to disturb the divine heart of nature.

We were unexpectedly greeted by a guest of the TS whom we had met in Madras, Baron Porcelli who often travelled in India in pursuit of his philosophical and religious interests. Eager to explore the mysteries of the holy city we found out that another familiar figure from Adyar, Radha Burnier was also staying at Varanasi and we had lunch with her on that day. She was the daughter of Rukmini Devi's brother, Sri Ram who had been president of the Theosophical Society. She had also married very young a wealthy European, the photographer Raymond Burnier, an heir of the NESTLÉ fortune, settled in India since 1938 who was a friend of the film director Jean Renoir and the musicologist Alain Danielou, a brother of the noted Catholic theologian, cardinal and archbishop of Paris, practically converted to the Hindu way of life. Together that trio was in the middle decades of the twentieth century the nucleus of a circle of talented Indophiles who spent time in an old palace on the banks of the Ganga. Renoir made his film "Le Fleuve" in 1949, based on a novel by Rumer Godden and it was awarded the Golden Lion trophy in Venice. We had been told that Radha's marriage had been unhappy because of her husband's other sentimental attachments and there was an edge in her demeanour and a sadness in her expression which betrayed that wound. She was a remarkably intelligent and cultured woman but her relations with her aunt had been icy for years. We assumed that envy of the more famous and artistically successful Rukmini Devi might have been the cause of that antipathy.

So lasting are first aesthetic experiences that the name Ganges still evoked in me reminiscences of those vast ceiling frescoes in German and Italian baroque palaces in which the holy river of India is evoked as one of the four streams of the biblical world in the garb of a copper-hued maiden surrounded by crocodiles, elephants and tigers. The exoticism of the imagination is very remote from the real strangeness of unfamiliar lands and the amphitheater of mankind that Kashi, the city of light spreads out before its everflowing liquid spectator has no equivalent anywhere on earth.

After a brief stay at the Theosophical Society we moved to the sprawling campus of Benares Hindu University, another institution partly inspired by theosophists in the spirit of native renaissance promoted by its founder Pandit Malaviya. I instantly felt a home in that park-like environment whose mostly ochre and pink buildings, constructed in a neo-mughal style are in visual harmony with the lush landscape.

The guest house was simple and pleasant in the midst of a manicured garden whose huge multicoloured dahlias, shaped like fireworks of petals, we tirelessly admired. We gave several lectures in a number of departments and met some eminent scholars including Professor A L Basham, the author of "The Glory that was India" after attending his talk. Since years he taught at the Australian national University and often came to India where he was an illustrious figure. I remember that we talked about Swami Vivekananda as we knew of his keen interest in that hallowed personality whose work he had studied at length. He thought that by reviving the spiritual conversation between East and West at a high intellectual level the Bengali activist monk had heralded a new era of civilizational synthesis that would continue to unfold during decades to come.

THE WEB OF TANTRA

Dr Alex Wayman, an authority on Buddhist philosophy from Columbia University was for a few days a neighbor at the guesthouse with his Japanese wife Hideko who participated in his research work. One of his salient books is "Introduction to Buddhist Tantras" which had come out a few years before our meeting. His area of particular interest was the history of Buddhist theories of logic but he said that he had retained from youth a fascination for the tantric literature which seems to have developed in many parts of India from undefined antiquity since it is rooted in the shamanistic traditions of the subcontinent and of greater Asia.

One can notice references to Tantric symbols and rituals in parts of the Vedas and the followers of the Buddha soon embraced its iconography and metaphysics in their own practices and teachings. Thus Buddhist and Hindu Tantra cross-fertilized and often mingled as the cosmology and theology remain related in spite of evolving variations. Tantra means weave, loom, web, method, strategy, technique for transcending the conditions of the mind and body and many other things, depending upon the context. Sanskrit is a network of relations and the words in it are active, evolving notions that constantly mutate depending upon their place in a given process, like the neurons and dendrites in the brain or the genes and viruses in biology. Now that we understand symbolic logic as a fractal mode of communication in which every image or gesture is a composite array of intersubjective signals we know why sanskrit provides a most suitable template for computer languages and Tantra combines syllables (mantras), precise gestures (mudras), positions (asanas), geometric figures (yantras and mandalas) and breathing patterns (pranayama) to channel and focus the mind towards the realization of its own transcendent inner nature or, as accessories, the mastery of supernatural powers.

We had various conversations with the Waymans over breakfast before going to our respective assignments. We discussed the lives and characters of various orientalists, many of whom he had personally known such as H. Nakajima, D.T. Suzuki and my heroes Coomaraswamy and Alan Watts. Wayman was impish and a bit sardonic like a Rinzai zen Roshi and he had kept the dark jewish sense of humour consonant with the Buddhist salve of detachment. "The tantras are like the waves of an ocean, he observed once, they keep hitting the shore of your mind, one after another and it never ends because most are huge, there are thousands and they all, in spite of the sheer complexity of their teachings, reinforce the same feeling in you: the unity of all things within a transcendent and radical consciousness."

Wayman had been studying the Buddhist Tantra tradition, also known as Vajrayana for three decades but he acknowledged that he had only grazed the surface of that seemingly bottomless corpus that had been created since a king of Shambhala in today's Orissa in Eastern India had authored the *Jnana Siddhi* not long after the Buddha had left his body, if tradition is to be believed. From that hazy origin, thousands of scriptures, mostly written in sanskrit, had circulated and sown their seeds all over the subcontinent and beyond, in Sogdian, Tocharian, Tibetan, Mongol, Chinese, Javanese, Khmer and Japanese translations all across Asia, possibly inspiring or influencing gnostic schools of thought on the Mediterranean shores as well. Some accounts held that there were tens of millions of Tantric liberated masters or Siddhas while the Tibetan Vajrayana hagiology records eighty four mahasiddhas, hailing from all parts of India and Tibet.

Another eminent mind we met in the University was professor TRV Murti whose major work, "The Central Philosophy of Buddhism," dedicated to Nagarjuna's *madhyamika* metaphysics I had read with great attention as my father regarded it as one of the best expositions of the Mahayana's understanding of reality. Murti's great merit was to have freed the Buddhist notion of universal negation from the nihilistic interpretations that mostly western students had given it. As he put it to us: "Buddhism in its essence is deconstructionistic but not nihilistic. It merely shows that reality is not describable by discursive logic nor by any mathematical or other rational means. Wittgenstein came to the same conclusion in our century. It can only be synthesized in the silence of meditation, not analyzed in speech or writing. All we can do is point to it." He felt that inevitably natural sciences were reaching the same realization and he has since then been proven right again and again, in physics as in cosmology and biology.

The head of the Music School of the University was Professor Gautam whom we had met at the end of a recital he had given at the Friends of India auditorium in Spain and he invited us to speak to his students on the philosophical roots of Indian musicology. We also attended a few concerts by the faculty and visiting musicians which made me more familiar with the Hindustani and Northern style, quite different from the Carnatic tradition I had studied at Kalakshetra. The dreamy drone of the tambura kept the pitch for the fevered or languid flights of the sitar or the sarod whose strings shiver under fluttering fingers like the wings of frantic birds in a silver cage. There is a resonance of eternity in the melodies that unfold, dissect and recompose the ragas as a carpet weaver knits together into geometric and floral designs the tense strands of his loom.

EAST OF EDEN

One of my talks was delivered in the department of ancient history and archaeology, headed by Professor Lallanji Gopal, a well known academic and an authority of topics as diverse as the history of Indian ancient agriculture and the "structuralist" Samkhya philosophy. I spoke on my research regarding the connections between various early historic peoples and places of India and of the Near and Middle East, with particular emphasis on Syria and Assyria and with regard to the countless Vedic and Puranic references to Suras and Asuras.

I recalled that, although no definite conclusion has been reached regarding the origins of the noun *sur* or *asur* it is generally held to mean "mighty" in ancient Sanskrit and applied to all the gods especially to the personified Sun Surya whereas Ashur was the ruling deity of the eponymous city that in turn gave its name to a kingdom and its people. It allegedly signified "overseer" and applied to other immortals as well. Syria owes its name to the same root, perhaps through the Surri or Hurrite peoples who invaded it from the East and the port-city of Tyre was called "Sur" in the local languages. The Sanskrit Surya is Hvar in Old Iranian which may be the same as Hurr.

I pointed to the solar connection of the radical in both language families (Indo-European and Semitic) and proposed that the names had a common origin in India and in West Asia as the abundant evidence of very old relations between the two regions by land and sea suggests. Long before the documented rise of "Indo-Iranian" cultures, represented by the Hittite and Mitannian peoples in Mesopotamia and Asia Minor in the eighteenth century BCE there was a robust commercial and intellectual intercourse between the Tigris-Euphrates valley and the Indus-Sarasvati area.

In the last section of the lecture I recalled how the asuras who acquired negative traits in the later Indian mythological context remained the chief deities of the Persians who turned the devas into fallen angels in an interesting case of "mirror inversion." I mentioned the lord of darkness of the Zoroastrians, Ahriman or Angra Mainyu, a forerunner of the Hebrew and Christian Satan and ventured to say that this king of the demons, *daevanam daeva* who has no real equivalent in Indian mythology may be an Iranian derivate from Angiras Manas. Angiras is the first Rishi who learnt from Atharvan the science of Brahman, the ultimate knowledge. He is said to have composed the fourth Veda and one of the most important books of the first one, the Rig Veda. His name means "breath" in Sanskrit, like *angelos* is "wind" in greek. Thus Angra Mainyu is the mind of breath and he evokes the vedic Varuna who is the lord of the *asuras*, like Ahriman is the prince of the daevas. The divergent evolution of the theology reflects the gradual estrangement of the Persian Aryans from their Indo-Gangetic cousins.

The presentation was well received and led to a lively debate which evinced the divide between the westernized historians, reluctant to admit strong connections between distant ancient nations and the more traditionally minded Indians who, in the spirit of global unity promoted by their philosophies, enthusiastically supported the concept of a universal Sanskrit civilization. Lallanji Gopal who was in the chair pointed out that the asuras are said in some scriptures to owe their name to the fact that, contrary to the devas or suras, they rejected the *sura*, the intoxicating drink concocted for the vedic *sautramani* ritual sacrifice and which gradually lost its importance to the soma that became a synonym of amrta, the elixir of immortality known as ambrosia by the ancient Greeks. A professor in the audience recalled that various "heretical" movements are attested in remote antiquity. For example, Vena, a grandson of the vedic rishi Atri who is called the first king of the world in some scriptures, became a Jain and, after being dethroned to the benefit of his son Prithu, retired as an ascetic on the banks of the Narmada in the Deccan. As such he is judged unfavourably in the later orthodox Hindu records but his story evinces both the great antiquity of the Jain faith, affirmed by its followers, and its rivalry with the Vedic tradition.

Forty years later it is even more obvious that for many thousands of years peoples, languages and cultures periodically if not constantly mingled and borrowed from one another across Eurasia, particularly between the Mediterranean and the Indian Ocean.

THE KASHIRAJ AND THE PURANAS

I had naturally invoked the Puranas at various stages of the lecture and in a subsequent conversation, Dr Gopal advised us to meet the Maharaja of Benares who had founded an institute of research on that huge collection of texts that embrace mythology, history, social and political sciences as well as many other topics. It was not the first time that we had been given this suggestion and we soon called on Kashi Raj or "the king of light" who is regarded as one of the essential keepers of the Hindu religious culture since the first such monarch, Divodasa, said to be a reincarnation of the patron saint of medicine Dhanvantari founded the holy city.

We crossed the shaky pontoon bridge that leads from the Tulsi Ghat to the suburb of Ramnagar where the vast 18th century fortified palace of the maharaja stands. King Balwant Singh who built it on the very spot where Vyasa is held to have divided the Veda into four, was the son of great Brahmin landlord who had recreated the long defunct kingdom of Kashi with the support of the British East India Company by acquiring cities and lands from the chronically bankrupt Nawabs of Oudh, the titular viceroys of the mughal Emperors. Balwant Singh and his successors had restored the city to its former glory as the beating heart of Brahmanical scholarship while enhancing its material prosperity. Even though the rapacious Warren Hastings had confiscated most of their possessions and deprived them of their political power by 1781, the maharajas of Benares had retained their prestige and authority and the current holder of the title, Vibhuti Narain Singh continued the tradition of his ancestors. He received us in a majestic room, adorned with crystal chandeliers and the usual panoplies of exotic weapons and towering royal portraits. He himself walked in escorted by a small liveried retinue holding the ceremonial fly whisks made from yak tails and the royal *chhatra* or umbrella above his heat, covered with a gold embroidered bonnet. He was a portly bespectacled man who had the slightly awkward and restless demeanour of an absent minded savant.

Having expected a prince clad in a three piece suit or worse, we were delighted by that noble sight and duly paid our respects. We were offered the customary tea, cakes and sweets while His Highness asked us some questions about our travels and interests. When he knew that we had drive across Asia in a expedition called "Dharma," he beamed that his ancestor had resurrected the hoary Dharma Sabha of which he was the living custodian as well as the head trustee of the Kashi Vishwanath Temple, the most sacred in the city, the seat of one of the twelve Jyortilingas (pillars of light) of Shiva . Tradition even saw him as the embodiment of the God of Kailash. He seemed fidgety and was often distracted by the other people in the room but kept on the conversation after each sudden pause as if nothing had happened.

"This palace contains a temple to Shiva built by Vyasa himself" he said. "This is the cradle of the Vedic Dharma and all the wisdom and history of mankind is recorded here" he added.

Noticing my remarks on aspects of Hinduism and local history the maharaja was kind enough to point at me with an amused smile and proffer: "This young man knows a lot about our culture. You are very smart." Before I could utter words of self deprecation the author of the praise was engaging in an aside with a passing secretary.

That fragmented chat led to an invitation to visit the Puranas Research Institute and the maharaja summoned some of the scholars in-house at the time who joined us promptly. One of them, Father Giorgio Bonazzoli was an Italian who, led by his passion for India and guided by our admired friend from Barcelona, Raimondo Panikkar, had thoroughly embraced the way of life and the culture of the place and we quickly sympathized. In that group we evoked aspects of the history of the Gangetic plain which had very early been ruled by the Ikshvaku Solar dynasty of Kosala, even older than the lines of Bharatas and Kauravas in the Sarasvati region and regarded as the first one in Jambudviva since its founder was the eldest son of the "first man" of the present era or kalpa, Manu Vaivasvata.

Puru's father king Yayati ruled from Pratishtana which is now Allahabad and other monarchs of Kosala, Trisanku and Sagara had victoriously battled their western cousins. A king of Kashi had fought in the Mahabharata war on the side of the Pandavas who were his cousins on the maternal side like their Kaurava foes. The maharaja held the ancestral belief that the Vedas which had been composed originally in Brahmavarta, the cradle of the *pancajanas*—the five original tribes—had been recovered and arranged in their present order by Vyasa (a lineage and a function and not a personal name) on the shores of the Ganges in the beginning of Kali Yuga when Varanasi had replaced Kurukshetra as the spiritual centre of India after the devastation wrought by the great war. Vyasa and his six main helpers had also recovered and rearranged the Puranas into the order in which they are known.

"This is the mystical axis of India, His Highness pointed out. It is the focus of the Hindu, Buddhist and Jain faiths. Even the Sikh gurus had strong bonds to Kashi. So many invaders tried to wipe out the Dharma by destroying temples and killing or expelling priests and Brahmins. Yet they were rebuilt and we have twenty three thousand Hindu mandirs within the city. Aurangzeb pulled down Kashi Vishwanath, broke the jyotirlinga, threw the pieces into the well of wisdom and built his mosque in its place. He changed Varanasi's name to Muhammadabad. Yet even this most powerful emperor failed. The temple was rebuilt just around the mosque, the linga was retrieved from the well and nobody took to the new name, not even Muslims." The maharaja ended the sentence with a delighted smile.

We returned to the Puranic institute in the following days and were shown some ancient manuscripts of those venerable texts which contain vast amounts of information on all aspects of India's history, popular traditions, religion and civilization. They represent, in the eyes of many scholars, the collection of knowledge retrieved from earlier and now lost documents by *Sutas*, royal chroniclers and archivists, traditionally born from Brahmin mothers and ksatriya fathers and as such belonging to a sixth varna (*anuloma* since their mothers ranked socially above their fathers) whose role it was to disseminate knowledge to the general population and especially to the military and merchant aristocracy. Accordingly Puranas tend to be couched in the form of a dialogue in which the answers are often provided by Lomaharsana, Vyasa's amanuensis and successor. There are eighteen surviving ones and they are separated into three groups, respectively affiliated to Vishnu, Shiva and Shakti, corresponding to the three main categories of living Hinduism and also symbolically to the three *dosas* or principles of reality, representing the concepts of energy, density and transcendence through harmony.

Like all things in India, they are enormous and the surviving material amounts to four hundred thousand shlokas or quatrains, some of which are repeated in more than one Purana but are said to be the remains of at least ten million stanzas, most of which were lost due to human or natural causes along many centuries.

The researchers who investigated those arcane books and published their findings in a dedicated, locally printed journal had many things of interest to say, complementing what we knew from our readings of Wilson and other orientalists. Puranas were written in many places since the remotest times and were periodically updated and expanded to reflect more recent events so that dating them is extremely difficult. Some are said to have originated in earlier historical cycles or kalpas so that they contain elements that are allegedly millions of years old, according to the Indian cosmological concept of an endless series of eras or *manvantaras* in which the same characters reappear to play the same role in the innumerable performances of the same play, each of whose versions varies slightly from all others however since nothing is ever identical to anything else.

A few Puranas are dedicated to predicting the future, a choice topic of India literature but curiously many of those texts, though listed in the tables of contents are now missing whereas some visible later interpolations trying to pass for predictions describe the various Muslim invasions, the arrival of Europeans and even the rule of Queen Victoria. The Bhavisya (future) Purana for one mentions the Biblical account of man's creation in Genesis and the first Hebrew prophets and alludes to a "blond, white clad" wise man in the Himalayas who has been regarded by some Christians as Jesus. The Matsya is famous for its description of the great flood from which Manu, the first man is saved by Vishnu who tells him to build an ark and then, in the form of a swordfish pulls the ship, laden with the seeds of all living things on earth to the polar mountain where the father of the future humanity disembarks and waits for the water to recede. This story that connects the "first ancestor" of India's race to the biblical Nuh or Noah has aroused an unsettled discussion about the origin of the diluvial legend. There is no doubt that the Matsya Purana is very ancient since the *Mahabharata* refers to it but the biblical story is borrowed from sumero-chaldean records and all that can be said is that many mythical traditions are shared between the Mesopotamian and Indo-Gangetic civilizations. In India there are sundry mentions of giant floods one of which must have resulted, twelve thousand years ago, from the post-glacial melting of polar ice caps and the consequent rise of ocean levels and some populations existing at the time are said to have taken refuge in the Himalayas

Since they were in part composed for the benefit of kings and noblemen Puranas contain exhaustive but often unverifiable genealogies of dynasties going all the way back to mythical origins and also many chapters on *Rajniti*, the science of ruling a state as well as religious prescriptions, descriptions of great sanctuaries, pilgrimage places and holy spots. Innumerable allegoric stories and symbolic icons that surface in many other parts of the world are also enshrined in the Puranas. Analogies have been drawn with early Christian texts, inspired by Manichean and other esoteric orientalising sources and certain archetypes of famous legends are easy to find. The blood of Vishnu fallen in the skull cup of Siva of the Padma Purana evokes images of the Holy Grail while the thunderbolt of Indra is a cross made of bones in the same text, which suggests a possible origin of that widespread symbol for mortal danger particularly used to warn against electrocution and to designate a pirate ship.

The same Purana like several others describes the universe in its many regions and the process of its creation and the Kasi khanda of the Skanda Purana relates the ascent to Vishnu's paradise of king Bharata. Like Dante was to be guided by Virgil and Beatrix in his otherworldly journey, the monarch is led by Sunanda who portrays for him the realms they traverse and the innumerable types of beings that dwell in them.

There is no end to the analogies to other traditions that can be found in those encyclopaedic repositories of Hindu lore and one of the most striking regards the prajapati (prince of creation) Daksha who is said to have the head of a he-goat since he lost his own. He is the father of Sati who is sacrificed during her wedding to Shiva Bhairava. The goat is *Aja* in Sanskrit which means the Unborn One.

The worship of the baleful god Bhairava (the fearsome one) ritually involved the slaughter of a black goat. The resemblances are clear with the symbology of Satan, witchcraft and the scapegoat in semitic religions which have, in keeping with their Manichean dualism, sought to ban the "left handed" cults while extensively using their iconography as a deterrent and thereby perhaps increased its power of fascination. In contrast, India's civilization tolerates the survival of archaic practices defined as parts of the *vamachara*. This was the conclusion also reached by Father Bonazzoli who had initially been somewhat disturbed, like most Christian and Muslim missionaries and laymen by the non-dualistic ambiguity of Indian thought and its acceptance of all aspects of creation, including the apparently evil ones. "In early days, Indra seems to have been the chief deity of the Ksatriyas while the Brahmans worshipped primarily Prajapati and for long periods there was a conflict between the two communities which both claimed sole mastery and right to teach the Vedas. The Brahmins appear to have won and there is at least one record of a wholesale massacre of the warrior class by Brahmin-led armies. The ksatriyas reportedly fell into insignificance and the ruling dynasties that replaced them were of tribal, brahminical or menial origin, according to the Vishnu Purana."

We agreed with him that semitic religious traditions, like Zoroastrian doctrines had sought to establish a radical incompatibility between two opposing principles of creation and were thence committed to an unending war between God and Evil in which hypocrisy was a necessary weapon since it is impossible to follow the principle of "absolute good" if one must destroy "evil" by all means, which implies resorting to violence and other condemnable methods. The Dharma on the other hand could be described as a compass for a relativistic world in which positive and negative factors and effects are inextricably linked. The Puranas in Bonazzoli's view exemplified the empirical flexibility of the Hindu attitude to life, shaped by many millenia of mythologized history which teaches the intractable complexity of the human experience.

"Think of the depiction of India provided in some of the medieval Puranas, the Italian priest said, they relate that kings belonged to the merchant and peasant classes. Those upstarts eventually claimed to be of ksatriya or rajput extraction and that was gradually accepted by society, beginning with the Brahmins. It is consonant with the many Vedic references to sages who came from the warrior caste and to Brahmin kings, like His Highness the Maharaja here.The western notion of a caste-ridden Indian society, socially frozen for ages in feudal inequality is fictitious. Jatis were constantly evolving and transforming, rising and falling in the ladder depending upon political and economic circumstances."

Anyone who reads the Puranas and some other texts, including certain parts of the Vedas, such as the Atharva cannot fail to notice the presence of many of the practices that in the West have been clustered for centuries under the chapter of witchcraft, sorcery or demon worship. In South Asia all known deities are given room or at least a wide berth and are acknowledged as ambivalent. Yama, the god of death is an unforgiving master as he is Kala, time which destroys all things but he is also Dharma, the inflexible divine law. Our father Yama gave us life and therefore also spelt out our demise. He is often depicted as a black dog like Cerberus of the Greek Hades. A wrathful ugly demon can be turned into a protector while an apparently benign deity may be pitilessly destructive. Rishis are often irascible and unpredictable. Things are only what they seem to be in a given context and change with it. The observer lends its perceived nature to what he encounters. It is no wonder that the gypsies brought with them from India many of the notions and practices that are still regarded generally as belonging to the black arts.

The picture that emerges from the traditional accounts of history reflects a contemporary rise of civilization in the regions of the

Sarasvati and Ganges with frequent conflicts and constant interactions. The original Vedic culture seems to have blossomed at the meeting point between the Eastern Ikshvakus and the Western Bharatas. Many of its ingredients came from the east, contrary to the prevalent indological theory which sees it as an import from the steppes beyond the Indus and Hindu Kush. The easterly gangetic culture produced the *Ramayana* whereas its occidental counterpart left the literary monument of the *Mahabharata*. The Westerners domesticated the horse early as they found it in the arid plains of Gujarat and Sindh perhaps before getting other breeds from Central Asia. In the Ramayana on the other hand we observe an agricultural and urban "Aryan" culture that was, according to the domestic sources, ancestral to the better known and archaeologically more visible civilization of the Indus and Saraswati. At various times, the cultural legacy of the past was lost and had to be revived and rebuilt with the help of the gods. The Vedas, Shastras and Puranas as we know them are pieces that were retrieved from oblivion and reflect the stories and institutions of long gone eras.

We were then taken to visit the museum of the palace, full of opulent bric-à-brac from the five continents, including a large collection of exotic musical instruments jeweled lotus-shaped palanquin thrones, silver and ivory plated ornamental horse carriages and vintage American and European limousines. While our curiosity was whetted by the disparate treasures assembled in that cavern of Ali Baba we were more interested by the thousands of precious ancient manuscripts in Sanskrit, Persian, Brajbhasa (the ancestor of classical Hindi), Prakrits and Arabic hoarded in the Vidya Bhawan library. "India has kept hundred million manuscripts from all times in its past" His Highness had affirmed "and most of them are not known or even understood by people today. It is the largest treasury of knowledge for the world of tomorrow."

He may have erred on the side of excess when quoting that fantastic number but we got confirmation in later years that there are indeed untold millions of ancient textual records still extant all over the subcontinent, in temples, ashrams, monasteries and private hands.

"More than twenty thousand temples in one city, my father said. What is that if not combined power of faith, generosity, business sense and the will to endure and revive despite the threats and entreaties of various colonizers? Hinduism is like a banyan tree rooting itself in its native soil with millions of tendrils. It lasted here because that is the alma mater. The Arya religions gradually vanished in Europe and Eurasia because they were cut off from the main trunk. This is the aswattha!"

ALONG THE GHATS

At the end of the 18th century, Jonathan Duncan an administrator of the city on behalf of the British East India Company had proposed the creation of a college dedicated to the study and preservation of Sanskrit language and literature. That institution has since become the Banaras Sanskrit University which gathers thousands of students and many hundreds of affiliated schools and colleges. We attended some seminars in that historic venue and were able to grasp the essence of at least part of the learned debates held in the language of the Upanishads among old and young pundits. One of the readers in the department of Vedas and Vedangas engaged us in a conversation at the end of a session and offered to guide us through some parts of the city that we might not have visited yet. We eagerly accepted his gracious suggestion as we understood the value of such a scholarly guide.

While we strolled along the ghats, lost in the observation of the colourful milling crowds we exchanged some reflections with him. He pointed to us various types of ascetics who sat on the banks or came down for their ritual dips in the river. Among them the most intriguing were the *aghoris* of various sects, the uncompromising renouncers who went to extreme lengths to sever their bonds with the world of matter and even to attract the rejection of society like Francis of Assissi and Benoit Labre in their day. Covered in the ashes of burned corpses, almost entirely naked, often smoking hallucinogenic short pipes known as chellums, some inspired fear and perhaps repugnance. Our cicerone thought that they were the models followed by the Sufi Malamati wanderers who are known as God's madmen. We knew that some of those Hindu followers of the left path spend nights meditating near funeral pyres and climb up the icy slopes of the Himalayas clad in their sole indifference to material conditions. When they leave their bodies they disappear tracelessly in nature like wild animals and indeed their common rules are graphically simple but harsh; they are to eat "like dogs," what they find or are given without judging the quality of the food, to move like foxes, carefully and slyly and to sleep like stones wherever they pause. However their minds must be constantly fixated on the invisible lord of creation, Shiva, the immortal ascetic who dwells on mount Kailash. In certain sects, they perform strange ecstatic dances paced by ritual chants like some derwishes. However extreme their ways may seem to modern western minds, the basic principles of their behavior are familiar to all traditionally brought up Indians, especially in the poorer masses whose attitude to life, food and religion are quite similar, and not simply due to an evident lack of material choices.

Whenever we went by the Manikarnika Ghats where funeral pyres burn day and night and contemplated the dead being consumed by the flames, many thoughts assailed my mind. The initial shock caused by the sight of this literal return of the body to dust had long been replaced by a quiet acceptance of a biological reality that western cultures try to deny by hiding corpses beneath the ground in supposedly hermetic boxes as a poor substitute for mummification. The puerile hope in a resurrection of the body is now a waning superstition but we cannot easily give up our patently unhealthy and wasteful custom of canning our dead in ever expanding enclaves of real estate as if they needed material lodgings even after their physical shells have crumbled into bone fragments. The attempt to somehow preserve the skeleton of a departed soul betrays the ultimate idolatry that Christians accuse the Hindus of practicing. I wondered if the ability to witness the destruction of the bodily frame by fire had not helped Indians to soar freely to metaphysical heights when the followers of semitic religions tended to remain earthbound around the graveyards of their forebears, in the expectation of their return in the flesh.

Prince Siddharta's spiritual quest was triggered by his successive encounters with old age, sickness, poverty and death and they are constant companions of a visitor to the ghats of Varanasi. Perhaps nowhere else does human misery and destitution show itself more starkly than in the holy city along the Ganga, although it is invested with a resigned and yet hopeful and timeless serenity. By its very inevitability and direness, poverty in India appears to be an anagogy, a metaphysical invitation to look beyond the transient and cruel world of appearances.

As we passed by the lofty dome and minarets of the Gyan Vapi mosque which towers over the surrounding cluster of temples dwarfing the hallowed golden spire of the Vishwanath temple we were reminded of the maharaja's allusion to the resilience of his country's religion. The sacred buildings of the Hindus are like the trees of a thick Indian jungle. If cut down, they grow again and eventually wrap in a tight embrace the spare geometrical architecture of mosques and churches like the trunks of Angkor's forest have enfolded the stonework of men.

"The jyotirlinga of Vishwanath is a beam of light, our benevolent guide noted; a linga is not a phallus as your western scholars are too happy to call it; the word means "link." The lingam is what connects us with the universal fountainhead, in our hearts and at the centre of the universe."

That observation led to a conversation on various aspects of traditional knowledge and on its factual accuracy which is generally discounted or denied in the contemporary rationalist perspective. What is objectively real and what is allegorical in the depictions of the universe provided by Hindu literature? We admire the philosophical insights of the texts and the sophisticated understanding of grammar and semantics they express but are they outdated and irrelevant when they talk of the physical world?

XV

Digging into India's Ageless Soul

The Gorakhpanthi

The pandit offered to take us to his personal guru, an ascetic of the Gorakhnath lineage who often passed through the city in the course of his constant peregrinations. We welcomed this rare opportunity to come in the presence of a member of one of India's most venerable Sadhu lineages which recognizes nine great masters since its origins. The founder gave its name to the city of Gorakhpur in Northern India several thousand years ago and the second, known as Matsyendranath ("the Lord of the fish") hailed from Bengal and is regarded as one of the mightiest realized souls, to the extent that some Christian missionaries tried to relate him to Jesus on the basis of his piscean emblem and because his name comes from "mada" and "madhu" the sweet wine that he offers his followers as a tantric eucharist.

On the next afternoon, we followed our pandit into a dilapidated old palace not far from the Ashwamedha Ghat used as a resting place for sadhus and we found our guide's guru in a little courtyard where he sat crosslegged, surrounded by a few devotees, most of visibly humble extraction. The Nath was a gaunt, dark, bearded man of indefinite age with large smiling eyes, clad in a loincloth. On his chest he wore a long necklace of rudraksha beads and his pierced, stretched earlobes supported heavy metal ornaments, according to the tradition which gives members of his order the name of kamphata, those who wear iron earrings. According to some accounts, the Buddha had similar ones before he reached sambodhi and statues show him with distended earlobes.

The Pundit paid respectful obeisance to the ascetic who greeted him with gentle warmth and beamed at us with the guileless satisfaction of a child. We sat in front of him in the little circle and for a few minutes watched him converse with his devotees in the local Bhojpuri idiom. It appeared that he was advising them on personal matters and briefly describing some holy places he had had visited. As we sipped tea that had been brought in earthen cups our guide, after answering a few questions from the Nath about us, asked if we had any queries about spiritual matters.

My father began by briefly retracing our journey so far and the objectives which motivated it. It seemed from his knowing smile and nods that the sadhu understood part of it right away although the pandit translated after every few sentences. My father rarely put his thoughts in the form of a question. In this case he emphasized our trust in the great value and veracity of Indian Shastras and noted that the materialistic, skeptical basis of modern ideologies did not allow intellectuals raised in the western worldview to accept the testimony of seers, mystics and enlightened beings.

The Nath slightly shook his head and spoke for a few minutes stopping every now and then to enable his *shishya* to translate in English while he sometimes looked at us knowingly or lowered his gaze and withdrew into a brief recollection. The gist of what he said is what I can still recall today.

"Guruji says that you are right to have come to India for your work. She is the jagadguru, the world teacher and mankind will be saved by India's wisdom which is the knowledge accumulated by many prior civilizations along many millions of years in this planet and in others. In the next generation or two people will rediscover it and find that it is all true."

This was an auspicious beginning and it made us duly attentive.

"What you read in the shastras about yoga and the tantras and the powers and blessings they bring is real. There is no limit to the human potential because God and man are one. The entire universe is in us and our physical body is only a vehicle we use to visit this dimension and to operate in it. It conditions us and makes us suffer because of ignorance of our real nature but it is the only way to acquire a distinct, stable identity for the duration of our lives at this material level. Our karma has given us this fate and this embodiment and we must wear them out before we can move away."

The conversation proceeded between our questions and the Nath's responses which were often expanded by his interpreter who brought to bear his own scholarship on the topics that were evoked. The time scale of the traditional chronologies was evoked, with its accounts of fourteen great time cycles or manvantaras, each subdivided into kalpas and yugas, whose length was calculated on the basis of zodiacal observations The four yugas of a cycle are in decreasing order of length, in the proportion of 4-3-2-1—the tetraktys of Pythagoras—and they are symbolized as the number of dots on dice. The Kali yuga in which we live is the shortest and also the first and represents the side of the dice which has one dot. It will end in destruction and recreation in the next Krita yuga, an era of innocence, wisdom and purity since it will bring forth the next incarnations of all the beings that come back with each "golden age" before the decay of entropy sets in.

From one era to the next all things are preserved in bija or potential form like seeds in the winter, awaiting the next cycle of germination, growth , blossoming and decline.

One very intriguing fact that was considered is that while there are only four yugas in the cosmic calendar, India's timekeeping system divides a year into six seasons, in keeping with the features of a tropical monsoon climate. Likewise a dice must perforce have six sides. The answer to that puzzle was that two sides of the dice of time are blank as they represent the periods of dissolution or night at the beginning and end of each kalpa when Shiva, as the Nath put it "opens his eyes, ceases to dance and absorbs the world into his mind." In contrast, the Vaishnavas philosophers say that their supreme god Narayana falls asleep on the coiled serpent of space time on which he rests and thereby pulls the universe back into the uncreated matrix. Instead Shiva dreams what we perceive as reality and destroys it when he awakes.

"We are Shiva," said the ascetic, "when we awake to his presence, likewise, all other things cease to be because they are our dream. Instead his radiant, blissful self fills us and we disappear in it. We have no separate identity."

He went on to explain the cosmology of his sampradaya (initiatic school). Although his words were often cryptic in the translation, our familiarity with Hindu thought helped us to follow the concepts. He talked about the thirty three kalpas, which are both time cycles and ritual forms and about fourteen manvantaras of which we are living the seventh. He emphasized that Creation is a game: *sristi leela* in which the Unborn One delights as time is nothing but his pastime and is therefore a mere periodic appearance of the timeless: *sarvatma,* Shiva or the soul of all things. The root of sristi is found in the latin verb *surgere*, describing an autonomous, outward rise.

The first name of God in the Vedas, he recalled, is Ka which is an interrogation meaning "who?" or "what?" or Kasmai ("To whom?") while kham is the name of dark empty infinity. The gods and all other creatures emerged out of the initial sacrifice. Diti, finitude gave rise to the daityas and her sister, Aditi, the boundless, begat the adityas or devas. The daityas ruled at a given stage but were egotistical and destructive, which brought about their overthrow by the adityas after they had been duped by their god Shukra, the lord of the planet Venus (or Lucifer in its latin name) into adopting an erroneous, materialistic faith.

Curiously Shukra, the master of magical arts who alone knows the secret *sanjeevini* mantra to resuscitate the dead, forbids his followers from drinking intoxicating brews whereas Indra and his hosts drink the *madhu* or mead that give them the strength to overcome their foes. A reflection of that eternal conflict is found in the vedic battle in which the lord of the adityas slaughters and dismembers Vritra, the reptilian embodiment of chaos. Such an ontological mystery unfolds over millions of our years and is repeated in a similar form in each manvantara. As our Pundit friend commented, Indra, like all beings, has to expiate the karma of killing his twin brother Vritra and loses his supremacy as a result even though his act was *haviryajna*: a life giving sacrifice. "Within death is immortality": *antaram mrtyor amritam.*

All men and other beings are born from Vaivasvata, Surya, the solar Manu who is one and multiple. The first royal race is thus solar and the later lunar dynasties are descended from it. History mirrors cosmology because "as above so below" in an infinity of reflecting overlapping scales of magnitude.

Although sight is our primary instrument of perception, the essential nature of reality is sonic and therefore hearing is the subtlest sense. Hence, all physical, visible and invisible things are structured according to musical harmonics, based on the tone and rhythm of their vibrational frequencies. Tradition holds that all castes are descended from brothers, i.e children of the same father, just as for Christians "Jesus is the Son of God and the son of man, like all of us." "There is no caste for unconditioned beings" the sadhu added "but conditioned beings create them for their needs so that society may function harmoniously. They can only be discarded as a result of spiritual progress, not through legal rules or political struggles as they will always reappear in some form."

The creator in each cosmogenetic cycle is helped by seven rishis, who are evoked by the stars of the Great Bear. Together, like the seven musical notes of the scale, they build the symphonic or rather polyphonic harmony that is the universe. Mental concentration is the fundamental source of things and in sanskrit it is called tapas, implying intensity, suffering and the generation of heat as when rubbing two sticks together to light the vedic altar fire. The Nath enumerated the nine stages of actualization that form the created world, from the three primary ones to the six subsequent components, including the seventh one: the *arnavas* who are the "children of the seasons" and include men, mammals, birds, reptilians, insects and plants. He also mentioned the seven elements, beginning with *mahattwa* (the essence of all things) and continuing with *ahankara* (self) which is the combination of that essence with the three gunas that we have already explicated and which lend it a temporary and fictitious separateness within the individual creatures formed out of this mix.

Then the five elements, ether, air, fire, water and earth arise in that order. The pundit clarified that they are degrees of density of matter rather than elements in the western physico-chemical sense. They generate each other in a chain by increasing condensation and it appears that the ancient Indian sages understood that water and fire are interrelated as the vedic expression apam napat indicates. The process is at once a psychological interpretation and a reflection of the material mechanism of emanation since "all truth is ultimately symbolic" as Keyserling understood in Benares.

The following explanation was even more intriguing as mention was made of the role of the pranas as breaths or animate beings who united to form the body purusa, the adamic first man and the creator of the world, penetrated by the indriyas or faculties of perception which shape and inhabit the sensorial organs. Then man who is a breath like all living creatures, becomes Indra, the perceiver and observer of the physical reality, said the Nath and being unlimited, he has no pratisthan or resting place. I thought in that instant of the hidden meaning of the words of Jesus that the Son of Man has no place to rest his head. Being everywhere he is nowhere. His voice is fire, his sight is the Sun, his heart is the moon, his hearing is space, his smell is the air, his navel is the apana, the outgoing breath which evokes death and has survived in the greek word apnea. Finally his sexual organ is water and his skin is the vegetation that covers the earth. When he casts out the net of his senses Indra captures the images and objects of the world in his mind and become caught in them, such is the meaning of the term aindrajala: the spiderweb of impressions, feelings and subsequent memories and beliefs that constitutes our phenomenal identity. Jala is also a word for water which, it turns out under the miscroscope, when frozen is a network of tiny star shaped patterns. Did the ancient Indians discover this in meditation?

The cosmic man is born and to rise above the animal stage he must internalize the natural law of the rythms and seasons, the *rtam* which reflects truth, *satya* and manifests as *shivam:* abundance and as beauty or harmony: *sundaram.* Then Indra is given the *amrta,* the nectar of immortality which flows from the Sun and he can fight, defeat and dismember Vritra, his mirror image in chaos in order to instore divine order. The followers of Vritra, the danavas or daityas flee from the gods of light and hide under the ocean. Men are procreated and multiply and they inherit the holy duty of carrying out the sacrificial rites to the cosmic forces in order to maintain the balance between *rtam* and *anrtam* (between growth and entropy would we say now). The four Vedas appear in each kalpa and they correspond to the four realms of nature, the Rg Veda is about the earth and its dwellers; the Yajur concerns the intermediate space in which the yajna is performed, antariksha; the Sama connects us with the heavens and their divine hosts while the Atharva opens up the underworld and reflects the most ancient mystery cults practiced by the forest dwellers and their shamans. There, said the Nath lies the origin of the vratyas, the followers of Shiva Rudra who were the first yogis and who passed on the tantric knowledge. They came from the lofty mountains and jungles in the East of India that is called purva, meaning both ancient and oriental.

We came then to the human condition and to other life forms. We were reminded about the doctrine that the atman or divine self in us is visible as a thumb sized light without a fire located in the heart. Because of his multi-dimensional existence, man has access to the devas who are above or in the north and to the pitris, ancestral souls of seven different kinds who live below him or to the South. If we follow the path of social duties and family life, we reincarnate "like grain" after we die. That is called the way of the moon which most people are bound to follow. However there are those in all times and places who take the road less travelled to the north, the way of the Sun and break out of the cycle of death and rebirth. Such is the choice of the sadhus who let themselves be taken in the noose of Hara, "the ravisher" as Shiva is known and thus gain complete freedom, whether on the rightward course or on the *vamachara*: the netherward journey of the kaulas who engage and master the infernal forces through the controlled use of liquor, narcotics and sexual power.

All those words brought to my mind flashes of images inherited from childhood readings. Was the "thumb sized" light of the self not the Tom Thumb of the fairy tale who, like the performers of vedic sacrifices, used white pebbles as markers on his initiatic journey and saved himself and his six bigger brothers from being swallowed by the baleful oger (*ugram:* fierce in samskrit which became the latin orcus) of earthly desires? Instead he tricked the monster into slaughtering his own seven beloved daughters, who are perhaps the Pleiades, and escaped with the magical boots of seven leagues, a symbol of spiritual liberation. In the tale he and his brothers had lost their way when he had used bread crumbs to keep track as birds had eaten those perishable vestiges, illustrating the fact that the consumables of this world are not a viatic to success as they offer no guarantee of future welfare.

Was Snowhite the atman cast in the forest of ascesis to escape death at the hands of the hunter of the black queen, the maya-samsara of the ego jealous of the image of the higher self in her mirror? The seven treasure-mining dwarfs are the nibelungen, powers of the senses and intellect that help Snowhite to attain liberation and come back to her true condition. The poisoned apple contains the temptation of greed and vanity which plunges her into narcosis. The Sleeping Beauty discovers her mortality as a curse from the evil fairy of life but is saved by the spiritual godmother who transforms her announced decease into a century long slumber, a Samadhi-like trance during which time stops in the enchanted castle. Only the prince of spring and resurrection will revive her in his embrace along with all her world but the mother of her savior is an ogress like the Mahakali of Tantra. She is Time that eats all who live. However the princess is saved and reaches immortality when time itself perishes. Total recognition overcomes death according to Vedanta which is in itself "knowledge's end."

Those beloved children's tales were indeed indo-european legends borrowed from a common store of initiatic lore and Indian philosophy provides the key to unravel their hidden message.

The Nath answered our questions regarding the ancestral cosmography of the Hindus. He mentioned the seven continents described in the Puranas and said that on the vertical scale, there are five spheres of lower density above the two we all see and feel (earth and sky) and each of those is the realm of our subtler envelopes, bodies respectively made of aether, breath, mind, consciousness and the blissful essence that we share with the supreme being. If we awaken those usually dormant faculties locked in the cakras that are psychic knots along our inner axis we can then discover and experience those higher dimensions: the swaha, maha, janah, tapah and satya lokas but they are only halts on a journey to the highest freedom which liberates us from all those intermediary conditions and makes all separate creatures cease to exist.

We did not ask the Nath to explain the nature of the five higher lokas as we had read about them and thought about the more or less accurate or confusing interpretations that have been given to their names. They refer to increasingly subtle substances. Tapah for example suggests intense radiant heat whereas satyam is the ultimate essence or truth of reality. In man they correspond to rising levels of meditative consciousness, leading up to the Samadhi beatific trance found in the thousand petalled lotus that lies at the crown of the head and is related in physiology to the pineal gland.

While listening to exposition which had naturally taken the format of an upanishadic dialogue I thought of one of Keyserling's striking formulas: "recognition does not lead to salvation, it is salvation."

In the human mind, hell is more intriguing than heaven, perhaps because it is far easier to access and the Hindu map of the otherworld confirms that prejudice. There are seven and they host a legion of diverse creatures, many reptilian such as our old friends the nagas who dwell in the lowest circle, the Patala ruled by their monarch Vasuki. Batlike vampires have their own realm, the vetala. Hells are called narakas which suggests their connection with man (nara) and also with narcos: the hallucinogenic state, since like all other relative realities, they are but mental states, figments of our consciousness generated by karma.

This periplum around the Indian mythological ocean ended with the by now evident affirmation that the history of the world is much older and grander than our rather skeletal modern accounts of it.

"Many continents vanished and many races and civilizations have perished although we are their descendents" the sage said, shaking his head and lifting his palms in a typically South Asian gesture. "In our temples we keep records of most of them: their languages and scripts, their gods and their histories. What they know in universities is a handful of sand from a vast beach. One of the ancient tongues, now almost forgotten is paisaci, the speech of the pisachas, the ghosts of the Old Ones. There are thousands of books written in it, hidden in some holy places and they hold many mysteries and magical powers . The Atharva Veda contains some excerpts."

GODS AND BUDDHAS

We understood he was not going to say more on this and the long session was drawing to an end as the pundit was getting weary in spite of the enthusiastic devotion to his master that had fuelled his eloquence. I joyously internalized the confirmation that the fantastic stories reported by Blavatsky, Saint Yves d'Alveydre, Churchward, Serrano and many others might be grounded in authentic annals of lost civilizations. The sacred and secret languages Senzar, Naacal and Vatan could have truly been spoken and written centuries of centuries ago. Perhaps the pisachas were the vanished Atlanteans of western tradition.

When one plunges into the depth of this ocean of preserved knowledge outer material circumstances cease to matter. The dirt, the grinding but colourful poverty, the disorderly neglect that pervade street scenes in India, all that Pierre Loti qualified as "a barbaric carelessness" when he wandered in the temple-city of Srirangam, appear as the mere torn and soiled trappings of a flashing jewel. Even in tawdry surroundings I can accept much of the Indian reality because of that glimmer of truth I spy in the complicit smile or glance of a casual passer-by, in the hieratic gesture of a godly statuette or in the fierce gaze of a garish effigy.

We thanked with calm effusion our teacher of the day. He beamed again and made a gesture of blessing. He had not tried to convert us to any creed or convince us of any theory. He had merely shared the truth he had been brought into and which he did not for a second analyse intellectually. He had spoken as if he had breathed, spontaneously. Keyserling had noted that for Hindus it is a deadly sin to influence by force or authority the faith of another. Emperor Ashoka in his edict enjoined on his subjects not to promote their own beliefs by demeaning those of others. One can only teach one who is ready to accept and understand; otherwise, a lesson has no meaning for the unprepared or unwilling listener. We were all the more grateful to the Nath and his translator because we were aware that "the desire for communication disappears in proportion to the advance in interiorisation" since one realizes that essential truth is inexpressible.

On the way back to the University of Benares we exchanged impressions with the Pandit and came back on the topic of supernatural powers. "They cannot be used without depleting the merit of the Siddha and slowing him down on his journey to God," the Pandit said, reiterating a well known warning of the shastras. "That is why the Asuras, the older 'gods', who resorted to them fell into the underworld. The yogi should not be distracted and waylaid by those tricks which deviate the course of natural laws. Sorcerers and magicians are always inferior beings as the powers they show prevent them from rising higher. Indeed they create karma, mostly of the bad variety instead of exhausting it through tapas and jnana."

"Is there any manner in which the application of the siddhis (paranormal abilities) can be virtuous and karma-free?" I asked, spurred by my juvenile fascination with miraculous omnipotence.

"Only if they are done in selfless way as a tribute to the Lord who alone has the might and grace" came the reply. "Any conceited or self-serving display of magic is asuric." That made me understand the reluctance of Christ to perform miracles and his refusal to take credit for them. In Islam the prodigies manifested through the prophets are of a different, far higher order than the superficially similar feats performed by magicians employing the abilities of jinns.

I thought again of the role of the Supernatural in religion when we visited, a few miles away from Varanasi the grove of Sarnath where the historic Gautama Buddha preached his first sermon and thus set in motion the Wheel of the Law. The contrast with the holy city of the Hindus was striking. There a noisy, dirty, overcrowded beehive of temples milling with pilgrims and citizens from all walks of life, here the pastoral quiet of a deer park haunted by scattered monasteries. In Kashi, the burning fervor of the cult of the Sun and the river lighting the pyres of the dead; in Sarnath the cooling embrace of meditation around the mystery of bucolic ruins.

The Vedic celebration of existence and the other world is replaced by the Buddhist contemplation of Emptiness as the cure for existential suffering and instead of long haired, bearded, half naked and painted sadhus one sees yellow draped monks with clean shaven heads from Indochina and the Far East silently gliding in and out of oriental-looking pagodas and convents. The call of mystical communion with the elements appears to be replaced by the rule of intellectual and devotional discipline. Yet, despite the contrast, the history of the Sakya Muni reflects the continuity of his mission with India's ageless Dharma. He was born in Kapilavastu in the foothills of Nepal and is said in canonic scriptures to be a reincarnation of the Kapila who founded the samkhya system which may be regarded as the cosmological and metaphysical spine of Indian philosophies. Siddharta Buddha is also called Angiras as if belonging to the hoary lineage of vedic rishis and he initiated his ministry in Sarnath which was then called rishipattana, the place where rishis come down to earth.

All Buddhas are reported to begin preaching here when they descend from the blessed heaven of Tushita into the world of men and one of the Jain Tirthankars, in whose succession perhaps one may find the source of the Buddhist tradition of multiple "enlightened ones," was born in Sarnath as well.

The Tathagatha's dhammacakra is the wheel of the law that Visnu displays in his statuary and it is the emblem of the Hindu emperors who are known as cakravartins. The Buddha's rotating symbol is flanked by the chital deers that symbolize fire and are associated with vedic rishis and sannyasis. The pain (duhkha) that he diagnoses and cures in men was analysed in the Upanishads and so was the virtuous conduct he prescribes and which is indeed a yoga in the line of Patanjali's doctrine.

If there is a major difference between the way of the Ksatriya prince turned ascetic and the brahminical tradition, it consists in the former's emphasis on moral and ethical tenets shorn of the complex rituals inherited from ancient forms of nature worship and exempt of pantheistic devotion. As a prince born in a clan of warriors Siddharta focused on the rules of individual conduct and social discipline. He favoured practical knowledge over ceremonial and secret esotericism but he manifestly did not seek to overthrow the existing order as he acknowledged in practice the role of Brahmins and the reality of the devas. It is well known that in the following centuries the metaphysical speculation and the elaborate liturgy from which he had refrained were revived and vastly developed in various schools of the tradition he founded so that Mahayana Buddhism at least is as "catholic" in its hierarchy and its pageantry as the most clerical versions of Hinduism.

One of the lectures we gave at the Benares Hindu University took place in the department of physics under the auspices of Professor P. Krishna, a specialist of crystallography whose name we had been given by his aunt, Rukmini Devi. Krishna was a charming, fairly young and rather highly anglicized man who combined his scientific interests with the theosophical tradition of his family and a great knowledge of Carnatic music. He invited us to his house to meet his wife and children and we almost instantly became friends. His understanding of the Indian tonal and chromatic scale theory had led him to conclude that it was based on a sophisticated understanding of sound geometry and was in turn reflected in the cosmology of the scriptures. The Vedas, in their complex metric, rhythmic and tonal structures encode that science of natural proportions that Luca Paccioli illustrated in his engravings of Platonic solids. The ragas are geometric crystalline structures made of sound according to the theory of musical numbers. In that view, reality can be depicted as made of infinitely small multi-dimensional pyramids inasmuch as it can be depicted through algebraic equations. I was years later to find a more elaborate and detailed description of this connection between the numerical, the aural and the visual in two books, both published in 1978, written by Ernest McClain and Antonio de Nicolas. Through that gnosis one discovers the correspondances between yantras and mandalas, musical octaves and their subdivisions into mathematically precise srutis. The wisdom of the Vedas is indeed "heard" because it is the music of the cosmos, the polyphony that Hildegard von Bingen perceived and described in her mystical writings but mapping sound patterns as geometric forms is only possible for the expert in both disciplines. Not all can see the virtual architecture of a melody and even fewer are able to hear the harmonics of silent patterns.

Just about the time when we were coming to an end of our stay in the world's oldest living spiritual centre the Emergency was repealed in order to allow the national election campaign to begin. We gave a lecture at the Kashi Vidyapeeth, a vast university founded by nationalist intellectuals in the final years of British rule in order to provide a homegrown response to the dominant systems of education imported from England and left soon after for Calcutta. From the heartland of Hindu civilization we travelled to the former metropolis of western imperial power.

XVI

Kali's Domain

"Rage Rage against the Dying of the Raj"

Calcutta, as it was still called then, cannot fail to evoke strong emotions because it overwhelms the newcomer by its baroque exoticism, its size, its overcrowding and the constant clash of extremes that joust and mingle in its perimeter. Abject misery crawls next to glittering opulence, Bengali extravagance invades severe neo-palladian classicism, the deafening noise of celebrating or angry crowds dies out on the manicured hedges of sprawling and secluded aristocratic clubs. For almost hundred and fifty years Calcutta was the second largest metropolis of the Empire on which the Sun never set, the London of the Orient; its influence extended to the distant shores of Burma, Siam, Indonesia, China and Australia. Far flung commercial emporia such as Malacca, Singapore, Hong Kong, Canton and Shanghai were its offspring or its satellites. Since the transfer of the capital to Delhi, Calcutta had been declining and independence, by cutting it off from its eastern hinterland which fell to Pakistan left a major wound that long-standing Communist rule had done little to heal. One could see the evidence of the decay in the once splendid imperial buildings and stately thoroughfares that suffered from the poverty-induced neglect typical of most Marxist administrations. Everywhere masses of people existed, did their chores, ate, drank and died on the pavement in broad public view. Our taxi driver explained in excellent though heavily accented English that most of them were refugees from the 1971 Bangladesh war of liberation.

We took our lodgings at the guest house of the university of Calcutta in Ballygunge and began to do our rounds, even though the sultry climate took its toll on our energy after weeks spent in the green campus of Benares University during the glorious northern Indian spring. One of our first visits took us to the venerable Asiatic Society on Park Street, one of the sanctuaries of early Indian scholarship that I longed to enter since I had read its history back in Spain.

The Asiatic Society was born from the vision of one man, a British judge called William Jones who was both a scholar and a lover of Indian letters. Jones penned the mission statement for the institution he desired to set up during the long sea journey from England in 1783. He was a gifted member of the Encyclopaedic movement which had swept through European intellectual circles and as such he desired to pursue and record all knowledge that could be gathered in and about Asia. Like many other leading minds of the Enlightenment such as Voltaire he had few religious prejudices and held Asian ancient cultures in high regard as being the older sisters of western civilisation. Unlike the Portuguese and Dutch who had come to trade and convert "natives" to Christianity, the British of Jones's days were increasingly involved in administering the lands in which they were settling.

The United Kingdom had just lost its thirteen American colonies but the East India Company was fast expanding and firming up its Asian possessions and needed orientalists and scientists to understand better the nations it had come to rule. Jones and many of his like minded and learned contemporaries such as Warren Hastings, Wilkins, Colebrooke, Halsted, Shore, Duncan and Wilson were fascinated by India in all its aspects even though they were also conscious, if not always approving of Britain's self-appointed mission to extend its rule over that huge land.

Scholarship was both a noble avocation and an instrument for comprehending and dominating the mysterious and complex society that circumstances had conspired to bring under Albion's control. Warren Hastings, India's first governor general since 1773, ably embodied that ambiguity. The impoverished scion of an old feudal line, he had risen by dint of his talent from the lowly rank of clerk or 'writer' while acquiring a deep and broad knowledge of his adoptive country's culture, languages and history. He saw himself almost as a local and was accepted as such. Indeed he could claim to be as Indian as the many Persians and Turks who still held dominant roles all across the land and he wished, like many other Britons of his generation, Hindustan and Britain to remain deeply involved with one another without necessarily planning to rule the entire country. Yet, he had a duty to the shareholders and to Parliament which Prime Minister Pitt had made directly responsible for the management of the East India Company. In the end Hastings had to relinquish his post, leave his beloved Calcutta and return home to face years of prosecution for his infractions. Although he was exonerated of wrongdoing in 1795, he gave up the dream of living as a Nabob in the Orient and dedicated himself to rebuilding the country seat of his medieval ancestors in Gloucestershire where he spent his last years as an English country squire. With him perhaps died the orientalist vision of a syncretistic new Indo-European civilization that is vividly evoked in the 18th century so-called Company School paintings. The self-assured Christian imperialists of the Victorian Age supplanted the deistic indophiles who had followed the first British merchants in their trading posts.

The "Asiatick Society," the Serampore Mission of William Carey and Wellesley's Fort William College, were the first implements conceived to further the Company's global ambitions. From Calcutta as a base, not only India but Asia as a whole was seen as open for economic, political and cultural conquest. Some enterprising British businessmen realized that the colonies of the Portuguese, Danish, Dutch and French powers could easily fall into their hands as a result of what was the first capitalist enterprise on a trans-continental scale. Their endeavour made their shareholders , and the British Crown as a consequence, immensely wealthy and India was already the capstone of that empire, the gateway to the Far East.

Despite their deep sympathy for "the science of the hindoos" the orientalists could not free themselves from the yoke of European "casteism" and they did not admit any Indian on an equal level in their circle. Only half a century later did the first "natives" from the most eminent Calcutta families join that bastion of Western indology and the nation which William Jones had called "the nurse of the sciences" had to wait until 1885 for one of its sons, Rajendra Lal Mitra to rise to the presidency of the venerable conclave. The Asiatic Society was after all conceived primarily for the benefit and under the total control of the expatriate English intellectual elite.

In spite of or perhaps due to its expatriate composition and foreign perspective the Asiatic Society had a crucial effect on India's intellectual evolution. For centuries, the indigenous scholarly and spiritual classes had held on to ancient knowledge often transmitted in a literal way and had sought thereby to protect their ancestral beliefs and practices from foreign conquerors. The political primacy of Muslim rulers was reflected in the preeminence of Islamic scholarship and philosophy generally conveyed in Arabic and Persian. As a result of that eclipse, much of what Europeans called the "sciences of the Gentoos" had become mysterious and incomprehensible to most Indians so that many critically alive spirits regarded it as superstition. The Asiatic Society did for Hindu literature, philology, grammar and jurisprudence what the Theosophical Society was to achieve for Indian religions and philosophies almost exactly one hundred years later; it made them relevant and prestigious again in the eyes of many educated local people hitherto tempted to convert to one of the foreign forms of monotheism and to adopt unreservedly the way of life and the mindset of the Europeans. Thus the Bengal Renaissance, which was to turn into a nationwide phenomenon began as a wide ranging endeavour to reform and revive the legacy of so many centuries. That movement sowed the seeds of the struggle for freedom from colonial rule.

We were met by the Secretary of the venerable society Dr D. C. Ghose who gave us a quick tour of the invaluable collection of manuscripts, books and other memorabilia held in the unfortunately dusty and poorly kept premises of an ugly modern building. He told us that the library boasted one hundred and fifty thousand volumes and almost fifty thousand manuscripts in twenty seven languages as well as eighty thousand journals. We knew that the first big addition to the original collection had been the entire library of the Sultan of Mysore which had come to Calcutta from Seringapatam after the defeat and death of its owner. We were shown the original volumes of the first four "Asiatick Researches," published from 1788 and admired some other relics, some of which were in a precarious condition that made us fear for their survival in the future. Our lecture at the Soviety was scheduled a few days later and we were free to pursue our discovery of that city in which many of Britain's eminent children in all fields of activity, including a great-grandson of the Lord Protector Oliver Cromwell, got their training in the battle of life. It turned out that we had more time on our hands than we had thought since, true to its reputation, the University was closed or at least paralysed by strikes, protests and other disturbances for much of our stay. We did however manage to deliver those two or three talks on the occasional working days.

RELICS OF COLONIAL DAYS

We spent an entire day in the cavernous Indian Museum, a building akin to a Roman neo-classical palace, after meeting the director who programmed our talk in that first of all Indian museums, another offspring of the neighbouring Asiatic Society. I remember a curator telling me that if a visitor were to spend just five minutes looking at every one of the objects stored in the collection, he would need more than three years to see them all, assuming he spent twelve hours of every day on that absorbing task. It is a repository of everything that attracted a Victorian gentleman's scholarly interest in the tradition of the schatzkammers, enshrining in close proximity priceless archeological and artistic exhibits as well as mineral and botanical samples and stuffed specimens of the infinitely varied fauna the subcontinent hosts, from the Bengal tiger to the horse-sized Himalayan antelope, the barkhor, from the giant flying squirrel to the gangly gibbon and from the massive one-horned rhinoceros to the tiny loris. We were surprised to learn that in very ancient days India had hosted species that are now confined to Africa such as great apes, giraffes and hippos whereas macaques, elephants, crocodiles and lions are still extant in South Asia.

However a greater museum was the city itself with its myriad monuments of many styles, ranging from the pastoral thatched hut which is the original "bungalow" to the gothic cathedral and the rococo mosque. The space allotted to specific buildings and their size denoted the hierarchy of values in a society. The British, seeking to rival previous imperial overlords displayed their power, if not always their good taste in their seats of governance and law since managing the economy for their own benefit and dispensing justice were major concerns. Additionally they competed with the local creeds by raising monumental temples of christian worship and evinced their dominance by laying out huge private enclaves, closed to the indigenes, where they indulged their favourite pastimes such as Port drinking, golf, cricket and horse racing.

We saw the testimonies of their insolent might in the Turf, Golf and Tollygunge Clubs. It has often been said that space is the greatest luxury and in crowded, throbbing Calcutta, luxury could not be better displayed than in those greens, ponds, hillocks and clusters of trees spreading as far as the horizon around white walled mansions in which the bureaucrats, soldiers and merchants of the empire, if not for the climate, might have imagined that they were still in their remote verdant island.

Although the clubs also betrayed the twilight in the fortunes of the city since the end of the Raj they had managed to survive with genteel nostalgia under the rule of the Leftist Babus. We were told that the Marxist oligarchy that had replaced the White Sahibs for most of the years of independence had been tolerant for these havens of privilege and had never tried to close them down despite their distinctly un-proletarian function.

At a concert of the Music Society, which had been founded by an expatriate French pianist Philippe Sandré, we were introduced to the wife of the Governor of West Bengal who hailed from Goa. Mrs Dias was an elegant woman who played the piano and had a western upbringing, like many in the region of her birth. We had a mutually respected friend in the Archbishop of Delhi Angelo Fernandes, also a Goan.

One result of that meeting was that we were invited for tea at the Governor's mansion which, apart from the pleasure of meeting her again with her husband, the Hon. Anthony Lancelot Dias enabled us to see from inside an eminent relic of Indian and western colonial history.

The Raj Bhavan, the former palace of the Viceroys of India was build at the dawn of the 19th century when Napoleon held sway in Europe and when the Irish Marquess of Wellesley was Governor general. It was modeled on Kedleston Hall, a grand country manor in Derby built in the neoclassical style then *de rigueur*. Surrounded by sprawling landscaped gardens, it sits as the symbol of the rising British power of that time. Another mute witness to its far flung reach is the Chinese bronze dragon brought from Nanking in 1842 when, as a solemnly laconic inscription attests, peace was "dictated to the Chinese Emperor by the military force of England and India" at the conclusion of one of the Opium wars. Perhaps for the first time, it occurred to me that the Chinese, who have very long memories, might still associate India with the soldiers who had fought and vanquished them for the sake of the British Crown and had expanded the borders of the Raj at the expense of the Middle Kingdom's sphere of influence.

In India on the other hand few people still remember the fundamental role that the sepoys played in the overseas wars waged by Westminster and the importance of Bombay's shipyards for the Her or His Gracious Majesty's Fleet.

The conversation over tea in the blue drawing room of the palace was followed by a rapid tour of the state rooms. In the throne hall we saw the *gaddi* of Tipu Sultan which had been brought from Mysore as an emblem of victory by the Company's troops.

The traces left by history can inspire many philosophical musings and there is much to say about Richard Wellesley, William Pitt's trusted second, who had transformed the Company's management of large parts of India into a real government. Although, in keeping with the libertine habits of his class he had lived for years in Paris with a French actress whom he had finally married after she gave him three children, Wellesley shared his nation's dislike for France, heightened by the advent of the 1789 revolution, and spared no effort to expel its agents from India where they had acquired deep roots. Taking advantage of the turmoil and wars which prevented successive regimes in Paris from exercising control over their colonies and probably raised fear of republican contamination in some Indian princes, the new governor proceeded to defeat the remaining independent powers in the Deccan and assert Britain's supremacy in the Bay of Bengal.

While London was fighting the First Consul on the continent, Wellesley, aided by his brothers, all but wiped out France's influence in India. During the Marquess's stint in Calcutta, Bonaparte had himself crowned Emperor in 1804. Wellesley left India for good in the following year when the battles of Trafalgar and Austerlitz reshaped the balance of power. As members of the rural, riding and hunting Irish Ascendency, the Wellesleys had been raised in a feudal setting and they did probably not find that aspect of life in India unfamiliar. They were Tories of their times, pragmatic, liberal in politics and ideology, relatively egalitarian in their upwardly mobile society and yet deeply convinced of the superiority of their nation and religion. However they were capable of tolerance if circumstances demanded it and probably realized that, to succeed in their political objectives they had to avoid interfering too much in the religious and social affairs of their Asian subjects.

From Wellesley's former abode to the Victoria Memorial, the distance is short but a century stands between them. While the former was built to house the chief representative of a new overseas hegemon, the latter is a mausoleum to the memory of an empire that was already drawing to an end. There is a well known link between the man who built the seat of British power and the man who ordered the construction of the Memorial. Nathaniel, Lord of Curzon who took over as Viceroy a hundred years after Wellesley, in 1899 happened to be the heir of Kedleston Hall and settled in the replica of his ancestral home when he reached Calcutta. Like Wellesley he was an Etonian, had attended Oxford and was a self-taught orientalist. Haughty, even pompous, erudite, a talented travel writer and an imperialist to the hilt he was one of the most interesting personalities the British ever sent to administer India. We had found his traces along our Asian itinerary in Turkey, Iran and Afghanistan where he was still remembered for his adventurous explorations and his diplomatic missions. To Calcutta where he had landed with great fanfare he brought his statuesque American wife, an heiress whose fortune had restored glitter to the hoary coat of arms of the house of Curzon but he was later reviled by many as the man who had divided Bengal, mainly on religious lines and thereby sown the seed of national partition.

Upon the death of the Queen-Empress, Curzon decreed the erection of a sort of British Taj Mahal in her memory. It was also a manner for this vainglorious man to celebrate the fact that he had saved the Indian original model from destruction. Since the end of the 1857 native rebellion, the English had declared themselves the successors of the Mughal Padshahs and in 1906 the visiting Prince of Wales played the role of Shah Jahan when he laid the foundation stone of that neo-Florentine political basilica of the imperial religion. We were graciously received by the director of that magnificent institution and gave a talk in what has become one of the major cultural cenacles of the city.

By then we had also spoken at the Asiatic Society where our talks revolved around the topic of Indology as a changing discipline. From being a colonial pursuit intended to map out and decipher India for the benefit of its western masters it had to become an indigenous rediscovery process, from both inner and outer perspective. In our view, shared by many experts, the old prejudices and methodologies adopted by foreign academics and explorers to study the natives of subjected lands and their civilizations endured and had been rather uncritically accepted by domestic institutions.

One can only get an impression of the wealth that accumulated in the former capital of British India by visiting one of the monumental, though often derelict, dwellings inhabited by members of the old business elite. The most famous of those mansions is the marble palace which still belongs to the descendents of its builders, the Mullicks. We visited that replica of a neo-classical European palazzo, a contemporary of the Hazardwari of the Nawabs of Bengal, built in the early years of Victoria's rule, with its own park, zoo and Chinese-style family shrine, filled with a lavish bric-a-brac of European paintings, sculptures, objets d'art and a myriad knickknacks from a time and a place that did not know of the word "kitsch" and where the rich unabashedly indulged their taste for any precious, visually enticing object that came from the far-away western metropolis. Several statues of Queen Victoria of diverse sizes and materials and vis-à-vis busts of her grandson George V on a chimney mantelpiece attested the owner's loyalty to the masters of the day. Bronze Wellingtons and Napoleons faced each other on horseback across a cavernous ballroom. Colossal Chinese cloisonné vases competed for space with outsized khmer incense burners and Mughal hookah stands on intricate marble floors. The gods, nymphs and heroes of Olympus and Rome exhibited their scantily draped physiques to the lotus eyes of Indian devis and Italian Madonnas. Cleopatra reclined near Giuletta, Jesus gazed at Buddha, Shatunkala looked past Francesca under the crystal cascades of Belgian chandeliers and all around, cages displayed macaws, orioles, parakeets, cuckatoos, pheasants, mynahs and doves whose warbling, trills, calls and whistles contrasted with the solemn silence of the marble and bronze crowd.

There are quite a few gems in this romantic repository, however, as Raja Mullick laid his hands on a few Old western masters from Italy, France and the Netherlands. Gazing at the real and imitation statues from Graeco-Roman antiquity and the Renaissance I was led to make a comparison with the Indian busts and faces we had admired in several public and private collections. The anatomy of classical western sculpture and painting is more accurate and realistic than the Asian one but in terms of expression and movement, there is in Indian portraiture an expressiveness and a sense of cosmic meaning that are seldom if ever found in European academism. Greek statues are magnificently athletic or sensuous and delicately shaped but their faces either stare blankly or express mundane feelings such as faint mirth, anger or strain and they often appear as perfect, rather mindless bodies whose frozen gestures have a mechanical character. Indian gods, goddesses and nymphs and other supernatural creatures dance, smile, welcome adoration or meditate. They manifest the existence of a throbbing and multilayered festive and dramatic invisible world while greek gods are in a state of suspended animation as if they had fallen under a spell while performing a mundane or self-absorbed action.

In the Victoria Memorial we had reviewed lines of Governors, Viceroys, Generals on parade, draped in the haughty aloofness of colonial power or sporting the phlegmatic detachment of European self-assurance. These conventional expressions of western portraiture are consonant with the theatrical decorum of classical art. In Hindu art, living men and women were rarely if ever depicted unless they were liberated saints. Painting and statuary were primarily reserved to the gods and other normally invisible beings and they are conceived as geometrically designed, conventional renderings precisely studded with symbolic attributes, wearing few and unobtrusive clothes. However the humanity, the serenity, the grace, the humour and the bliss denoted by these icons, whether they are devas, buddhas, tirthankaras, yakshas or apsaras are overpowering.

In the age when the Marble Palace was in its prime, Calcutta prided itself on many other such lavish houses in which the leading merchant and landholding families, British, Hindu, Jain, Muslim, Armenian and Jewish, displayed their opulence and sophistication. All were keen to adopt Western traits at least in their ways of life and external appearance but in effect created a multi-cultural synthesis which was often bewildering. The Suvarna Choudhuris, Mullicks, Boses, Duttas, Sinhas of Raipur, Roys of Nadia, Kapoors of Bardhaman, Roy Chowdhuris of Barishal, Seths of Burrabazar, Sens of Janbazar, Mukerjees, Mitters and other bankers, industrialists and zamindars, who often owned estates as large as small nations, may have aspired mostly to social and political syncretism but other more intellectually gifted Indians sought to bring about a spiritual fusion between the various religious systems as well, according to a constant Indian tendency that Emperor Akbar himself had displayed.

HINDU REFORM AND RENAISSANCE

Two of those reformers were from leading families of the province; they were Dwarkanath Tagore, a merchant tycoon, and Rammohun Roy, who came from a distinguished dynasty of administrators. Together they sought to devise for their countrymen an alternative to Christian conversion which was becoming popular among high class Bengalis. In 1829 they set up the Brahmo Sabha, a "monotheistic" and philosophical version of the hindu tradition that focused on the one Universal God alluded to in the Upanishads and common to all people, devoid of the "idol worship" that so disturbed Christians and Muhammedans.

Bengal has for many centuries been dominated two apparently contradictory denominations, the tantric cult of Kali, the fearsome and yet radiant black goddess who is the wife and embodies the might of Shiva and the sweet mystical adoration of Krishna, the cowherd king from Vrindavan who is the latest Avatar of Vishnu and whose devotion was revived by the great 16th century Bhakta Chaitanya. Whereas the former practice is steeped in tribal magical beliefs and rites and still requires or at least admits the sacrifice of animals, such as black goats, the latter is strictly vegetarian, non-violent and preaches a loving surrender to the dancing lord of the gopis. Ram Mohan's father was a follower of Vishnu while his mother came from a family of Kali devotees. As an offspring of this unusual mixed marriage, he sought to get back to the vedantic source of the religious traditions and thereby planted the seeds of the religious renaissance that produced many great spiritual figures, from Ramakrishna Paramahamsa to Sri Aurobindo.

In the course of time, however, the religious movement started by Roy proved to be limited in its spread although it had a major influence on India's reformist intellectuals. It was too simple, abstemious and perhaps too "Victorian" in its tenets and liturgy for the euphoric and tropical exuberance of the Indian spirit. It never expanded beyond the ranks of an anglicized urban elite in Bengal. While Roy had no direct successor, his legacy was maintained by the Tagore family which was in the course of an entire century to produce a real-life gallery of eminent artists, thinkers and literateurs.

One of the delightful experiences Calcutta offers is to visit Jorasanko, the estate of Rabindranath Tagore and his clan, on whose campus the university of Rabindrabharati has been established. The sprawling red mansion in the typical hybrid style of 19th century Bengal evokes the polyfacetic personality of the great poet, playwright and mystic as well as the diverse gifts and talents of his ancestors and relatives. Like Italy in the Renaissance or France in the Baroque Age Bengal teemed with towering artists, writers, scholars, scientists, political thinkers and revolutionaries during the Victorian and Edwardian eras. Among them, Rabindranath Tagore became the uncrowned monarch and his renown in India and especially in his native region is extraordinary. Not even Victor Hugo in France or Leo Tolstoy in Russia have retained the same universal appeal, partly because they were ideologically and personally controversial while Tagore at least in Bengal is not. Goethe is perhaps the nearest equivalent as a truly national literary and philosophical icon in his own country. Our lecture at Rabindrabharati, surrounded by many memorabilia of the great man was a harbinger of our planned visit to the university he had founded in Shantiniketan.

At the crossroads between South Asia and the Far East, poised between the Bay of Bengal and a densely populated fertile hinterland that reached up to the Himalayas, Calcutta could claim to be the queen of the Orient but outside the ornate palaces of the British rulers and the native grandees, amidst the poverty-stricken masses the religious heart of the land was beating in the cavernous, dark temples that many of the sophisticated *bhadralok,* preferring the aristocratic intellectual rites of the Brahmo Samaj, did not visit.

It was from the then new temple of Dakshineshwar that the mystical sun of India shone the brightest in the humble but radiant personality of Ramakrishna. His influence on his country and the world was more powerful than that of any of the polished erudite intellectuals of the great city. After visiting the Kalighat temple, a shaktipeeth which is the shrine of the *genius loci* that gave the city its name and where one feels the primal fervor that lies at the core of the worship of the mother goddess we went to Dakshineshwar where Ramakrishna spent most of his adult life in a temple where his brother was the head priest. Gazing at its cupolas, I was reminded of the neo-byzantine architecture that became popular in France not long after the period in which this hindu basilica was built, illustrating the unpredictable cross-fertilization that constantly takes place between various regions of the world. It was intended by its founder, Rani Roshmoni a woman of humble birth who had married one of the wealthiest men of the area, to be open to all, irrespective of caste and creed and so it has remained.

Ramakrishna himself, born in a Brahmin family, shed all connections to his community and embraced a life of renunciation and spiritual ecstasy. He at various times practiced the rites of several religions in order to experience divinity in different guises. He claimed to have come into the presence of Jesus and to have fallen into the sufi mystical union called *fana fi'llah.* However he remained faithful to the family and temple deity at whose feet he found the ultimate enlightenment shortly before leaving his material body at fifty in the hermitage of Belur on the banks of the Hooghly river, the vital artery of Kolkata and of the western part of Bengal.

At Belur which has now become one of the many Vatican-like enclaves that dot the Indian continent, we felt the spirit of the Saint of Dashineshwar and of his chief disciple Vivekananda. The sylvan serenity of the park prepares the visitor for the ecumenical majesty of the main sandstone temple which successfully integrates in a harmonious synthesis the sculptured motifs of a mandir with the dome of a mosque and the lofty nave of a vihara that reminds Christians of a Romanesque church. There again we found the syncretistic yearning that the Ramakrishna worldwide mission expresses after the Brahmo Samaj called for it. However, while the latter movement split in two between the Hindu party led by the

Tagores and the Christianized faction first headed by Keshub Chandra Sen, the Ramakrishna movement remained resolutely vedantic, in the spirit of its founders who realized that only in the infinitely broad frame of Hinduism could such a universal ideal find its full expression, free from the dogmatic and historic borders that define semitic creeds. The Hindu revival acquired its definite form as socially reformist but textually and culturally traditional. Its goals included the alleviation of poverty, the rejection of socially unjust practices such as caste segregation, widow suicide and untouchability and the introduction of modern notions borrowed from the west in education, in response to the wishes of British and Indian reform-minded administrators and activists.

Although the Vedic scriptures refer to Rishis who are almost all married and demand chastity of the Brahmins only in their youthful years of study prior to their attainment of the householder status, there is a very ancient tradition of lifelong celibacy in India, followed by ascetics or sadhus of both sexes. Buddha did not inaugurate the monastic institution and the vows that regulate it. Swami Vivekananda followed a hoary Hindu practice when he founded the Ramakrishna Mission. When we asked one of its swamis why all religions, including Islam in some of its Sufi branches, have provisions for chastity, the answer was that spiritual and scholarly discipline requires dedication which is not easily combined with family obligations and which eventually reduces the interest one has in the latter. At my age then this seemed hard to believe but over the years I came to experience the truth of this pragmatic though unromantic observation.

THE RAMAKRISHNA MISSION AND MOTHER TERESA

The matter of social work and public welfare in India was of great interest to us as it is concerned with one of the habitual accusations laid at the door of Hindu civilization by its detractors and even by many of its sympathizers. Swami Vivekananda preached and started a programme of charitable action and economic upliftment at the national level. Although some western scholars claim that he borrowed that concept of religion as service to the poor from Christianity, he always referred to precedents and injunctions in the Hindu religious texts.

The notion of helping the downtrodden to save oneself is a fundamental Christian and also Islamic notion tied to the missionary character of those faiths but there are many exhortations to charity, solidarity and sharing one's wealth with the poor in all the native Indian religions, beginning with those that predate Christianity by many centuries. However the concept of the duty to others is a bit different as the Secretary General of the Ramakrishna mission Swami Gambhirananda, a renowned scholar and prolific author, explained when we called on him. He had, like the founder as well as all the members of his order genuine respect for Jesus and the religion inspired by him but he smilingly drew a distinction between the original meaning of conversion and the use that was made of it by the churches and other monotheistic confessions.

"Conversion is akin to conversation," the Swami observed.

"It means turning all people's souls and minds towards a common goal, that is salvation or liberation from ignorance. To everyone his path so that I cannot impose or even prescribe my religious discipline to others for whom it may not be suitable if they belong to other traditions. Likewise, our approach to charity is dictated by the law of karma. Unlike Christianity which sees all men equally damned by the Original Sin and granted one life on earth to redeem themselves or descend into hell or purgatory, the vedantic doctrines all talk of an infinite number of livetimes during which the soul can accumulate merit or guilt which will be carried into the next birth.

No one can change someone else's karma, he added, so that people have to bear with the suffering that is their lot and strive to purify themselves from the negative backlog they inherited. Conversely, if they are blessed with good material conditions, they must beware of spending that positive capital by indulging in the pleasures afforded to them and falling into a much less privileged state in this existence and in future ones. Therefore charity must be performed mainly for one's own sake and one cannot force others to accept what they are not ready to take."

We saw an illustration of that philosophy in the discreet but effective work carried out the Ramakrishna monks around their premises both in Calcutta and elsewhere, providing a refuge, food and spiritual comfort to the most destitute and bereft persons who came to them in that vast battlefield of poverty and suffering, where many could still be seen dying from disease and malnutrition in the sight of all. However, the most celebrated organization was and still is Mother Teresa's Missionaries of Charity. Though she had not yet been awarded the Nobel Peace Prize, she was already universally famous and no one who came to Calcutta could fail to notice her organisation's presence. Although her mission had adopted many local features in its trappings and methods, Christian zeal was quite noticeable in contrast with the more traditional hindu attitude. More than once we were told by Indian friends that Mother Teresa's admirable work had been given global fame by the powerful Catholic promotional system while older and equally dedicated homegrown charities had no access to such a mighty loudspeaker and could not summon as much support from far and wide. There is little doubt that the heroic Albanian nun was used as a symbol and a magnet by an image conscious Roman Church, keen to project itself as coming to the rescue of those abandoned by their own mostly pagan society.

Other critiques were also raised about Mother Teresa's methods which were focused on providing shelter for terminal patients in order to let them die with dignity, instead of trying to heal them medically. Some suspected, not without reason, that a goal of the missionaries was to make people turn to Christianity in their last moments as part of the unceasing evangelic endeavour to harvest souls. However we were repeatedly assured that in her Nirmal Hriday all the patients and the dying were ministered to with full respect for their respective faiths upto the last rites unless they specifically asked for Christian sacraments. Thus Hindus were blessed with Ganga water in their final moments.

It is always easier to criticize than to act and we could only feel respect and reverence for the abnegation displayed by the missionaries and their volunteers we watched at work in the most wretched quarters of the city, in scenes reminiscent of Rumer Godden's novels. Dominique Lapierre was to make their grim but uplifting epic famous in "The City of Joy" a few years later.

Suffering calls for yeomanly efforts on the part of all those who can help and no one can reasonably find fault in those who dedicate their lives to its mitigation but it appeared to many dispassionate witnesses that mother Teresa, brought up in a rural province of the Ottoman empire in the late 19th century and conditioned by the ideal of mortification that characterizes much of Christianity, sought to share in the pain of those she helped as much as she intended to improve their circumstances. She did require her nuns to live in harsh conditions and generally opposed proposals to make their work easier and their lives more comfortable with the help of technology. She had come to India in an era of penury when few consumer goods were readily available and her organization had very humble beginnings. When it grew to command thousands of nuns and co-workers and to gather vast amounts of charitable donations, Mother Teresa who was already old then did not change her philosophy or practice and continued to operate as when she had run a small shelter in a slum with a few recruits. For that reason she was misunderstood by more than one secularly minded observer who thought that more could have been done to change the lot of the destitute she ministered to. She however resisted suggestions to modernize her Spartan facilities to turn them into proper medical centres, fearing that they would become gradually gentrified nursing homes and that the spirit of devotion and poverty would be lost.

One can appreciate her reasons when one sees how many religious organizations the world over have transformed into commercial enterprises. The Christian "Saint of Calcutta" wanted to preserve the medieval spirit of charity and hospitality.

XVII
How East and West Meet

The Christian Quandary in India

We had met at one of our talks two elderly Belgian Jesuits from the famous St Xavier's College, who had lived in Bengal for decades and were intimately familiar with the city and its people. They both dwelt in a tiny old flat crammed with books and papers, above the small inter-cultural centre called Shanti Bhawan set up by one of them, Father Robert Antoine in South Calcutta. They were scholars of indology of no mean repute, fluent in Sanskrit and Bengali as well as in Greek and Latin. Antoine was recognized as a philosopher whose book "Homo Viator" (Man, the Wayfarer) was a collection of essays on Eastern and Western spiritual traditions. He liked to say that if the Orient was best symbolized by the Buddha, Tantalus the eternally unsatisfied and craving figure of the Greek Hades was an apt allegory of Western man. We spent more than one evening with them discussing over dinner comparative Upanishadic and Christian theology and the significance of charity in the western and Indian contexts. My father did not always agree with their predictably conditioned views that mitigated their personal affection for vedantic philosophy nourished by the outstanding scholarly library their college has inherited from Archbishop Goethals. Antoine had famously written that "we must love Truth more than Christ because before he was that, he was Truth" and that posed no mean problem in the Indian context.

They felt for instance that Hindu ethics prescribes harmlessness to other living beings but is reserved about "do-goodism" as it tends to enjoin preferential charity to brahmanas, religious institutions and sadhus but falls silent on the duties to the lower castes and untouchable even when they starve. We argued that in a society organized in clan-like and occupational communities, solidarity is naturally at play within each jati or caste and largely replaces the concept of global indiscriminate charity. On the other hand, Brahmins were generally men of learning who, with their families dedicated themselves to the cultivation of knowledge and the preservation of a shared spiritual heritage and not to material pursuits, unlike all the other castes. Therefore they were given priority in the support system provided by kings, businesspeople and landowners. It is another matter that, as in all man-made institutions, entropic degeneration had turned many Brahmins into greedy confidence men or lazy parasites, as the medieval literature attests.

Our ecclesiastic friends conceded that the same fate had affected monastic orders and the clergy of the Catholic Church. Corrupt Brahmins, insincere and ignorant Sannyasis and money-minded priests did not however negate the pristine values of the Sanathana Dharma anymore than depraved monks or unscrupulous padres could be taken as proof of Christ's irrelevance. Yet, it is all too natural for people to find fault with another civilization without being willing to admit to similar or worse failings in their own. Acknowledging the tremendous poverty and the glaring inequality that characterize Indian society should not imply that the Hindu religion is at fault for it. Most Christian societies were no better in that respect before the advent of the modern social welfare systems and the amount of organized violence in these "advanced" nations was probably much higher than in the South Asian region.

As one of them Father Fallon said: "It is convenient for Europe to claim that they colonized and exploited other peoples because they were more advanced than their victims. The fact remains that the forcible annexation of foreign lands was a sin."

Pierre Fallon had known Mother Teresa for years and he first mentioned something that became better known years after her death. While discussing the great challenge to their faith that Christian priests face when they witness the piety of average Indians and inevitably come to question the unproven and explicitly irrational foundations of their own creed, he mentioned incidentally that Mother Teresa herself, immersed in a mainly Hindu milieu, had many times faced a nagging doubt about the dogmas she had been taught as a child. Was that questioning a reason for the relentless and almost fierce energy she deployed in her practical task? "She has the role of Martha in the Gospel, "Father Fallon said shaking his head," she complains that she cannot really understand the doctrine or feel the presence of Christ, Surrounded by misery and hardship she does not see how a benevolent God can let things be the way they are or even make them that way and yet expect us to gain salvation in the Next World...."

Faced with the natural logic enshrined in the spiritual core of the Hindu worldview, Christians are indeed at pains to reconcile their own unquestionable dogmas with the conditions of what they are expected to accept as a real, God-created and yet Devil-ruled Vale of tears. We could sense that Christian missionaries, cast afloat in the vast, living and yet seemingly unchanging ocean of Indian religions, have to take shelter either in uncritical obedience to the Church's precepts and rules or in a mystical quest for a grand synthesis between the beliefs they were taught and the surrounding climate of supra-denominational spirituality that pervades the land's many cults. Thus social reform and upliftment becomes the focus of Christian messengers to justify their claim to relevance in an environment where they cannot expect unconditional acceptance of their catechism from people used to looking at the metaphysical roots of religion.

Fallon and Antoine were remarkable men gifted with great charity, compassion and breadth of vision. They sought to bridge the gap between the Hindu civilization and the Catholic worldview with intelligence and devotion but they could not fail to notice that the great religious synthesis they hoped for would not be acceptable to Christian theological authorities. Their endeavour could only result in a respectful and enlightening philosophical dialogue between two traditions. The Church's requirement of harvesting new souls for

Christ necessarily creates ambiguity in the attitude of all its priests towards other religions and faced with the sophisticated metaphysics, apologetics and eschatology of Indian spiritual systems, many experience an inevitable sense of inferiority. "We are children in front of our Hindu elders, father Antoine quipped once, but perhaps the simplest and deepest truth comes out of the mouth of children."

Much of Christianity's seemingly naïve and spontaneous conceit is encapsulated in that sentence.

The Bengali Francophile

One morning an elderly gentleman introduced himself in flawless French at the end of one of our lectures at the University. He was a resident of nearby Chandernagore and one of the leading experts on the biography and work of the 18th century French orientalist Anquetil du Perron who had first translated fifty Upanishads from the Persian version left by Dara Shikoh into French and thereby decisively influenced European philosophy from Schopenhauer onwards.

"Notice," the old Bengali remarked with a mischievous glimmer in his eye, "how Anquetil came to India in 1755 not to study the Vedas about which almost nothing was known then in Europe but the Zoroastrian scriptures which were seen as a fount of wisdom and a source for Christianity. However in 1775 or so, back in Europe he got a copy of Dara Shikoh's farsee text and he discovered the gnosis of the Upnekhat as he transcribed it. His latin rendering, smattered with Persian and Sanskrit words is almost unintelligible but it was enough to get some people thinking in the West. Of course they still thought the Persians came first because Zoroaster is present in the Bible so that it makes him more familiar and acceptable to Christians. Also Zarathustra is a Messiah or a Prophet like Jesus and that makes more sense to followers of a religion revealed by one God-Man; so Voltaire and others were disappointed to discover that the texts of the Avesta translated by Anquetil were prayers. The speculative philosophy was in the Upanishads, not in the Mazdean fragments."

The name of our new friend was K C Karmocar and being a francophone Bengali and a former student of the illustrious gallophile scholar Kalidas Nag he liked France even more than his compatriots who have a soft corner for the land of good food, revered intellectuals and the Revolution. He had been awarded the prestigious Palmes Academiques by the République and was delighted to find visitors from his second motherland. We had many hours of conversation on sundry topics with him and he invited us to the University of Burdwan where he had been a lecturer before his retirement.

Karmocar was a mine of knowledge on the history of his land and he told us many stories about the great scientist Jagdish Chander Bose, a pioneer and an inventor who may be regarded as the true father of wireless communications and a forerunner in the use of semiconductors. Bose was a polymath and a humanist who probably created the science-fiction genre in Bengali and corresponded with many of the leading minds of his day, from Tagore to Romain Rolland. At Karmocar's urging, riding once more the city's ancient and rusty trams we visited his stately red-brick house on APC Roy Road and admired many of the original memorabilia collected by the great man. Father Fallon had pointed out that J.C. Bose had learnt physics first from the eminent Jesuit Eugène Lafont at St Xavier's but Karmocar who did not hide his antipathy for the two priests whose attempt to christianise Hinduism he distrusted, argued that the pantheistic philosophy of Bose was typically Hindu.

"He was the first to show with scientific methods that plants feel and communicate like animals and he even demonstrated that metals feel stress and fatigue like living substances," our friend said. "For holding such 'eastern mystical view' he lost credit with many orthodox scientists of the day and yet now he is found to have been right. Bose was the real discoverer of biophysics and some of his students, such as Meghnad Saha and S. N. Bose were as important to the advancement of science as he himself had been. Marconi, being a European, got credit for inventing the radio but Bose preceded him."

Looking beyond his explicit Bengali chauvinism, we found it hard to deny that he supplied real facts.

Karmocar was a scholar in many areas, apart from his dedication to Anquetil's work. He made us realize how influential French literature, especially since the days of Alexandre Dumas, Victor Hugo and Emile Zola, had been in his native province, notably with Bankim Chandra Chattopadhyay, perhaps the greatest fiction writer of his century in his language. A number of classical French novels and plays had been translated into Bengali by no less a person than Jyotindranath Tagore, one of Rabindranath's many brothers and Baudelaire had enjoyed great popularity among the local literary elite, beginning with the precociously talented Dutt sisters, perhaps because of his exotic flavour and "oriental" sensuousness. Conversely, Rabindranath Tagore's poetic style was emulated at times by French authors as diverse as André Gide and the symbolic bard and diplomat Saint John Perse.

Like most Bengalis, Karmocar also had detailed knowledge of Subhash Chandra Bose, the heroic leader in the independence struggle who is no relation to the afore-mentioned scientist but is a pioneer in many ways too. The first nominal head in exile of a free Indian state, Bose, who was elected Mayor of Calcutta in 1930 reportedly died in an air crash in Taiwan shortly after the Allied victory in the second world war, leading many to think that he might have been assassinated. In 1943, after trying to muster military support from the Axis powers in Europe, Netaji (the leader) as he had become known, was sent to Madagascar on a *Kriegsmarine* submersible and went aboard a Nippon submarine on to Japan where Admiral Tojo received him and helped him recruit an Indian army among the prisoners of war captured by his forces in South East Asia.

There is always a less known aspect to every historic saga. Karmocar told us about how even before the War, Bose had established relations with a unit of the Japanese Secret Service headed by I Fujiwara, an officer who belonged to the most illustrious clan in the Empire of the Rising Sun, closely related to the Mikado's bloodline. This contact was made, according to him through a mysterious European woman who lived in Calcutta and published in 1939 an influential document entitled "A Warning to the Hindus."

He asked us if we had met Savitri Devi as she lived in Delhi at the time, unbeknownst to us. I had read once about that eccentric French born Graeco-British female scholar and writer who had come to India in the early nineteen thirties to explore the repository of Aryan civilization. In Calcutta, she had donned Indian clothes, adopted the Hindu way of life and married a Bengali intellectual and political activist A. K. Mukherji. Together they had founded a cult of the rising German Fuhrer, Adolf Hitler whom they saw as the new Aryan Avatar fated to bring back the Golden Age of Hyperborean civilization.

Among many original twists and turns taken by strands of Hinduism, this was surely one of the strangest but the performance of religious pujas dedicated to the new Indo-Germanic Messiah had not prevented the couple from playing an important role in the effervescent metropolis during the war years. Savitri Devi and her husband secretly passed on intelligence to the Nazi and Japanese Imperial regimes to facilitate their planned invasions of India and supported Bose's action for national liberation from British rule. Savitri Devi put Bose in touch with the military rulers in Tokyo. Although the Mukherjis risked their lives by playing that clandestine role they were not arrested and, after leaving her husband, Savitri returned to Europe in 1945 on a British passport and spent the next years traveling on the continent and promoting her vision of Aryan occultism and mystical pantheism. I was to find her trace many years later among people who had known her well. Although her delusion about Hitler's destiny had led her astray she was but one of countless people in all walks of life and nations who had been mesmerized by the dark charisma of the Austrian politician.

Savitri Devi was otherwise a highly intelligent and cultured woman whose writings betray a visionary grasp of the hidden realities beneath apparent turns of events. She realized the unlimited scope and depth of Indian philosophical and political thought which she compared favourably with the relative intellectual poverty of semitic belief systems. Like many in her age and in other times, she regarded Jews as promoters and beneficiaries of a self-serving social system entirely controlled by economic and confessional criteria and thus highly destructive for other traditional civilizations founded on the "Indo-Aryan" notion of the cosmic law in which metaphysics and the understanding of the natural order regulates all other activities. Her ideas were clearly well received by many Indian thinkers at the time and Netaji Subhash was one of those who took her appeal and her vision into account. "He was inspired by the Vedic wisdom and the message of the Bhagavad Gita revived by Swami Vivekananda. He sought to practice the doctrine of karma yoga in all his actions" Karmocar pointed out "and as such he did not judge people and ideas by British-set standards. He kept an independent evaluation of things and had above all, a strategic way of thinking."

We asked him if Netaji had been tempted to embrace the national socialist ideals professed by Savitri in an age when the Axis powers were regarded by many as the chief hope for colonized peoples because of their opposition to the imperial western states. In response our friend pointed to Bose's often reaffirmed commitment to democracy and socialism although he openly favoured an authoritarian or even paramilitary form of government at least for the first years after the achievement of independence. He was not alone in that view and I later realized that all "leftist" theories related to Marxism share certain features with Fascist doctrines, much as they may deny it.

National Socialism and its international namesake may have become fraternal enemies but siblings they remain from the time when they had not yet parted ways. Calcutta, the historic capital of Communist power in India had also been more receptive to Nazi influence or at least to Japanese pan-Asianism than most of the country, perhaps because it was more deeply westernized and also due to the tremendous economic inequality and rampant poverty that the British Raj had only increased.

Comparisons are often drawn between the fiery, urbane and martial Bengali, S C Bose and the monk-like Gujarati Gandhi. Despite the evident contrasts, both were lawyers totally dedicated to the task of freeing India and they represented two facets of the country's civilization. Bose, following the call of the ksatriya attempted to break the nation's shackles through the conventional methods of armed struggle while Gandhi chose the path of civil disobedience, pleading, negotiation and moral remonstrance. Each thought that the other was on the wrong track but in the end Bose's military appeals undermined British control over the colonial Indian army and had, according to some authoritative testimonies at least as much influence in convincing Westminster to give up its empire as Gandhi's grassroots campaigns. In Calcutta I found that people had a natural preference for the son of the soil and looked at Gandhi with some resentment as he was well known for having undermined Bose's leadership of the Congress and opposed from the start his project to overthrow the Raj by military means. Gandhi's unconditional rejection of violence could not accommodate Bose's strategic plans even though the Mahatma was not opposed to Hitler's Germany and advocated India's non-cooperation with Britain after baldly advising the British not to resist the Nazis in Europe. It is hence unsurprising that not a few Indians accuse the Father of Nation of either duplicity, inconsistency or both. However Gandhi and his supporters in the Congress stuck to their general policy of working for freedom through a gradual process of emancipation from colonial rule instead of seeking a quick and forced break. India was probably spared much bloodshed by this conscious choice although the country's partition took place amidst a huge massacre that negated the main benefit of the non-violent method.

SATYAJIT RAY

We had met a few of Bengal's storied intellectuals and artists but did not have the chance to visit the ailing Suniti Kumar Chatterjee, the best known savant of the city at the time who would die a few weeks later. However we made an appointment with India's foremost film maker Satyajit Ray and went to see him in his spacious, rather dark flat located in an Edwardian "Wren-naissance" building on Bishop Elfroy Road.

Ray had become internationally famous for such classics as *Pather Panchali* and *Charulatha* and he acknowledged his debt to French

"New Wave" cinema and to Jean Renoir who had oriented him towards the making of feature films. In 1977, after completing his Calcutta Trilogy he was finishing *Shatranj ke khiladi* (The Chess Players) which was his first hindi language production featuring a distinguished international cast of actors. I found him courteous but haughty and rather melancholy in his gaze and expression. His face reminded me of the brooding mask of a khmer statue, with a broad nose, high forehead and full lips. We talked about cinema, literature and Indian culture and quickly discovered his ambiguity about the Hindu traditional philosophy which he visibly associated with backwardness, prejudice and oppression. He was no formal Marxist and, like Visconti to whom he could be compared in some aspects of his work, was guided more by aesthetic appreciation than by ideology. As many of his compatriots he had been repelled by the exploitation of mass poverty that had been characteristic of the Indian social system for centuries and he had scathingly indicted it by portraying the decadent oligarchies of the colonial period on the background of stark and widespread destitution. His predilection for Italian neo-realism could perhaps be traced back to a conscious minimalistic reaction to India's love affair with unruly profusion. I could sense silent disapproval when my father mentioned our action for the introduction of fundamental citizens' duties in India's polity and Mrs. Gandhi's support for it as he clearly disliked her. He felt that the country was at risk of becoming a dictatorship and was not convinced by our pointing out to the current electoral campaign which contradicted predictions of permanent tyranny.

We should probably have avoided political subjects but I left with the impression that here was a man of exceptional, multi-faceted talent who repressed a naturally playful, humorous and surrealistic bent of mind to direct his austerely realistic, understated and slow paced classics. He might have been happier churning out colourful and fantastic tales for children as his parallel writing and graphic design careers indicated. Did he wish to be seen as the Indian De Sica or Truffault or was he really following his spontaneous inspiration? The question remains open. I think that some of his films have not aged well but others are unforgettably personal and powerful. He deserves even more respect for putting artistic ideals ahead of commercial concerns.

FIGURES OF SAGES

As our stay in the city of palaces and slums came to an end we moved, on the invitation of Karmocar to the quaint old outpost of Chandernagore, for centuries a speck of French soil on the banks of the Hooghly that had often provided asylum to Indian opponents of British colonial rule and also to people who had fallen foul of the rather strict Victorian laws on morality.

We stayed at an ashram in a garden on the shore of the Hooghly near the usually sleepy Strand, the main promenade on the river front where one can see some architectural remnants of the Gallic presence, such as the columnated Doric-fronted palace of Dupleix and the spires of the church of the Sacred Heart, reminding all that France long ago had dedicated itself to that hoary universal symbol of faith. The ashram was affiliated to the Yogoda Satsangha Society, the body founded by the illustrious Paramahamsa Yogananda who had spread the technique of kriya yoga worldwide. The head of the ashram was a distinguished and cultured old man who had been in his youth a disciple of Sri Yukteshwar, Yogananda's own master, reputed as an astrologer and a great enlightened being whose own ashram is located not far away, in the old Dutch settlement of Serampore also on the bank of the river.

Sri Yukteshvar's spiritual lineage went back through his own master from Benares, Shyam Lahiri to the mythical Mahavatar Baba, a mysterious allegedly immortal Siddha yogi from the Himalayas who remains invisible to those he does not choose to meet. Several members of Lahiri's sampradaya have reported coming across the Babaji in diverse locations and his picture, drawn according to Yogananda's indications, has become famous thanks to the YSS, its international outlet, the Divine Life Society and to the Beatles who for years followed the kriya yoga discipline.

The Society's headquarters in India are in Dakshineshwar and it is particularly present in Bengal. Our stay in that small haven of pastoral peace overlooking the placid flow of the river gave us time to learn more about the teachings and miracles of the various masters of that tradition which Yogananda described in his books and especially in his "Autobiography of a Yogi."

Bengal was, in the latter part of the 19th century under strong Christian influence because of the old and well established European presence. Both Sri Yukteshwar and Yogananda hailed from the region and they studied in Christian schools so that they constantly sought to highlight the philosophical and mystical bonds between the Gospels of Jesus and the Hindu holy texts in order to bring the two traditions closer, in keeping with the Bengali tendency early evinced by Ram Mohun Roy and the Brahmo Samaj. Yogananda had said, following his masters, that Christ had come to India and had met with Mahavatar Baba.

This subject was familiar to us and we could converse for hours with our host, the head of the ashram on the many common symbols, allegories and similar rituals. The parampara of Yogananda evinced the flexible nature of the Hindu spiritual tradition; some of its masters had been householders and raised families while others had embraced celibacy and withdrawn from the world and a few toured the globe in order to spread the message. There was no apparent regard for social class either. Sri Yukteshwar was an aristocrat by birth while his teacher Lahiri had been a petty administrative officer. The spontaneity of the freely chosen relations between guru and disciple contrasted with the strict hierarchy one notices in all major Christian denominations and even in Buddhism.

Whereas some Hindu traditional schools have an understandable suspicion of Christianity which has generally acted as a conquering, expansionistic creed, there are no such reservations among the followers of either Sri Ramakrishna or Mahavatar Baba but instead a genuine desire for communion together with a natural sense of their separate and distinct identities. They do not seek the light of truth in Jesus but rather they wish to show the relationship between separate doctrines of wisdom seen as branches of one universal tree. We reflected together on how the Christian baptism reflects the Upanishadic verse *Apojyotir raso'mritam brahmair*:" water is the light, the nectar of eternal life, Brahman" and why the Vedas allude to the sacrifice of Fire as the First Born in the water to which he is entrusted in a reed basket or raft, thus evoking the story of the newborn Moses.

John The Baptist tells his followers that he who is to come after him will christen people with fire and not in water. When Jesus appears on the bank of the Jordan to be baptized by John, a dove flies down from Heaven to manifest the Son's divine election. In the Brahmanic scriptures, the divine bird Gayatri flies up to the solar Agni and brings forth Kumara, the eternal child, showing the origin of the symbol of the Holy Ghost. The kumara is concealed in a cavern like the divine offspring of Mary in the cave of Bethlehem.

In the vedic hymns, Agni is saved from the river of death by the virgin moon who adopts him as her child. Agni is etymologically related to the latin Ignis and also to Agnus: the lamb who is the emblem of Jesus. Prajna, the highest knowledge is the offspring born of Maya and of the still, contemplating consciousness as Jesus is immaculately conceived by Mary when she is visited by the Angel Messenger. The Virgin Mother is the vedic Viraj, the divine feminine principle and her scion is Anilaya, an eternal wanderer without abode ("for the son of man has no place to rest his head") who like Prajapati is both mortal and immortal, man and God at once. Prajapati must be sacrificed so that all creation may arise from him and feast on his flesh and blood. Then the eternal child is reborn and the cycle can begin anew.

"It is a cosmic and cosmogonic myth which religions enact in a human setting when the symbols incarnate in human forms, It was known in India thousands of years before Jesus was born in Judea" the old man said. "How few however remain aware of the universal truth beneath the seemingly historical accounts which become part of sectarian traditions!."

We regretfully left that abode of tranquility next to Chandernagore to proceed on our journey but not before visiting the exquisite and ancient terracota temple which exemplifies the typical architecture of Bengal in which sanctuaries are lovingly turned and sculpted like ornate potteries. They give its full meaning to the widespread allegory that represents the body as made of clay and alludes to God as the supreme potter. The guru embraced us with touching emotion and we really felt we had found a spiritual family in that nook of Bengal.

We reached Burdwan where we lectured at the university housed in the rambling former palace of the toponymous maharajas whose family still dominated the Calcutta social scene, vying with the princes of Cooch Behar for primacy. In that district, in the village of Palitpur a famous guru called Soham Swami ("Master That I am") but popularly known as Tiger Baba who had been a wrestler and a bodyguard renowned for his prodigious strength , had established his ashram. He was a disciple of the mysterious spiritual master Tibbeti Baba, legendary for his supernatural powers, who was variously regarded as either a Bengali Hindu or a Buddhist Tibetan and who wandered across the length and breadth of Asia and Siberia. Such biographic and religious ambiguity is quite frequent in India where denominational and philosophical streams converge and branch off freely.

Tibbeti Baba taught, like Soham Swami, what may be described as a non-sectarian synthesis in simple language of Advaita Vedanta and Mahayana which rejects the worship of a personalized deity. Soham Swami, shortly after his teacher left his body in 1923 published a collection of the latter's utterances entitled "Commonsense" that may be regarded by "western" eyes as an atheistic message insofar as God is seen as a material being. Indeed various renowned Communists and agnostics in India took this book as their vade mecum but both the Babas are to be seen as representatives of the apophatic current in Indian thought and are no more atheistic than the Buddha. They are venerated by many as "godmen" and their influence should help confused foreigners understand the de facto symbiosis that prevails in Bengal between the iconic cult of Kali, Tagore's spiritual syncretism and Marxism. I was reminded of the paradoxical interest of some of the Bolshevik leaders for Tibetan metaphysics and symbology revealed by the history of the Roerich family.

The palace of Burdwan is a pink tropical avatar of a Palladian regal mansion that could have been designed by a feverish Robert Adam and I felt intensely there the nostalgic lure of life on a great country estate in colonial Bengal but we were impatient to reach Shantiniketan, the university founded by Rabindranath Tagore in a rural setting which was our next stop.

TAGORE'S ABODE OF PEACE

We had been warned of a disappointment since Visvabharati as its founder had called it (meaning "Universal Indian") was no longer the pastoral academy where the master had spent many years of his life. It had grown into a conventional university with multiple departments and had adopted the mandatory syllabus and examination system which Tagore had always deeply disliked. Both my father and I felt attuned to Gurudev's theories of education, inspired by the personalized *guru-shishya parampara* and based on communion with nature.

The sage of Shantiniketan with his finely chiseled face, contemplative glance and flowing snowy beard that give him the appearance of a Greek river god offers many analogies with Leo Tolstoy, another illustrious aristocratic author and thinker who used his wealth to reform his society, devise a new educational method and seek the spiritual unity of all religions. Tagore is however far more refined and subtle than the colossus of Yasnaia Polyana. He was an artist in almost all fields, poetry, painting, music and decoration while, despite the wonderful power and beauty of his prose Tolstoy affected a disdain for art belied by his sensitivity. Like the Russian count, the Bengali grandee was a pioneer in various fields. He worked tirelessly for Asian unity within the global community and in that sense he inspired Netaji Subhash although he did not approve of militant nationalism and was probably in his last years horrified by Japanese belligerent expansionism. In his attachment to peace and international amity he was close to Gandhi much as he disliked the deliberately plebeian aspects of the Mahatma's ideology.

Tagore, like Gandhi, Vivekananda and Aurobindo envisioned a peaceful world, connected by the innumerable bonds of wisdom, art, culture and human solidarity in which Asia could give the best of her ancient civilizations. As he put: "each country of Asia will solve its own national problems according to its strength, nature and needs but the lamp they will each carry in their path to progress will converge to illuminate the common way of knowledge."

Tagore's influence on China was very great in his time and he was only forgotten in the dark days of the Cultural Revolution. The Chinna Bhavan at Shantiniketan remains a testimony of the importance he attached to the millennial bonds between the Middle Kingdom and India. He invited some eminent Chinese scholars to teach there and the faculty hosts a precious library of sinic literature in many areas and started the first regular course of Tibetan language and literature in modern India.

Our lecture at the Music Faculty was attended by the Vice-Chancellor's wife, a respected musician and that evening we were invited for dinner by her and her husband Dr Surajit Chandra Sinha who presided over Visvabharati in those years.

Sinha, a refined and courteous man of letters belonged to the princely family of Susang, in what is now Bangladesh. He dedicated himself to anthropology and had produced pioneering studies on the tribes of various parts of India. It was traditional in aristocratic houses of that region to pursue an academic vocation, contrary to the prevailing culture of Rajputs in the North of the country who usually confine themselves to martial, sporting or political activities. His family, some of whose members were prominent Marxists, had known the Tagores for more than a century and he himself had met Gurudev often in his youth at Shantiniketan where his parents had a country house. We spent an evening, evoking the great man's shadow and discussing some of the many celebrities who had stayed at the school, such as the orientalists Giuseppe Tucci and Sylvain Levi as well as several renowned European and South American poets. The Vive-

Chancellor evoked a conversation he had had with Julian Huxley and the latter's fascination with the mysteries of consciousness to which his brother Aldous had dedicated much of his life work. "The major task of the scientist today, Sinha said, quoting Huxley, is the exploration of the inner life. The study of the mind has just begun." He also enlightened us about the French influence in Tagore's life work. Gurudev had invited a respected educationist from the pensionnat of Sainte Marie of Neuilly, Christiane Boissennec to head the girls' section of Shantiniketan and the Art School Kala Bhavan had long had on its faculty Andrée Karpeles. In subsequent years, Alexandra David-Néel, the well known explorer of Tibet had visited it and so had Alice Boner, the Swiss orientalist and artist whose great canvases inspired by Indian symbology we had seen at the museum of Benares Hindu University.

The poet-laureate was serious in his commitment to universalism and he tried to give as much importance to the West as to the East in the institution's curriculum.

One of the questions that often comes up about Tagore regards the true value of his poetic gift as the English translation of his verse can at times seem trite or maudlin. Without knowing Bengali in depth it is probably not possible to appreciate the real beauty of his original expression and Dr Sinha, who was not an unconditional devotee of Gurudev gave a balanced opinion.

"It is possible that his Nobel Prize was given partly for political considerations, as such prizes usually are" he said "After all the British, and the West in general, wished to honour those members of the Indian elite who supported Euro-American rule and were well integrated in the colonial empires. There was also a growing need to break out of the circle of eurocentrism which already looked painfully outdated. Tagore, as a prominent figure in Calcutta, the heart of the Raj was an easy choice but as a Bengali writer Tagore was a bard of the soul of his land. He brought village folklore into the drawing rooms of the *bhadralok* and he embodied the Indian ancestral fusion of non-denominational mysticism and cultural universalism. Thus every Bengali and every Indian could find himself in his productions."

Since I had first read him I had always appreciated the exquisite inspiration, so simple and yet so refreshing, so full of inner light that Tagore manifested. I remembered lines such as:

"I dive down in the sea of form
Hoping to gain the pearl of formlessness."
Or: "O master poet I have sat down at thy feet
Only let me make life simple and straight
Like a flute of reed for thee to fill with music."

Tagore speaks the cosmic language of all mystics. His poetry could have been written by a Persian Sufi, by a medieval minstrel, by a Spanish Carmelite or by a Hindu bhakta. Likewise his face and effigy evoke the rishis, peers and prophets of all ages and times and timelessness is what India enshrines through the constant and tight combination of all the periods of history. A universalist in his poetry despite the intensely regional flavor of his themes Tagore was as cosmopolitan in his worldview as he was catholic in his spirituality and polyfacetic in his interests and talents. Science, history, international politics, education and social upliftment were all studied by this man who like Bacon took all knowledge as his province.

The Sinhas advised us to explore the countryside that still surrounds the Shantiniketan campus and where Tagore had spent much of his childhood. At that time the property of his grandfather was surrounded by other great feudal estates such as Taltore and Surul which belonged to friends of his family. We enjoyed some enchanting hours walking about the lush fields and groves crowned by the scruffy plumes of palms in which villages looked like naturally grown clusters of mud and thatch. Herds of dark nonchalant buffaloes bathed in greenish ponds together with laughing naked boys while flocks of mynahs and parrots fluttered noisily about. More than once we swam into the still water of a "tank" to find shelter from the damp heat and dried ourselves beneath the canopy of overhanging roots of banyan trees. The crimson bouquets of palasas rose high in the mauve evening skies that echoed the cuckoo's insistant appeal. The battle of Plassey which gave to Robert Clive and the East India Company's army the control of Bengal was named after those very trees.

Many a time when in the Indian rural surroundings I think of the vast literature that details the age-old poverty and hopelessness of most of its human denizens. Yet I cannot but compare the idyllic repose of its atmosphere with the dirty agitation and cramped quarters of cities in which most migrants from the villages find themselves. Conventional socio-economic thought holds the fate of town dwellers to be better because of improved access to poorly paid work, rudimentary education (at least for the next generation) and medical care, although those facilities are more potential than really accessible. We are told that country life for the poor is stultifyingly monotonous, boring and petty minded and that the stimulation and opportunities afforded by an urban existence, even in a slum amount to an improvement in their lot. However I cannot relate to that assessment and I feel like Gandhi that uprooting vast numbers of rural people is a disastrous process and that real upliftment would consist in making them more affluent and independent in their traditional setting so that they may learn to enjoy the priceless gift of the environment that has shaped them for thousands of years. Yet men are restless and hardly ever content with their lot so that they are on an endless race to escape from themselves unless they are paralysed by the sheer weight of their conditioning.

Indian wisdom has shown long ago that the only real freedom lies within us. Physical endeavours to evade hardship always disappoint unless they take us inward, where true development takes place. Would modern India keep that in mind in her halting struggle against poverty?

XVIII

Viceroys, Lamas and Kommissars

Simla

The "toy train" had for hours zigzagged up and down fir and pine clad hills and valleys, crossing more than eight hundred bridges, large and small and plumbing the darkness of a hundred tunnels to reach our destination, nestled atop a high ridge, two miles above the steamy Indian plains. Before us a grey stone Jacobean manor rose on a flower edged lawn of the greenest turf. We had come to Simla, the summer capital of the British in India and our temporary home there would be the former residence of the viceroys which had been turned into the national institute of advanced studies by the country's philosopher president S. Radhakrishnan.

As a child, Kipling and other bards of the Raj had left in my memory various tales about Simla, that simili-English resort town in which the rulers of the immense Indian empire found the clubby atmosphere that they were used to in their hierarchically conscious society. They could almost forget that they were in Asia and share their time between golf and cricket games, horse races, hunting and fishing parties, high teas, evening cocktails in smokings and gowns and all male confabulations over Port, whisky and cigars.

Since Governor General Sir John Lawrence picked that wooded range of the "Indian Switzerland" as a refuge from torrid and humid Calcutta in 1863, his successors had spent the hottest months of the year in that haven of sunny coolness. Lord Lytton, perhaps the most romantically inclined of all viceroys had, from the year of his arrival in India in 1876 planned the summer palace in which we were staying as a nostalgic paean to his homeland's Elizabethan past. However it was

Lord Dufferin of Ava, the man who annexed Burma to the Indian empire who first stayed there and paneled the soaring inner walls and ceilings with the precious teak wood collected from the land he had conquered.

Having come into being to fulfill the needs of the colonial military and administrative elite, the town took the appearance of a neogothic, red and green village with a duly bell towered white Christ Church, a theater, a golf club and many castle-like buildings which till today evoke the ballads of Walter Scott. The governor of the vast Punjab province and his staff also moved their summer headquarters to Simla and so did high ranking functionaries and leading businessmen. The natives were only reluctantly admitted and generally circumscribed to the other side of town, as far as possible from Observatory hill which was the Viceroy's exclusive domain. Along the crest of the ridge the Mall was laid out as a pedestrian promenade on which only the carriages of the highest representatives of the British crown had right of way. On the opposite hill, the Jakho dominated since ancient times by a Hindu temple, many wealthy part-time residents built their mansions and chalets. Simla came to be known as a village of manors. The Maharaja of Patiala who owned much of the land around the town became unwelcome as his ostentatious display of wealth annoyed the parsimonious and understated Englishmen and, true to the belief that living well is the best revenge, built a magnificent estate for himself and his vast entourage on the nearby Chail hilltop, pointedly chosen for being higher than Simla. There it remains and displays a golf course which was then the loftiest in the world and may still be.

This mountainous region of India has more in common with the Alps than its landscape; for instance it had as many principalities as there are cantons in the Helvetic confederacy. Our research and lectures at the Institute of Advanced Studies and at the local University left us with plenty of time to explore the town and the region. Simla was still dominated by the peculiar anglo-indian culture preserved by its boarding schools, its churches and its local aristocracy. We had another experience of the Raj's legacy when we were received for tea by the urbane and literate Governor of the State at the old viceregal lodge which carried the unexpected name of Peterhoff.

His Excellency Aminuddin Ahmad Khan happened to be, as we discovered incidentally, a brother-in-law of the recently deceased President of India, Fakhruddin Ali Ahmed who had received us in Delhi a few months earlier. The governor was born a heir to the little state of Loharu near Delhi, carved out by an Afghan military chief who had settled there in the 18th century. He was probably a bit bored by the provincial atmosphere of Simla and enjoyed meeting foreign visitors. We ended up spending a few afternoons with him and other occasional guests in his drawing room. He told us a few things about the history of his official residence which had been lived in by viceroys before the construction of the monumental lodge where we resided.

The first occupant of Peterhoff had been the 8th Earl of Elgin, son of the Scottish peer made famous by his controversial purchase of the Parthenon marble friezes from Athens. Elgin the younger was an avid explorer of the wilds of what was then known as the Punjab hill states and died in 1863 while crossing a mountain stream near Dharmshala, in the region where he lies buried. Much later it was in the selfsame mansion that the assassin of Gandhi, Nathuram Godse was tried as the building had by then become a court of justice. The governor however could not account for the house's Tzarist name. "The only thing I know that relates to this is that the Consul General of Russia who also resided in Simla in the hot season was at one time a certain Nabokoff, an uncle of the writer" the Nawab chuckled.

He had many other stories to tell about Simla whose history fed his—and my—interest in gossip about illustrious figures. He advised us to visit the golf club at Naldehra, a place which had given her middle name to a daughter of Lord Curzon as she had been conceived in that very location.

The exotically called beauty, Alexandra Naldehra, nicknamed Baba, a God-daughter of the Queen of England, grew to become the first love of Prince George, Duke of Kent, the future George VI before marrying the Prince of Wales's equerry and confidant and going through a string of high profile affairs. Her happy admirers reportedly included Lord Halifax, Mussolini's dashing ambassador to London Dino Grandi and Sir Oswald Mosley, the head of the British Fascist party who was married to her elder sister. She personified the glamorous high society of her day which had discarded Victorian prudery to throw itself into the decadent whirl of the swinging twenties.

Not much remained of the rather self-indulgent society life of Simla in British days when it attracted most of the elite of the country, including such future celebrities as the prodigal daughter of Indian painting Amrita SherGil and her admirer the journalist Malcolm Muggeridge or the art critic Mulk Raj Anand who had set there in the thirties his novel "Coolie". The town had become a sedate watering hole for middle class families from Delhi and the Punjab plains but it remained a major garrison as it hosted the western command headquarters of the army. We met the commanding officer, Lieutenant General IS Gill, the son of a Sikh soldier and a Scottish mother who arranged for us to speak to a small gathering of some of his top officers about the relevance of Indian ancient culture to military and strategic matters. The General himself looked and spoke like a tried and true soldier and a gentleman of the old British Indian army. Talking to him made us realize the profound influence of the colonizing power over the institutions it had fashioned in its image. However India, as land of castes and communities absorbed that foreign implant while injecting in it some of its ancestral features and without feeling too perturbed in the seemingly unchanging core of its being.

We had an opportunity to explore that process of inculturation with a couple of officers who invited us at their club shortly after our session with the Western Command higher Staff. We all came to the conclusion that occupational classes are similar in most nations. An Indian Rajput is closer to a nobleman of military extraction in any part of the world than to a businessman in his own country. Likewise a western intellectual or administrator tends to find affinities with many a Brahmin. The British military officers easily formed bonds, despite the racial and religious prejudices, with their Indian subordinates who often became brothers-in-arms. Likewise English Royalty felt a kinship with the local princes even though the latter were not even admitted in the local associations and clubs set up by the expatriate middle class that managed the Empire.

Such considerations brought us to the sensitive but important question of the Indian army's role since Independence. Contrary to its neighbours, Pakistan and Bangladesh that shared its colonial past India had never experienced or even been threatened by a military takeover despite several wars and difficult situations, including the state of Emergency that had then only recently been lifted. The answer of the officers was predictable but it confirmed our opinion that the armed forces fashioned by the East Indian Company and the succeeding Raj had remained a professional weapon that took no part in politics and had no interest in ruling a country whose size and diversity could discourage even ambitious generals.

The nation has been held together by a consensus expressed in the Constitution which provides enough stakes to all its ethnic components to stay together provided the highest power is not openly and violently usurped by a faction. The instinctive feudal loyalism fostered by the Hindu political doctrine keeps most people in their traditional places. Rulership is divinely sanctioned by inheritance or election but there are few examples of a non-Muslim war leader rising in the ranks to seize the throne. In the political domain the country was divided for most of its history into countless kingdoms and locally self-governing units and hence since the abolition of the Mughal Empire no prince, no monarch however prestigious, could claim the allegiance of a large section of the populace across the land. The Nehru family had picked the mantle of supremacy in a democratic format in the wake of the Independence struggle but their predominance was open to constant challenge and in that summer of 1977 many expected Mrs. Gandhi, made unpopular by her experiment with authoritarianism, to lose her mandate which she did shortly thereafter by a huge margin of votes. Her party was decimated in Northern India and the coalition of her opponents came to power with surprising ease and speed.

In the military circles of Simla we heard a version of the process that led to India's partition which several other sources confirmed in later discussions. Muhammed Ali Jinnah was seen as a British agent who had been used by the colonial power to divide and weaken the nationalist movement by convincing a substantial proportion of influential Muslims that their prosperity and even their survival were at risk if India became independent with a Hindu majority. While Jinnah's ambition was to be a national leader, the Crown wanted to split India along confessional lines and retain decisive influence over the various countries which were expected to emerge out of the breakup of the Raj. In particular, the North Western region, because of its proximity to the oil rich Persian Gulf and to Soviet Central Asia was seen as critical to the maintenance of Anglo-Saxon supremacy in Asia. Winston Churchill among other statesmen had adopted the views of Sir Olaf Caroe, an influential high official long posted in Peshawar and had 'turned' Jinnah and through him the Muslim League into fierce campaigners for an Islamic British protectorate "from the Hindu Kush in the West to the Brahmaputra in the East." Such a new "mughal nation" might have encompassed most of the Indo-Gangetic plain and drawn in other Muslim-ruled states in the south of India such as the Nizam of Hyderabad's.

WHIFFS OF OLDEN DAYS

Until their departure many British colonial authorities, guided by their monarchical instincts, expected the Indian princely rulers to play major parts in post-colonial India. Some conservative Indian politicians thought that they would retain their limited sovereignty under a federal status. However the staunchly republican convictions of Nehru and the resolve of his first Home Minister Patel not to let old feudal divisions imperil or weaken the survival of the new country put paid to those speculations. Many maharajas and nawabs saw that their age was coming to an end and they tried to react in various ways to the inevitable abolition of their fiefdoms and prerogatives.

One who was not reconciled with looming fate was Harinder Singh Brar, the Sikh maharaja of Faridkot, a small but prosperous and densely populated state of the Punjab, close to the future border with Pakistan. His ancestor had founded, almost a century earlier, the Singh Sabha, a movement for the reform of Sikhism. He saw the possibility of acquiring a very large estate in Ethiopia where he often went hunting for big game. Accordingly he requested the Negus Haile Selassie to grant him sovereignty with all the privileges of nationhood over a territory as vast as a small country that he wished to purchase.

The Ethiopian Emperor might have been open to the Maharaja's offer that would have brought a large infusion of Pounds Sterling into the depleted Treasury of the realm but his advisers thought better of it and opposed the alienation of a large piece of the national patrimony which was already threatened by several regional separatist movements. Hence the Lion of Judah had to reject the offer of the Lion from the Punjab.

I could say if it were not a bit cavalier, that we got the story from the horse's mouth as it was the maharaja himself who narrated it with relish after the three course formal lunch that we attended at his manorial chalet located amidst the apple orchards of Mashobra, a few miles away from Simla. Before getting to the main residence we had paused at various smaller buildings on the estate to be welcomed by majestic turbaned Sardars and at least on one occasion we thought we were being greeted by His Highness in person until it became apparent that we had only met one of his ADCs. I read later that the Ethiopian king of kings had experienced the same kind of misadventure. The Maharaja kept an entourage of handsome officers and paid an unexpected price when one of his daughters married one against her father's will. Finally the portly and mercurial Harinder Singh himself received us with gruff cordiality in a drawing room enlivened by the blaze of logs from a stately fireplace.

During the lunch, served by liveried valets in silver and flatware stamped with the Faridkot crest a black tied band played popular

European and Indian tunes in an adjoining gallery. There must have been a dozen guests at the long table, all military officers, landowners and government servants in the region, except for a couple of young and glamorous women who happened to be quite well known in the power circles of the capital at the time as we found out later.

According to a general habit in India most guests left shortly after the end of the luncheon but the host, visibly used to long postmeridian chats over digestifs was relieved when we agreed to stay. Our decision was made easier by the continuing presence of the elegant young things, one of whom I found adorably flirty to the point of naughtiness. The afternoon proceeded quite agreeably and that is when I heard the story of the maharaja's projects and adventures in Africa despite the distracting presence of my neighbor on the sofa, whose shapely body was more revealed than hidden by her narrow, armless bodice and gossamer saree. Her unselfconscious indulgence in the fine wine served by the amphitryon contributed to her joyous mood and possibly to the frequent slippage of the upper strip of her dress that covers the bust—the pallu. What we would now call a malfunction made her look like a siren swimming waist-deep in a river of silk.

I learnt during the afternoon that the alluring beauty was a favourite of Sanjay Gandhi, the Prime Minister's second son.

The Maharaja's conversation was interesting because of its wickedness. He was known as a rake and his immense wealth brought him less fame than his alleged breaches of morality. There were stories about his three daughters in their youthful years not being able to bring their girlfriends home for fear that they would fall prey to their philandering father. When he died a decade later his fortune was estimated at an astronomical amount in Rupees, equivalent to several billion Dollars although popular exaggeration may have played a part in that evaluation. However, he had several palaces, vast amounts of lands, dozens of limousines of various makes and the usual troves of jewelry, gold and precious heirlooms that distinguished any self-respecting Indian prince. Despite his bon vivant cynicism, we found that his weak spot was his only son who was visibly the apple of his eye. Fate struck when the beloved heir died in a car accident a few years later, plunging his father in a sorrow from which he was not to recover. In Harinder Singh I was reminded of the brash, sometimes perverse childishness of those, such as Johannes von Thurn and Taxis. whose inherited wealth and privilege protect from the fear of consequences of their words or actions. Is mankind in general, by its tendency to adulate the powerful and to hold them above the common law not as responsible for their behaviour as they themselves are?

Around that time the Commonwealth Expedition reached Simla all the way from London and paused for a few days at the former Viceregal Lodge. It was made up of a number of British, Australian, Canadian and other young people who annually were selected to visit various countries of the erstwhile empire and revive bonds between citizens. On the evening after the group gave a spirited variety performance of song, dance and doggerel recitation in the Gaiety Theatre, one of the most endearing relics of the Raj, there was a "sit-down" dinner around the very long table in the state dining room of the manor on whose walls the names of several viceroys were inscribed in gold letters. The memories of Milords Lansdowne, Minto, Hardinge, Willingdon, Linlithgow and other beribboned. hermine-draped, white stockinged supreme representatives of the former overseas suzerain presided over the gathering and the atmosphere of the evening was unabashedly nostalgic although "Rule Britannia" was obviously not intoned.

I continued the evening in the drawing room with a beautiful British young female member of that globe trotting cast who made me see additional virtues in her nation and lent a new charm to those premises of a bygone colonial age.

We enjoyed our society outings in Simla but appreciated the intellectual environment provided by the Institute. Some of the best scholars of the country were in residence there and we met a few other foreign visitors including the well known Welch philosopher and Druid Hywell D Lewis who spent a few weeks at Rashtrapati Niwas as the former viceregal residence was known.

However this being India, high philosophy could be found in unexpected places. We formed a friendship with a semi-retired grocer from the town bazaar, a deeply religious man who had read books and practiced spirituality all his life. He was a humble sage of the sort that traditional societies breed and who are rare in our modern specialized and materialistic cultures. I remember long conversations over *chai* with him and my father in his wooden home perched on the steep slope of the hill in the maze of interconnected dwellings that cascaded down into the valley. One had to walk gingerly along a few roof edges to climb into his surprisingly cozy though exiguous penthouse. The cramped quarters had been built after a great fire had burned most of the old bazaar in the late 19th century. The British administration had turned the top of the hill razed clean by the blaze into the wide Churchyard and the Mall, forcing the locals to rebuild their lodgings on the precipitous decline on both sides of the crest, near their shops located on either side of the main throughfare. Rudyard Kipling in *Kim* described that labyrinthic warren in which he situated his picturesque Lurgan Sahib, inspired by the real life figure of the art dealer A.M. Jacob. That mysterious personage was of undefined origin as he was believed to be either a Parsi, a Jew or a Muslim and rumored to provide intelligence to the Tzar's government. He traded in antiques and jewelry and famously sold the huge diamond that bears his name to the Nizam of Hyderabad. Indeed at one time was fancied to be the richest man in Simla.

Our grocer was eloquent and proffered simple advice in an unassuming tone of voice, quoting aphorisms from various popular sources gleaned in diverse religions and countries. I remember how he explained once that marriage should not be based on love at first sight but rather on a deliberate and well thought out decision reached together by both parties and their families. "Instant love is merely a physical impression that is often misleading" he pointed out. "It seldom stands the test of time and the subsequent disappointments can lead to great unhappiness and confusion. In the West people have tried to break with tradition by exhorting people to freely pick their spouses through chance meetings and trials at intimacy without commitment. When you grow in maturity and experience you come to realize that married life needs to be founded on a mutual pledge of devotion and support involving a great deal of forbearance. Wanting to marry in order to get physical pleasure and excitement is a misleading approach."

At the time my adolescent romanticism found it hard to accept his testimony but life has since made me feel that age-old ways of building families are the most reasonable. They can end in failure but probably less often than our contemporary reliance on individual instincts that we tend to justify under the blanket name of love.

THE GERMAN PROFESSOR

During one of our walks on the mall on a beautiful sunny afternoon we came across an old western gentleman who was also taking a stroll. As he was admiring the majestic panorama of forested peaks we stopped near him to soak in the vista and engaged in a conversation. Thin, blue eyed and a bit formal and stiff he revealed that he was German and had lived in India for many years. His name was Lothar Wendel and he had taught European literature and philosophy at the Birla Institute of Technology of Science in Rajasthan until retiring. He now shared his time between India and Germany. He was a student of Keyserling's philosophy, which forthwith endeared him to us and knew a lot about German travelers and scholars who had visited India in the last two centuries. We had tea together in the old Cecil hotel on the Mall and he told us many interesting things about literary influences that his native country and India had had on one another.

"In the first thirty years of the twentieth century, many Germans, Baltic Germans in particular, were fascinated by the past of Tibet and Central Asia, following the expeditions of Aurel Stein and Sven Hedin and their discoveries. Indian culture seemed a bit too soft, tropical and chaotic to many of them but the Roof of the World held many secrets and its civilization looked more congenial. The famous Takla Makan Tocharian mummies turned out to have been red haired, clear skinned tall people who could have been Scandinavian. In 1908, a

Russian archaeologist, Kozlov discovered the mysterious ruins of Karakhota in Turkestan. There were, reportedly very ancient sarcophagi of the Uyghur, a vanished civilization that had founded a Central Asian empire many thousands of years ago. That was the realm that Genghis Khan revived much later."

We had long been intrigued by the enigma of the Uyghurs who, according to Churchward had taken refuge in deep underground cities beneath the Mongolian and Sinjiang plateau after the destruction of their capital. In his famous travel book "Men, Beasts and Gods," Ferdinand Ossendowski related the local traditions that describe the hidden kingdom of the "King of the world."

Wendel knew of various missions that had been sent to Central Asia and Tibet before and during the second world war in order to locate that occult realm, believed to hold great treasures as well as the key to universal power. We talked about Nicholas Roerich and our meeting with his son Svetoslav in Bangalore.

"Roerich was convinced that a talisman that could save mankind and resurrect the original Aryan civilization was hidden somewhere between the Himalayas and the Altai range" said Wendel. "He set up the Urusvati Institute in Kulu on his return from his first expedition in 1928 to pursue that quest and in 1930 he published his book entitled "Shambhala, in Search of a New Era." He, as well as other investigators was inspired by the saga of Baron Ungern von Sternberg who sought to claim Genghis Khan's Eurasian legacy in order to defeat the Bolshevik revolution and bring about a new Buddhist-Orthodox civilization. Roerich, like Ungern, was familiar with a book entitled "Descended from Shambhala" written in 1915 by Albert Grundewel which reported that the Romanovs were believed in some circles to have the kings of Shambhala as their remote ancestors. That notion was propagated in higher spheres of the Russian empire by Akvan Dorjieff, the Dalail Lama's representative at the court of St Petersburg and Ungern saw himself later as the incarnation of *Begse*, one of the eight fierce Mahayana *dharmarajas*, or guardians of the eight quarters.

One of Roerich's goals in exploring Tibet, Turkestan and Mongolia was to revive peacefully the great trans-civilizational project heralded by Ungern only five years earlier. He was hoping to find traces of Prince Poulzig who has been sent by Ungern on a quest for Shambhala and Agartha in 1921 and had disappeared somewhere in that region."

We had in mind our conversations with the German professor when we reached Naggar, the old capital of the small erstwhile Kulu kingdom where the Roerichs settled for many years. In that magnificent site looking out to towering peaks we could contemplate the mental horizons of the Russian thinker and artist, haunted like many of his compatriots by the legend of Genghis Khan and seeking to retrieve the lost spell of his power.

The Roerich house is out of character with its setting; it is a stately home that could as well be in an elegant bourough of Paris or Berlin. Yet it faces the mysterious snowy and rugged Walhalla that has been called the third pole and where many Asian cultures situate the axis of the universe, the Meru mountain.

The seal and crest of that supernatural kingdom is the svastika, also a mongol symbol which Ungern had stamped on his banner. In 1890, according to various esoteric sources the Living Buddha of Urga had made a prediction about the return of Genghis Khan in the shape of a white man and the rebirth of his empire. That was the year when the young French theosophist and explorer Alexandra David-Néel first landed in India and formed the design to reach Tibet which was then closed to foreigners.

An esoteric ritual of the Lamaist tradition, the *kalachakra* in its higher "stage of perfection" is said to bestow invincibility to the Chosen One in his endeavour for universal supremacy. It is a ceremony dedicated to Mahakala, the tantric embodiment of Time and Death who is invoked as a war god by the Mongols. The supreme God of the Shamans, Tengri, the sky or *Sien Fung* in Chinese would then confer his protection on the world leader and his election would be manifested in the possession of the staff of Genghis Khan, an ebony cane allegedly endowed with prodigious powers, circled by silver rings, capped by a cube with flattened angles and inscribed with the names of Genghis and Tengri in Chinese characters.

In the wake of the devastation of the First World War which had brought about the cataclysmic end of three European empires and plunged China into widening chaos, predictions of that type had a deep impact on many minds in Russia and Central Europe. Some saw the prophecy of Narabanchi as a beacon of hope against the red tide of Bolshevism and related civil wars. Ungern and other White Russian and German conservative generals tried to harness that mystical revival to stem the Bolshevik flood and the Roerichs, as Buddhists and theosophists were a part of that movement. Another believer was General Karl Haushoffer who founded the *Vril* Society in Berlin in 1918 and the Institute for Geopolitics in Munich a few years later. The Vril was the name given to the superhuman energy whose secret was in the hands of the hidden Asian masters.

However opposing forces were at work. In Western Europe and in Northern America a few well informed and influential individuals, conscious of the power of myth for mass mobilization, realized that Asia united with Eastern Europe could quickly become hegemonic over the world. They believed in Mackinder's verdict that "whoever controls the heartland of Eurasia controls the planet" and they acted to prevent an outcome that would have been fatal to their own cultural supremacy and colonial empires.

In the course of his encounters and researches around Europe my father had learnt that in the year 1920, while Ungern was carving out his new Eurasian state under the magical guidance of the eighth Living Buddha of Urga, the blind Bogdo Ghegen Khan or Jetsumdamba Hutuktu in Mongolia, a secretive wealthy Belgian occultist had travelled in that region with the goal of uncovering the secret that Ungern also sought; the hidden site of Genghis Khan's grave, said to be located at the foot of the sacred mountain Bogdo Ol near Urga.

On the cliffs of the Altai range around the sacred Belukha mountain, are caverns that, according to local traditions, provide access to the underground realm of Shambhala or *Dejung* in Tibetan.

Raised in a country where the Supernatural has remained very present in the minds of a ruling class closely allied with Britain and the Anglo-Saxon sphere, that elusive investigator, possibly an honorable correspondent of HM's government, whom we will call X, undertook two expeditions (code-named respectively KHANNE and VITRIOL) and, with the help of the Chinese Triads—the Hong or "Red" Society in particular—with which he had special relations and mining companies in which he was a large shareholder, reportedly managed if not to access Agartha, at least to retrieve the staff of Genghis Khan and, allegedly to prevent Baron Ungern from achieving his objective. In what way he did the latter is not clear from the few records available but it is a fact that the "mad Tantric baron" was defeated and captured in 1921 by special units of Trotzky's Red Army allied with Mongolian Communist leader Damdin Sukhbataar after being reportedly betrayed by the Hutuktu.

Ungern was summarily tried and executed by a revolutionary court. There are reasons to believe that he had been vanquished by the covert and paradoxical alliance between the Bolsheviks in Moscow and the Anglo-Saxon powers, united in their opposition to the Eurasian geopolitical projects fostered by the former Russian imperial leadership.

Coincidentally or not in that same year a young German ex-soldier in Munich, trained and indoctrinated by the mystical and occultist poet Dietrich Eckhart, fascinated by the Indian *mayavada* philosophy, took control of the new National Socialist Workers Party. In 1920, a few months earlier he, Adolf Hitler had designed its flag carrying a black swastika set in a white circle against a red background. History was unfolding in a new direction and the meeting of Scandinavian legendary lore and Central Asian esotericism was to generate the immense and ruthless might of the Third Reich. The Hutuktu and the famed "white stone prophecy" had predicted the rise of three new empires on the world and the Axis powers, Germany, Japan and Italy claimed to embody them.

In 1924, Nicholas Roerich and his family, venturing into Tibet and Central Asia through Kashmir, travelled across the area for four years. They were also on a quest for the roots of the spiritual civilization of the roof of the world but instead of seeking to gain political hegemony by the force of arms like Ungern they aimed, under a guidance of their mystic master Mahatma Morya, for a psychic and cultural resurrection of mankind through a "Sacred Union of the East." In the same year Alexandra David-Néel reached Lhasa for the first time and spent two months there in order to further penetrate the hidden message of esoteric Buddhism.

From his readings, our German friend Wendel had acquired the conviction that the main goal of Roerich's expedition was to bring back to Shambhala a fragment of the *chintamani* stone he had retrieved from an American art collection.

"That is the wish-granting jewel of the Buddha," he said in a detached tone and in Germany it was described by our medieval minnesinger Wolfram von Eschenbach in *Parzival* as the *Lapis Exilis*, the stone of the Grail that fell from the sky. In India they say that it is the stone found on the *makara*'s forehead. The makara is a mythological sea animal but in medieval Europe we knew of the narwhal fish and kings had cups and hunting horns made out of its ivory. The gem is often described as being green, like the *tabula smaragdina* of Hermes which is cut out of a giant emerald. The Chinese believe it is of the purest jade which is why they prize that material above all other minerals. In Tibet it is inscribed with the mantra *Om Mani Padma Hum: the Gem in the Lotus* but Roerich interpreted the full Tibetan inscription as:

Through the Skies I come
I bring the chalice covered with the shield.

Roerich believed in the theosophical tradition that the chintamani had been brought from Sirius by space traveling superhuman beings and that it had been later fragmented into three pieces although the largest piece is still at Shambhala in the custody of the king of the world. Another fragment was kept in the Tashilhumpo monastery in Shigatse which the Roerichs visited when their expedition crossed Tibet. The Russian artist thought that he was carrying the third piece which would grant him access to Shambhala and he evoked that apotheosis in some of his paintings. The reunion of the three stones is to pave the way for the dawn of the new age of universal peace and harmony. He represented it by three rounds within a larger circle on the banner of peace that was accepted by many governments as an emblem of the sanctity of the artistic heritage of mankind."

THE HIDDEN RACE TO SHAMBHALA

We all knew that in Europe, in the years of the Roerich expedition the Nazi party was rising and assuming the legacy of the Russian Eurasianists under the sign of the cosmic and solar cross, the svastika of the kings of Agartha. As usual in human affairs, the lure of force and violence prevailed over the entreaties of wisdom. It was in 1924 as well that the German agent Wilhelm Fischler published his book "Sturm uber Asien" on the Great Game played between the rival empires of Russia and Germany before and during the last war.

While the Roerichs explored the Central Asian wilds, the new Soviet regime in Moscow was also paying attention to Tibet and the feared Trotskyist Kommissar Yaacov Blumkin, who at the time ruled Mongolia with an iron hand on behalf of the Kremlin, was dispatched there in 1926, much to the concern of the British authorities in India who feared Communist subversion among their Asian subjects.

Blumkin may have connected with the Roerichs in Turkestan although that is not established but his superior, the Deputy Chairman of the OGPU, Moskvin whose real name was Mikhail Trilisser met them in Moscow during that same year, when they went there from Mongolia in order to present to the Soviet Foreign Minister Chicherin holy soil from the land of Shambhala to be placed in Lenin's gasket.

It remains a great mystery how Roerich, a spiritualist Old Regime aristocrat who had been naturally hostile to the 1917 revolution, was able to win over the support of the Marxist revolutionaries who ruled the new Soviet State. His expedition was discreetly but efficiently assisted by the Bolsheviks in spite of the fact that—or perhaps because—he was looking for Shambhala and wished to bring all Central Asian peoples into a Buddhist cultural renaissance that somehow might be reconciled with the Russian Communist creed. In the previous years he and his family had lived in the USA where they had garnered wide and influential support and the British Raj offered him hospitality in Kulu on his return from Tibet, even though his travels and intentions had drawn extensive suspicions within His Majesty's Intelligence services.

As bizarre as it may seem some Bolshevik leaders delved in the esoteric beliefs of certain members of the former Tzarist high hierarchy and acquired a fascination for the occult rituals of Mahayana Buddhism, if only because they sought to gain the prodigious powers they were said to confer. One eminent follower of this path was Gleb Bokii, one of the few non Jewish top members of the Soviet Cheka who had become the head of the special department of the OGPU and was one of the supervisors of the Gulag system.

As an eminent cryptographer and mathematician Bokii was regarded as a genius and just about the time of Roerich's exploratory mission, he and his colleague Alexander Barchenko practiced advanced tantric rituals and mounted an expedition to locate Shambhala. They were however unable to carry it out due to the opposition of other powerful factions in the regime which did not condone Barchenko's theory that the "new communist man" might be created through Buddhist esoteric rituals intended to replace the human personality by a divine one.

The lure of the supernatural Himalayan realm was shared by both Russian and German successive regimes which competed to gain control over it since Lama Dorjieff had incited Emperor Nicholas II to claim the legacy of Shambhala in order to become the protector of Tibet, Eastern Turkestan and Mongolia. Dorjieff joined the Bolshevik side right after the revolution and convinced many that a synthesis could be achieved between Lamaism and Leninism. The Roerichs subscribed to that view and even thought that Lenin was a reincarnated Buddhist deity. We had read various statements by the present Dalai Lama to the effect that Buddhism and Communism are not incompatible since the former can provide a spiritual foundation for the latter. He remains in that way faithful to the ideological perspective of many earlier Mongolian and Tibetan religious leaders.

When the Roerichs entered Khotan from India through the Karakoram passes in 1924, Rufus Isaacs, Lord Reading was the Viceroy, the first Jew in a nomenclature of old Britannic names and titles, to occupy that exalted position and only the second follower of that religion to enter the Cabinet. There are reasons to believe that his administration regarded Roerich as a Russian agent and yet the latter was welcomed in India, as he would be upon his return from Tibet four years later.

Lothar Wendel believed that this seemingly universal interest in the Roerichs' mission was an effect of the global influence of the Theosophical Society and other related secret associations that extended even to the USSR with which the western powers then maintained clandestine relations much more amicable than was officially admitted since Lenin had signed a treaty with Great Britain a few years earlier. Wendel also felt that the Jewish identities of most Soviet kommissars—including Trilisser and Blumkin—and of many secret, often double agents, some being kabbalists who dabbled in the occult doctrines of various traditions, accounted for their ambivalence towards supernatural forces over and above their addiction to complex conspiracies and intrigues.

That point of view was not surprising in a German of his generation but it is well known that a visible rise in global Jewish power took place in the aftermath of the First World War, when Israelites became the leaders of the new revolutionary regimes, in Germany, Central Europe and in the former Russian Empire while rapidly expanding their political and financial power in the United States. In 1917, Lord Balfour in his famous declaration had promised the international Jewish leadership a home in Palestine and in 1921 the American automobile king Henry Ford published his influential book "The International Jew," accusing a Zionist cabal of having led the world into the mass butchery of 1914-1918 to serve its own political and economic interests. That book was read and discussed in Nationalist Socialist circles and Hitler himself was inspired by it.

In that uncertain and confusing climate the rise of the Nazi ideology, with its esoteric "Indo-Aryan" and "Arctic" background and trappings, was welcomed on many sides, both in the imperial west and in the newly communist east. There were sympathisers in high places in European and American capitals.

XIX
Hill Wanderings

Mandi and Suket

We gained further insights into mostly forgotten aspects of history when our periplum through Himachal took us to some of the small former princely states that dotted its political map. In Mandi, Maharaja Joginder Sen, an avuncular elderly gentleman with exquisite manners, a warm smile and dreamy eyes, had many stories to tell about his ancestors who had come from Bengal in the Middle Age to establish their rule in that hilly region.

"They were younger members of the royal dynasty that ruled much of Eastern India at the time," the Raja told us.

"For religious pilgrimages and also for economic reasons many Bengalis came to these parts and that is how the kingdom of Shambhala, located around today's Sambhalpur, also a part of greater Bengal then, gave its name to the Zhangzhung realm on the upper Sutlej, near Manasarowar and Mount Kailash. The local rulers had Bengali pundits, poets and administrators at their court and for centuries that connection continued as we know from the many Bengali Buddhist scholarly monks who went to Tibet to teach Mahayana, up until the eighteenth century. Our family, including my nephew the Raja of Suket are among the descendents of that Bengali diaspora along the Sutlej."

Joginder Sen's story captured our attention. Shambhala was now being given a concrete, almost reachable location. Its history was tied to the sacred Sutlej, the only affluent of the Indus which springs from the holy Manasarowar lake, through the adjoining Rakshasa Tal, the pond of the Rakshasas. On its way towards the Punjab it irrigates the

Garuda valley before crossing the wild land of the Kinnaras, today known as the tribal district of Kinnaur.

The local legends were familiar to both the old Raja and his relative, Lalit Sen of Suket who received us in his former capital of Sundernagar, or rather in the new town built after the old capital had recently disappeared under the water of a reservoir created by a huge dam. The valley had been turned into a construction site for the Beas-Sutlej Link project and hundreds of technical professionals resided on the site for the duration of the work. We were invited to speak to them by the supervising engineer on the suggestion of the Raja and had a chance to express both our regard for the great expertise displayed there and our misgivings regarding the ecological and human hazards inherent in those massive undertakings.

We asked Lalit Sen and his son Hari, a mature and intellectually gifted youth, about the traditions tied to the fabulous or supernatural beings of the Himalayan region. Lalit Sen was a handsome man with an unfailingly gracious disposition who had played various roles of distinction as a member of Parliament and a secretary to the former Prime Minister Lal Bahadur Shastri. His pragmatic perspective did not incline him to flights of fancy. However he païd due regard to the folklore of his land and knew much about the bordering Kinnaur district that merges with Tibet several miles to the east.

"The culture of Kinnaur is still little known to outsiders, he told us during a family lunch served on the verandah of his hacienda-like residence built in the traditional style of the region. The language is not Indo-European and belongs to the Tibeto-Burmese group. I am told that it is more complex and more extensive than Sanskrit, in terms of the sounds it uses. Legends have it that it is derived from the ancient tongue of Shambhala. Kinnauris still worship the supernatural creatures of Vedic and post-vedic mythology. The Garuda valley also known as Hiranmaya is named after the *girdh*, the huge Himalayan vulture which gave its name to the bird of Vishnu and which is supposed to dwell there. The girdh however, which the British called the lammergeier is very real and big enough to carry away a young sheep in flight. It is our Indian condor.

Similarly, the kinnaras are horse or bird-headed beings who, like the yakshas and gandharvas inhabit the Himalayan region and rank somewhere between gods and humans. The gandharvas were the mountain tribes that dwelt in the Hindu Kush and the Pamirs and gave their name to Gandhara, today's Afghanistan while the yakshas are located in Alaka, where the Saraswati and Alaknanda river begin, and around the Kailash peak. They all had their respective kings but the paramount ruler of the Northern mountains is Kubera, the golden master of mineral wealth who holds court on Mound Gandhamandara near Kailash. There are large underground caverns as well and I suppose that is how the myth of Shambhala originated although I am not sure where the name Agartha came from. If you have a chance to meet The Dalai Lama again, you should ask His Holiness or a high ranking Tibetan monk to tell you more about it since he is an heir of that tradition and is believed to be a reincarnation of the second monarch or *kalkin* of Shambhala, Pundarika."

We thus learnt that there is a Saraswati stream in the upper Himalayas, which tradition knows as the remaining upper stream of the extinct vast river of the same name celebrated in the Vedas. That Tibetan waterway crosses the Mana pass, named after Manu who followed its course from Kailash into the newly emerging Indian plains after the great flood receded according to the Hindu legends. Like Lake Manasarowar, the pass carries the name of the "first man" and geologically it is located near the faultline that joins the Indian subcontinent with ancient Laurasia since the two landmasses collided and came together, thereby pushing up the Himalayan chain.

Could the legend of Manu landing on that island peak of Kailash during the Deluge enshrine the memory of an age when a vast ocean filled what is now the Tibetan plateau? The many salt lakes that remain there are vestiges of that long vanished sea which has also left vast deposits of marine fossils.

Lalit Sen also had a personal experience of the events that preceded and surrounded the proclamation of independence and he told us that, in his view, the British India Office had first promoted

Muslim separatism through Sir Mohammed Agha Khan who was a protégé and a loyal ally of the Crown. Later on the baton had been passed to Jinnah who was entrusted with the task of bringing the Pakistan project to fruition. Strangely enough both men were Shiites and for that reason seemed ill suited to lead Indian Muslims into what was called by some the new Medina out of "pagan" India but the deep rift between Sunnis and Shiites was not so apparent at the time.

"The British wished to create an Islamic feudal nation similar to Iran over which they then exercised a de facto protectorate. I am sure the documents that prove the collusion between the Crown's secret services and the leaders of the Muslim league still exist somewhere" said the raja of Suket with his customary indulgent smile "I believe in French you have an expression to define the British state: *la perfide Albion*."

FORGOTTEN PLOTS AND DREAMS

A few weeks later we were the guests of another great raconteur in a square wooden castle crowned by a high stone keep, set in a green valley surrounded by steep conifer clad hills. The nearby village was Jubbal and we had been invited to spend a few days in that remote glade which evoked the atmosphere of a tale by the brothers Grimm.

Raja Joginder Chand and his wife were a young couple whom we had met in Simla where they owned a small manor called Hainault. He was cheerful and lively and she demure and graceful. They had five children, four maidens aged between twelve and eight and a five year old crown prince, the impish cynosure of the clan. The girls had this deliciously romantic shyness that has vanished wherever co-education has replaced the segregated convent schools of old and they moved together like the *apsaras* of Indian legends or closer to our age, the daughters of Tzar Nicholas and Alexandra . Every evening I found on my pillow a white perfumed champa flower and discovered soon enough that I owed this sweet good night present to the eldest of the young ladies, a dreamy budding beauty to whom alas I had no real chance to speak as she kept herself out of reach although she more than once floated into my dreams as a white petal lazily adrift on a slow moving stream.

The Raja opened to us the castle's library which was full of rare historical books, some printed as early as the first years of the nineteenth century. I spent there many a captivating hour devouring richly illustrated annals of British and Mughal India and chronicles of various Hindu kingdoms in Himachal and in other parts of the country. I was also intrigued by the towering keep which contained the temple of the family deity, the treasury of the former state of Jubbal and the most valuable heirlooms of the family. However on that subject our host was tight lipped and did not venture beyond making general statements in response to my adolescent curiosity.

He was more prolix on the biography of his late father who had been a remarkable man. The first in that ancient dynasty to have gone to university in England, Raja Digvijay Chand had become the leader of the many princelings who ruled the region's fiefdoms and had formed an ambitious political project.

We were told the story on a rainy evening after dinner, while we sipped tea from bone china cups in the teak paneled drawing room, decked with hunting trophies and ancient weapons. A tiger skin lay at our feet and the glassy eyes of a snow leopard, a sloth bear and a Himalayan *thar* or ibex unblinkingly stared at us from the walls. I should have have felt uneasy with those mute relics of a cynegetically obsessed age but I was conditioned to accept them as a part of the heritage I had been familiar with since my childhood. The word "politically correct" had not yet been invented.

"My father saw that Indian independence would bring about the end of the maharajas, Joginder Chand said, and he tried his best to avoid it. During the second World War, he got most of the feudal rulers of this region to support him and he went to meet Maharaja Hari Singh of Jammu and Kashmir, the father of Dr Karan Singh and asked him to plan for a merger between our states and his at the time of independence which was expected to come soon, in one way or another, whether the Germans or the Allies won the war."

"Hari Singh being an indecisive man hesitated. He did not feel he had the ability to keep his Muslim and other subjects under control once British rule would end. One of my father's ideas was to link up with Nepal, a sovereign Hindu kingdom and Tibet which was in effect independent at the time and tied to the Indian empire by a treaty that would lapse with the Raj. If the Dalai Lama and the king of Nepal, along with the rulers of Bhutan and Sikkim could be persuaded to form a federation with the Indian hill states and Kashmir, that would have become a vast Central Asian state. I believe that the British were secretly in favour of that plan just as they supported the idea of Pakistan. Of course that would be seen as treason now but then there was no clarity as to what would become of India at Independence and many thought that it would splinter into many countries or might become a communist dictatorship or even lapse into civil war.

Had it not been for the hold of the National Congress over the country and for the iron will of Sardar Patel, we might have seen a very different map of South Asia take shape. The bigger monarchs, Hyderabad, Travancore, Bhopal, Jodhpur, Gwalior, Tripura, Junagadh tried to secure their independence in various ways when their treaties with the British paramount power lapsed. However, my father saw the writing on the wall when Maharaja Hari Singh had to appeal to the Indian Government to save him from the Pakistani invasion. Now Tibet has long been gobbled up by Maoist China and we in India have just seen the end of a national dynasty which replaced our ancient provincial monarchies. *Chacha* (uncle) Nehru became a democratic no-frills Great Mughal who made sure to leave his throne to his only child" he concluded with a wicked grin.

It seemed to me that the sort of loose confederacy envisaged by Joginder Chand's father, landlocked, mountainous and surrounded by India, China and the USSR would not have been viable but I was told that the Raja of Jubbal and his "co-conspirators" sought to set up a system similar to the union of Malaysian sultanates that has resisted the hegemonic designs of its larger neighbours Indonesia and Thailand.

We had to ask him about the kingdom of Shambhala and as we had hoped, he recalled many interesting stories from the local historical records and folk traditions.

"My brother-in-law the raja of Bushahr should know even more than I do on this" our host remarked. "His former state encompasses part of the Kinnaur land that belonged to Shambhala and if you go up the course of the Sutlej you will reach the ancient fortified capital Kyunglung. The headquarters of Kinnaur district is Kalpa named after the mythical headtown of Shambhala. Tibetan lamas call Shambhala the kingdom of Kalachakra and its king is Kalki. In Hinduism we expect the coming of Kalki, the tenth and last avatar of Vishnu who is to bring about the end of this age. Now the Kinnaras were described as being horse headed and our Kalki, the destroyer of darkness is said to ride a white horse. I believe that this part of the Hindu religious lore is of Himalayan origin."

We had often wondered why the Kinnara hill tribes were totemically associated with horses and felt that they must have originated in the Tibetan and Central Asian plateau where their ancestors had ridden the small and sturdy Tibetan and Mongolian mounts. Central Asia is one of the cradles of the equine race and even today it harbours some of the last remaining indigenous herds of *Takh* named after Colonel Przewalski who first reported their existence in Europe in 1879. In Tibetan esoteric iconography, the wishfulfilling chintamani jewel is shown shining on the back of a divine wild horse, the *Lung Ta* and the baleful goddess who is the protectress of Lhasa and the Dalai Lama, Palden Lhamo is often depicted astride a charger.

There was also a symbolic link with a hidden wisdom which is said to be taught by a horse headed god in one of the vedic traditions and the old expression "from the horse's mouth" may carry a dim memory of that image. The centaurs who remind us of the kinnaras are also described in greek myths as wise teachers.

Joginder Chand supported the theory of a Central Asian origin for those Himalayan tribes. "The Kinnaras came from the North and may be survivors of a great Central Asian empire of which they kept distant memories" he noted. "We must have had documents about ancient times in the regional archives but in 1803 the Gurkhas invaded from Nepal and plundered, stole and burnt records and heirlooms until the British pushed them out in 1815. Because of that occupation much of our history is now forgotten. In Bushahr for example no annals are older than the early 19th century."

That brought a stark reminder of this constant feature of human history; the periodic and seemingly inevitable incursions of peoples into each other's territories result in the utter loss of the collective capital of mankind and force new generations to reinvent the wheel every now and then. The urge to wipe out the achievements of others in order to affirm primacy is at least as strong as the motivation to create and build. Mankind is, like Penelope of Ithaca unraveling at night what it weaves during the day and only fragmentary glimmers remain of the prior twilight.

One conclusion we drew from our investigations into the enigma of Shambhala is that the legends and factual history reflected each other, howbeit in a faint and distorted way. Tibet and the adjacent mountain valleys provided a haven to many branches of the religious and intellectual civilization of India since times immemorial. The kalachakra tradition that can be traced back to Bengal, Orissa and the region of Amaravati in the Deccan almost disappeared there in the wake of the Muslim invasions but was integrally preserved in the Tibetan highlands which still claim the heritage of the first Shambhala merged with the autochthonous shamanistic symbology. However the Sakya Muni himself came from the Himalayan area where some of his own teachings seem to have originated so that his doctrine may be said to have retreated back to its ancestral home.

Before leaving the pastoral valleys of Himachal we had one last dinner with the Raja and Rani of Mandi in their small but comfortable mansion. Joginder Sen had explained that after one of the earthquakes which frequently upset the region had destroyed most of the old palace, his grandfather had never wanted to stay under a solid roof again and lived his remaining years in a regally appointed tent set in his garden. However his son had built a more permanent abode and looking around I felt I could have been in Paris and not in at the foot of the great mountain ranges bordering Tibet. On a corner table in dull silver frames sepia coloured photographs of princes clad in brocaded finery and jeweled turbans when not in smokings and black ties smiled alongside slender velvet eyed ladies in long satin gowns and chiffon sarees with 1930 haircuts and diadems. For a second I realized that they were the ghosts of a patrician hothouse flora born from the cross-fertilization of the Indian feudal past with European elite culture. Our hosts were among the last of that vanishing hybrid species.

Joginder Sen of Mandi had wanted to give us an introduction to the Maharaja of Dhrangadhra, the former secretary of the defunct Chamber of Princes whose achievements and intellectual abilities were highly regarded. The envelope sealed with Mandi's crest was addressed to his fellow ruler in the formally ceremonious way of old. Much later we got to know its contents. In Victorian English he had expressed with Asiatic periphrastic flourish the importance he gave to our action for a revival of the notion of Dharma and we realized how easy it is in the Hindu perspective to assimilate man to God when the former speaks on behalf the latter. We were designated as "divine messengers of the Almighty" and some of the praise showered on us was so dithyrambic that I refrain from quoting it. We did not take that choice of words as a childish or insincere exaggeration but merely as a spontaneous recognition of a higher call that had come to him through us.

FROM BIOGRAPHIES TO HISTORY

By then, after our sojourn at the Rashtrapati Niwas, the former viceregal residence had ended we were staying at the house of the Catholic parish of Simla as guests of the local priest who had invited us to speak to his flock. The Church had been built in gothic style in the early eighteen eighties under the patronage of Lord Ripon, a viceroy converted to Catholicism who because of his new faith could not be a member of the British cabinet. I was struck by the fact that a country held to be a standard bearer of liberal democracy and freedom and ruling an empire on which the Sun never set, encompassing almost every race and religion in the world had laws that until rather recently prevented a substantial proportion of its own population from participating in the government.

The United Kingdom was and perhaps remains even today living proof that relative economic and social liberty can be combined at least in theory with theocracy and extreme inequality.

As many Indians were fond of saying, the British were at ease with Indian mores and customs because of their familiarity with the caste system which they perhaps made more rigid than it was before they took over the country.

In Simla, on the reference of the Jubbals we called on Virbhadra Singh, the Maharaja of Rampur Bushahr at his house, Holly Lodge, on Jakho Hill not far from where Allan Octavian Hume had lived in the grand Rothney Castle in the manner of a Scottish laird. Rothney has long disappeared since a monsoon landslide brought down the steep hillside that it once crowned.

Hume was both a civil servant of the Raj and the heir to a large holding in the former East India Company. He belonged to the family of the famous sensualist philosopher and the politician Joseph Hume was his grandfather He had resources to invest in his scientific, spiritual and reformist interests and he became a theosophist and a supporter of Helena Blavatsky through whom he came in contact, according to his own testimony with the Himalayan Mahatmas. Mrs. Blavatsky was at various times his house guest in Simla but their relation ceased after she performed some "miracles" at Rothney which Hume's skeptical friends believed to be fraudulent. Hume had been unceremoniously sacked from the government by Lord Lytton in 1879 for his opposition to policies that were both unfair and oppressive to the native population. He then dedicated his life to ornithology and amassed a spectacular collection of stuffed birds from all over India at Rothney.

When Madame Blavatsky was accused by both Christian and rationalist organizations of being a charlatan dabbling in spurious magic as well as a Russian spy, Hume succumbed to pressures and abandoned theosophy. He was a powerful advocate of Indian autonomy and, with the support of Viceroy Dufferin seeded the creation of the Indian National Congress in 1885, the year when the Theosophical Society established its seat in India. That and the fact that various British subjects were its presidents in the following years give credence to the view that the Congress party was an offshoot of British colonial policies aimed at controlling "native" nationalism.

Hume left his adopted country in 1894 and returned to Britain where he died eighteen years later. His collection of Indian birds was gifted to the Victoria and Albert Museum where it is still on display and his grand mansion in Simla, after being for years the summer residence of Germany's Consul General in India, fell into disrepair. Nearby there are several other historic dwellings, including the Priory which hosted the famous Prince Soltykoff in 1858. Holly Lodge had first housed the girls' school founded by the widow of the Rt Rev. Cotton, the Anglican bishop of Calcutta. The school later shifted to Auckland House in whose visiting faculty quarters we were staying for a few days at the time. We had become friends with the headmistress Mrs. Hakim, a great-grand-daughter of the personal physician to Prince Duleep Singh, heir to the "Lion of the Punjab" Ranjit Singh and I retain sweet memories of that garden of young feminine flowers from all over India and South Asia. Whenever we passed by the school yard on our way in and out the uniformed teenage girls would line up and greet us with sonorous "good morning Sir" followed by shy smiles and peals of excited laughter. I felt like a matinee idol reviewing a parade of female fans, not sufficiently aware of the fact that adolescent females secluded from male company were bound to find any young member of the opposite sex an irresistible object of curiosity and attraction irrespective of his personal merit.

Our conversation with the 123rd prince of Bushahr, a shrewd and influential politician whose dynasty is held to go back all the way to Lord Krishna himself, was rather brief but interesting. He advised us to visit his former state and stop over at the old capital of Sarahan which, he felt had a historic connection with Saraha another great mystic of the Indo-Tibetan tantric tradition and he pointed out that the religious beliefs still held by some of the tribes of that border region reflect very ancient theologies later adopted by both Hindus and Tibetan Buddhists.

"Shamanism is the oldest creed common to Asia, from Siberia to Japan, the Raja said. The root is *shama*, which means peace or *sama*, harmony in Sanskrit and the Buddhist monks are *shramanas* or *samanas.* That concept of group mendicant celibacy predates Buddhism and it was readily accepted in the Himalayas and Tibet because it had roots in the local tradition. In India it died out because the Hindu sadhus are wandering individuals. They congregate for ritual occasions but they don't live together in a common building. In ancient Brahmanical India, permanent religious centres were occupied by married teacher-priests, not by ascetics who instead isolated themselves in forests and mountain caves."

Virbhadra Singh's perspective confirmed us in the view that Christian monasticism was seminally influenced by Buddhist missionaries just as Mahayana ecclesiastical institutions may have later imitated Christian models.

We had another meeting in the same period with Shanta Kumar the Chief Minister of the State which, like many members of the new Central Government in Delhi belonged to the Jan Sangh, the political party created by the RSS to represent Hindu nationalist forces. He struck us by his efficiency and decisiveness and showed interest in our suggestion to make Himachal Pradesh a model state governed according to the ancestral Hindu-Buddhist Dharma as the land sits at an intersection between Vedic and Lamaist cultures and was in the recent past occupied by many small traditional kingdoms.

The concept of setting up an institute for the promotion and development of this socio-political concept took shape in our minds there and although we proposed to the Chief Minister to locate it in his state it could not be realized in spite of his favourable response but similar initiatives were more successful in other part of India.

The hold of the Hindu conservative party in Himachal, whose people are known for their tolerance and moderation and for their particularly close links with the British rulers during 150 years, proved in our mind the lack of fanaticism in that ideology. We expected to find a similar acceptance from the new ruling coalition in New Delhi where, at the end of the monsoon season we now were headed.

In Chandigarh, the deliberately non-Indian planned city designed by Le Corbusier according to Nehru's wish we entered again the heartland of Sikhism. Le Corbusier is still known for his indifference to traditional cultures which he wished to replace, in the spirit of his time by a functional and minimalistic building style that could supposedly be adopted everywhere and anywhere. Much later I was to live for a few years in La Chaux de Fonds, the Swiss birthplace of the celebrated architect near the French border and I detected in that austere, grey industrial Calvinist town set amidst dark fir-covered hills and meadows the source of his own humorless and drab worldview. He should have been made infamous for his wish to raze Stockholm in order to rebuild it as another concrete leggo. In Chandigarh he was given a *tabula rasa*, an empty agricultural space in which he could materialize his concepts and although the city has a refreshingly spatious Helvetic orderliness the cement of his buildings was soon sullied by the contrasted subtropical climate. Those geometric blocks make me think of the fossilized angular remains of gigantic dinosaurs. Fortunately the colours and rumours of Indian life, which Le Corbusier probably despised, provide this otherwise anonymous landscape with a saving grace.

SAGA OF THE SIKHS

We were happy to land in the modern and elegant guest house of the university which reflected the city's cleanliness and greenery. If Amritsar had shown us the eighteenth century opulence of Sikh pageantry at the Golden Temple, Chandigarh symbolizes the easy acceptance of contemporary living by the that same community which culturally and demographically dominates the region.

While we lectured on the usual variety of topics at the university and later at the one in Patiala, also in the Punjab, we took the opportunity of familiarizing ourselves more with the faith that hails Guru Nanak as its founder.

By Indian standards, Sikhism is a recent religion and that may also account for its ability to embrace modernity. Guru Nanak was born in the 15th century near Lahore, at a time when all of Northern India was under more or less tolerant Muslim Afghan rulers while a native spiritual renaissance was taking place in various provinces. The Punjab was heavily influenced by Muslim culture and had probably lost much of its memory of pre-Islamic times. Few people there were familiar with the ancient complex and esoteric rituals and arcanes.

Thus a revival had to appeal to popular piety and borrow its inspiration from the various living traditions coexisting in the land. Guru Nanak brought out the best in both the Sanathana Dharma and Sufi Islam and composed many prayers and hymns to instill high moral values and a spirit of equality and fraternity among all people. He appears to have had a universal vision since he undertook major travels across the subcontinent and visited the holy places of the Middle East, including Mecca, Medina, Jerusalem and Baghdad. Thereby, he imbibed his message with many elements found in the Christian and Mussalman scriptures. His creed was propagated by the nine masters who followed him and achieved its definitive form under the tenth and last guru, the heroic Gobind Singh.

By then Sikhism had become a force to be reckoned with as it was followed by millions of people in all walks of life throughout the Mughal empire. The Padshahs had originally ignored or tolerated the growing community which Akbar had regarded with favour but his successors predictably were warned by the *ulema* that this well organized body headed by a charismatic and sacred personality was a potential threat to their political power and to the authority of Islam on the land. Waves of repression periodically emanated from Delhi, separated by periods of truce and finally the ruthless Aurangzeb decided, according to his customary method, to crush this martial "state within the state" that was drawing together the larger Hindu populations from which it was in no way separated.

Guru Gobind Singh who was raised as a knight and a war commander found himself forced to fight for his survival and for the welfare of his followers. He spent most of his life fending off and generally defeating the attacks of the Mughal forces until he was murdered in 1708 by two Pathan "hitmen" sent by a local governor. The year before Aurangzeb had breathed his last and his son and successor Bahadur Shah sought to make an ally out of the revered Sikh leader. He had even allowed him to be proclaimed in Agra the *Hind Ke Peer*: the spiritual lord of India. The Mughal empire was declining fast and the *Khalsa*, the Sikh community grew and prospered but it would take another century for the first Sikh kingdom to emerge. Had he not died at the peak of his strength and prestige, Gobind Singh might have become the redeemer of Hindustan from its decadent foreign rulers. He had the moral and physical attributes to personify the native spirit at its best and in his widespread iconography he still appears to lead his nation into battle astride his blue black charger, with all the trapping of kingship, often holding a beloved falcon on his wrist. His heroic and tragic figure reminds me of Hazrat Husain, the sainted Imam of the Shi'ites who was murdered at Karbala.

Contrary to the Hindus, the Sikhs have an acute historical awareness and take great care to document and research their own past. Later in Delhi we would meet Prof. Gurbaksh Singh regarded as the greater living scholar on the history of that religion. In Chandigarh and Patiala we talked to various academics and spiritual teachers who gave us insightful perspectives into the nature and the evolution of their tradition.

"The Sikh Gurus could have unified India while the Turkic state was crumbling, one of them told us but we were unlucky in one way. Guru Gobind Singh was not strong enough to defeat Aurangzeb who was still in control of the empire although he had to face several insurrections in the South. When Ranjit Singh built the first Sikh state the British were already too strong and had defeated the other native forces so that they were able to destroy his kingdom shortly after his death. He ruled over a Muslim majority, therefore his sway was fragile as he also had to combat the permanent threat of Afghan invasion from the West. In the early 18th century the best chance for India to remain independent and to restore its unity was provided by the successes achieved by the Sikhs in the North and the Marathas in the South. However those two great peoples almost never cooperated and fell prey to their internal rivalries. The Sikhs showed the way to a casteless, vigorous and progressive India, willing to accept the best from all foreign countries and integrate it within its own civilization. In a way Ranjit Singh locally was an earlier equivalent of the Meiji in Japan."

Although we had to agree with the professor we felt that Sikhism was too steeped in Punjabi culture to appeal to the other ethnic and linguistic groups and that its egalitarian gospel was too radical for conservative ruling classes outside its geographic cradle. The Marathas likewise were seen as upstarts by the old nobility and their propensity to plunder discredited them in the regions they took over. As a result of those enduring divisions the European invaders were even more successful in their conquest than their Central Asian predecessors but then India, in terms of size and diversity is comparable to Europe and it was equally difficult for any national group to take over the whole. Was French, German or Spanish dominance ever accepted in other parts of the European continent when these respective nations extended their rule over much of it? Indeed India, because of its ancient national religious and literary sanskrit culture is at least potentially far more unified than Europe and it has been more than once brought together under a single ruler, though not for long.

The British were exceptionally deft in using the animosity of the Sikhs towards the Mughals to their advantage, thus making the former some of the most reliable supporters of their Raj. As result of that alliance Sikhism evolved into an independent religion increasingly separated from its Hindu fountainhead.

While in Simla we had been in touch on the telephone with Amrinder Singh the young maharaja of Patiala who said we might call on him if we came to his ancestral city. We did pay a visit to the new Moti Bagh palace where he lived after his father had donated the gigantic old palace with its thousand rooms to the government to set up a national sports academy. The maharaja was friendly and pleasant but he was in the unenviable position of being constantly compared with his formidable grandfather Bhupinder Singh, a towering figure of pre-Independence India whose gargantuan appetite for jewels, women, medals (he had been awarded most of the national and royal orders of Europe) limousines and pageantry was only rivaled by his interest in mysticism, new technology (he built the first monorail in India in his capital) and global politics. His libido and his extravagance did not deprive him of will and purpose. He served in the general staff of the imperial armies during the first World War on various theaters, was made a Major General and was elected for ten years as the chancellor of the Chamber of Princes, India's equivalent of the House of Lords. He met many of Europe's monarchs and presidents and at times flouted British warnings by dealing with foreign leaders such as Hitler and Mussolini who received him in their respective capitals. To his imperial critics, he responded that he was informing himself about international affairs but he came to be seen as a rebel and he was indeed animated by the urge for independence that led his contemporary Subhash Bose to seek the same foreign contacts. His neighbour the Maharaja of Kapurthala made himself known for his predilection for everything French, thereby showing his disdain for the British and their hegemonic culture and he often stated that he liked the European continent inasmuch as he found Britain dull and small minded.

The "magnificent Maharaja" of Patiala as he was called became predictably unpopular with the paramount power and a widespread belief amongst his former subjects is that he died from poison, perhaps at the behest of the colonial overlords who were suspected of having much earlier killed Ranjit Singh's exiled son through alcoholism and opium. When Bhupinder Singh expired at 47, he left more than fifty children from his ten wives and many concubines. Four of his spouses were sisters from a small kingdom of Himachal and they were said to be his favourites. In that final salvo of the maharajas, from a generation that produced some highly capable and enlightened rulers, he was the last of the larger-than-life potentates who strode on the Asian stage with panache and fanfare even though he had only inherited a small tributary state. Had he been at the helm of a large independent kingdom, he might have been compared to a legendary medieval raja such as Harischandra or closer to our age, to Fath Ali Shah of Persia or Mehmet Ali of Egypt.

Those who condemn Bhupinder Singh's profligacy and carnal self-indulgence forget that he behaved by standards radically different from if not opposed to those of democratic politics. In the Asian tradition the king is not a corporate manager but a father of his subjects who must inspire both admiration, affection and fear in them. He embodies their dreams and aspirations and in various

Indian ancient texts he is compared to fire that can never be fully trustworthy or reliably contained but is an indispensable source of light and life.

In the few days we spent in Patiala which kept then even more than now its memories as a royal seat we came across some of the members of the local aristocracy, most often related to the prolific Bhupinder Singh and his polygamous forbears. We found that the town's denizens cultivated the romance of their former king and in a country where legends are far more meaningful than history, often implausible tales were repeated about him. Many believed, for instance, that he had been banished from Simla for eloping with the Viceroy's daughter after a tryst with her at a spot since called Scandal Point. Then they claimed that he had built Chail to console himself from his exile; yet there is no factual basis for this story and nobody could name the viceroy whose daughter had allegedly caused such affront to British propriety. Chail in any event was built by his father when Bhupinder Singh was only ten. There is every reason to believe that the romance was invented in keeping with his reputation as a Don Juan but it would be too much to expect his former subjects not to swear by it.

XX

Meetings and Musings

Some Other Nehrus

After a short journey from the quasi-Ruritanian atmosphere of Patiala we were back in Delhi where one could perceive the political change that had taken place in our absence. The rulers of the former regime were now in virtual retirement and could be seen much more frequently about such places as the familiar India International Centre. We were invited to lecture there again as well as in various colleges and cultural institutions and had a few weeks to make some enlightening acquaintances apart from the now familiar Lokesh Chandra, Karan Singh and J.C. Kapur. We called on the senior diplomat B.K. Nehru, a nephew of the first Prime Minister who was regarded as the most accomplished in his family in terms of administrative experience and political savvy. He had been India's ambassador to the USA during the Kennedy and Johnson presidencies and had just returned from London where he had been the High Commissioner. An Oxford and LSE alumnus he had married early a Hungarian Jewish young woman, Magdolen Forlath or Friedman, familiarly known as Fori in India, who had shared his life in high places and had been highly popular during her husband's stint in Washington where Vice President (and later) President Lyndon Johnson was known to be very fond of her and often called informally on the couple at their residence. Those were years when India and the USA had cordial relations, in spite of growing ideological differences regarding the Cold War, the Vietnam War and the Soviet intervention in Hungary. We briefly evoked with Ambassador Nehru the circumstances that led to the steady deterioration of the political climate between the two nations and created the open antagonism between the Nixon administration and the government of Indira Gandhi. The personal equation that Mr. and Mrs. B K Nehru had with the top members of the Democratic Party, who saw in him a countervailing influence to Foreign Minister Krishna Menon's vocal anti-Americanism, was never recreated with the succeeding Republicans whose Kissingerian *Real Politik*, a throwback to the Eisenhower-Dulles years, despised India's increasingly socialistic tendencies and Non-Aligned principles.

It had become public knowledge by then that, contrary to widespread belief, John Kennedy had not been impressed with Jawaharlal Nehru whom he regarded as a sanctimonious and self-righteous leader. However, the equally sophisticated but less opinionated and sentimental B.K. Nehru won his respect. India's diplomatic cadre at the time was very small and few citizens of the young nation had been groomed in the exacting science and abstruse protocol of old fashioned international etiquette. Two or three of them belonged to the Nehru family. One was R.K. Nehru, a cousin of the Prime Minister who had served as India's Envoy to China between 1951 and 1958 at a time of high hopes for a close and comprehensive partnership between the two Asian giants. R.K. Nehru had left Beijing a year before the flight of the Dalai Lama to India brought an end to the bilateral cordiality and sowed the seeds of the 1962 war.

It was not coincidental that the deterioration of Indo-Chinese relations was contemporaneous with the visible rapprochement between Delhi and Washington which resulted in the not so covert US military support for India against the People's Republic, intended to back and bolster the Tibetan rebellion against the Chinese occupying forces. R.K. Nehru was an elderly and frail man when we got to know him but his wife Rajan, the daughter of a knighted civil servant under the Raj, was the graceful and vivacious sister of P.N. Haksar, Indira Gandhi's highly influential principal secretary and adviser. The couple and their children loved Europe, like most members of their family and they seemed to view their own country, as many of their eminent contemporary countrymen did, through the prism of an elite English education. They were both romantic and pragmatic in their perceptions and naturally proud of India's cultural achievements. I recall that we once talked about their ancestral family home, Anand Bhawan in Allahabad known to Hindus as Prayag, at the confluence of the three sacred rivers, which seemed destined to provide India with its first national leader. "The ashram of Bharadhwaj, one of the greatest Hindu Rishis, was located in what is now a public garden in front of Anand Bhawan" Rajan pointed out "and Bharadhwaj means the flag of Bharat, that is India."

My father noticed that Bharadhwaj is described as a master of advanced technologies in various areas and a builder of sophisticated machines. Pandit Nehru thousands of years later was a committed promoter of science and technology and started many ambitious national programmes in areas such as aeronautics, heavy engineering and space exploration. It was as if he had been inspired by the soul of the legendary "genius loci."

At that point in history, we felt like we were talking to members of a recently dethroned, uncrowned royal family. Had their star now fallen for good?

"When we were building a partnership with a major power, my brother tended to appoint someone from his immediate family, but sometimes when that relative left, it seems that the relationship was scaled down" Vijayalakshmi Pandit told us, matter-of-factly while we had tea with her in her simple but elegant flat in South Delhi.

She was Jawaharlal Nehru's favorite sibling and enjoyed his complete trust. Few women had as distinguished a career in public service in those days. In 1953, she had been the first female president of the United Nations General Assembly before becoming India's Ambassador to the USSR and then to the USA and finally High Commissioner to Great Britain. However she had turned against her niece Indira Gandhi not long after the latter had risen to the prime ministership. Many claimed to detect some jealousy in the older lady who felt that she had considerably more skills and accomplishments to her credit than the initially shy and insecure daughter of Pandit

Nehru. She also disagreed with some of the political views of her niece but she made it clear that what she really opposed was Indira Gandhi's increasingly authoritarian ways, her weakness for what Mrs Pandit described as her son Sanjay's arbitrary and capricious ideas and her reliance on a small coterie of pliant subordinates. "This has led her to disaster, she told us with obvious irritation, and it has left India in the hands of a feeble and divided government, many of whose members are old Congress stalwarts who jumped ship when my niece's policies alienated them.

Who would have thought when we became independent that a Prime Minister from our family would be jailed by our own government for abuse of power and illegal actions?"

This was not long after Mrs Gandhi had been released from Tihar jail where the Home Minister Charan Singh had sent her on charges of subverting the Constitution and plotting to kill opposition leaders. Such charges could not easily be proven and the latter were ludicrous so that the government had to let her free after her imprisonment aroused a nationwide wave of sympathy for her. It was not the last mistake the new rulers made shortly after taking office.

THE NEW LEADERSHIP

We had requested to meet the Prime Minister, Morarji Desai in the interest of our mission and were very curious to experience directly his personality which had always been controversial. Some regarded him as a Gandhian ascetic saint and others as an eccentric politician whose unusual dietary practices (he lived on nuts and milk and drank his own urine in the morning) attracted much derision. He was eighty two years old at the time and kept an impressive health and form which spoke in favour of his self medication in keeping with certain Indian traditions. When he received us at his office in the South Block of the Central Secretariat he slowly and stiffly rose and after greetings were exchanged sat down behind his desk and listened to us with impassive serenity. He looked sphyngian in his immaculate white kurta and Gandhi cap and soon came back with one of his typical sharp retorts: "You want to give lessons to India? India has taught the world for many centuries." My father was quick to respond that we merely sought to serve India for the preservation and revival of its precious heritage and by passing on its message.

Morarji Desai was, like his late mentor and fellow Gujerati Sardar Patel known to be more socio-economically conservative than Mrs Gandhi and her supporters and that ideological rift, combined with personal rivalries, had brought about the original split in the Congress party. Indira Gandhi regarded her enemies as allies of the USA and Britain whom she had come to see as her double Nemesis. Desai and many of his colleagues in the government he headed held the former Prime Minister to be a hostage of the Soviet Union who had needlessly attracted the hostility of the West through her policies. Indeed some ministers in the Janata cabinet were known to have had contacts with the CIA and other anti-communist agencies although some of Mrs Gandhi's subordinates were probably also in one way or another in touch with the Americans. In that half an hour meeting we could sense the sympathy of Morarji Desai for the US and the liberal economic system even though those topics were not nominally discussed. He had a well known soft spot for Jimmy Carter, the serving American president and told us that he saw him as an ideological heir of Gandhi and Martin Luther King.

The Prime Minister wished us well in our endeavour but we could quickly feel the relative weakness and uncertainty of the Government, cobbled together by a coalition of disparate parties whose sole common ground was their opposition to Mrs Gandhi. While the backbone of the new regime was the nationalist conservative Jan Singh, other components were Left Wing Trade Unionists and regional politicians. Many members were former Congress veterans, including Karan Singh who had joined the new team at the eleventh hour. The decisiveness and authority of Indira Gandhi, the *Desh ki Neta* as she had been known, was clearly missing since it is an eternal truth that power may not be easily exercised absent an uncontested leader.

To get a better perspective from the major force in the system we reconnected with our friends from the RSS and went to meet Nana

Deshmukh, perhaps the most formidable personality in that ideological sector. Although he had been depicted in circles close to the Congress as a feared and enigmatic figure, we found him to be a soft spoken and quiet elderly man. Born in a poor Brahmin family and orphaned as a child, he had dedicated his life to social work within the RSS and had remained celibate as required by that organisation's code of conduct which sees national service as a monastic vocation for its leaders. In 1972 he had founded an institute dedicated to researching and propagating the legacy of his intellectual mentor Deendayal Upadhyaya, founder of the doctrine of integral humanism.

Nanaji, unlike the usually privileged and foreign educated Congress leaders, reflected the humble circumstances of his life in rural Maharashtra and was spartan in his appearance and speech. He had spent many years in the villages of Bundelkhand where he carried out organizing work under the banner of a campaign for self-reliance. He had also founded in Chitrakoot, a picturesque holy place of that region an agrarian university or *Gramoday Vishvavidyalaya* which helped many thousands of peasants and artisans to autonomously improve their living standards. Although, like all his RSS colleagues he was customarily described as a champion of a "far right wing ideology," his ideals for India's reform were actually quite close to Mahatma Gandhi's objectives and he had participated in Gandhi's disciple Vinoba Bhave's well known *Bhoodan* (spontaneous land donation to the poor) campaign, alongside foreign spiritual and social reformers like my father's friend Lanza del Vasto. That made us wonder once more whether, had he lived longer, the Mahatma might not have been seen on the side of the RSS and other advocates of small scale farming and handicraft ranged against Nehru and his socialist policies supportive of Soviet-style heavy industry and centralized bureaucratic government.

During our various interactions with RSS office bearers and volunteers they had appeared austere, often unsophisticated in the cosmopolitan, academic sense, but not fanatical or violent. During the time of Emergency they had unreservedly supported leaders like the socialist Jayaprakash Narayan and the liberal Morarji Desai inspite of doctrinal differences. It seemed clear that the stigma attached to them was largely manufactured by political rivals eager to ingratiate themselves to fearful religious minorities.

We had a long talk with Deshmukh on various matters and realized that the Jan Sangh was not strong enough in the current dispensation to implement its programme. The durability of the coalition was questionable and the ageing though mercurial Desai was Prime Minister only due to a compromise justified by seniority. Already the lack of experience and professionalism of some of the cabinet members and the growing infighting between factions took its toll on the Janata's popularity.

Deshmukh pointed out that the writings and speeches of leaders such as Hedgewar, Golwalkar and Upadhyaya had no relation with the European Nazi and Fascist theses. He remarked that Upadhyaya had elaborated the theory of integral humanism as an indigenous response to the Marxist and atheistic versions of humanism promoted in the West. My father noted that the French Catholic theologian Jacques Maritain had been perhaps the first to use the term of integral humanism, applying it in a Christian context to reconcile the message of Jesus with the agnostic propositions of the secular humanists. Upadhyay had done something similar for Hindus but unlike Christianity which requires unconditional faith in the divinity of the historic Jesus Christ and acceptance of the tenets and dogmas of the Church, Hinduism said Deshmukh did not require any particular creed or form of worship to be adopted and adhered to by all.

"Our opponents accuse us of trying to spread a military, uniform kind of religion, copied on western monotheism" he argued. "We never promoted any Indian tradition as opposed to another.... Our followers can practice at will Vedanta, Arya Samaj, Tantric worship, Sikhism, Jainism or Buddhism, any other or none at all. The only thing we demand is devotion and loyalty to Bharat Mata, mother India and a commitment to serve and improve the lives of its children. That is what some minorities, especially among the Muslims object to. They claim that although they live here their primary loyalty is to the *Umma* and their spiritual home is Mecca. They say that they cannot admit idol worshippers as their brothers. In the views of those people, who are probably not a majority among Muslims, the only rightful outcome is for India to be ruled once again by Muslims and converted to the right religion in order to become like Pakistan. We cannot accept that but if Muslims keep their faith private and regard themselves as Indians like all others, we have no problems with them. Likewise most native Christians are loyal Indians but some feel beholden to western nations or the Vatican and support conversions to their faith in order to change the spiritual culture of the nation which they describe as pagan. The Congress and Leftist parties have constantly tried to woo and humor Muslims and Christians, treat them as separate nations and promise them privileges and special protection to get their votes. Yet the Muslim social ideology is the most opposed to Marxism and their alliance is opportunistic and counter-natural."

His words showed us the deep divide that existed between the Jan Sangh's vision of India and the goals espoused by various parties located on the other side of the ideological spectrum. In a way the Congress and the Communists for better or worse had become heavily dependent on the support of religious minorities with which they had no special affinity beyond the shared commitment to keep the RSS and its allies out of power. They constantly accused the "Hindu Right" of fostering tensions and conflicts between communities but they were doing precisely that when they raised the scare of pogroms by the Hindu majority among the naturally insecure Muslims who tend to listen only to their own clerical guides. Can a democracy have any meaning unless citizens evaluate issues at stake as individuals and not as blind followers of a leader or party?

IN THE POWER CIRCLE

In that uncertain context we called on Mrs Gandhi at the residence she occupied at the time. We did not wish to fail meeting her in times of ill fortune. She received us promptly and was attentive and courteous although we could feel the tension in her demeanour and the preoccupation in her features. We learnt later that she was methodically preparing her comeback as she had sized her opponents' weakness and determined that she could defeat them if they were forced to call anticipated elections. One of her advisers confided that she was convinced that her defeat had been engineered or at least aided by Anglo-American covert action and that, had she not lost the election a coup might have removed her as Allende had been overthrown and slain in 1973. She had voiced that suspicion to Fidel Castro years earlier and now felt that her misgivings had been vindicated. She particularly suspected the Rockefeller-Kissinger coterie in the US Government and felt that they had turned some of the powerful Indian business houses against her. It was no mystery that the principals of the premier among them, the Tata group of companies had been quite hostile to the declaration of Emergency and that the famous lawyer Nani Palkhivala who was the master strategist of that business empire was a staunch ally of Morarji Desai's government.

Mrs Gandhi saw a league of right wing Hindu forces, pro-western liberals and international capitalists arrayed against her and her policies.

Almost every day, through our friends including Lalit Sen who was in Delhi for the season, we had meetings with notable and interesting personalities in diverse areas of activities, scientists, scholars, military officers, judges, politicians, artists and diplomats. During tea with the chief of the armed forces staff, General Raina whose French wife carried the storied name of Marie Antoinette, I expressed my fondness for horses and my interest in joining in some way the 61th Cavalry which was the last mounted regiment in the Indian army. The General, a highly decorated veteran who had lost an eye in one of many conflicts, going back to the second World War was amused by my enthusiasm but pointed out that such as request could not be granted to a foreigner and further he advised me that the living and training conditions were probably too harsh and demanding for a European in the Indian climatic conditions.

Raina was a Kashmiri Pandit, like Mrs Gandhi who was known to favour fellow Kashmiris but the General was known as an incorruptible soldier of the old school and had pointedly warned the Prime Minister that the army would not back her if she violated the Constitution. Because of his apolitical integrity he was popular with the Janata Government.

One of our most pleasant conversations took place when we were received by HH Fatehsinghrao Gaekwad, the Maharaja of Baroda who resided on Dupleix Lane when in Delhi. He carried on his name the legend of fabulous wealth of his ancestors which had fascinated western imaginations since a Maratha warlord of peasant extraction (Gaekwad means cowherd) carved out a large and prosperous fiefdom in Gujarat and signed a peace treaty with the British India Company. Thereby protected from potential rivals and enemies the Gaekwads grew to become perhaps the wealthiest Hindu monarchs of the time through prudent and enlightened management of their estates. They dazzled even the British overlords with their jewels, palaces, carriage collections, private zoos, hunting parties and receptions. However, since the late 19th century when the gifted and wise Sayaji Rao Gaekwad rose to the throne they were progressive and practical in their magnificence and promoted irrigation, road building, urbanism, lower and higher education, women's welfare, banking, trade, science and technology for their subjects so that when Independence came the region they had ruled was among the most affluent and literate in the country.

The Maharajas of Baroda had also, unlike most of their peers, actively supported the freedom movement and patronized intellectual leaders such as Dadabhai Naoroji, Swami Vivekananda and Rabindranath Tagore while not hesitating to challenge and even upset the British rulers at the risk of their own political survival.

Fateh Singh Rao bore this weighty heritage gracefully and with humour as a former star cricket player and a bon vivant. "Jackie Baroda" as he was familiarly known, kept many friends all over the world and was worldly but with simplicity. He had been heavily criticized by many of his fellow rulers for not resisting the imperative demands from the Central Government when he had been the President of the Concord of Princes, the "union" of former monarchs and noblemen entrusted with the task of defending some of the old privileges conceded to their class. While Karan Singh had gone over to the "enemy" side and taken the side of the Government against his peers, Fateh Singh Rao, also a politician in the Congress party probably felt that the position of the feudal chiefs was not tenable in the new republican order and, being the heir to an extremely wealthy family he could afford to forego the privy purse on which many other smaller and poorer princes depended to maintain their traditions, dependents and social status. He confided casually that his great grandfather Sayaji Rao, who had been seen by many of his contemporaries as a future national leader of India had not desired to preserve the princely states which he regarded as anachronistic relics of an outdated feudal age. "As long as India was under foreign rule, one had to do the best one could to improve the condition of one's own fiefdom and the common people in Baroda were generally better off than Indians in British India but once we got independence, the preservation of our privileges became a rather petty minded concern that was hardly defensible" he mused.

However, we thought that, looking beyond the issue of the mere status of Maharajas, what was more meaningful was the perpetuation of local cultures fostered by royal patronage and ritual. The republican form of government with its bureaucratic and egalitarian anonymity was proving lethal to the survival of those institutions. The new dispensation had also done away with the traditions of locally accessible and responsible administration. A maharaja's state was his ancestral home and he needed the acceptance of his people to ensure the survival of his line. Administrators sent from the capital for a limited period of time could not be expected to have similar concerns. Of course, as HH Baroda and other princes frankly pointed out to us many rulers were worthless, spendthrift and decadent but does the modern system not display major dysfunctions and faults as well? As always, so much depends on the men who rule, whether they are hereditary, selected or elected. Sayaji Rao himself was reputed to have changed his views in the last years of his life when he came to advocate a sovereign Indian federation comprising the former British provinces and the princely states that could be turned into constitutional monarchies on the European model. He had seemingly lost some faith in the republican form of government.

In many ways, the genial, jet-setting and portly Gaekwad was the antithesis of his fellow Maratha Nana Deshmukh although he was a proud Hindu too. He was a nature conservationist at heart and a wildlife lover after having been a big game hunter in various parts of Asia and Africa in his youth. However he had had a change of heart before the age of thirty after realizing that wild animals were threatened with extinction everywhere. Accordingly he had set up the Wildlife Institute of India and the Indian Society of Naturalists while heading the national chapter of the World Wildlife Fund. "Maharajas are seen as the hunters who massacred thousands of tigers and other endangered species" he said ruefully "but in fact in those days wildlife was plentiful and we took good care to keep it that way since we needed to have lots of game to shoot. That may have been a wrong motive but since the great hunts stopped, forests shrunk and animals, losing their habitats are vanishing as well. That is how from a hunter I became a conservationist. Don't they say that robbers make the best policemen?"

He invited us to visit his former capital city of Baroda, reputed for the university built by his ancestor and of which he had been long been the Chancellor. "Come before it is spoiled by growth and modernization" he told us jovially. "It used to be a model city in India but the way things are going it may not remain that way for long. We have managed to save some animal sanctuaries and nature reserves even within the town limits. Our Fine Arts and Music Faculty is one of the best in the country and our people tend to be well mannered, hospitable and cultured."

By him and others, we were introduced to Justice Nagendra Singh, then a judge of the International Court at the Hague who was spending some time in Delhi at the time. He was a senior ICS officer who had been a secretary to the President of India, a reputed scholar in his field and the secretary to the international bar association. A scion of the illustrious princely house of Dungarpur in Rajasthan, he could be proud to belong to the eldest line of the Gehlot Sisodia clan of Suryavanshis, or children of the Sun. Although the premier state of that clan in terms of power and size is Udaipur, small Dungarpur was the fiefdom of the firstborn of that millennial blue blooded race. Yet this heir of one of the world's most aristocratic theocracies had been republican India's chief election commissioner a few years earlier and had in that capacity coordinated the largest democratic exercise in the world.

Compared to Nagendra Singh and his Suryavanshi kin, FatehSingh Rao of Baroda was a wealthy newcomer to the royal pantheon who could not claim Surya, the god of light nor any other deity as his first forebear. The elder brother of the Judge and current head of the Dungarpur line, Lakshman Singh was reputed as a stalwart representative of the virtues of his ancestors. The conversation with Nagendra Singh was of particular interest to us as he was keenly aware of the connections and differences between the Indian notion of Dharma and the western concept of rights and duties. The complicated equation between traditional legal culture and mores on the one hand and western contemporary juridical norms on the other concerned other luminaries and officials, including members of the Supreme Court of India. We were able to confirm that state of affairs when we discussed such matters with justices P. N. Bhagwati and Krishna Iyer.

"A major difference between western law and Indian ancient jurisprudence, said Nagendra Singh, is that the former takes the individual as its referential and starting point whereas the latter has the natural order and society as its viewpoint. Law must evolve, of course, but should it follow and reflect ideas and realities or rather correct and reshape them? If the individual is king, then it is difficult to find reasons to limit his freedom to do as he pleases."

ECHOES FROM GREECE

Among the serving foreign diplomats the Ambassador of Greece Vassilis Vitsaxis stood out as a scholar and a poet who loved India where he found many echoes of his own nation's culture and religion. We spent hours with him comparing the meanings of homophonous words in Samskrit and ancient Greek. Although the Vedic Yavanas were certainly the Ionians and the Hellens the Alinas of the Puranas, there was some doubt as to whether the Achaians were the Haihayas and the warlike Dorians the relatives of the Mahabharata's chief villain Duryodhana. The Sanskrit *swapna* or dream had become the Hellenic *hypnos and Dyaus* was known as *Zeus* while *Danava* had remained almost unchanged as *Danaus. Jara,* old age in samskrt was spelt *geros* in greek and Crete, the landing place of Europe, the legendary Eastern princess who gave her name to the continent kept her indo-european name Kriti that is applied to the first or golden age of the *caturyuga* cycle. The evolution of meanings across time and space was a source of reflection and amusement for the three of us. For instance *hasta*: the hand in samskrt had become *esthos*, a sense such as hearing or sight and given rise to the notion of aistheis or esthetics. Likewise *amnaya*: remembrance had left a trace in *mnesis*: memory whereas the indic *sukha* (happiness) had turned into psyche: the soul.

We agreed that the legendary origins of the Athenian polity were related to the great common pool of Indo-European origins, evoked by the father serpent-god Erechteus whose name contained the samskritic root *raksh*, signifying protection. The founding ruler Cecrops is said to have come from Egypt but he symbolizes the centre and the wheel (*kukros, kuklos* in Greek, *chakra* in Samskrit) associated with royalty as shown by the title of the Vedic paramount ruler: the *chakravartin*, he who holds the wheel over the earth. The ambassador pointed out that the noun Cecrops could be interpreted as the "round faced one" which might allude to the Sun but it assimilates that mythical hero to a cyclop, a one eyed giant. "The notion of the third eye, *triophtalmos* in the centre of the forehead survived in Hellenic religion, he concluded. It is the equivalent of Shiva's eye which remains always open when the others are closed in meditation. Cecrops is a male counterpart to Europa, the broad faced one (the moon) and can be compared to Pelops who settled in the peninsula that bears his name, the Peloponnese."

Vitsaxis, as a writer was keenly interested in theater and was inevitably drawn to compare ancient Greek and Sanskrit plays which were all inspired by very similar mythological and legendary lores. However he saw the difference between the Hellenic dramatic repertoire which is divided between well codified comedic and tragic genres and the classical Indian stage productions that more properly belong to what came to be known, much closer to us in the West as the baroque and romantic drama containing elements of both tragedy and comedy as real life always does. He felt that the fall of Greece under Roman rule arrested the development of dramatic literature there since the new imperial civilization produced almost only comedies of the farcical or social type whereas the "Aeschylian" hieratic theater became a rather frozen relic of the past.

India's surviving classical plays on the other hand belong mostly to the early centuries of the Common Era, when the western world was being transformed by the adoption of Christianity which long shunned pagan entertainment. However both the Indian and Greek stage works must have been originally inspired by religious rites, as enactments of divine and human stories in which music, dance and recitation were used to narrate ancient events. Singing of the Vedic hymns may have gradually evolved into a performance miming the actions described just as the theogonies of Hesiod and other archaic poets provided the material for Hellenic tragedies, perhaps in the form of religious mysteries at first. In their final form, Indian plays are like novels or fairy tales enacted on stage although they retain a religious and didactic character in their scripts and contextual references whereas Greek tragedies, with their choirs, masked actors and hieratic choreography stay closer to their sacramental sources.

THE SUFI AND THE POLITICIANS

As compared to the rather continuous indo-european universe of thought and culture, Islamic civilization stands apart as a primarily semitic creation in its perception of God, man and the latter's role. We could feel that difference much more clearly than we might ever have understood it by reading about it when we visited, more than once, the Dargah of Nizamuddin Auliya and were privileged to meet its nineteenth head or *Sajadahnashin*, Syed Bukhari Pir Zamin Nizami, a direct descendent of the Saint and one of the leading Sufi masters in the world. He was a frail and wiry man of about seventy five years of age who seemed to slowly glide along the corridors of the sanctuary and spoke gently in a thin voice. With his pistachio turban, long caftan, cloudy glasses and thin grey beard he embodied the agelessly medieval quality of Islamic spirituality and seemed to still live in the days of the Delhi Sultanate as if his remote ancestor had reincarnated in him. The people who surrounded him also appeared to move in a time warp, oblivious of the changed world that surrounded with its noisy technologies and opulent hotels the ancient structures, contemporary hovels and smelly lanes and passages clustered around the Dargah. Living among the green-draped tombs, the milling beggars and the white clad praying crowds, the Sufi Peer and his entourage seemed to hold the material advances and comforts of civilization in utter contempt.

With his stature and following, the saintly Zamin Nizami could have lived in a modern palace like many princes of his faith but he was content to remain rooted in the archaic and untidy but poetic labyrinth of his forbears' community. He invited us once to join him for the evening prayer, the *Isha* and we found this moment of intense piety in the hallowed precincts deeply touching. The Peer was known to spend much of the night awake reciting the *Namaz e Tahajjud,* which consists in the low muted recitation of a number of Qur'anic surahs beginning with the *Salah* during the cycle of prostrations that typifies Islamic orations. As Massignon the leading Arabicist has justly observed, the exercise of piety in Islam is a heroic struggle against the tendencies and temptations of human nature, contrary to the "virtue as moderation" taught by most Hellenic philosophers. A devout Muslim is expected to fight sleep, hunger, thirst and other desires through an exacting regime of constant prescriptions designed to make him indifferent to pleasure and pain. Such a hard discipline however is not within the reach of everyone and it seems that too many who have the faith but not the wisdom end up feeling frustrated and guilty for breaching those severe rules. Some believers can then turn into embittered bigots or unfeeling fanatics as they attempt to make up for their doctrinal failings through violent displays of hatred against others who are regarded as even greater sinners. Were not many Islamic rulers atoning for their personal lapses by killing infidels in the name of God?

It occurred to me that Peer Zamin in his devout humility personified the contemplative and otherworldy face of Islam, its mystical poetry, its disdain for the glories and cravings of this life and its yearning for celestial eternity. The other face of that Janus was the Shahi Imam of Delhi, also a Bukhari, Syed Abdullah, known throughout the country as a wily politician who used his power and influence as if he were still the theological mentor to the long vanished Mughal emperors. Both the men remained linked to the Muslim Ancien Regime and more than one Hindu had told us that the two faces were inseparable. Islam had been spread by the Book and the sword. The mystics who prayed and converted their disciples paved the way for the jurists and soldiers who enforced their political rule. The silken glove of the *Tariqa* covered the iron hand of the *Sharia* and the *Shahada*, the divine testimony, was sooner or later followed by the *Firman*, the royal decree and the *Fatwa,* the cleric's edict.

Unlike Hindus who regard religious practice as a personal and family affair, Muslims often invite followers of other cults to pray with them. That tendency to include and embrace all people is heartwarming and wins many converts but it is rooted in the notion that all children of God should be brought into the fold of the monotheistic *Deen.* Diversity is thus absorbed in the unity whereas the Hindu conception is culturally determined and regards every form of belief and worship as related to one's origins and status in society that should be respected as it is. Hindus are thus often accused of being sectarian and indifferent to those who don't belong to their community but that clanishness tends to ensure tolerance. Universalist creeds by nature intend to replace or at least reform all others.

A living example of the continuous conversion process that had taken place for centuries was provided by the high profile Chief

Minister of Jammu and Kashmir, Sheykh Mohammed Abdullah and his family. Like many Kashmiris, that formidable figure was a second generation Muslim as his own father, a Brahmin had embraced the faith under the influence of a local Sufi master in the final years of the nineteenth century. Sheykh Abdullah could have easily been a character of Kipling's novels. Towering in size and charismatic, he had entered revolutionary politics very young and had taken the mantle of power from the last Maharaja. By then he was married to a half-European Kashmiri lady whose father was the son of a Croatian businessman, by the name of Nedou, settled in Srinagar where he owned the leading hotel of the town. The Abdullah and Nedou clans had thus become intertwined by marriage and together held great economic influence in the valley.

Rumour had it that there was more to Sheykh Abdullah's wife past than her official biography admitted. According to some she had been briefly married before to a mysterious Arab who vanished when he was exposed as a spy of the British Intelligence Service. Some claimed to have proof that the elusive foreigner was none other than Lawrence of Arabia who was indeed posted in India in that year 1928 for an undisclosed mission in the service of the Empire under an assumed name.

Those who liked conspiracies and believed the British capable of hatching the most convoluted covert operations alleged that Sheykh Abdullah when he married Lawrence's divorced wife also became an asset of the Raj and was subsequently helped from London in his political career. If there is any truth to this account then he would belong to that exclusive club of leaders selected by the Crown to maintain influence over some strategic regions or communities such as the monarchs of Jordan (the present ruler is half-English) and the Agha Khans.

As a matter of fact since Independence Kashmir had been a fiefdom of Abdullah's family despite the latter's uneasy relation with the central government in Delhi due to the fact that the Sheykh had constantly vied for more autonomy and even toyed with the possibility of winning sovereignty for his state. His son Farooq who was a physician also had a British wife and shared his time between Delhi and Srinagar. I don't recall through what channel we contacted him and were invited for an informal brunch at his house near the Lodi area of the capital.

Farooq Abdullah and his immediate family greeted us with great cordiality and we soon were seated at a long table laid with many of the delicacies that make breakfast so delicious in different ways in Britain and in Kashmir. While we ate, we talked about our travels and our objectives and it quickly appeared that our host had a very British, ironic sense of humour which bespoke a certain amount of polite cynicism. He was clearly an adept of the Enlightenment and had a skeptical take on religion and spirituality. It struck me then that someone born between two very different worlds: the realm of Islam and the Anglosphere would be likely, if not electing to belong to only one of them, to find refuge in amused detachment.

Cultured Kashmiris, children of a valley nestled at the crossroad between great political and religious empires, must often cultivate an enigmatic ambivalence to the many ideologies and doctrines that flow through their land. Their only constant loyalty is to their small motherland.

Before the end of those few months spent in Delhi we had a chance to meet briefly the Minister of Foreign Affairs Atal Behari Vajpayee who was to become Prime Minister several years later. Already a veteran politician renowned for his shrewdness and Delphic inscrutability, he seemed to us a true "homegrown" statesman, far more comfortable with the Hindi language and the traditional culture of Northern India than with Anglophone South Delhi. He was, like most leaders of the Jan Sangh markedly different from the cosmopolitan Indira Gandhi but, true to the Indian vernacular spirit he showed himself to be a better consensus builder than the imperious and fiery daughter of Pandit Nehru.

Despite the RSS's reputation for authoritarian and sectarian leadership, Vajpayee, although closely associated with that conservative Hindu force turned out to be patient, pragmatic and reasonable to the extent of disappointing those who expected him to implement his party's allegedly hardline socio-religious revivalist projects. It can be said that both Nehru and Indira Gandhi had been more ideologically radical and occasionally ruthless in enforcing their 'social democratic' policies than their "far right wing" foes. Vajpayee was true to his style with us, smiling, affable but sparse with words although he was known as an entrancing orator and was also an esteemed Hindi poet.

XXI

Exploring Many Paths to the Pathless

At the Frontiers of Science and Legend

Back in Madras we reconnected to familiar surroundings and personalities and spent time in both Adyar and Kalakshetra. In that year 1978 Rukmini Devi produced a new dance drama based on the lovely story of Nala and Damayanti that I have already alluded to and in which a golden swan, the symbol of the heart and the Sun in vedic iconography acts as the messenger between the two far apart lovers. She had coincidentally been tapped by Prime Minister Desai to become President of India in the face of opposition from left wing parties but she declined that greatest of honours, preferring to continue devoting her time and energy to her favourite causes and staying away from politics.

Various intriguing occasions emerged to unravel some little known aspects of the Indian past. We attended an international congress of traditional astronomers and astrologers dedicated to the study of ancient history in the light of the data provided in various scriptures and texts beginning with the Vedas themselves. Those texts contain very detailed and precise descriptions of the positions of constellations in the sky at the time of the events being narrated so that a trained astronomer, familiar with sanskrit names for stars, planets, zodiacal signs, meteors, eclipses and asterisms, unlike most western orientalists, finds or confirms chronologies that had generally been rejected by modern researchers for going too far back in time. In the light of zodiacal coordinates, the happenings recorded in many hymns and epics could be dated and in most cases the findings agreed with the traditional annals which set at least some parts of the Vedas back to the eighth and seventh millennia before the common era and locate the Ramayana more than five thousand years before the advent of Christ. Such estimations seemed fantastic and implausible to orthodox scholars and had long been dismissed out of hand but ongoing archaeological discoveries and verifications of calendars with the help of modern computational technology have given a new lease of life to the ancient chronicles. In some parts of India advanced urban societies on a wide scale left many traces and relics that go back in time as far as the Vedas were said to date. We remembered what the Gorakhpanthi Muni had told us in Varanasi some months earlier and could only conclude that contemporary investigations lent credibility to both traditional legends and historical records. The former contain many symbolic myths but they also enshrine a kernel of factual memories associated with specific dates.

Some time later, after we had given some talks at the Madras Indian Institute of Technology, including one lecture on the UFO phenomenon and its apparent connection with ancient records, we were invited for lunch by an unknown gentleman who turned out to be a leading industrialist of South India. He received us in his modern, understated but sprawling mansion and offered us a refined Tamil meal composed of the many usual goblets arrayed on wide silver *thalis* (trays). He had invited a man whom he introduced as his adviser on spiritual and astrological matters and who was as loquacious as the host was laconic. The conversation took an unexpected turn when the astrologer revealed that he was keenly interested in the enigmas surrounding Mount Shasta, the revered Californian volcano which was a sacred peak for many West American tribes such as the Klamath. Many years back a writer called Harvey Spence Lewis writing under the pen name of Vishar Cerve had popularized a legend according to which Shasta was the gateway to an underground world in which the survivors of the vanished prehistoric continent of Lemuria had taken refuge millions of years ago. He relied on the allegedly direct testimony of another American, Frederick Oliver who in 1894 had reported seeing some of the Lemurians around the mysterious mountain.

Our Tamil astrologer was, it turned out, a disciple of the Dravidian writer and ideologue Devanaya Pavanar who was almost eighty at the time. Pavanar was an icon of the Tamil revival movement which gave great credit to his claims that the Tamil people and language were descended from the oldest of all cultures, the Lemurian civilization originating in the sunken continent of Kumara Kandam located to the south of India until 16000 years before the common era when a massive rise in ocean levels swallowed it.

India and Madagascar are, according to that version, remains of the submerged land which retain traces of its geology, flora and fauna both fossil and living, especially in the various loris and lemurian species of mammals. The 19th century hypothesis proposed by Haeckel has now been discarded after the discovery of continental drift but for Pavanar and his followers, Kumara Kandam was no other than Lemuria and had been the first seat of the Pandyan dynasty, the most ancient in South India (*pandu* meaning "very old" in Tamil) whose crest carried the two fishes that are so often found in Hindu and Buddhist religious and heraldic symbology.

We had been exposed before to the mythology of Lemuria which Blavatsky described as the continent of the third "root race" on earth although we had obvious trouble making the connection between Kumara Kandam and far away Mount Shasta but we were told that day that the Lemurians had expanded in their time all over the planet and that a few subterranean colonies were left, one of which lay beneath that Californian volcano. The version adopted by some Dravidianists is thus a synthesis between the North American account inspired by Native traditions and the local memories of an antediluvian home even older than Atlantis.

There are however some problems with the theory defended by those rather chauvinistic South Indians who generally wish to affirm their superiority over the "Northern" Sanskritic civilization and assign purely "lemurian" origins to figures, words, concepts and places that often have sanskrit names and etymologies. We pointed out to our hosts that what is usually defined as the "Aryan" northern Indian culture may well have come from the South and evolved over many thousands of years after the disappearance of the common geographic cradle. The Ramayana and Mahabharata both mention the Pandyas and their land and the latter epic records that their army fought on the side of the sons of Pandu whose name seems related to theirs. "Pandu" meaning pale in Sanskrit, may reflect the "white haired" old age that the tamil phonetic equivalent designates.

In the Ramayana the king of Lanka Ravana is said to own a magnificent flying vehicle as if the Southern people had kept some samples of advanced technology unknown to Rama and his subjects. Another seeming allusion to the advances of a great civilization is to be found in the legend of Rishi Agastya, the most illustrious figure from Southern India whose name is linked with the ocean and with the region around Cape Comorin, at the tip of the subcontinent. The star Canopus is called Agastya after him in Indian astronomy and he is said to have been born from a pot in which his mother had placed the foetus. In ancient Egypt, Canopus gave its name to a town famous for the making of pots in which the remains of the dead were kept. Were those traditions vestigial of a largely forgotten civilization whose last survivors brought with them an ancient knowledge to younger cultures?

Our astrologer was convinced that many of the UFOs observed all over the world are lemurian craft, some of which are based under Mount Shasta. There was nothing we could say for or against that explanation although it surely makes as much sense as other accounts of the "flying saucer" enigma. We found it intriguing that intellectuals and prominent supporters of the Tamil revival had integrated some of the data related to UFOS into their national cosmogony. When "official" academic science ignores certain discoveries those are often eagerly adopted and used by religious and political leaders to promote their own projects.

One of our neighbours in the Adyar compound where we had returned for a few days was a lean young woman whose fresh beauty attracted my gaze when she zoomed past on a bicycle with a quick nod and a contagious smile. We eventually made her acquaintance and found that she was an Italian research scholar in samskrit dramatic literature and traditional dance. One of her areas of study was the history of ancient greek relations with India. Having heard of our own interests one day she unexpectedly brought a book written by friends of hers from Rome and published in Italy a few months earlier. The title was "2000 A c Distruzione Atromica" by David Davenport and Ettore Vicenti. The authors had carried out investigations on the archaeological sites of the Indus Valley and claimed to have detected traces of a nuclear explosion going back thousands of years ago. They made the connection with the highly destructive weapons evoked in the Mahabharata and in other old texts. That suggestion would obviously not be accepted in academic circles but Fabrizia Baldissera, our new friend saw that it coincided with our reasoning and thought that it deserved consideration. She was to become one of the leading Indologists in Italy and now teaches at the University of Florence.

LISTENING TO KRISHNAMURTI

Nothing could be more antipodal to our meeting about Lemurian secrets than a talk by the famous philosopher Jiddu Krishnamurti who came to Madras every year and spoke in a building that belonged to his foundation. We had been invited by his long-time friend and follower Sunanda Patwardhan who belonged to a prominent family of Brahmin intellectuals and social reformers. One evening we sat on the floor in a large, well lit and sparsely decorated room and watched the former protégé of Annie Besant, thin, white haired, clad in spotless white walk in quietly, sit very straight on a chair and deliver in his usual quiet and thoughtful style a peroration on how the essential reality of being might be realized by all.

We had seen before many images of his chiseled Grecian features, straight nose, enigmatic gaze and melancholy, ascetic expression; his beauty as a youth had fascinated many men and women; we were equally familiar with his method of analysis, from books and recordings of earlier talks. He was hostile to organized religion in any form and to any invocation of traditional or supernatural concepts and he affirmed the ability of human beings to transcend all such belief systems and grasp things as they are, without intermediary. If one breached his commandment and sought an ancient established equivalent to his way of thinking, Zen readily came to mind and intellectually he was closest to Buddhism in general, particularly to those schools of "immediate awakening" through intuitive methods. However Krishnamurti rejected comparisons and I sensed how in his early years an overdose of abstruse theosophical metaphysics and occultist scholarship had turned him against his own esoteric baggage. Yet to me his approach also revealed an insufficiency related to his very refusal to provide any context to his advice. It ended up being dryly intellectual and abstract as well and I could not resist asking him, in the final question and answer session how he could ask people (as he had a few minutes earlier) not to make any comparisons in their minds about whatever they perceived at any given moment. I briefly pointed out that the human mind proceeds naturally by comparisons which enable it to make sense of newly discovered things and identify them.

The impassive Krishnamurti replied that one needed to acquire a new state of consciousness, uncritical and transparent to be able to capture the totality of things. I think that is more or less what he meant. I got the feeling that he was not particularly interested in discussing this point further as if it was an obvious fact. That perhaps was the gist of his message and also the problem with it; in many decades of such talks all over the world he seemed to have remained the same and his sessions had become predictable gatherings of generally well heeled, cultured people in secluded affluent surroundings, hearing him as if they were at a recital by a beloved soloist. For many it had become a part of their lives but once he departed this world there was no successor, no transmission and his books might gradually fall into oblivion. He probably helped thousands to feel better about themselves as long as they could attend his meetings but it would be difficult to sum up his message or his legacy in any practical way. Krishnamurti's "anti-theosophical" minimalism consisted only of his own personality. He did not want to leave a lineage or even an institution and accordingly a curtain fell when he died.

THE HAVEN OF SRI AUROBINDO

For a long time we intended to spend some time in Pondicherry, the old capital of the tiny former French possessions in India. After spending a few months in Madras one day we took the road that hugs the seashore on the green, coconut shaded Coromandel plain and arrived in the whitewashed enclave made famous by Dupleix and Suffren in the 18th century. It had fallen into a long slumber after Britain had put paid to the last French hegemonic dreams in the subcontinent. until in 1910, an illustrious Bengali poet and revolutionary was given refuge in that small port city when British authorities banned him from the empire. It was often the case that dissidents of the Raj were given protection by the French but Aurobindo was no ordinary rebel and his arrival in Pondicherry gradually gave that sleepy enclave a new global renown.

Auobindo Ghose hailed from a thoroughly westernized family of the upper bourgeoisie; his rationalist father claimed to have abandoned his Brahmo Samaj faith to embrace the scientific theory of evolution. Aurobindo, a King's College scholar had first defined himself as an atheist, which in India is not necessarily contrary to spirituality, and soon dedicated his youthful energy to the struggle for national liberation. In London he was introduced by a member of the Cotton family of East India Company fame to Maharaja Sayaji Rao of Baroda, became his secretary and later vice-principal of the college that was to grow into the university of the same name. The Maharaja, a great-grand father of prince Fateh Singh Rao who had so warmly received us in Delhi, quietly encouraged a movement for emancipation of British rule in his state and supported several freedom fighters and reformers. Aurobindo gradually became a leader of the hardline wing of the National Congress and coordinated a clandestine campaign to attack British interests in the country. One of his colleagues in this movement was his cousin Virendranath Chattopadhyaya, a brother-in-law of Kamaladevi whom we had known as well and also a brother of the famous poetess and freedom fighter Sarojini Naidu. Another secret correspondent was Surendranath Tagore, a sibling of the great poet. It was an elite organization mostly made up of British educated young men, born in anglophile families, destined by their upbringing to become supporters of the Raj who, perhaps predictably turned against it upon imbibing the western notions of democracy and self-rule.

The very high-mindedness and relative inexperience of those aristocratic scions may have caused the failure of their initiative. Several were arrested and Aurobindo, defended by the prominent lawyer Chittaranjan Das spent one year in solitary confinement at Calcutta's Alipore jail. He came out a changed man, claiming to have been visited supernaturally by Swami Vivekananda. After repairing for a short period time to Chandernagore, he moved to Pondicherry to dedicate himself to a spiritual quest. His "night of illumination" had shown him the insufficiency of political action to better the human lot.

Aurobindo, like so many of his countrymen along the ages had discovered that only spiritual liberation is real since the material world is a mere shadow play. Western thinkers almost never admit that conclusion unless they embrace a strictly religious vocation under the authority of a Church, so entrenched among them is the belief in the reality of earthly existence. In India, a revolutionary movement often came to a stop when its leaders answered an otherworldly calling. Like Aurobindo, his fellow clandestine insurrectionist Jatindranath Banerjee also listened to an inner voice and sought a spiritual master. Eventually he became one himself under the name of Niralamba Swami and founded an ashram in his native village of Channa near Burdwan although his life style and teachings could be seen as unconventional from the Hindu standpoint but then is there really anything like conventional Hinduism outside foreign notions of it?

As an increasingly recluse writer in his modest lodgings of the rue Francois Martin where he still received some his revolutionary relatives, including the indefatigable Viren Chattopadhyaya,

Aurobindo might have faded into obscurity under the indifferent watch of the French colonial administration if on the eve of the First World War an unusual French couple had not visited the exiled philosopher and felt deeply touched by his doctrine and personality.

The Richards were well-heeled and widely travelled Parisians; the husband was a politician and the wife, of Jewish sephardi ancestry, a student of occult doctrines. Her maiden name was Mira Alfassa and she was reputed to have para-normal abilities; she had spent a long time in an esoteric community in Algeria as a disciple of a Kabbalist who looked like an old Testament prophet and called himself Max Theon. He had founded a Masonic order, the Hermetic Brotherhood of Luxor in 1884 and with his wife, who seems to have been related to the British judge and Tantric initiate Sir John Woodroffe, known under the pen name of Arthur Avallon, he was the head of a "Cosmic Movement." Mira Alfassa had established in Paris a "cosmic circle" known as *Idée Nouvelle* which had drawn many noted intellectuals of the time, including the young Alexandra David-Néel.

In Pondicherry Mira, who had befriended many great artists such as Rodin and Monet fell under the spell of Sri Aurobindo and after the war, which she spent mostly in Japan with her husband, she separated from him and settled with the Indian master who soon became her mystical partner. Together they founded the Ashram in 1926 and she gradually became known as the Mother. Neither he nor she would ever leave this sliver of land on the Bay of Bengal for the rest of their lives.

In this former French outpost we found two separate towns, the Aurobindo Ashram which had spread across the territory of the erstwhile colonial enclave, and the rest of it which reflected a tricentennial blend of Gallic and Tamil influences and hosted several thousand French citizens, many of them retired functionaries from the colonies, especially from Indochina. The two communities coexisted without affinities and the skeptical or staunchly Catholic Franco-Indians were usually suspicious and critical of the Ashramites whom they regarded as conceited hypocrites. Many saw Aurobindo as a pedantic "pataphysician" and the Mother as an opportunistic witch and we heard many such peremptory verdicts justified by various allegations and claims. The very relationship between Aurobindo and the woman he called the embodiment of the Divine Mother, so peculiarly Indian in nature, was quite incomprehensible to those small town rationalists who only noticed that Mira had left her second husband to live with an Indian guru and build a cult around herself.

The Ashram's Mother had a striking personality in more than one way; she had always been elegantly dressed and wore exotic jewelry; she had a magnetic gaze surely honed by years of psychic training. As we became familiar with the history of the extraordinary couple, we learnt that Mira Alfassa had been born and had lived the first twelve years of her life in a building of the Boulevard Haussman in Paris where my father more than half a century later had an office. Her own father was a French government official in Algeria where my paternal family had been settled during more than a century. She had passed away in 1973, on the year we had resolved to undertake a journey to India for "mystical" reasons without knowing of her demise. Those striking coincidences impressed us deeply. I must say that we felt much more attracted to Sri Aurobindo and to his writings, often abstruse and even longwinded in their peculiarly "Victorian" style than to the Mother's message which I sensed to have been intuitive and unspoken as her own written or recorded teachings appeared rather lightweight and commonplace. Clearly there was much more in her than what transpires in her printed words.

On the surface there was not much in common between Sri Aurobindo, the product of high brow Oxbridge education groomed for a prestigious administrative career and Mira who was largely self-taught, aside from the conventional schooling of an upper class Frenchwoman of the time. Aurobindo had taught himself Sanskrit to read Hindu philosophy after returning to India, since his formal studies had included Latin, Greek, French and German apart from the Queen's English but no Indian language or literature. The Mother had dabbled in esoteric lore rooted in Hebrew and Egyptian occultism, in line with the prevalent orientalism of the age. Aurobindo had discovered spiritual philosophy in the Hindu and Buddhist traditions and had then broken away from the western secular formation of his academic youth. Those two exceptional people met at a decisive stage in their lives and together they exercised a powerful influence on many other renowned thinkers, scientists and religious reformers. I had read about Aurobindo in Paul Brunton's popular book and in René Guenon's writings but one can see his enduring legacy in the work of the California Institute of Integral Studies, inspired by Indra Sen's integral psychology and set up by Stanford professor Spiegelberg and Harinder Chaudhuri who had died in 1975.

The founder of the Lindisfarne Community William Thompson was one of many eminent thinkers to have spent time at the ashram. A lifelong but discreet resident disciple had been Margaret Woodrow Wilson, a daughter of the American President. There were other distinguished persons from remote lands at the Ashram in the year of our arrival and, although we did not join it, we met many and befriended some in the course of the several months we spent in Pondicherry.

Readers will have noticed how certain names keep returning in this narration. We felt likewise that we were flowing in a stream of thought and inspiration that had brought together for many years the people we met and those we had long known about. Sri Ramakrishna, Swami Vivekananda, the Tagores, Sri Aurobindo, Helena Blavatsky, Annie Besant, Rukmini Devi, the Maharajas of Kashmir, Benares, Baroda and Mysore, Raimundo Panikkar, the Roerichs, Sri Ramana Maharshi, Indira Gandhi and several others, seemingly unrelated by background or occupation, mysteriously took roles in that unfolding pilgrimage as if they had been in the play we had chosen to both watch and act in. Many will say that it is merely their fame that brought some of them into the frame but there was a connecting thread which guided Theseus out of the labyrinth.

We particularly benefited from our conversations with A.B. Patel, the venerable writer and editor of the World Union Journal who had heeded Sri Aurobindo's call for building a planetary federation in order to eliminate fratricidal conflicts between nations. M. P. Pandit was a distinguished philosopher as well as a mystic while the Navajatas, the father and son team who headed the Ashram were far more business oriented.

There was a strange mixture of sophisticated intellectualism and personal devotion at the core of the community which was also known for entrepreneurial acumen. We had trouble understanding the seemingly absolute faith in the Mother's divine nature that most members of the Ashram combined with their otherwise very pragmatic and worldly sense of reality. Complete acceptance of a supernatural "truth" is perhaps a condition or at least an ingredient for successful action in a material sense and it may be noticed that the Theosophical Society lost its momentum and dynamism when its budding "world teacher" turned against it. Likewise, modern secularized and quasi-rationalistic Christianity has become a feeble and tepid doctrine if we compare it to the passionate, triumphant and often fierce character of the Church in its days of hegemony and missionary expansion. Aurobindo's movement, true to the Indian spirit of plurality and tolerance, was never a militant body but its members appear to derive quiet strength from the undisputed messianic nature of the couple they revere.

We could not fail to notice instances of failure among the experimental projects associated with the Ashram. For one, the Mother's ideas on pedagogy seemed utopian and impractical. Thus the school that had been set up under her guidance appeared to provide little focus or discipline to pupils who were expected to learn by themselves with minimal supervision. There was, we felt, room for a sensible compromise between the overly regimented and competitive systems enforced in most educational institutions and the excessive reliance on a child's preferences and assumed desire to study. Just as Krishnamurti's Rishi Valley school had forged a curriculum that remained academically rigorous and made only implicit reference to the founder's philosophy, likewise the Mother's schools would need to build and impart the required intellectual structures for as long as the Supramental consciousness heralded by Sri Aurobindo has not descended upon mankind at large.

We deliberately avoided interacting only with followers of the Ashram and the dwellers of nearby Auroville, the city of the future envisioned by the Mother. We formed a group of local residents from diverse backgrounds and set up a small institution, with the blessings of the Dalai Lama called the Vishwa Dharma Kendra. Some of our sympathizers and supporters were the French-Indian veteran professor Ambady Narayanan, the ex-Chief Minister of Pondicherry Farooq Marekar, Dr Sainte Rose, a French physician of mixed Indian and Caribbean parentage who offered us a generous hospitality and a few Hindu Pondicherrians who had long associations with the French culture and language. We held wide ranging discussions on certain days of the week and I used some of my free time to learn basic Korean and Chinese martial arts from a friend, Yvan Laporte who served in the French army's elite forces but was on long leave with his local family. I found in Taekwon Do and even more so in Kung Fu a physical illustration of the worldwiews shared by Eastern philosophies and was reminded of an early exposure to Aikido in my childhood through Sensei Ueshiba's disciples.

The exotic elements of our lifestyle included the daily mix of South Indian, Vietnamite and French cuisine prepared by a lady cook from Saigon. The colourful blend of East and West that characterized Pondicherry's culture then perhaps more than now was apparent in the old fashioned academic and juridical titles and idiosyncrasies displayed by some of the town's elderly Franco-Tamil residents, quite attached to traditions that went back to the reign of Louis XV. Some like Ambady Narayan were familiar with the latest Parisian left bank literary trends and argued about Sartre, Foucault, Derrida and Nizan in chaste French but they were no less proud of Indic philosophical achievements.

ANANDA ASHRAM AND SWAMI GITANANDA

A most rewarding experience was to spend some time staying and studying at Ananda Ashram, the yoga centre of Swami Gitananda on the outskirts of Pondicherry in the quiet sylvan surroundings of Thattanchavady. Swami Yogarishi Gitananda, born to a wealthy Sindhi father and an Irish mother was a Canadian citizen and an imposing figure, stout and white bearded as a Hindu Santa Claus with a mercurial but kind personality, sparkling wit and infectious good humor. When we saw him he immediately conjured in our minds the effigy of a royal lion with his vast silvery mane and sonorous voice "from the belly." He ran the Ashram with his American wife Meenakshi Devi, "converted" to Hinduism and their six year old son, Ananda Balayogi was already an accomplished hathayogi who amazed us by his flawless performance of athletic asanas. As an only child of a relatively older and unusual couple he reminded me a little of myself when I was little boy cared for by dotting parents in the Canary islands.

The Ananda Ashram occupied the land of a Math (or Madam in Tamil) named after Sri Kambali, a legendary saint of the southern Shaiva Siddhanta tradition. Gitananda had been entrusted with that old seat by the chief guru of that order although he himself belonged to the northern lineage of Rishi Bhrigu. He often pointed out that there was no separation between the various Hindu sampradayas which were merely converging paths traced by diverse likeminded teachers towards the highest common goal. Once we asked him about the legendary Bhrigu who is credited with many technical inventions, and the Swami confirmed that the descendents and followers of the Rishi, the Bhargavas who were concentrated in the coastal region around the port city of Bhrigukachcha or Broach were expert engineers and architects, according to tradition.

Swami Gitananda, served by his encyclopaedic knowledge of Hindu lore had original albeit shastra-inspired views on most subjects and he expressed them eloquently. He was unstoppable on the subject of westernized modernity and its deleterious effect on health, spirituality and the quality of life. He carried a wide ranging experience as a former physician, member of the Royal Navy, US Government and UN officer who had returned rather late in life to the spiritual calling of his youth. Like all yogis and indeed like most

Indian thinkers he upheld the necessity to practice an abstemious, simple and largely self-sufficient existence close to nature in an uncontaminated rural environment, quite the opposite of all that technological progress promises and imposes in the shape of urbanization, complex gadgets, energy intensive amenities and means of transportation and a massified, industrial food supply and distribution system. Anyone in his right mind has to agree that the former option is the most reasonable and easiest to achieve but we are irresistibly carried away by the flood of economic growth and Swami Gitananda was one of several wisemen left preaching in the desert although he personally practiced what he taught as far as he could.

His career and personality made me aware once more of the flexibility and breadth of the Indian Dharma, with its ability to draw and absorb the most diverse human types and temperaments in one or another of its myriad branches. Similar observations may be made of other religions but while monotheistic creeds or even Buddhism are centered on one personality or one book by definition, Hinduism encompasses all possible types of gods, goddesses, messiahs, saints and prophets while still leaving plenty of room for those who don't worship any or become gods or messiahs themselves to their followers.

Swami Gitananda's outspokenness, his international eminence, unyielding defence of tradition and disdain for the contemporary politicians had made him quite a few enemies and he had bad relations with the local government in which some leftist and "tamil chauvinist" officials campaigned against him. He was accused of being a foreign agent, a reactionary ideologue, a charlatan and an obscurantist. He mostly laughed at those biased charges but had to fight them in court because his detractors wanted to take the Ashram's land from him, claiming that it should have belonged to the public. Irrespective of the legal merit of those claims we could see the great benefit his activity had brought to Pondicherry since the Ashram attracted students from far and wide and was impeccably maintained. One could only guess to what self-serving use the petty politicians who denigrated him might have put that property which had lain waste until the energetic Canadian yogi adopted it.

THE UNIVERSAL HINDU LEGACY

An eloquent promoter of India's ancient achievements, Swami Gitananda was not shy to point to likely or possible legacies of the hindu religion and literature surviving in other cultures the world over. He was convinced that the episodes of the greek epic in which Herakles (*Hari-kulesh*) and Achilles (*Akhilesh*) disguise themselves as women and live in harems were borrowed from the passage of the Mahabharata that described Arjuna's similar adventure. Likewise he saw the story of Lot's wife and daughters being turned into salt statues in Genesis as a reminiscence of the Indian tale about a rishi who likewise turns women sent to seduce him into salt effigies. The even more famous story of Moses, a solar horned figure being entrusted to the river by his mother in a wicker basket and found by a princess is an echo of the legend of Karna, semi-divine son of the Sun who was likewise put in a box and cast into the Ganges by his mother before being rescued from the stream by a charioteer and his wife. When we asked how one could be sure that such popular themes had originated in India and not in the Near East, as most western scholars tend to believe, the yogarishi replied authoritatively that Indian civilization had invented innumerable ideas, concepts and plots, being far more creative than others in that regard, whereas the Bible had been put together at a relatively later age and bore the signs of many heterogenous inputs. If one accepts the traditional dates attributed to the Indian vedic and epic scriptures one would have to agree with him and recognize Bharat as the mother lode of myths and legends, in keeping with Voltaire and 18th century orientalists who saw all things coming "from the shores of the Ganges," contrary to the Euro-centric positivists who have come to dominate the area of ancient history.

We had once a talk with the Swami and one of the students of the ashram who turned out to be master of chess, a game that has produced a few international champions in South India and it led us to reflect on the symbols and roots of what is in essence a craft of the mind.

We knew that the very concept of chess is rooted in Indian cosmology and social organization. Like the four suits of card games which, in their various names correspond to the four *varnas* (in ancient Egypt they were known as swords, clubs, cups and coins, referring to the respective estates), the four classes of pieces, apart from the royal "couple," stand for the four forces of an army in antiquity: the *chaturanga* or four services: horsemen, chariots, elephant and infantrymen as well as the fourfold division of the "Indo-Aryan" social order. Those pieces are ranged in ranks and files on a board of 64 light and dark pieces which represent the pattern of alternative night and day. The two contending players also hold black and white colours and enact the contest between light and darkness which interact and defeat each other; however both have a white square at their right corner of the board and a black one on opposite extremity. There are twice as many squares as there are pieces, evincing that the empty shadow is as large as the form and the geometric centre of the board is at the intersection of the four innermost ones since fact there is no centre in creation but only an abstract point at the boundary of separate but connected realms.

The pawn which is the least important piece can however rise to become a queen (known as a vizier in the Persian version of the game) if it reaches the eighth rank on the opposite side of the board. That is the Ogdoad of the neoplatonics, the supreme degree 'beyond the seventh" which signifies illumination or liberation from one's birth condition so that the pawn's progress on the checkered board may be seen as a metaphor for initiation. While the "bishops" or "elephants" run diagonally in straight lines and draw a cross of St Andrew in their motion, the knights in their vaulting leaps design a swastika or solar cross, shaped like a bird in flight, reminding us that the horse is a symbol of the Sun in the Vedas and that the horses of the Sun were winged and flew across the skies like birds. Rooks go straight along ranks or files and the Queen, the Shakti of the King can move in any direction, straight or diagonal although she cannot jump like the knight. Finally the King is severely limited in his actions and depends on his troops to shield him because if he is checkmated or made a prisoner, his side automatically loses. The apex of power is also, paradoxically the weakest point and "uneasy lies the head on which rests the crown."

Swami Gitananda pointed out that Claude Shannon had computed the sum of moves possible for all pieces at the astronomical 10^{120}, a number which carries his name and the chess master added that according to various statistical studies experience is more important than sheer IQ to develop proficiency and that a heightened perception and a precise memory are critical since the strategic ability to gauge the state of play may be more useful than the mere aptitude to plan complex moves long in advance. That was the reason, according to the Yogarishi, that chess was called the game of kings as it helped train statesmen and military leaders and honed their decision making skills.

That conversation took me back to the contrast eloquently drawn by Claude Levi Strauss between games and religious rites and also to the source of the games theory. A chess game begins between two symmetrically equal partners and, absent a draw –which implies that the game has aborted - ends with the victory of one over the other through the symbolic submission or annihilation of the latter. On the contrary, an initiatic ritual portrays the allegoric ascent of the worshiper toward the deity and culminates in their essential or gnostic union. The endgame is *Shakhmat*: the death of the king or surrender of the ego to the higher power that alone remains. We instinctively wish the light (white) to win but in truth, as I noted earlier, are blank (from *blanc*: white in French) and black not different spellings of the primal and final non-being in which all colours are fused and extinguished and which encompasses both the bright and the obscure?

XXII

Crisscrossing the Centuries

The Lure of Golkonda

After the months spent in Pondicherry, we were on the move again around the country. A friend who belonged to one of Hyderabad's princely families had persuasively suggested that we come to his city whose gilded romantic past haunted him. "I can only show you a shadow of its former glory, a mere memory of its heyday," he said in that florid style that the members of his class were famed for, "but at least I will help you to see what is still standing and may not remain much longer, even in people's mind."

It was not easy in the bustling but dusty and indolent provincial capital, as we saw it first, to imagine the oriental Camelot that had flourished in its walls. Our friend the Nawab was a survivor of that age, ceremonially courteous, flighty and fatalistic. The refined environment he had been raised in coloured all his thoughts and emotions. He could not find any interest in the republican India he lived in, born as he was in one of the world's most unequal and hierarchical kingdoms, an Indo-Turkish Avallon where the traditions of the long vanished Mughal court were cultivated in the hothouse of the Deccan and where aristocrats from all over the world came to taste the increasingly rare fruits of absolute monarchy.

The term absolute was perhaps never accurate and not even in Hyderabad. In fact, that state, almost as large as England and endowed with many natural resources and a vast population, belonged mostly to a few families, beginning with the descendents of Mir Qamaruddin Chin Qilich Khan, known by the ceremonial title Asaf Jah, a Turkic Vizier of the Delhi government who made himself independent in the old kingdom of Golkonda when the Mughal Empire broke up. The other clans that owned the bulk of the land between them also hailed from Central Asia and Persia and still spoke their original languages although the local brand of Urdu was the elite's "lingua franca" while Telegu, Marathi and Kannada were in use among most of their overwhelmingly Hindu subjects.

Language, writing systems, religion, race and culture separated the paramount rulers from the ruled. The situation reminded me of the first centuries after the Normand invasions in Britain when the local Celts and Saxons were under the sway of the invaders from France.

The great families that ruled the kingdom, whose sovereign took the title of Nizam, were fiercely attached to their ethnic roots and intermarried although one could observe in many of them an admixion of Indian blood. The royal princesses were always given as brides to the offspring of the second ranking house, the Paigahs whose ancestor was a companion in arms of Asaf Jah. The Nizams claimed descent from Abu Bakr, the first Khalif of Islam and the last reigning one married a daughter of the last Ottoman Sultan and Khalif, thus reviving the old bonds with Turkish imperial blood. Below the Nizam and the immensively wealthy Paigahs the Salar Jang family, a Shi'ite dynasty of Persian origin, which gave three prime ministers to the state came third in rank before the *Umara Uzzam*, the fifty odd great noble houses which traced their origins to Mughal grandees and held vast *jagirs* or feudal estates comprising hundreds of villages granted by the monarch from generation to generation. The top sixteen tributary *jagirdars* were customarily entrusted with military responsibilities while lesser ones headed the various departments of the state administration.

Only three Hindu families hereditarily belonged to the inner ruling circle, the Peshkars who were vice-Dewans (or deputy prime ministers) and two other lines of high treasury and land revenue officials, the Rai Rayans and the Malwalas. Below came the lesser, mostly Muslim aristocrats, numbering about five hundred and fourteen Hindu vassal rulers whose states were called *samsthans*.

Muslims usually held military and religious offices while Hindus were entrusted with civilian posts. The Mughal system of feudatory administration was thus superimposed on the older Hindu social structures.

Because of their vast resources and the stability of their regime protected by British power, the Nizams and their courtiers could enjoy the best the world had to offer. Like today's Arab oil emirs and sheikhs they vied in building splendid mooorish palaces or sprawling Palladian villas and in collecting fleets of luxury motorcars, unique gems, old master paintings and other art treasures along with all the trappings of cosmopolitan wealth and refinement. Several of those grandees were known for their eclectic taste and we saw the remains of one of the most sumptuous and diverse collections in the Salar Jang Museum, a real cavern of Ali Baba, which keeps many of the masterworks from East and West accumulated by the eponymous grandee, the third of the name.

Our *cicerone* liked to evoke the glittering surroundings he had known in his childhood sheltered by hundreds of servants as well as personal physicians, governesses, tutors, ladies in waiting (often hired in Europe), astrologers, entertainers, secretaries, accountants, chauffeurs, equerries, dressmakers, shoemakers, cooks and guards. He alluded to mansions cut out of bohemian crystal such as the Salar Jangs' famed *Aina Mahal*, furniture of repoussé silver and carved ivory, seemingly endless dining rooms lit by tall polychromous chandeliers when hundred or more guests in formal attire sat at the very long tables of precious timber to savour five course suppers served by scores of liveried valets supervised by ceremonious maitres d'hotel. He helped us visualize the carousels of gilded carriages sailing through streets studded with banners, ornate pavilions and ceremonial arches covered in embroidered cloth, flowers and tinsel. The victorias, breaks and landaus of the royal house were escorted by the flamboyant horsemen of the Nizam's cavalry and by his Arab and Ethiopian slave bodyguards followed by the usual procession of caparisoned and painted elephants, ponderous camels and colourful turbaned retainers.

After the Russian Revolution when the Bolsheviks sold many of the Tzar's jewels, the Nizam acquired that fabulous collection which heightened his reputation as the world's richest sovereign but it could not have escaped him that many of the diamonds had been unearthed at his own mines in Golconka centuries earlier and were hence being returned, through the vicissitudes of history to their land of origin.

In formal circumstances the local aristocrats wore the long ashkans and the typical Hyderabadi acorn-shaped immmaculate *dastar* or red *fez;* when not in purdah the ladies glittered in brocade, silk or Parisian chiffon gowns and dazzling jewels. When they went abroad or in select occasions at home, however, those cosmopolitan gentlemen sported bespoke suits and the top, bowler or canotier hats that were in style while young boys wore the obligatory sailor costumes I had seen in my own old family photographs. Women would be decked in the latest Parisian fashions, including the elaborate and expansive hats of the period, with their huge ribbons and sundry feathers and flowers. Those frills had a deliciously outlandish appearance and made their bearers look as if they had been acting a play from the *Belle Epoque* in front of a turbaned, white draped and bare footed audience and I recited a ballad by Tennyson, a favourite poet among the westernized Indian royals whose house coincidentally had been acquired by the ubiquitous Sayaji Rao of Baroda in 1920. The stanzas end in the refrain:

"A goodly place, a goodly time
For it was in the golden prime
Of good Harun al Rashid"

"Yes, I wonder who was exotic in those circumstances our host replied with a grin.... The local people who carried on looking and living like they had for centuries or my grandparents who had transplanted bits of the Strand and Neuilly here. It all depends on the point of view, I surmise. The Mughal emperors in Delhi had also kept many habits and fashions from their Central Asian home and in winter they wore tall astrakhan caps, long embroidered, fur lined caftans and ornate leather boots as if they were still in Bokhara. The elites always look to distant lands."

We admired testimonies of that that bygone elegance in family portraits and old photographs that reflected the rarefied distinction of those figures from a vanished age, with their chiseled olive hued faces, beaked noses, dusky eyes, curled up beards and moustaches and long manicured hands. In the zenana, children wore brocade clothes and jeweled crowns on formal occasions and had their hair tied in long plaits as if they had been Chinese subjects of the contemporary Ch'ing dynasty.

Keyserling was right when he noted that only societies ordered by a semi-theocratic hierarchy enable their hereditary elites to acquire and maintain the sense of grace and majesty as well as the exquisite manners which elude more democratic polities. The Nizam's state rested on deeply unjust principles from the standpoint of human equality as it was primarily run for the benefit of a small oligarchy of foreign conquerors and their descendents but, like a well tended botanical garden it produced the most delicate and exotic flowers in its glasshouses.

Apart from the lavish parties, traditional *mushairas*, polo games and splendid state ceremonies, a frequent pastime for the Hyderabadi ruling families as for most princely clans in India was the hunt which was practiced on the rugged Deccan plateau and jungle covered hills that spread outside the capital. British and other foreign visitors were often guests at those large scale expeditions mounted to bag tigers, leopards, boars, wild buffaloes, all kinds of antelopes as well as fowl of many species. Distinguished visitors from the United Kingdom and from the royal families of Europe and Asia expected to be entertained in "maharaja style" and often wanted to shoot at least one tiger. Most Indian rulers and great nobles sought to oblige them since, apart from honoring the tradition of hospitality, it was important to win the goodwill of influential Britons. The latter often used and even abused the privilege conferred by their colonial status and few may have felt the need to reciprocate those generous invitations back in their island home. Eminent guests expected to kill a tiger no less than ten-and-a-half foot long and many Indian hosts sought to satisfy their vanity even by cheating with measurements if there was no other way to achieve that result.

Vast cavalcades, and later motorcades, escorted by columns of servants carrying food, drinks, tents, furniture and all the amenities desired by the hunters ventured into the rural hinterland, riding or driving past villages frozen in the medieval past. The pampered lords of the palatial estates came in sight of their often poverty-stricken sharecroppers recreating an immemorial scene that seems to be a leitmotiv of the human condition; however that situation, blessed for a few and harsh for too many was to come to a close. The last years of the Raj saw the rise, under communist inspiration, of a widespread rural rebellion that had been simmering for years and the "police operation" of Indian troops soon after the end of British paramountcy led to the annexation of Hyderabad forcing the Nizam to abdicate.

We had heard in Delhi that Prime Minister Nehru had been reluctant to send the army into the state, which was formally independent after the automatic lapse of its treaty with the British colonial government. Nehru wanted to maintain the principle of non-violence and constitutional propriety that the Congress leadership had espoused under Mahatma Gandhi's leadership. However, there was a risk that the Nizam would merge his kingdom with Pakistan and the threat of Balkanization was staring India in the face. To defeat the internal rebellion, a militia of fanatical Muslim volunteers—the *Razakars*—unleashed a brutal repression in the rural areas.

Faced with the worsening situation, the government in Delhi had to intervene and the energetic Patel prevailed over Nehru's hesitation. Thousands of people died during those troubled days. The Nizam's forces could, however, only offer token resistance and soon surrendered. The monarch renounced his powers and many of his great vassals left the country. Those who stayed faced a rapid decline in their fortunes and prospects. The forlorn or abandoned palaces fell into disrepair, were sold, demolished or parceled off. Ugly office and apartment buildings and cramped slums took over many of the immense gardens, golf courses and parade grounds. The golden time of Harun al Rashid, the Indo-Saracenic Camelot had come to an abrupt end like most things that may seem, at least on the surface, too good or to beautiful to be true.

It appeared that Nehru had been personally disturbed by that outcome which was at odds with his desire to be a man of peace relying on good will and diplomatic methods to achieve his aims.

"He was also quite close culturally to the nobility," our Hyderabadi host commented when we discussed that episode of history in his family's drawing room, still exhaling the musty atmosphere of a storied past. "Despite his socialist ideology, Nehru was at heart an elitist groomed in the Darbari (court-like) environment of his privileged family. The story goes that he called his daughter Indira after the famous and beautiful Maharani of Cooch Behar who was a daughter of the much admired and influential Maharaja Sayaji Rao of Baroda. He did not believe in the monarchical forms of government, at least not in the princely states but he liked the polish and the social graces of that class with which he felt at home. In that regard he was a man conflicted between his democratic convictions and his aristocratic instincts."

Glancing around, at the old Persian carpets, at the chintz covered sofas, billowing brocade curtains, alabaster lamps and porphyry Grecian busts that sat on gilt bronze edged corner tables near Satsuma vases I felt once again that, like the phoenix the age of luxury dies only to be reborn from its pyre. The Nizams and Nawabs of yore might have lost the glow that fortune lends but up and coming oligarchies were eager to purchase the exquisite relics of their golden days so as to revive the feast. It would take time however to recreate legends as mesmerising as those which surround the kings of Golkonda and Hyderabad.

BARONS OF BOMBAY

After nostalgic, still Moorish Hyderabad, Bombay, the milling, hectic seaport acquired by the Portuguese and gifted to Charles II as a wedding present was a study in contrast. We had introductions to some eminent members of the Parsi community and also to a few of the old business families, which in that day completely dominated the industrial and financial scene since not many new great fortunes had yet emerged after Independence.

The magnificent natural landscape of Bombay surrounded by a bay that rivals Rio de Janeiro's, Lisbon's and Hong Kong's had enabled the British city planners to lay out an elegant and stately garden city between the blue sea and the verdant hills. However unchecked urban sprawl and high rise construction was rapidly destroying the indo-gothic tropical symphony composed by the foreign rulers. The grand mansions and palaces that dotted the forested Malabar Hill were all being replaced by drab residential skyscrapers, once secluded neighbourhoods were cluttered with shanties and the sandy waterfront had been blocked by rows of concrete apartment blocks while the famed beaches had become far too dirty to enjoy. Old residents were generally dismayed though resigned to the defacement of their city of which they are vibrantly proud. An incongruous mixture of Manhattan, London, Cairo and Sao Paulo is the result of that rapid and anarchical evolution, which tends to support the view that democracy in practice is injurious to order, beauty and impervious to wisdom. In the name of serving the majority's immediate interests it tramples on concerns about long term desirability. Only a few can see far ahead, the masses cannot look beyond daily worries and desires.

Metropolitan trading seaports are usually not meccas for the sages and the contemplatives but Bombay, being in India has its share of philosophical souls and through some of our Zoroastrian friends who were also theosophists, we were received by the highly respected Parsi priest Dastur Nowroz Minocher Homji, whose first name referred auspiciously to the Iranian New Year. That venerable, erudite and gentle personality was highly approachable, like most religious and political dignitaries traditionally are in India, and he willingly expatiated on some key features of Zarathustra's faith, which he pointedly contrasted with the formal Zorastrian religion as it had survived in India.

The Dastur regarded the pioneering 19th century intellectual K.R. Cama as the most important reformer of the tradition which, after studying the surviving ancient texts with French orientalists in Paris, he had defined in a seminal treatise, the *Zarthost Dai* as the

Daenyao Mazdayashnoish (the creed of Mazda). Although Homji did not share the somewhat "modernist" views of Cama who had been much influenced by the evolution of western Christianity in his judgments, like him and another great religious scholar, Dastur Dhalla, he regarded the *gathas*, or hymns, similar in form and contents to the RgVeda (*gatha* in Avestan is the synonym of *gita* in Sanskrt) as the authentic source material. The five books of those millennial songs are popularly known as the *Panj Bokti* (the five saviours).

"*Gati* (progress) and *Khordad* (perfection) are the goals of the Mazdean path," he uttered solemnly and they result in the achievement of *Amurdad* (eternity) in bliss.

"The religion's viatic is *Arbab Guiv*: give and survive. Our tradition is a sister of vedic Hinduism, free from many of the superstitions, tribal practices and social superstructures that over time have come to clutter the original brahmanical message.

Naturally we have acquired our own superstitions as well, he conceded. See for example the importance given to the cow in India. In our language the word *gao* also has come to apply to the cattle but initially it means the world at large and life in general. Thus, the veneration of life has come down to the worship of the cow and Hindus who, in ancient days sacrificed cattle and still do in Nepal, now hold them to be sacred. From the general we have come down to the particular, perhaps because man cannot easily relate to abstract notions so that he sooner or later reduces them to concrete images and beings."

The Dastur advised us to visit the Institute named after K.R. Cama on Apollo Street in which many of his papers and a wide amount of literature on the Parsi religion are kept. Before leaving we asked him why his community had become renowned for its Masonic secretiveness on matters related to its ritual traditions.

"We probably are in that way like the Brahmins of old," he chucked. "We like to keep our practices private to ourselves and don't welcome the attention of outsiders. Perhaps are we also carrying the stigmas of centuries of persecutions in Iran after the Muslim takeover. That is why our ancestors came to India more than ten centuries ago.

Here we never had any problems with our Hindu neighbours. We became yet another caste and we share much of their philosophical worldview. As the proverb goes: *Vahdak dar zad kafarat dar shifa*: "unity in fundamentals, diversity in the details."

Indeed, the Parsis are a riddle in more than one way. They are usually cheerful, amiable and quick to joke and laugh but their sanctuaries have a mysterious, Delphic atmosphere, pithily reflected in the ubiquitous signs posted on their walls: "Forbidden to non-Parsis." Yet, we got the impression that the religion as practiced today consists in a moral code illustrated by some simple and beautiful ancient rites and an unostentatious liturgy. Parsis are few in number but quite often gifted, industrious and creative as their immense contribution to Bombay's and India's economic, social and scientific life testifies. The British colonizers quickly developed a predilection for them in view of their business sense, reliability and self discipline. The "Aryan" blood purity of those Persian immigrants seduced the racially conscious Victorians and they noticed that these diligent drogmans, agents and compradores devoid of caste prejudices shared the British pragmatism, business sense, humour and penchant for eccentricity. In return, most Parsis became loyal supporters of the Raj and admirers of European culture despite the fact that they often resented British haughtiness and the fundamental injustice of colonial rule.

Even though they, as a small minority traditionally had no political role, influential and wealthy Zoroastrians became involved in the power game both in India and Britain and one of the most eminent, Dadabhai Naoroji, who had been a Dewan (chief minister) of Baroda and a business partner of K.R. Cama, became the first Indian-born member of the Westminister Parliament in 1893 and a respected voice for India's political emancipation.

Their resentment of British petty prejudices and domineering attitudes led many cosmopolitan Parsis to seek a more congenial environment in France and its civilization. French scholars, beginning with Anquetil du Perron had been the first to do research in Zoroastrian scriptures and their contribution created a bond which was reinforced when Cama's daughter-in-law, Bhikaji Cama, also born in a wealthy and distinguished family moved to France and from her apartment of the rue de Ponthieu in Paris spearheaded a league of expatriate Indians fighting for national liberation.

Those early patriots of the early nineteen hundreds came from diverse backgrounds, Hindu, Muslim, Sikh, feudal, intellectual and commercial; they associated with the socialist international movements, not always out of Marxist convictions but simply because they saw in the revolutionary parties the only allies in the struggle for decolonization. When the German empire began to stake its claims to various territories in Africa and Asia against British and French hegemony, some of its diplomats lent a sympathetic ear to the entreaties of Madame Cama and her allies. High ranking officials such as Bernstorff and von Oppenheim intervened on their behalf and arranged for meetings with members of the Hohenzollern Imperial family during the first world war. Not long before our visit to Bombay, we had learnt of the death at an advanced age of one of Madame Cama's colleagues the raja of Hathras, Mahendra Pratap Singh, who had founded in Kabul, under German protection, the first Indian government in exile in 1915.

The francophilia of the Parsis is deep rooted although it has faded in recent decades. The uncrowned king of Bombay and the pontiff of India's business community was then the much admired JRD Tata, the Paris-born scion of the premier Zoroastrian family by a French mother. JRD Tata was a combination of John Rockefeller II and Gianni Agnelli in Asia. His Hollywoodian good looks and dashing personality matched his Romanesque past as a former French legionnaire in North Africa and an alumnus of the Lycée Janson de Sailly, where he had kept company with several Iranian and Afghan royals and French aristocrats. His social attributes did not conflict with his business acumen, which had enabled him to multiply the ventures started by his forbears and grow the family empire which became almost hegemonic under his sway. He was also the country's most eminent philanthropist and had set up, in true Parsi tradition, many of India's foremost scientific, cultural, charitable and educational institutions apart from starting the national airlines as a pioneer aviator himself.

There was always a mystery about Tata's success as a capitalist in the increasingly socialist India under the rule of the Nehru family, which tended to look suspiciously at anyone powerful or prestigious enough to cast a shadow on its supremacy. Tata however had been careful to stay clear of politics and ostensibly to take no sides between parties although his sympathy for the liberal Swatantra Party of Rajagopalachari was well known. During the emergency JRD kept a studied silence but some of his lieutenants at Bombay House, the venerable headquarters of the Tata empire made no secret of their opposition to Mrs Gandhi's power grab. Her Nemesis was Tata's right hand man, the eminent lawyer "Nani" Palkhivala, a staunch critic of the arbitrary measures adopted by the Prime Minister before and during Emergency, who had also fought to defend the Princes' case when their privy purses and titles had been withdrawn .

Palkhivala had been appointed by a grateful Morarji Desai as India's ambassador to Washington and he had recently returned from that post when we met him in his office. His welcome was rather cold as he saw in us sympathizers of the now dethroned Mrs Gandhi. He however warmed up to the topic of the Dharma which was one of his favourite themes. He had equated it in a famous speech and in various papers to the "institutional morality," which he held to be as important as institutional legality. His juridical philosophy was rooted in a respect for the sanctity of unwritten rules of decency which originated in his Zoroastrian tradition and its emphasis on *asha vahistha* (highest righteousness) as in the Vedic notion of Rita. It was interesting to compare his perception of human law as a reflection of a deeper natural and divine set of precepts, also enshrined in the basic structure of India's Constitution, to Mrs Gandhi's views, and we found Palkhivala's awareness to be shared by other legal luminaries we met, including Supreme Court judge P. N. Bhagwati.

The former Prime Minister had sought to use the concept of Dharma in furtherance of her political ideas. She more than once asserted that the interests of the nation or its people must override the legal conventions when the latter are found ill suited or detrimental to the required social transformation, a typically Marxist notion of law.

However inevitably her views were influenced by her personal desire to hold on to power and, as it has almost always come to pass, her intentions to better the lot of the poor and oppressed had translated into the adoption of self-serving measures designed to increase and extend her personal power and crush her opponents.

When we met with various directors of the Tata group we realized that they were a careful mix of old families from the Parsi elite with some new names, such as Palkhivala's, that had been raised from the lower middle class into the exalted inner circle. After being an almost exclusively Zoroastrian enterprise, the conglomerate had grown to attract ever more Hindus and members of other minorities. That evolution reflected the larger trend in India as a whole and when we came in contact with heirs of the prestigious Parsi business houses of Mody, Sabawala, Mistry, Jussavala, Petit and Mehta at parties in their South Bombay flats or at their beach houses at Juhu, which had unfortunately lost much of their pre-independence glamour, we saw that, like most old ruling classes everywhere in the world, they were on a decline accelerated by the well known infecundity of the community whose numbers are shrinking year after year, contrary to the rest of India's population.

"This only shows that the will to survive is inversely proportional to the level of education and achievement," said once an eminent older Parsi, half-seriously. "We are victims of history's fatigue. Fickle fortune has now turned her gaze on new blood. If it were not for the house of Tata and perhaps two or three other major corporate families, our race would already have vanished into nostalgic insignificance, like many impoverished Zoroastrians have."

The Parsis had heavily invested in what was a waning age for Indian civilization. They had pioneered or revived industries such as shipbuilding, overseas trade and steel making and embraced the European way of life and western languages and customs earlier than anyone else in the country. Their eclectic spiritual interests had made some of them theosophists and anglophilia had perhaps inspired a few to embrace Christianity. One of the ladies who gave us tea and conversation at her stately home on Malabar Hill was Sophie Wadia, an American *née* Camacho, the widow of an international leader of theosophy, the late B.P. Wadia. Her husband's family was perhaps the oldest business dynasty in the country to have achieved international notoriety since it built some of the best Royal Navy ships from the middle of the 18th century. The vessel on which the American national anthem was composed while its crew bombarded Baltimore and Nelson's admiral man-of-war at Trafalgar were both Wadia built ships. During the American Civil War, other members of the family benefited from the blockade of US seaports by launching, with some of their peers the cotton growing, spinning and milling industry to replace the British imports from the Confederate States. This new activity inflated their already large fortune. Much later one of the Wadia heirs, owner of the Bombay Dyeing Company married Dina, the only child of Muhammed Ali Jinnah whose Islamic faith did not really extend to his personal life so that he welcomed her marriage to a non-Muslim tycoon.

Sophie's husband had dedicated his life to theosophy since Madame Blavatsky appeared to him in Adyar many years after her death. He had joined the United Lodge of Theosophy founded in the USA by some American dissidents, who rejected the direction given to the Adyar-based movement by Annie Besant and Leadbeater.

No mention of sea vessels from Bombay would be complete without a reference to the powerful owner and manager of India's largest commercial ocean shipping company, Scindia Lines, Mrs Sumati Morarji. We met her in her office and saw once more that women in India have, without losing the trappings of femininity, as uncanny an ability to rule and operate countries, companies and foundations as to run their own homes and families, unlike many contemporary feminists who seem to turn militant protest into a full time occupation in lieu of any other.

PHYSICISTS AND PHILOSOPHERS

The Tata Institute of Fundamental Research is a shining example of what Tata's patronage has done to turn sheer wealth into scientific excellence. We had a meeting with the Director B. V. Sreekanthan and spoke to a few of the main research physicists on the current trends in the field and the emerging connections with Indian epistemic philosophy. Predictably some hardcore scientists were skeptical on this issue while others, more in touch with their roots, welcomed it and shared some reflections related to the insights of Raja Ramanna, Yash Pal, George Sudarshan, D S. Kothari and Fritjof Capra.

A stalwart of the institute at the time, Jayant Narlikar was a former student and junior colleague of the illustrious Sir Frederick Hoyle and, sharing his concept of a steady state cosmology, remained a dogged and embattled opponent of the dominant 'Big Bang' theory. It struck us that his position stood against the traditional cosmology of Vedic texts which describes the world as emerging and expanding out of a golden egg in which it was enclosed in seed form. Narlikar's playful response was that India had given birth to many cosmological systems so that any new theory could find sanction in some scripture or another. Hoyle's perspective on panspermia, or the propagation of life across the universe in the shape of microorganisms travelling aboard comets and other meteors is certainly compatible with the Indic notion of life being all pervasive.

The discussion gave rise to some enlightening give and take about the real contribution of ancient India to scientific knowledge, as distinct from the often fantastic claims made by some of its enthusiastic but naïve admirers. It is true that Sayana, an authoritative commentator of the Rg Veda who flourished some six hundred years ago gave a surprisingly accurate of the speed of light when he said that it travels 2202 *yojanas* in half a *nimisha* but various lengths are given for the yojana—the Indian "league," a very ancient indo-european distance measuring unit—at different times and places in India and the duration of a nimisha is also open to more than one interpretation. However, given that this is not a symbolic round figure but a specific number, there is reason to give credit to Sayana and the knowledge that he shared.

It is indisputable, on the other hand, that Pingala describes the *meru prastara* which is no other than Pascal's triangle, almost two millenia before the French mathematician. Likewise the *sulba* theorem that is part of vedic literature (in what is known as the vedangas or limbs of the Vedas) is none other than that which is called after Pythagoras in the West and the *sulba shastras* very probably predate the greek sage who was known to have studied in India.

One of the scientists at the meeting recalled that Heisenberg had recognized that Vedanta's analogical reasoning was useful to quantum physics which could not be understood in terms of conventional logic. An astrophysicist who defined himself as a follower of Sankaracharya pointed out that the great master in his commentary on the *Prasnopanishad* clearly alluded to the force of gravity that prevents solid bodies from both flying away into space and collapsing on the ground. "In this regard, he added, there is a very interesting mention of the fact that it acts on the life breath (*apana*) which holds bodies erect and enables them to fight gravity. Thus, Adi Sankara traces a link between what keeps us physically on the surface (gravitation) and what enables us to rise and remain standing (life). Is gravity then tied to life and the soul?"

We already knew the symbolic significance of the sacred number 108 in India in which the first of the three digits stands for the undivided unity of the source, the middle one for the nothingness of maya and 8, the third for the infinite plurality of beings and things summed up in the five senses and the three higher organs of inner and outer perception: the soul, the intellect and the self. We were given another technical reason for this number which accurately represents the rate of the diameters of the Sun and Moon to their respective distance from the earth. I was struck by the fact that this mathematical relation in nature is at least as surprising as the evidence of the ancient Indians' awareness of it.

Despite the obvious pleasure they drew from those reminiscences of an ageless knowledge, I found those eminent scientists a bit reluctant to indulge in that heady game. Their academic training had made them wary of drawing parallels from their respective fields into an area that was regarded as unrelated and off limits to serious researchers. Even Capra was regarded with suspicion for his highly popular endeavour to interpret scientific theories and data in the light of venerable religious texts. However the spiritual genie of India was out of Aladdin's lamp and it was, like a poltergeist, haunting the minds, labs and cyclotrons of the modern-day magicians. It could no longer be put back into its dusty bottle on the shelf of archaeological relics.

This impression was heightened during the time we spent at Bombay's Indian Institute of Technology, a premier centre of scientific research where we lectured in various departments. We were asked to speak about the topic of UFOs by teachers and students who were intrigued by that enigma and we evoked the connections with the ancient Indian texts, in particular Bharadwaja's *Brihad Vimana Shastra*, completed and published by Swami Parivarjak in 1968. We alluded to the various types of propulsion systems described in that long treatise and also to the many machines and instruments that allegedly made the vimanas such advanced vehicles, endowed with formidable military capabilities.

Some intriguing things reported in that and other texts are *yodhayantra* (fighting machines or robots), *varijayantras* (hydraulic mechanisms), *dwarapalayantras* (artificial gate keepers), *visvakriyadarpanas* (a sort of telescope for panoramic long distance vision), *puspini darpana* (an artificial lightning generator) and many others. In fact the *Samarangana Sutradhara* states unambiguously that "anything can be made by machines when not otherwise." The materials used to make them are diverse as well and the tripura vimana for example is said to be built out of mica (or of whatever transparent shiny material which was called in Sanskrit by the name we associate with mica).

When we see how many synonyms and homonyms exist even in our more precise technical vocabulary, we can understand the uncertainty surrounding the meaning of nouns used thousands of years ago in a civilization of which we know little.

The various power sources listed in the same compendium are liquid, solid, incandescent and gaseous. The solid ones are called *mani* (gems or crystals), whether they are found in nature or are manufactured. One of the rather well defined ones, consisting of fourteen mineral and organic components is called *chumbak mani* and is a magnet.

After the lecture, we had a long discussion with some members of the audience of the implications of the information found in those arcane books. A natural skeptical reaction was to inquire whether vimana-related literature might have been "updated" by modern creative editors, desirous of glorifying the achievements of their ancestors. The obvious response was that several of those texts had been known and kept for centuries and could not have been substantially modified in recent times without detection. Even if no verifiably ancient manuscript of the Brihad Vimana Shastra is known, many other documents containing a wealth of technical details or observations about the flying vessels and the underlying technology are proven to be several centuries old at the least.

In another register, the Mahabharata quotes a *nagara yantrasutra* which reportedly dealt with the technique of making and using fire arms. In the 4th century BC the pragmatic statesman Chanakya mentioned in his *arthashastra the akasa yodhinah* or air warriors and the greatest poet of India Kalidasa accurately portrayed a long flight above India by the hero of his play *Meghaduttam as* if he himself had been able to watch the countryside unfolding thousands of feet below his vantage point. The famous tale of the ten princes *(dasakumaracarita)* which is at least eight centuries old alludes to a chemically prepared wick that produced a light without fire, in an uncanny anticipation of the electric bulb.

The conclusion was that such a widespread awareness reflected during centuries of literary and scientific production could not be devoid of a factual basis. Why would so many writers and acknowledged astronomers, chroniclers, chemists, mathematicians and teachers of various disciplines provide detailed and often matching accounts of all sorts of man-made contraptions if they had never existed? Yet, the prejudiced minds of contemporary scholars tend to remain closed to the persuasive evidence which contradicts the prevailing notions of history and human evolution.

Little did we know that three decades later the very *chumbak mani* of the Shastra was to be manufactured and tested by three graduate students in chemistry of the same IIT and found to have interesting properties, metallic when heated upto 400 degrees C and semiconducting above that temperature. At 1250 degrees it becomes a magnetic, shiny material and under certain conditions reveals superconductivity.

Along with the chumbak the researchers duplicated two associated products, a metal compound called *panchaloha*, well known to the metallurgists of ancient India and a yellow liquid known as *pargrandhik drav*. Those three ingredients were reportedly used in ancient India to build a *guhagarbha drasta yantra*, literally "a device to see or detect things hidden underground."

There is not even a probability that our interactions at IIT Bombay in 1980 played a role in the initiation of that research in 2013 but I find the coincidence inspiring and encouraging since it confirms the view that some long-forgotten seeds (the samskrit *bija*) can one day grow into mighty banyan trees through what appears to be a purely serendipitous process.

THE GANDHIAN TYCOON

We were not done yet with our forays into the mysteries of science in Mumbai as we found out when we went to meet GD Birla, the seniormost industrialist who had been perhaps Gandhi's greatest backer. The Mahatma was shot dead at the Delhi mansion of the tycoon where he was staying on 30 January 1948.

GD Birla, the eighty six year old head of a business conglomerate that was second only to Tata's and extended in many areas across the length and breadth of India was a feared and admired man whose personal intelligence network was said to be unrivalled. It was whispered that nothing could be said in the house of the Prime Minister that he would not know within a few hours. His business methods were faithful to the modus operandi of the Marwari community to which he belonged, famous for secretive practices tied to the traditional money lending and trade financing activities that made them wealthy. GD Birla and his large family clan were less westernized in their upbringing than the Tatas who were not suspected of applying similar conspiratorial ways and means, perhaps because they were more discreet in that regard. The critics of Birla and his empire liked to accuse him of having used Gandhi's name and influence to further his own ends but that could hardly be unexpected of a man who had expanded his fortune into India's largest by challenging some British industrial monopolies such as jute-processing and car-making. Some of the other major Hindu businessmen, such as the head of the house of Bajaj had also been closely associated with Gandhi unlike the Tatas who had kept a lower profile in the Independence struggle, probably because of their greater proximity to the rulers of the Raj.

Birla had asked us to come for breakfast at his flat high above Bombay on the forested crest of Malabar Hill in the luxurious Il Palazzo building. The gaunt, bespectacled, sharp featured potentate received us with the majestic self assurance that power bestows on its possessors and proceeded to ask us a number of questions on our ideas and activities. Suddenly he stopped us with a raised hand and pointed to the book that was lying on the coffee table between us.

"The Tao of Physics" by Fritjof Capra, he announced emphatically, it is my bedside reading. It shows that Indian philosophy holds the key to understanding the universe."

Like most important entrepreneurs, the Birlas had kept themselves in good terms with all political forces and were known to have financed most of them, possibly not excluding the Communists. The patriarch of the family might have seen the coming to power of Hindu nationalists within the Janata coalition with some favour because of his staunchly religious convictions and his alleged sympathy for the United States which he shared with Morarji Desai; however when we met him the Congress was making a rapid comeback in public opinion in its new avatar under Mrs. Gandhi's leadership and we knew that the Birlas had major stakes in the reborn party which was also in need of their support.

G.D. Birla had sponsored in the early years of freedom the national economic development plan that carried his name and advocated state capitalism through major government undertakings in strategic industries. He had, in this, been heeded by Nehru's government which however intended those state enterprises to remain permanently under sole government ownership and control whereas Birla's proposal was to privatise them within a given number of years, as a businessman was wont to. The bank nationalizations implemented by Mrs Gandhi had probably not endeared her to him although his own family interests had not been too directly affected by her left-leaning policies.

We were advised by GD Birla to pay a visit to the institute he had founded in his hometown of Pilani, the BITS that had become internationally reputed and where our friend from Simla, Lothar Wendell had taught for years. Those were his final words before we left another legendary figure of the nation's recent history whom we were not to meet again. He died three years later.

XXIII

The Nostalgia of Maharajas

REMEMBERING SAYAJI RAO

From Bombay to Baroda, now known by its original name of Vadodara the trip was short and direct. We found with pleasure the green and clean city described by FatehSinghrao Gaewad and settled in the University Guest House which was comfortable and surrounded by a lush garden much favoured by langhurs, the retainers of the moon god, who, like lanky old dark faced gentlemen in grey furs and fluffy white balaklavas held assemblies on our balcony and sashayed into the room if we forgot to close the sliding door. The university, which had hosted various eminent figures such as the young Sri Aurobindo and been a seething cauldron of clandestine action against the British Raj remains reputed, especially for its fine arts department which was, with Shantiniketan the incubator of much contemporary creativity in painting, sculpture and design. As in all former capitals of princely states, the imprint and memory of the Maharajas, and especially of the true father of the modern city, the great Sayaji Rao were ubiquitous. In the absence of his living heir, the royal secretary showed us around the magnificent LakshmiVilas Palace, named after the goddess of fortune which, even in its lonely and silent state that reminded me of the tale of sleeping beauty, preserved the legacy of refinement and eclecticism of its builder and the latter's equally gifted wife Chimnabhai. The most talented artists and artisans from Italy, Belgium, France, Britain and India had contributed to the decoration of the palace and Murano glassmakers had created the floor mosaic of the grand Durbar Hall featuring Indian mythological themes in the syncretistic style that was in fashion at the turn of the century. The ceremonial courtyard which frames one side of the Durbar is studded with Falicci's marble fountains and neo-classical statues. In its heyday, the palace hosted the royal couple, their children, sundry relatives and more than two hundred regular servants headed by a multi-national team of chamberlains, majordomos, butlers, secretaries, military attachés, ladies-in-waiting of the maharani, chefs and personal valets.

Many of the European old master paintings and *objets d'art* collected by the maharaja during his worldwide travels had been moved to the city's art gallery and museum housed in another palace on the grounds of the royal estate but there were still enough treasures from the past to fill many an antiquarian's storeroom.

Remembering as I did my readings of Rousselet's travels in India I wondered about the fate of the fabled full scale gold and silver cannons and many other precious objects, not to forget the huge emeralds from Colombia that successive monarchs had acquired over the decades. I also rued the apparent disappearance of the royal zoo, lyrically evoked by Jules Verne in his "La Maison à Vapeur" as an impressive ménagerie of rhinoceroses, crocodiles, tigers, lions, zebras, giraffes, cheetahs, panthers and many other rare mammals.

The Baroda aviary had also been famous but all those wonders had gradually vanished after the eclipse of the local dynasty. The vast park landscaped by the head gardener of Kew gardens, despite its visible neglect was still full of songbirds and migratory fowls and afforded sweeping vistas of the palace's "mughal neo-baroque" asymmetrical array of towers, spires, pavilions, arcades, colonnades and helmet-like kiosks (*jharokas*) at the confluence of East and West, as a sort of oriental Neuschwanstein which emphatically proclaims the triumph of imagination over regularity.

The Baroda Royal Library has many claims to fame in view of its impressive collection of rare books and documents which include one of the ancient manuscripts of the *Brihad Vimana Shastra* that probably dates to the eighteenth century or earlier and hence invalidates suspicions of modern forgery.

We were busy during our stay with the lectures and seminars that were arranged for us in various faculties of the beautifully laid out university which stands witness to the maharaja's quest for beauty, in contrast to the often calamitous taste or lack of it evinced by many architects and contractors in the decades since Independence.

One of the talks took place at the reputed institute for the study of comparative religions also established by "Sir" Sayaji Rao – only the British would dare to bestow a knighthood on a ruling king and make him a subordinate to one of their salaried functionaries. We learnt that the maharaja had been inspired to set up that centre by his friend Sir Francis Younghusband, the India-born explorer of Central Asia and invader of Tibet who had become a visionary spiritualist on his return from Lhasa.

Sayaji Rao had an syncretistic philosophical mind and defined himself as a rational theist who had little patience with the many ritual, ceremonial and magical aspects of Hindu religious culture. In his childhood his British tutors had raised him in the tradition of Victorian morality, faith in science and philanthropy while instilling distrust for the "heathen" beliefs of his subjects which he thought would gradually be corrected through liberal education. He believed in the merit of comparing and highlighting the highest values taught by all major creeds and supported Younghusband's endeavours which culminated in the World Congress of Faiths.

I was intrigued to find out that Younghusband claimed to have had a transcendent vision while travelling back from Tibet in 1904 and had become convinced that other planets are populated by higher beings headed by an exalted universal leader dwelling on the star Altair. He called this great being Stellair and described his belief in various books such as "Life in the Stars," published in 1927 and "The Living Universe," three years later which had a wide influence on British society. The founder of the Scout movement, Baden Powell appeared to subscribe to Younghusband's gospel. We did not know if the maharaja of Baroda also sympathized with the doctrine expounded by the famous Englishman whose mystical epiphany, in the aftermath of the massacre which his expedition carried out in

Tibet reminds one of Emperor Ashoka's own conversion after the great slaughter of the battle of Kalinga.

In retrospect Younghusband's theosophical *metanoia* was in tune with India's ancestral spirit as well as with the *zeitgeist* of the times when so many orientalising seers, prophets and would-be messiahs appeared in the western world.

The Maharaja was in his later years afflicted by the untimely deaths of some of his children and grandchildren to whom he had given a cosmopolitan education first at the palace school and then in Europe and the USA. More than one had fallen prey to alcoholism, a common ill among the rich and idle. The western education and habits they had been imparted contrasted with the traditional environment in which they lived and, like many other Indian aristocrats, they became misfits in their own society in which they felt useless although they remained strangers in the racially conscious and often bigoted European circles that they haunted.

The story of Baroda's ruling family, one of the richest in the world then, reflects by its misfortunes and sorrows the eternal but eternally neglected truth that great wealth and privilege tend to be harbingers of pain and self-destruction. The British design to breed cultural hybrids between feudal India and colonial Europe produced many charming, attractive and glamorous figures, yet deeply conflicted, unhappy and marked by misfortune. Sayaji Rao, an accomplished and hyperactive teetotaller who had been adopted by the earlier regent maharani in a poor family of distant relatives at the age of ten was deeply disappointed by his spoilt offspring who did not follow his example despite his frequent admonitions.

As often, some of my choiciest memories of Baroda are drawn from conversations with people in diverse walks of life, especially some of the professors whose familiarity with their national ancient lore often produced enchanting spiritual lessons. I recall the old philosopher who pointed out that in Vedic literature the *raksasas* and *asuras,* who are the closest equivalents to the demons, vampires and other evil creatures of our popular western pantheon wax in strength at night and always try to disrupt any meritorious endeavour performed by gods and humans, to which they are attracted like moths to the flame. "What devas do, asuras imitate but they do it in a bigger way, as a counterfeit" he said, quoting the Brahmanas. I saw the equivalent image in the latin proverb *Daemon est Deus inversus* and in the theological metaphor: "The Devil apes God."

Some of the Indian scriptures go deeper when they explain that the devas see the hidden meaning in all things and don't like literal statements : *paroksaiva priya hi devah pratyaksa dvisah*, contrary to asuras who follow the letter which, said Paul, kills while the spirit giveth life. The language of the gods is even called *sandhyabhasa* or paradoxical tongue and a large section of esoteric Sanskrit literature is written in that coded style and vocabulary.

THE SUN'S HEIR

Much as we had been prepared for what expected us in Udaipur, the lake city set amidst the hills of Rajputana, we were enraptured by the magic beauty of the site. Like Venice or Istanbul, Udaipur, albeit on a smaller scale, always overcomes visitors by the miraculous harmony of its palaces spreading along the island specked, tree ringed mirrors of water that reflect their majestic walls, towers and *chhatris*. The colossal dwellings of the kings of Mewar, white as a string of pearls form an enclosed town that dominates the city. Like many other traditional capitals, Udaipur was shaped after a new landscape was created by damming a river in a valley in the 17th century. The result was a lovely symbiosis of art with nature achieved in keeping with a millenary tradition of city planning codified in the *Sulba Shastras*.

Shortly after our arrival we were received by the master of that legendary abode, HH Maharana Bhawat Singh, the seventy fifth holder of that throne which had for many centuries been held above all others in India, due to both the illustrious origins of its titularies and the heroic feats several of them displayed to resist the invaders from the North-West. A virtual federation embracing most of the present states of Rajasthan, Gujarat and Central India took shape around the kings of Mewar whose living heir, as president of the Vishwa Hindu Parishad, the universal Hindu Council, was still seen as a spiritual emperor, a living though symbolic embodiment of the chakravarti.

This was the reason why we had written to him and it was in that capacity that he had invited us to visit Udaipur. He was a man of middle height with long dark eyes, a calm bearing and an inscrutable physiognomy. Like Sayaji Rao Gaekwad he had been adopted by the childless previous maharana, crippled from birth, in a poor and rural younger branch of the royal clan. We would discover that such adoptions had been rather frequent so that several of the famed potentates who dazzled the West in the last two centuries by their glamour and wealth had been born in modest circumstances and elevated to the royal seat by fortuitous events.

The origins of the house of Mewar itself were wrapped in mystery since the clan owed its dynastic name, Grahilot, to a remote ancestor who fourteen hundred years earlier had been born in a cave in which his persecuted widowed mother had hidden to escape the enemies of her kin. The child named Grahiladitya (the Sun of the cave), raised by the local Bhil tribesmen had grown to become their leader and an invincible warrior. This made modern historians assume that he was himself a Bhil but the family's genealogy, apocryphal or not, makes him a scion of the ancient house of Vallabhi ruling in Gujarat since the fifth century of the common era, which was itself descended from Lava, the eldest son of Sri Rama and as such gives the Sun God Surya as the first ancestor. Maharanas were the hereditary heads of the Sisodia branch of the Grahilot lineage of Suryavanshis, begotten by Grahiladitya, and their adventures, wars, romances and actions fill many volumes compiled by generations of chroniclers and sung by an uninterrupted succession of bards who carry the same name, *bardai* in the local version of Hindustani spoken in Rajasthan.

The ancient records keep the trace, according to Colonel Tod's profuse notes, of a Persian invasion under the rule of Darius the First although official history does not teach that his troops reached so far to the East. Yet the annals of Udaipur state that they were led by a prince Bahman, or Vohumana, who is said to be the 34th descendent of Rama, in keeping with the traditional view that the Achemenids were relatives of the Hindu ksatriyas. This seems to suggest that the royal house of Mewar originated from this Persian conqueror. Other more "rational" versions of history make the "Solar Clans" descend from Scythian, Kushan or White Hunnic invaders from the first centuries of the common era and assumes that they were gradually assimilated into the old ksatriya caste like many outsiders before and after them. That they worshipped the Sun or might have been followers of Zarathustra before becoming Hindus would, according to this account explain their "suryavanshi" patronym which Tod relates to the Sauromatae of Iran.

When this question was broached in our conversation with the Maharana he was quick to point out that Indians had a very ancient kinship with the various "Aryan" tribes of modern Afghanistan, Iran and Central Asia so that there was no real ethnic controversy in the traditional context.

"Many of our rajput clans wandered off beyond the Khyber Pass and the Hindu Kush since untold centuries, he said and some came back home much later so that there was no argument about their real origins. The Bhattis, our Yadava brethren of the lunar race who are descended from Lord Krishna went all the way to Afghanistan—where they founded Ghazni—Iran and Syria more than three thousand years ago and some came back in the Middle Age. One branch established the Hindu kingdom of Jaisalmer in the western desert while others sunk roots in Gujarat and others still remained in Sind and Beluchistan where over time they converted to Islam. Sakha means branch in Sanskrit and the Scythians or Sakas are in fact branches of the great Indian family, like the Medes, Persians, Sarmatians and Jats who were known as Getes in Europe if I remember right. In fact Sakas are already mentioned in the Mahabharata as they fought in the great battle. We share many traits with the Mongols in their language and culture because some of our ancestors settled there many thousands of years ago and Mongol official history records that. Our languages have many words in common with theirs. Our fortified cities are called "kots" like their own.

As he spoke I realized once again that as in all traditional civilizations "rooted in the sky," India's history allows for various parallel versions of events, the mundane "factual" one coexists with the mythological or legendary narratives that invest every character with a super-natural or divine nature and source. Kings could readily believe that they were the offspring of stars or planets because all life is made of cosmic dust and solar energy, as bio-chemistry also tells us. By denying that transcendent aspect of reality, so-called scientific materialism simply closes our eyes to the bigger picture.

The Maharanas saw themselves as dewans or ministers of the real monarch of the State, the god Krishna whose hallowed Srinathji *murti,* the tutelary four headed deity of Mewar is enshrined in the sanctuary of Nathdwara near Udaipur since it miraculously stopped there after being taken out of its earlier temple at Mathura in order to escape destruction at the hands of Aurang Zeb's iconoclastic soldiers.

We were hosted in the palace built in the 19th century by Maharana Fateh Singh for his guests. Our suite was located high in the corner tower that faces the lake and from our windows and the adjoining gallery we were able to tirelessly admire the calm expanse of water, periodically rippled by the wake of boats that link the Lake Palace to the shore below. Further away on another island, palm trees rise above the milky arcades and pavilions of Jag Mandir where the future Emperor Shah Jahan whiled away many days of exile when he was the disgraced crown prince. On the other bank in the distance, above forests and orchards, the sere hills of the Aravallis frame the azure sky and the eyrie of Fatehgarh stands like a Rhenish Burg atop the highest peak.

During various conversations, some of which took place over lunch on the Sun-drenched terrace of the royal residence we talked about many things with Bhagwat Sinh who, although not a scholar, had a high awareness of his heritage and a precise notion of the political system that his ancestors had managed for so many generations. He would have naturally been accused of partiality by ideologues of democracy but an open minded listener could see that there was a genuine knowledge of human nature in the old regime, unlike our current institutions, many of which seem to be based on a denial of psychological and biological factors and are thus constantly and gratuitously fighting the decrees of fate.

"The last few maharanas before me were keen reformers," he told us proudly, "but for thousands of years there was no notion of progress. The role of the monarch was to maintain a balance according to immemorial laws. His duty was to protect his people from invaders and from injustice and for that he was respected, upheld and obeyed. If his subjects became prosperous, he benefited from it. If he was capable and trained his children to perform the same role, why would anybody have wanted to vote for someone else? Do the sailors in a ship elect a captain and do soldiers elect one of them to be their general? Not unless their leadership is remiss and found wanting. Abolishing royal legitimacy is an invitation to all to fight for power and that is how civil wars erupt."

I remember my father saying in response that all political systems require a permanent underlying principle to justify their existence and claim legitimacy. In a democracy it is the purported voice of the hypothetically sovereign people but that theory is highly questionable given that a people as a whole are never fully informed on their choice, almost never unanimous in their views and that there is no clear reason why a majority, however narrow should enforce its choice on the minority by giving a few people a mandate to do what they claim to be in the common interest.

In one of those luncheons there were a few other guests and the Maharana played host with his Australian wife. We were soon told that this relationship, quite common in other princely families –does the Veda not mention the four consorts of the monarch, beginning with the *mahishi*, the head queen and the *vavara* or favourite? - was exceptionable in the conservative house of Udaipur and had led to a split between him and his official wife who was from Bikaner. The heir apparent Mahendra Sinhji had taken the side of his mother and was estranged from his father who made no mystery of his preference for his younger son, Prince Arvind Sinh who lived in another palace in the countryside.

What was irreplaceable in the feudal and paternalistic regime of India was the personal bond of loyalty and affection that united the ruler and the ruled, over and above the personal judgment that subjects passed on their lord. As in a functional family, the sentimental relation was stronger than the passing feelings of disappointment or resentment. There was no place for envy and personal ambition in the commoners who were generally proud of who they respectively were and did not, unlike modern citizens of democracies, aspire to rise in status and power in order to find meaning for their lives. The combination of the jati system, similar to the guild-based order of western medieval societies, and of the belief in karma and reincarnation gave to most the mixture of security, resignation and hope that affords contentment.

"In Udaipur as in other princely states, our people felt like they were at the centre of the world, Bhagwat Sinh ruefully said. They did not sense that they were under the British yoke because in their eyes we were the rulers and our kingdom was the most beautiful and illustrious of all. Now we are in a backwater far away from the imperial capital where most decisions are made and locally there are only anonymous bureaucrats who change every now and then. My ancestors never visited Delhi when it was under Muslim or British control because they would not submit to any foreign overlord. The viceroys would come and see us here but we would not travel to their headquarters. The king of England was an ally, not a suzerain. When the world wars came, my predecessors refused to send a contingent to fight for the British, unlike many other maharajas and nawabs who vied to serve under their flag. Maharana FatehSingh famously said: "if we had a war here, would Britain send soldiers to take side in our quarrels?"

I had to point out respectfully that indeed the United Kingdom had sent its armies not only to fight in Indian wars but eventually to submit the land. "So, said our host without hesitation, our men would only have gone to England as conquerors, not as tributaries. The British knew our position and they tolerated it because they did not want to humiliate the Dewan of Eklingji, aware that it would trigger a wave of anger among all Rajputs. The maharanas had not left India in many centuries and never sailed on the ocean. They were rooted in their hereditary soil like a banyan tree. However they respected the Raj because it had rescued them from ruin and oppression at the hands of the maratha marauders. Colonel Tod created a strong bond of friendship between his nation and us and we knew the British would not destroy and desecrate our shrines like so many Muslim invaders had."

THE HILLS AND FORTS OF MEWAR

Bhagwat Sinh arranged for us to visit some of the main sites associated with the history of his house. After the holy seats of Eklingji with its hundred and eight sanctuaries and Nathdwara, the abode of Krishna's icon we discovered the ancient fortified capitals of Nagda and Chittore which had witnessed so many sieges, heroic deeds and fights unto death culminating in the mass voluntary holocaust of all the warriors' wives and daughters. We also explored some of the lesser known attractions of Udaipur, including the library established by order of Maharana Sajjan Singh under the supervision of the illustrious savant and poet Kaviraj Shyamaldas to collect and safeguard many valuable manuscripts and books in several languages.

The Sajjan Vali Vilas contains one of the oldest and most beautifully illustrated versions of the Ramayana and a large number of texts that have not been yet translated into European languages. We were guided in our explorations by an old and trusted personal secretary of His Highness, Pandit Tarkeshvar Sharma who had served the preceding king and was the keeper of many secrets as his disarmingly gentle but inscrutable manner suggested. Once while we were near the palace, a wisened and frail looking old man in frayed clothes and unassuming turban introduced himself. When after a few words of polite conversation we sought to find out who he was he simply stated that he was the father of the Maharana. In the shadow of the grandeur of his son who was driven around in a pennant flying emblazoned Rolls Royce, he continued to live as modestly as he always had and travelled second class in the train as we discovered eventually. While we were rather disconcerted by that apparent lack of filial generosity on the part of our royal host, we never noticed a hint of bitterness or reproach in the proud and yet humble old Rajput. Later we were to hear some severe judgments passed on Bhagwat Sinh by his some of his relatives and former subjects but from observing the traditional ways and customs we realized that, once adopted a child lost his bond and obligations to his natural progenitor whereas the latter could not expect any enhancement of his own economic status from the elevation of his offspring.

Like a Dalai Lama whose family usually had no connection to their infant son's deified status or J Krishnamurti who had been taken away from his father by the Theosophical Society, the father of the ruler was the king who had adopted him and we found out that the Maharana's biological sire was mostly taken care off by his two other sons, Arjun and Narendra who owned small hotels in the town. We got to know them well as they were both gracious and hospitable. In Narendra's apartment we were introduced to one of his personal guests, Hossein Dawoodi who was then serving as Iran's ambassador to Afghanistan. Dr Dawoodi was, like many of his upper class countrymen, a literate and versatile man. We had long talks about the nature of Persian Islam in which he was deeply versed and he explained the belief in the Mahdi, the hidden twelth Iman Mohammed Al Muntazer who awaits in a cave the End Time leading to the *the yawm ed deen* or day of judgment that will witness his reappearance and his victory over the *Dajjal*, the devil. The ambassador saw Shi'ite eschatology as a result of the influence of apocalyptic Christianity, Mazdeism and also of the Hindu and Buddhist prophecies about the advent of Kalki Avatar and Maitreya Buddha respectively.

"Iranian Islam is the closest to Indian civilization for historic reasons, he commented, and His Majesty The Shah is aware of that and wishes to bring the country back to its spiritual roots as a land of syncretistic mysticism, far more adapted to modernity than the rigid Sunni orthodoxy that is practiced in most Arab countries."

Soon after, the turn of events in Iran would put a sadly ironic ring around his words as the spirit of free philosophical inquiry (at least in non-political domains) was to be stifled for several decades by the regime that arose on the ruins of the Shah's empire.

Thanks to Pandit Sharma and the palace secretary, a Southern Brahmin called Subramaniam we met a few of the more intriguing and notable personalities of the town, such as Mohan Singh Mehta, the imposing figure who had founded Udaipur's major cultural and social welfare institution, the Seva Mandir and whose son Jagat was at the time India's foreign secretary. Mehta had been a member of the national constituent assembly before becoming ambassador to Pakistan and holding various other distinguished posts. We also had a long talk with the distinguished physicist and Udaipur native D S Kothari, a former student of Ernest Rutherford—father of the "saturnian concept of the atom"—and a pioneer in the endeavour to link the cosmological insights of contemporary science with the concepts developed in ancient Sanskrit philosophical doctrines.

Some of the most fascinating ideas came however from an old scholar met at the palace library and who was familiar with many of its contents. We compared some of the notions expounded by Tod with the information he retained from his readings of the ancient annals. We were interested to hear the persistent tradition that gives to the nouns "mongols" and "moghuls" a Sanskrit origin in *mangal*, meaning fortunate and used to designate the planet we call Mars, the symbol of the god of war. In Indian Sanskrit texts the Mongols are Turvashas or Takshaks, which is akin to Tajik, another Central Asian people. The noble Turks called themselves *Jigits* that, according to our Hindu pandit, is derived from the Sanskrit root *jag*: to move, whence *jagat*, the (moving) world. The Jagatai were horse riding nomads and saw themselves as world rulers. They were a branch of the larger Indo-Asian family of nations and periodically rode into India out of their northwestern abodes. The successive Turkic and Mughal invaders were hence not seen as strangers to the subcontinent but rather as returning relatives of the native people although their conversion to Islam changed the nature of the interaction since, unlike their Kushan, Saka and Huna precedessors, they no longer practiced variants of the indigenous tradition but sought to impose a new faith.

THE SCIENCE OF SERPENTS AND HERBS

In an old quarter of Udaipur, reached through a narrow lane, a rather dilapidated house hosted one of the most respected practitioners of India's ancient plant medicine, the *rasayana*. The Vaidya (man of knowledge as physicians used to be called in Europe until the 19th century) said he was almost ninety and looked duly venerable. He was in the quasi-constant company of his disciple, a dark, fiercely handsome young man whom he introduced as a repented dacoit (a highway man) to whom he was teaching his art. His specialty was the dangerous and vanishing science of healing with vegetal and animal poisons from which he made concoctions with simple grinding, pounding, cooking and filtering utensils, such as pestles, mortars, jars and kettles that evoked the laboratory of a medieval alchemist. His supplies came from all parts of India and even farther in the forms of bulbs, tubers, dried leaves, flowers and roots and phials of snake venom through various channels, mostly within the saffron cloth pouches of wandering ascetics and mendicants. Those more or less holy men provided an informal but immemorial courier services spanning the vast subcontinent from the mangroves of Bengal to the steppes of Tibet and from the savannahs of the Deccan to the dense forests of the Ghats. They were compensated for their services with offerings of foods and, when they needed it a place to sleep.

An old Sanskrit tale is about a student of medicine who, upon completing his training is sent as part of the required examination to find a plant that is of no pharmaceutical use. He comes back empty handed since all natural lifeforms have some therapeutic properties and thereby demonstrates his mastery. That remains the philosophy of Indian medicine since the days of its semi-legendary founders Dhanvantari, Charaka and Susruta among others. Those pioneers even had an understanding of the existence of potentially harmful micro-organisms such as viruses and germs, some visible and others imperceptible to the human eye which they called *krimi*, a name that evokes the latin root of the word we use to describe harmful actions to be prevented or punished.

Contrary to our modern civilization which seeks to maximize desires, conveniences and consumption and therefore requires ever more energy and creates ever more waste the Indian tradition sought to reduce needs and expenses to the minimum, except for the few who held political and economic power. No wonder that such a system is anathema to the advocates and promoters of GDP as a measure of human achievement.

Owing to Pandit Sharma's introduction we were allowed to peer into the Vaidya's age old pharmacopeia while he confided a few of the secrets of his science, which included the preparation of the *medhwa*, the mead traditionally consumed by the rajput warriors, whose name survived almost unaltered in ancient anglo-saxon Europe and which in India consists of several ingredients but mainly of the liquid pressed out of the *mahua* flower mixed with pomegranate juice and honey. He told us about the *sanjeevini*, the legendary Himalayan plant that supposedly bestows immortality, about the *kushta* plant mentioned in the *Atharva Veda* and used to treat malaria and about the *arjuna* which in the Rig Veda is described as a healing salve for heart disease. He explained the distinct properties of the respective venoms of the cobra, the krait and Russell's viper, three of India's deadly reptiles and gave us hints about the various uses of the digitalis, the datura and several kinds of opiates and hallucinogenic mushroom extracts. "The more powerful a poison the greater its healing properties," he explained in his native Mewari which his disciple translated in halting English. "In our tradition we have methods to transmute the harmful ingredient in poison while concentrating its essence so that it becomes safe and beneficial."

It was difficult to avoid the thought that in times not so remote the skills of such experts in poison would have been used to prepare deadly decoctions intended for foes and rivals. We did not resist the temptation to ask the gentle Vaidya whether such preparations had been requested by certain clients. It would have been insulting to infer that he might have obliged them. We knew that all practitioners of his ancient profession were required to swear an oath in many ways similar to the famed Hippocratic pledge and perhaps older than the greek version.

"As a vaidya I am only allowed to heal, not to harm or kill but some others in our tradition, the black tantrics may use their knowledge to evil ends," he replied cryptically. He however inspired such confidence that we did not hesitate to sip two of the potions and swallow some of the mysterious pills he gave us, both to cure a seasonal cold and to boost our resistance to the summer season that had already begun. We even wrote an article about him and his *materia medica* which was eventually published in some journal.

ARCANES OF THE JAINS

Of all the monuments in and around Udaipur, the most magnificent is probably the great Jain temple of Ranakpur, a vast white marble mansion crowned by many intricate pyramids mushrooming like celestial anthills around a central dome and supported inside by a forest of one thousand four hundred and forty exquisitely chiseled stalactite-like pillars, each of which is different in its sculptured design. One can spend days and weeks examining the stone lace work that shimmers in the changing light that filters in from outside.

I was mesmerized by the relief that depicts Jambudvipa, the cosmic image of India according the Jain tradition with its fifty two pavilion-like hills clustered in four equal groups of thirteen around the central spiral-shaped mound of Mount Meru. Ranakpur is said to have been built on the spot where its founder saw or dreamed of a *vimana* flying in the sky and instructed the architect to design a sanctuary shaped like the heavenly vehicle he had beheld. Images of divine spacecraft come to the mind all over India for the visitor in the know.

The temple and its iconography made us eager to know more about the Jain religion which motivated the bulding of this and of so many other temples as ornate and precious as *repoussé* jewels. Jains are particularly well represented in Rajasthan and Gujarat although in antiquity they appear to have been more numerous and influential in the Eastern Ganges valley, which is their cradle, and in South and

Central India. Thanks to D.S. Kothari, who was a Jain, we made the acquaintance of a local scholar from that community. We found him to be a shy, thin bespectacled elderly man with the austere and intense demeanour that often characterizes the adherents of the faith of Mahavira. His study was full of books on religion and history, many of them on his tradition. He was encouraged to open up when he realized that we were not unfamiliar with India's philosophical culture and willingly provided some explanations about that relatively mysterious creed generally held to be as old as Buddhism.

According to the Jains themselves their *sampradaya* or lineage began in the epic age with prince Rishabha, son of Nabhi, the king of Kosala and father of Bharata. As such Rishabha belonged to the solar race of Ikshvaku, a name derived from *ikshu*: the sugarcane plant that India was first to cultivate and he must have been a close relative and contemporary of Sri Rama who is also called rishabha "the bull." The hallowed founder of Jainism is associated with central figures of the Hindu tradition of which his faith is a part, collateral with Brahmanism, Shaivism and other lineages of the Dharma.

After Rishabha, also known as Adinath, "the first lord" who is said to have attained liberation on Mount Kailash, came twenty-three other *tirthankaras* or "ford crossers" (over the river of illusory existence), the last of whom is the historically recognized Vardhamana known as Mahavira, a prince from Kundinapura in the merchant republic of Vaishali in modern Bihar who probably lived around the sixth century before the common era and was a contemporary of the Buddha, with whose life and mission his offers many parallels, and, according to indigenous beliefs, of Sri Krishna as well.

Someone familiar with greek myths would recognize in the sanskrit root *ankara,* "he who masters or overcomes" the origin of Charon, the name of the passer of the dead over the river Styx, the stream which separates the realm of the living from the Hades, the hellenic netherworld. The *tirthankaras* are ascetic enlightened beings whose total nakedness evinces their renunciation. They are at the apex of a pantheon of superhuman entities which includes thirteen *salakapurusas,* twelve *chakravartins* or universal emperors, nine *baladevas,* nine *vasudevas* and an equal number of *prativasudevas,* who are violent and destructive and are killed in every cyclical era of the eternal universe by the *vasudevas.* The latter are however also doomed to go to hell by that act of murder and are reborn to play the same role in the following age of creation.

This fatalistic concept of cosmology, represented by the wheel of *kalachakra* in jain iconography seems to leave little space for individual or collective freedom but a fundamental and tempering factor is the principle of *anekantavada,* which implies that no perspective or system is complete or true in the absolute. Hence, Jain philosophy defines itself as *syadvada (syad* means "perhaps") and therefore provides through the uncertainty of relativism a degree of liberty that, on reflection, appears unconditioned.

Our erudite host unfurled for us an old colourful scroll which depicted the universe in the Jain tradition as an anthropomorphic being within which the earth, seas, skies and all their features and beings were allegorically drawn and designated. This concept is faithful to the notion of *mahapurusa* or the cosmic man that is so lyrically expounded in hymns of the Vedas and finds its counterpart in many hermetic, gnostic, kabbalistic and Taoist esoteric doctrines in other parts of the world. That organic vision of the world contrasts with the geometric abstract renderings specific to Tantric metaphysics and it made me understand Jainism as an early but complex apprehension of the holographic and fractal structure of reality recently revealed by physicists and mathematicians such as Mandelbrot, Pribram and Penrose. The dynamism of the quantic and relativistic theories is also implicit in the tradition of the Tirthankaras, which identifies dharma or reality as the essence of motion whereas all that is at rest is called *adharmatattwa*, outside the laws of life.

After being introduced to the Jaina worldview and to the practices and virtues it cultivates in order to attain illumination, such as serenity, introspection and renunciation we talked about the practical attitude of its adepts to everyday life. It stands to reason that the rejection of all violence against any form of life in thought, word and deed may seem a utopian rule and inevitably requires accommodations. For that reason, our guide explained, Mahavira's religion accepts that there are various levels of compliance with that precept and that laymen cannot be expected to observe it as strictly as *munis* or monks who are not immune from breaching the rule but are expected to make amends for those inescapable lapses. He commented that in centuries past, many kings had followed the Jain faith but had waged wars as monarchs are wont to. Even some soldiers were jains since the creed acknowledges the need to fight and kill for self-defence.

There is even some controversy as to whether Ashoka, the illustrious emperor who propagated the Buddha's gospel in far away lands was a Jain since his grandfather Chandragupta and other sovereigns of his dynasty are known to have practiced the dharma of the Tirthankaras. A careful observer must conclude that, contrary to the beliefs of many modern historians, spiritual traditions coexisted in symbiosis in the ancient world and were followed concurrently by both the aristocracies and the common people. The idea of a single "true" faith excluding all others was not yet known and one can hardly fail to see the advantages of such an inclusive understanding of religion.

It is quite likely that Ashoka practiced, like many of his contemporaries, the precepts of the Buddha and those of the Jainas all the while remaining faithful to the Hindu Dharma, which was literally "the law of the land." The depiction of Buddhism as an egalitarian rationalist revolution against theocratic brahminism is in part an anachronistic myth cherished by modern scholars trying to find parallels with current social processes.

One of the last questions to our patient Jain doctrinal cicerone had to do with the fact that Jainism, despite its attested antiquity which dates back much earlier than Mahavira, remains to this day an almost entirely Indian phenomenon unlike Buddhism which spread across the globe in the last twenty centuries.

"Jains were reluctant to leave the sacred *bhumi*, the land of Jambudvipa (the roseapple island) where all their sacred sites are and where they had a social support system, he said in his low monotone after considering our query for a moment. Their living precepts were strict and austere and perhaps Ashoka and others who spread the Buddha dharma felt that Jainism was a personal way of life that was not for foreigners. Our munis, especially the digambars—the ones who are clothed in space (i.e. naked)—are like the naga sadhus of Hindus who mostly keep to themselves and never leave Bharat, unlike the Buddhist bhikshus who travelled across Asia preaching the Cakya Muni's word."

Suitably for a Jain, he had prefaced his explanation with the word perhaps.

PEARL BUCK, THE MISSIONARY AND OTHER ANECDOTES

During the months we spent in Udaipur, we got to know the few European Catholic priests who lived in or near the city. The youngest of them, a refined, handsome and pensive man from Ireland gifted us a book he had written about his life and experiences in Rajasthan. He had literary talent and depicted vividly the local way of life which had changed little in many centuries. The book also recorded his friendship with the present maharana who had honoured him with his trust and even hinted at a somewhat romantic but platonic bond with the latter's wife. Whether that was a fictional ingredient added to spice up the story or was faithful to the facts I do not know but we were under the impression that he had gifted a copy to Bhagwat Sinh. I was more interested however in the account of his dealings with the villagers and townspeople of all classes which evinced the respect that Hindus in general display for other creeds because of their acknowledgment of the sacred in all things. The notions of heathenism or false gods are foreign to them. One passage of the book related how a Brahmin had once gently wondered why as a priest the *Angrezi* ate meat and drink alcohol, to which the quick-witted Irishman pointed out to his fellow cleric that he was living a life of chastity unlike the married pandit. "We practice different forms of abstinence," he had quipped.

Our Christian man of God had also accompanied the Maharana on some hunting parties and prided himself on being a good shot, which Indians took in stride with their habitual tolerance of foreign ways.

One story that the father narrated while having tea with us one day in our palace suite has remained in my memory. He talked about the visit that Pearl Buck had once paid to Udaipur as a guest of the Lake Palace and how, after conversing with her, he had given to the famous writer the manuscript of a novel that he had recently completed and was trying to publish in the West. He never heard from Buck again despite writing to her twice but was surprised and even dismayed to find out years later that her own novel "Mandala," published in 1970, wove a plot similar to his and even contained passages almost identical to what he had penned. We never saw his unpublished text and could hence not compare Pearl Buck's work to his creation but he had nothing to gain by taking undue credit and it would not be the first time that a celebrated wordsmith makes up for lack of inspiration by using willing or unwitting ghost writers.

We grew very fond of the diverse and often harsh landscape of the Aravallis around Udaipur with their stark rocky outcrops, deep dry valleys thick with thorny *kikars* and *babul* trees, rare glades shaded by *khadirs, bilwas, plakshas* and *neems* and narrow passes guarded by ruined forts. The most awesome of those fastnesses is Kumbhalgarh built by the heroic Maharana Kumbha around a high plateau as large as a small country. With its many miles of crenellated and turreted walls, it is perhaps the largest ancient citadel in the world and the many temples and deserted monuments that lie inside are crowned by the solitary eagle nest of the Rana's palace still owned at the time by the royal family.

Outside the towns, most of Mewar was and is still inhabited by tribes of Bhils and Meenas. Contrary to the manichean vision that many have in India and abroad, those hill peoples were not discriminated against like Australian aborigines and American

Indians under western occupation. They were left free to carry on with their traditional hunting and food gathering lifestyles and the Maharanas regarded them as their trusted allies. The effigy of a Bhil stands guard on one side of the royal crest of the Suryavanshis and one of them, during the coronation, smeared the brow of the newly anointed monarch with his blood as a sign of recognition.

"The tribals were not regarded as inferiors to be civilized, converted, resettled or gotten rid of," the Maharana remarked during a conversation. "They provided our troops with some light auxiliary fighters and archers. We protected them and they would willingly die for us although they had their own kings. The Indian Republic has taken upon itself to improve their lives but often only succeeds in driving them from their wilderness into slums or making them indentured labourers or factory hands," he shrugged.

His skeptical assessment of the social policies of independent India resonated with our own misgivings about the theory that all people should aspire to live in flats, own motor vehicles and watch television even though it may take generations to bestow upon most of them such modern comforts that mankind never knew during millennia of its prior existence.

One evening, while we were attending a typical marriage ceremony celebrated in an open enclosure outside the old town of Udaipur, my sight was suddenly drawn to the limpid sky above us whose stars were only dimmed by the illuminations of the party. I beheld a bell shaped dazzling meteor that was travelling at high but even speed above our heads. My father and many people in the assembled crowd saw it as well. What was extraordinary was the long shining tail of that object which consisted of an array of laser-like parallel beams along each of which smaller bells or bulbs of bright light flickered and pulsated like fiery rings sliding down a pillar. The entire vision conveyed an impression of serene and rhythmic regularity heightened by the total silence in which it moved. Another image that later came to my mind was that of a sea anemone or octopus trailing its straight tentacles speckled with intermittently flashing pods behind its body. In a few seconds, it had gone beyond the horizon, leaving quite a few or amazed witnesses in its track.

In the following days we were asked to give our impressions to a journalist who reported for the *Times of India* in the Udaipur region. He wanted to have our opinion as he knew of various talks we had given on the subject of UFOs and related matters. We expressed the view that what had been seen was probably a flying mechanical device propelled by a pulsating type of engine and not a falling aerolithe since there had been no sonic bang, not recorded crash and the object flew too low to be a "shooting star" while being markedly different from a meteor shower. An astronomer from the local observatory had, it turned out, tried to follow the mysterious flying object on his motorcycle, hoping to locate its landfall but had seen it disappear in the sky where it followed a horizontal course.

In that period many observations were reported from a large part of India, along an arc that stretched from Bombay in the South to Delhi and Chandigarh in the North. Several newspaper articles quoted us while mentioning the "UFO wave" and featuring various opinions about the nature of the objects. To this day I remain convinced that the stunning sighting was not caused by a natural phenomenon but rather concerned a large-scale vessel that gave an impressive pyrotechnic show while cruising over that part of India.

IN THE SEVEN KINGDOMS OF RAJASTHAN

During the cooler season we took the opportunity to travel around Rajputana, the "land of the seven (principal) kingdoms" that were gathered, after independence into the state of Rajasthan. There had been more than thirty theoretically sovereign principalities prior to 1947 since the ancient polity of India rested on a fractal order of ever larger units patterned after the family and village that were their basic model. The realm of Mewar was divided into a number of *thikanas* (fiefdoms), each of which with its thakur, rana or rawal, generally from one of the twenty four sakhas of the Gehlot house, its fortified palace, its chief town, its priests, merchants, peasants and military nobles looked like a miniature replica of the state of which it was a part.

I keep in my memory glimpses of a few of those small towns, huddled around the towering walls of the local lord's abode. The central square verges on a deep stepwell or tank, a *baoli* where people come to bathe, wash clothes and gossip. The women cast off their cholis while doing the laundry and children play around and dive noisily in the still verdant water. The contrast of the bronze and copper hued bosoms with the many coloured, embroidered and mirror-strewn robes in the bright Indian sun weaves a striking picture, as if a medieval temple bas-relief had come to life in a kaleidoscopic firework.

In Ajmer near the holy shrine of the great Sufi Moinuddin Chishty, we were hosted by the regional police chief, a swashbuckling Rajput who drove in an open jeep and favoured jaunty ranger hats, designer dark glasses and safari suits. His duty was to patrol a vast mostly desertic area and he clearly saw himself as a sort of sheriff in the American West, an impression confirmed by the library he kept at home. However the Ajmer district was peaceful, at any rate more than Bharatpur, an ancient and rather dusty town where a friend, Brigadier Ghasi Ram arranged for us to stay in a small fort that he owned in the open country. I duly enjoyed the exciting romance of living behind four crenellated walls in a tower, albeit of modest size which overlooked a vast sparsely cultivated plain. When we went to the walled city of Bharatpur in the mornings a few miles away we often came across a line of mustachioed, fierce or sheepish looking men led in chains by bored policemen to the local jail. They were *dacoits*, highwaymen who haunted in large gangs the nearby Chambal ravines and regularly fought the forces of law and order in bloody encounters. Some of those shooting matches lasted for hours and pursuits in that natural labyrinth of gullies, canyons and brush-cloaked hills stretched over weeks. The feared bandit queen Phoolan Devi was on the rampage in that untamed region where she was soon to carry out a large-scale massacre of men from a rival caste to take revenge on those who had gangraped her.

Unlike our simple abode in Bharatpur the magnificence of Umaid Bhawan in Jodhpur was cosmopolitan in its "Indo-art deco" neo-classical grandeur; many of the hundreds of rooms of that secular sand and honey-hued basilica are brightened by exotic frescoes. The palace was not easy to heat in that frigid late January and the mournful cries of the peacocks pacing the leafless park did not make for a festive ambience. However, during the day the sun enlivened the sky and lent added glory to the stupendous Mehrangarh fort that towers above the horizon as a mute but colossal witness of the glories of the royal Rathor dynasty of Marwar.

Gaj Singh the "erstwhile" but very present maharaja is, like his cousin in Udaipur staunchly committed to preserving the multi-centennial heritage of which he is the hereditary custodian and he told us about some of the initiatives he had taken to keep alive the traditions and ceremonies of his realm. The Rathors are descended from one of the last Hindu paramount rulers of Northern India, Harshavardhana of Kanauj and although they claim to be scions of Sri Rama as well, legend gives them a mixed ancestry since their mystical forbear Rishi Kasyapa, whose traces we had found all over Asia married the daughter of Hiranyakasipu, an asura whose blood all Rathors share. Unlike the indomitable rulers of Mewar, the desert kings of Marwar, "the land of death" allied with the Mughal rulers in Delhi, served as generals in their armies and even sent some of their daughters to marry the Timurid emperors. An old proverb was that the conquests of Akbar, Shah Jahan and Aurangzeb would not have been possible without *lakh talwar rathoran* (the hundred thousand swords of the Rathors).

Aurangzeb partly owed his accession to the contemporary Maharaja of Jodhpur, who denied his military support at a critical time to the hapless older brother Dara Shikoh. That fateful decision may have been perverse in its effects for the future of India and of the empire but it contributed to the security and prosperity of the Marwar state.

"Our flat sandy soil did not give us the protection that Mewar enjoys behind its mountain ranges," the Maharaja pointed out during a lunch in the private dining room, attended by his wife and his mother, the imperious dowager maharani Krishna Kumari, a sister of our royal philosopher the Raja of Dhrangadhra. "We had to stay in good terms with the power of Delhi to survive. Otherwise our land would have been overrun, even if we could have held a long siege at Mehrangarh."

Like their neighbours and kinsmen the rulers of Bikaner, the kings of Marwar had easily shifted their allegiance from the Mughals to the British and were known for their martial loyalty to the Raj. I recalled reading a travel book by the French novelist brothers, Jerôme and Jean Tharaud who described their brief stop over in Jodhpur on the "long courrier" flight from Paris to Saigon before the last world war. They had kept the memory of a polo match played on the grounds of Chittar Mahal, later known as Umaid Bhawan, then under construction. The players wore the characteristic horseman's breeches that are named after the city.

Gaj Singh, whom everybody in the region and beyond called "Bapji" according to the patriarchal tradition of Rajput kingship, duly attended Eton and Oxford where he had majored in political sciences. He scheduled and graciously chaired a lecture in the palace auditorium by my father and me. We were impressed by the gentle dignity and a thoughtfulness reflected in his expressive, soft gaze and quiet unassuming demeanour. He had lost his father in an airplane crash at four and must have had a rather lonely childhood in English boarding schools. I wondered how many politicians risen out of the rough and tumble game of electoral politics could boast of such a natural authority inherited from centuries of breeding. A sense of timelessness pervades the institution of royalty whereas time is what democratic leaders never feel that they have.

I found Stefan Norblin, the polish artist who had decorated Umaid Bhavan with scenes illustrating the great Indian epics an outstanding representative of an exoticised, hieratic and yet sinuous Art Nouveau style, echoing the sharp outlines and glowing enamels and pigments of Byzantine icons, in the line of the school of Gustave Moreau and Odilon Redon. His manner is, at least in my view, not unrelated to certain South Indian techniques, such as those displayed in the stunning Matancherry palace frescoes in Kerala for in most things, contrary to what Kipling thought, East and West have indeed met and blended since time immemorial, whether by design or coincidence.

Bikaner, the former capital of a desert kingdom which seceded from Marwar in the 15th century, where we spent a few days is not a particularly attractive city but it enshrines an extraordinary collection of palaces of various styles and ages within its huge fort and the heir of its ruling family received us in the latest among them, the Lallgarh, an imposing monument of delicately carved red standstone built under the reign of his grandfather General "Sir" Ganga Singh, perhaps the maharaja most respected and trusted by the British in his days because of his military acumen, intelligence and administrative competency. He was in their eyes the ideal king, loyal to them without being obsequious, reform-minded and capable, and his martial style and manner made him even more popular. After participating in 1901 expedition to China sent to crush the Boxer uprising, Ganga Singh had been a stalwart on the French theater during the First World War as the only Indian member of the Imperial War Cabinet and was chosen to represent India at the 1917 Imperial War Conference and at the 1919 Paris peace conference. In 1924, he had led his country's delegation to the League of Nations in Geneva crowning thereby a uniquely distinguished career of service both to India and the British paramount power.

His grandson Karni Singh, who had been an Olympic shooting champion appeared to me a sensitive, tormented man with a touch of eccentricity as many highly privileged heirs are. Since my father wished to show him some documents related to our activities regarding the Indian tradition and its political legacy he warned us that he was allergic to dust and could only read pages under a plastic or glass cover. Once his initial diffidence subsided he easily engaged in conversation and sought our views on certain aspects of religion which seemed to concern him. As a crack shot descended from a long dynasty of big game hunters—his grandfather had bagged more tigers than almost any of his contemporaries and the stuffed busts of some of his fierce victims silently snarled above us on the walls - he had enjoyed killing animals but was aware of the rapid loss of wildlife in the country which brought to mind the relevance of the precept of ahimsa. Like his peer in Baroda he was a conservationist at heart and justified the ancient rites of the chase as legacies of an age when people had to feed themselves and the ksatriyas, assigned to the protection of the land were required to kill game in order to remain fit for war.

"In Bikaner we practice "pig sticking" every year in the spring and the viceroys were often our guests, he recalled. In fact, this is a tradition found in the Vedas. The monarch had to kill the *varaha*, the old boar of winter to usher in the new year in *vasant* and bring good crops."

We pointed out that similar customs existed in other "Indo-European" cultures of Europe and Asia and that the mythological hunts of the boars of Erymanthus and Calydon belonged to that widespread lore.

"Traditions go through various phases, my father concluded. The animal that is essential to sacrifice in one era becomes sacred or intangible at a later stage. Thus the bull offered as part of the archaic Aryan hecatomb later was protected with all its kind. The same is now happening with the tiger, from being a trophy the totem is now taboo. The black antelope, *ena* was killed in oblation to a dead father and Rudra, the forest dweller, who is known as Orion in western lands with his dog Sirius pursues and kills the starry deer *nabhaskara taramriga* in vedic symbology. As the emblem of the latter, the spotted deer or chittal is also held sacred and now protected."

BUBBLES, AYESHA AND THE ROMANCE OF JAIPUR

Jaipur, huddled beneath the titanic fortress of Amber rising like a Walhalla above the arid Aravalli hills, was befittingly our final discovery in Rajasthan, which we had crisscrossed in the course of several months of residence in Udaipur. Like their relatives in Jodhpur the maharajas of Amber or Dundhar, who had moved their capital to Jaipur in the eighteenth century loyally served the Mughal emperors who had richly rewarded them by allowing them to expand their domain. When the British took over North-Western India much of the land around Delhi, Agra and Mathura in the Yamuna valley belonged to the Rajas of Jaipur and the Taj Mahal had reportedly been built on one of their properties. Three centuries later, the seat of power in the new imperial capital of New Delhi was also ceded by them to their colonial overlords. Their fabulous wealth combined with some political ambitions had contributed to their misfortune under the rule of Indira Gandhi. Using the Emergency law provisions, her government had charged them with tax evasion and had thrown the dowager queen in jail for six months after raiding their various properties in a quest for hidden gold.

It was widely known that a momentous decision of the beautiful widow of the last ruler Sawai Man, Maharani Gayatri Devi had been, in the late sixties to join the newly created centre-right Swatantra party, which sought to dethrone the ruling Congress Party in alliance with the Hindu Nationalist and anti-communist Jan Sangh. The family had paid a heavy price for daring to challenge the power structure.

Gayatri Devi was then a member of parliament, enjoyed overwhelming popularity in her constituency like many other princes and could therefore pose a major challenge to a weakened Indira Gandhi in a climate of economic crisis and popular discontent. The Prime Minister used all her wiles and the resources of the state to fob off that threat, nationalizing banks, expelling several American companies and passing fairly draconian acts to repress opposition by invoking critical risks to national security. By the time we met the Jaipurs, a reorganized splinter of the Congress led by Mrs Gandhi had come back to power with a commanding majority and the opposition was in disarray. Gayatri Devi and her kin had lost their fight against the Left.

We were received in the picturesque hill-top manor of Moti Dhumri, posed as a jewel on the city's crown as its name suggests, by the head of the Kachchawaha dynasty the affable Maharaja, Colonel Bhawani Singh, known to many as "Bubbles" in a study whose walls were incrusted with enamels and mother of pearl motifs. A low table between us supported an array of books on horses, polo and heraldry. We quickly noticed how shaken the prince still was, despite his Harrovian poise, by the reverse and humiliation suffered by his family although he had personally been spared, protected as he was by his heroic military record in the last war with Pakistan. His impeccable breeding could not fully conceal the lingering anguish that the events of the last few years had caused him. He probably felt that the returned Prime Minister in Delhi remained inimical to his House and that, unlike prior Mughal and English rulers, she wished to erase the influence still wielded by feudal princes who even by joining her Party might not be protected from continuous demotion.

Though an accomplished soldier, Bhawani Singh, whom we got to know well in later years, was a gentle and shy man who was ill equipped to face the ruthless world of contemporary party politics.

His mother-in-law Gayatri Devi, third wife of his late father, was made of sterner stuff and her Indianness defined her as a diamond lotus, like the vajras of Tibetan iconography. Her exotic and celebrated beauty owed faint oriental features to the North Eastern origins of her Bengali father. Her mother, princess Indira of Baroda, the rebellious daughter of Sayaji Rao was reputed to have been as beautiful and had dazzled the high society of her time with her cosmopolitan glamour. She had called her youngest daughter Ayesha after the heroin of Ridder Haggar's *She*, her favourite novel, and the Maharani carried side by side her dynastic name for official occasions, reserving the other for her inner circle.

We saw Gayatri Devi in the exquisite setting of the Trianon-like villa that her late husband had built for her on the grounds of the majestic Rambagh palace. Her simple saree and apparent casualness did not hide the regal hauteur of her demeanour. With the passing years, the feline "Siamese" face had lost some of the exotic dreaminess of her youth and seemed to have put on a mask of cosmopolitan distinction. She had, it seemed to me, the mannerisms of the "Marlborough House Set" and indeed she had spent much of her childhood at the family house on Hans Road in Knightsbridge when not at an English boarding school and before joining Tagore's

Shantiniketan which also hosted her nemesis Indira Gandhi, two years her senior, in 1934.

During the conversation, I thought at times of the Maharani's romantic ancestry. It included the tribal, hard drinking and quarrelsome rulers of Cooch Behar who had turned in the last two generation into the most polished and anglophilic of India's aristocrats. One of her great-grandfathers was the charismatic Keshub Chandra Sen who for years had led the Brahmo Samaj community with a firm hand while becoming a popular preacher and moralist in Britain where he had attracted the admiration of Queen Victoria.

Sen had worked to reform the Vedic faith so much that he had made his version of it into an Indian equivalent of High Church Christianity. His daughter, princess Suniti was equally supportive of the Raj, busied herself with social reform and upliftment of Indian women and wrote sweet novels typical of the high minded prose of the age. Her own son, Gayatri's father penned delicate love poems in the Edwardian vein while slowly drinking himself to death.

Ayesha's mother as I already hinted was famous as a hunting Amazon, a trend setter in fashion and a passionate though mysterious *femme fatale* who managed to maintain her royal aloofness while quietly pursuing, after her husband's early demise, intriguing and prestigious affairs. It was whispered that one of Indira's flings involved the then prince of Wales. She counted a galaxy of Hollywood stars, tycoons and crowned heads among her friends and shared her time between mansions in Calcutta, Darjeeling and London, palace hotels in the great European capitals and casinos, spa resorts and hunting lodges of East and West where she was famous for her unique dressing style, her gold cigarette holders and her fabulous jewelry. She partied and jet-setted with the likes of Prince Aly Khan, Mary Pickford, Douglas Fairbanks, Doris Duke, Noel Coward and Marquis Boni de Castellane with a freedom and panache hitherto forbidden to Indian blue blooded womanhood.

The best-selling French society novelist of the inter-war years, Maurice Dekobra, who had met her during his worldwide travels, made Indira the character of his 1934 book, "Princess Brinda," also entitled "La Prison des Reves" after evoking her, five years earlier in his equally famous "Les Tigres Parfumés, aventures au pays des maharajas." His books and other later ones, such as the risqué novel "Maharajah" signed under the pseudonym of Richard Cargoe and also based on the Maharani's supposed private life further impressed the European collective mind with an indelible and romantic picture of India that still survives in spite of the changed realities.

The lush little kingdom of Cooch Behar on the northern confines of Bengal, shrouded in thick elephant haunted forests, bedecked with the liquid mirrors of its rice fields and wrapped in the meanders of lazy rivers, had a magic all its own and we noticed that in Gayatri's memory it remained as an enchanted land.

The Maharani's mixed heritage from a fairly iconoclastic and atypical princely clan contrasted with the conservative feudal and religious background of her late husband who could claim descent from the second son of Lord Rama, Kusha as well as from the legendary king of the Nishadha tribe, Nala whose romantic story is featured in the Mahabharata and was expanded upon by the great poet Sriharsha in his long poem the *Naishadhiya.*

The handsome and brave Nala had received great boons from four gods, including the gift of making himself invisible at will and in exchange had sworn to fulfill any of their demands. When he was made aware, through the descriptions he was given by a golden swan of the existence of the beautiful princess Damayanti he was madly enamoured before even seeing her and his winged messenger also infected her with passion for him. The two lovebirds remain in Indian literature symbols of the burning desire for an unseen and unknown ideal, a mystical and erotic archetype. Eventually, Nala went to visit his far away beloved but was tasked by his four divine creditors to act as their emissary since they all lusted after her. That episode evokes parallels with the Greek tale of Eros and Psyche. To fulfill his vow, Nala was forced to argue on behalf of the gods to Damayanti but predictably failed to convince her to give him up for the sake of any of them. A more difficult test came up however when at the *swayamvara* or spouse-selecting ceremony, the princess had to tell the true Nala apart from the four superhuman impersonators who appeared exactly like him. Yet, the clairvoyance of love triumphed and she was able to pick what Americans would have called "the real deal," thus winning the right to marry him in an appropriately lavish ceremony.

As could be expected of an Eastern story that was not the end and the couple suffered many other adversities, in part because of Nala's addiction to gambling. In spite of all trials, Damayanti and her difficult husband had a posterity which after many centuries came to rule the region around Amber, became related by blood to the Mughal emperors and counted among their greatest descendents the monarch who built the geometrically planned city of Jaipur in the 18th century.

We talked briefly with Ayesha of her niece Uttara "Honey" Maharani of Kotah whom we had met in Delhi with her husband and who also had inherited the Cooch Behar's delicate high-cheek boned, almond eyed, ivory skinned loveliness. My father brought up gingerly the politics of the time and hard days of the Emergency and the name of Mrs. Gandhi brought a passing flash to the famed eyes of Gayatri.

"I'd rather not talk about it," she said, "but it was unfortunate to see the liberal heritage of Nehru being dissipated in this Third World-style coup d'état. By 1959 Rajaji (the venerated first Governor General of independent India Rajagopalachari) left the Congress Party when he saw it turning into a family property where critics of Nehru's rule were no longer allowed. Many of us Rajputs joined it when we saw it as an alternative to the sovietization of India that went along with increasing corruption in high places. By then Nehru was old, he suffered a costly defeat at the hands of the Chinese and relied increasingly on his immediate family and confidants. I hope that after her defeat and imprisonment the Prime Minister has now learnt a lesson and will never again be tempted to become a dictator."

We were hearing once more the severe but perhaps justified assessment that many all across the country had given us. The nepotism of Nehru and the methods of governance of his daughter may have been a natural consequence of the state of Indian society, which had remained largely feudal and dynastic in its ways of thinking. To retain the favour of their electorate the Nehru family practiced a form of paternalism and distributed concessions and handouts to the poorer sections of society and the minorities while cajoling the Marxist parties and carefully curbing the rise of any potential rivals for power.

Rajagopalachari had been one of those threats to the family's hegemony and to discredit his conservative, pro-Western tendencies, the Nehrus had steered the ship of state ever more to the left. The Maharani on the other hand had been Rajaji's Star performer. She had rallied many of the princely families to his Swatantra (freedom) party and as she recalled proudly, had been elected to the Jaipur seat in Parliament with the largest majority in national history.

The maharani promptly reverted to more pleasant topics and fondly evoked her youthful vacations in Le Touquet and her happy days at Brillantmont the house she had shared with her husband near Lausanne.

"I very much enjoyed seaside holidays in Brittany in Dinand," she said wistfully. Her modern education had enabled her, with the Maharaja's support to break a multicentenary taboo by shedding the purdah and showing her face to her subjects in public.

The glamorous Jaipur couple, the toast of London's high society, had spent a few very pleasant years in Spain where Man Singh had been sent as Ambassador in the years of my early childhood, about the time when my parents had moved to the mainland from the Canary Islands. There was perhaps some irony in democratic socialist India sending one of its most distinguished feudal figures to Franco's monarchical Spain but it was much appreciated in Madrid where Ayesha was triumphantly welcomed by the aristocracy and made many friends. The couple's legend had a whiff of cold war drama since the Jaipurs had been received for an intimate dinner at the White House by John and Jackie Kennedy in October 1962 at the height of the Cuban missile crisis. In his private musings, whose recordings were to be released years later, President Kennedy recalled how he was momentarily distracted from the anguish of those days by the glamorous royal couple invited by his wife. It was as if a symbol of India's graceful and laidback spirit had intruded on the dark tapestry of nuclear power politics and it seems that JFK told Ayesha that world war might begin on the next morning. To himself he probably whispered "Armageddon."

Gayatri Devi made no secret of her sadness at the state of India as she saw it. "Jaipur was clean and free of slums and uncontrolled urban sprawl," she reminisced. "The lakes and canals were sparkling. Look at them now. The Indian Republic has not preserved the country's well because most civil servants are incompetent or corrupt and the elected politicians are mostly interested in making money and pandering to their voters by avoiding unpopular decisions."

It was hard to disagree with her. Independence had consecrated in India a form of democracy which made it difficult to enforce discipline in the public services. As a result, the concern for cleanliness and rigor had generally taken a back seat to the desire to make people feel free and equal even if they were not.

Punctiliousness, obedience and thoroughness were associated in the popular mind with the former colonial and feudal times and it became more difficult to require those virtues. The galloping population increase and the lack of competent supervision, hitherto entrusted to the British administrators did the rest. India had become more crowded, messier and more incurious than it had been in centuries and those in power did not seem too bothered by that state of affairs.

XXIV

Gazing at the Hidden Realm

Opening Tibetan Diplomatic Annals

The road crossed verdant paddy fields set in a flat landscape framed by thick forests under the darkening evening light. In front of us rose a brightly painted, golden-roofed corniced building. It was crested by the small gilded "precious bottles" that symbolize the five buddhas of contemplation. From bottom to top they enshrined the lotus for Amitayus, the wheel for Amitabha, the bell for Amogasiddhi, the treasure vase for Acala crowned by the jewel of Ratnasambhava. They also evoke the five elements of nature and the five directions of space.

"Jangtse Thoesam Norling Gompa," our guide said proudly.

We were in Mundgod, one of the Tibetan settlements established on land hospitably granted to the refugees from the roof of the world by the Government of India. In twenty years the 4000 acres around Mundgod had become a well cultivated, densely populated array of eleven villages clustered around the construction sites of its two main monasteries, named after the five centuries old Doeguling University of Mahayana Buddhism located near Lhasa and devastated by Mao's Red Guards during the cultural revolution. The intent of the Dalai Lama was to build a smaller Tibet in exile for the diaspora within the Indian spiritual motherland. There it was hoped that those who had fled Communist rule at home could maintain their knowledge and tradition until the time when they or their descendents might be able to return.

We had been invited to to the community, located on a plateau a few hours's drive from Bangalore, by a younger brother of His Holiness, Tenzin Choegyal with whom we had corresponded. We had already exchanged some views with Tenzin Geyche the Dalai Lama's private secretary in Dharamshala, the refuge of the Living Buddha and his government in exile in the Himalayan foothills.

After settling down in the guest house that we were taken to, we were summoned to the dining room where a young man in well cut informal western clothes clothes introduced himself in fluent English. He was Tenzin Choegyal. Poised and articulate the youngest sibling of the Living Buddha is himself a Tulku, the reincarnation of Lama Ngari Rimpoche but has not embraced monastic life. He looked after political and diplomatic issues for the community.

The conversation over dinner lasted for almost two hours and ranged over various topics. However our main purpose was to seek his reaction to a proposal we had informally presented to the Chinese Ambassador in Delhi. It entailed for Beijing to grant a Vatican-like status to Lhasa or at least an area around the Potala as an international capital of Buddhism where the Dalai Lama and his court would be granted diplomatic or extra-territorial status, thus being able to return to the holy city. The benefits for China would be the drastic reduction of foreign condemnation of its policies in the autonomous region, a reconciliation between the former theocratic ruler of Tibet and the People's Republic and the likely end of attempts at armed rebellion by the Tibetans. On the other hand, many exiles would probably return to their homeland once their sovereign was reinstated in his seat and dignity and his person protected by international law. Religious and cultural tourism could be expected to rise substantially to Lhasa in particular and China in general while tensions between China and India were likely to subside once this major apple of discord was out of the way. On the face of it, it was the proverbial win-win situation.

The difficulties were of course substantial. China would have to implicitly renounce its claim that the Dalai Lama was a traitor, apart from recognizing the existence of a special enclave similar to what Hong Kong or Macau would become almost twenty years later. On the other hand, the Tibetans could never be assured that China would keep its commitment and the Dalai Lama would have to give up his political authority and hence the dream of eventual independence. The compromise would be similar to the Lateran treaty between Mussolini's regime and the Holy See whereby the Roman pontiff had forsaken his territorial claims in exchange for recognition as the symbolic head of a tiny state.

Tenzin Choegyal and the two advisers present at the dinner listened carefully and raised some expected objections. "I don't think His Holiness would or should ever agree to return as long as the political situation and living conditions of Tibetans have not been drastically improved by the PRC," he stated.

"Once in Lhasa he would be surrounded by Chinese agents and informants and would have few if any means to intercede on behalf of our people since Beijing would see that as a breach of the agreement. He would be a figurehead in a virtual prison and would quickly lose his moral authority. As long as he is abroad he can at least help and support those Tibetans who fled and have taken refuge here or in other countries. See the Panchen Lama.... He is a tool of the Politburo and cannot object to anything the Communist leadership decides."

We retorted that the Panchen Lama was nevertheless highly revered by Tibetans and in some way at least helped to keep the tradition alive by his presence and ceremonial role, as several other great lamas and former feudal lords who had more or less resigned themselves to Chinese rule. It was also worth noting, we felt, that the return of the Dalai Lama would dissuade Tibetans from attempting to violently protest or rise in rather futile rebellion, always with dire consequences for themselves since such actions only resulted in greater repression and arguably stood in the way of improvement of the overall situation.

"I will talk to His Holiness and to others in his circle," Tenzin said, "but I think we are far from seriously considering such an outcome even if the Chinese were prepared to discuss it."

In those years we had various occasions to exchange ideas on the future of Tibet with some other eminent members of the diaspora. One of their most respected leaders was the Venerable Samdhong Ripoche director of the Central Institute of Tibetan Higher Studies in

Sarnath, near Varanasi where he had invited us to stay and give various talks. We had proposed a plan to set up there an international university of Hindu and Buddhist Dharma and held various meetings with local dignitaries of the several Buddhist denominations represented in that holy place.

In Sarnath, Dharamshala and Mundgod where the Ganden Norling monastery was headed by the venerable *Tripa* (abbot) Zong Rimpoche, a teacher of the Dalai Lama himself we conversed about some little known aspects of Tibet's secret diplomacy during the first half of the twentieth century.

On the advice of the Kushok Bakula, the influential abbot of the Spituk monastery in Indian Tibet, who was one of the highest ranking *tulkus* in the lamaist hierarchy and a member of Ladakh's royal dynasty, we met a senior lama, more than eighty years old who lived in the mountains of Himachal Pradesh not far from Dharamshala but still travelled between the various Tibetan centres and communities spread across India. We were told that he had been a clerical official in the *Kashag*, the cabinet of the thirteenth Dalai Lama in the staff assigned to relations with foreign countries. He told us in halting but clear English that he had been attached to the office of Reting Rimpoche, the regent of the theocratic kingdom during the minority of the present Dalai Lama and had met Emil Schaffer and his German scientific expedition that had visited Tibet in 1939. That immediately attracted our interest and brought us back to our conversations with Lothar Wendel and Svetoslav Roerich. We asked what he knew of the various Soviet missions to the roof of the world.

SOVIET MISSIONS TO THE ROOF OF THE WORLD

At first the old man was hesitant to respond but, then, probably recovering old memories conceded that he had witnessed the arrival of Kommissar Sergey Borisov to Lhasa in 1925, where he had had an audience with the Dalai Lama. We found out later that Borisov was in charge of the Tibetan-Mongol Section of the Comintern in Moscow and had been given the mission of rallying the Living Buddha of the

Potala to the Bolshevik state in exchange for Soviet protection against the British Empire.

Borisov was one of the Communist leaders who believed in the possibility of building a Mahayana version of the Soviet ideology, given the "atheistic" nature of Buddhism, in order to unite Inner Asia and China with Russia under Communist rule in line with the vision of Boris Shumatsky, who headed the Eastern Department of the Comintern.

That strategic theory, rooted in the geopolitical theory of the "heartland" professed by Mackinder and General Haushoffer, found a philosophical counterpart in Barchenko's and Gleb Bokii's adoption of the Kalachakra as a psycho-physical technique to transform man into a superior enlightened being who would be a true communist by rising above selfishness and greed.

"At that time the 9th Panchen Lama, Thubten Chokyi Nyima was in Mongolia," the old *geshe* recalled.

"He had taken the succession of the expired Hutuktu Bogdo Ghegen in 1924 and cooperated with the local pro-Soviet Communist regime in Urga while keeping strong relations with the Republican Government of China. He claimed to be mandated by the King of Shambhala and aspired to rule Tibet with China's support, challenging the Lhasa *Kashag* which accused him of sedition. The governor of Western Tibet took his side and also looked to Moscow for support. The Soviet mission intended to bring about a reconciliation while pulling all of Tibet out of the British-Indian orbit."

It struck us that, coincidentally in 1922, three years earlier Alice Bailey had split away from the Theosophical Society and founded the Tibetan Lodge, better known as the Lucis Trust which was the real ancestor of the American New Age movement. Theosophy in its various avatars was inseparable from the great ideological and esoteric movements of the last hundred years. Bailey announced the dawn of a new era with the revelation of the Himalayan masters of wisdom and secret knowledge.

The archives show that in 1925, Bokii headed the Special Intelligence Section of the Soviet Foreign Affairs Commissariat, in charge of cryptography, code breaking and paranormal issues. He was advised by Barchenko who had earlier travelled in Central Asia on a semi-clandestine mission and by the Buryat Lama Badmaev. As we have said earlier Bokii had planned to lead a major scientific expedition to Central Asia and Tibet to look for Shambhala but was prevented from doing so by the Foreign Kommissar Chicherin, the very same one who received Nicolas Roerich and his wife but was jealous and suspicious of Bokii's growing influence. Instead, Borisov was sent to Lhasa with a merely diplomatic brief while Yakov Blumkin, already posted in Mongolia and trusted by Chicherin, was given a secret assignment to collect any knowledge pertaining to ancient Tibetan civilization and the hidden powers enshrined in the *dukhor* (kalachakra) gnosis.

We asked the Lama about Blumkin and he also acknowledged hearing that name but whether he did not have more information or did not wish to share it we never found out. Blumkin, as a clandestine agent, had probably been little noticed. He had carried secret missions in Central Asia on behalf of the Politburo since 1920 but survived only four years after his enigmatic 1926 Tibetan journey on which little documentation exists. In 1929 he was reportedly accused of being a Trotskyist (which he was) and of passing secret information to Germany and executed after a summary trial, taking his secrets with him to the grave. Only in 1939 did the head of the 5th section of the RUGB NKVD Dekanozov receive a four-page account of the conversations of one of his agents, Savelev with a German scientist, Werner Girke, at a time when the Reich and the USSR were allied under the terms of the Molotov-Ribentropp pact.

The report, addressed to first deputy Kommissar for Internal Affairs Merkulov, referred to Blumkin's findings during his journeys in Tibet and Mongolia and claimed that the Third Reich had put to use much of that scientifically relevant knowledge through various research programmes conducted under the aegis of the SS and *Ahnenerbe* and supervised by the well known Professor Hans Gunther who had taught first at Berlin and then at Karl Ludwig's University in Munich and was regarded by the Nazi regime as one of its scientific luminaries.

It appeared later that some outcomes of those programmes were the advanced aircraft, infrared sensors, electromagnetic propulsion systems and even the atomic weapons that German laboratories were building when the country surrendered after the fall of Berlin.

Also in the year 1926, Sven Hedin, the Swedish explorer, who represented mainly German strategic interests, went to Mongolia and met the Panchen Lama whom he had known much earlier in 1906 when he had visited him at his monastic capital of Shigatse in Southern Tibet in the course of his third expedition to Inner Asia. However he had not been authorized to enter Lhasa and had hence not been received by the Dalai Lama. Hedin opposed Soviet influence in the wider Asian region and sought to bring China's Kuo Ming Tang regime and West European powers together to combat communism. While the thirteenth Dalai Lama was regarded as an ally of the British since Younghusband had practically turned the Lhasa government into a protectorate of the Indian Empire, the Panchen Lama asserted his sovereignty. He sought allies in China and Russia to stake his political claims, which he supported by recalling his hierarchical precedence as the ruler of Shigatse's Tashilhumpo monastery built by the first Dalai Lama Padma Dorje Gandun Drupa in the 15th century of the western era, almost two centuries before the successors of Tsongkhapa moved to Lhasa's Potala.

As if to attest the seniority of the Shigatse seat, the first Dalai Lama is entombed in that monastery.

THE ESOTERIC GEOGRAPHY OF THE LAMAS

We naturally asked the Lama whether he was aware of what information about Shambhala might have been sought and gathered by the Soviet and German scientists.

"One of their fields of study was human history and the origins of various races," he replied. "They wanted to confirm that Tibetans are related to the Nordic people of Europe."

That was well known and I remembered that in the eighteenth and nineteenth centuries many scholars subscribed to the view that Swedes had come from Central Asia where they located the mystical city of Äsgard and where the red-headed white skinned mummies of the Tokharians had been found in the oasis of Turfan in the Takla Makan desert. Hedin lent credit to that theory and had explored and mapped the ancient kingdom of Kashgar in Turkestan, believed to be the cradle of the Scandinavian race.

"They also looked for technological knowledge for such things as space flight and very powerful weapons, did they not?" my father enquired.

"They particularly wanted to access Shambhala and contact the *Rigden Jampo*" (the monarch of Shambhala, also known as the *lokeshvara*), the old man replied, "but they understood that it required an initiation since Shambhala is not on the plane of matter we live in. it is also material but on a subtler level as the fifth Panchen lama explained in one of his books."

This matter-of-factly statement brought to my mind the very guarded and careful position of the Dalai Lama on such topics and his reluctance to allude to the supernatural dimensions of his tradition. I asked the *geshe* whether that was politically motivated. He remained grave and pondered his response for a minute.

"His Holiness has political responsibilities," he noted, "and he does not wish to make anyone uncomfortable with ideas that may be seen as irrational or conflict with other peoples' beliefs or conviction. It would not be helpful to the cause of Tibet."

We then asked him about the ancient Tibetan teachings regarding another world inside the earth.

"This is part of our cosmology," he said softly. "Our tradition teaches that the planet is hollow and inhabited inside by various classes of beings, much older than the human race, who migrated underground when great disasters struck the world. It is lit and warmed by an inner rotating Sun which accounts for the magnetism of our planet. Shambhala is located on one of the inner continents."

This was of course accepted by some of the German scholars and engineers who held pride of place in Nazi Germany. They studied Tibetan geographic texts, related to the Indian accounts of inner or lower worlds known as patalas, and took them seriously either because they had seen proof of the veracity of its depictions, as a few claimed, or because they trusted the ancient knowledge accumulated in the secluded Buddhist theocratic empire.

"Do the texts make any reference to the poles?" I asked, hardly containing my excitement.

"The inner world can be accessed either from Tibet where one of the openings is said to be beneath the Potala, or through the Sumeru mountain that stands on the axis of the earth," was the reply.

"However it is not visible in the normal condition because it exists in the vajra space, the universe of the diamond-thunderbold, superimposed on ours but parallel to it. We have to awaken our conscious awareness to our subtler body in order to locate Shambhala and enter it. It is as real, in fact more real than the visible world of every day but the time-space coordinates are different. That is why the kalachakra ritual enables its initiates to access that sphere. It is made of light like ours but the light is of sharper quality, of higher frequency, beyond the infrared," he ended with a brief laugh.

The Nazis had taken such statements and the various artistic depictions of the hidden realm literally and understood that the poles and the Antarctic continent in particular contain gateways to the Tibetan Promised Land. They dispatched the *Schwabenland* mission to what is now known as Queen Maud's land in order to secure that access, as the Savelev report indicates. However, if Shambhala lies in a different spacetime frame of reference, it would presumably not be visible even if one went deep into the earth, whether or not our planet is a hollow sphere. Developments in physics make it increasingly probable that reality is far more extensive and complex than what we perceive with our ordinary senses and the living beings we can see are merely those that exist on the same frequency so to speak.

"As a young man I read the autobiography of Captain Count von Lückner, who reportedly headed the supply and support organization for Schwabenland," my father recollected nostalgically. "When he was the Kaiser's freebooter during the First World War his ship was called the *See Adler*—The Sea Eagle. His great-grandfather was the

French Marshall of the same name decapitated during the Revolution."

We asked on various occasions the eminent Tibetan lamas whether they could confirm the stories about the enormous hidden treasures that the Germans, the Russians and others were said to have been looking for. Given the vast amounts of gold used to make and decorate hundreds of thousands of statues, funeral stupas and other sacred objects in the Potala and in many other Tibetan *lakhangs* (sanctuaries) and *gompas* (monasteries), it is easy to believe that many more precious substances and gems are lying undiscovered in secret places. The responses we got were predictably evasive. "According to tradition, one of the geshes said, Shambhala is full of gold, jewels and other rare minerals and the *vajra* itself is a diamond-like weapon that holds the power of the thunderbolt so that it can destroy entire cities or, if used in a different way, can also melt the hardest stone or make it light and easy to transport by remote control with the power of the mind."

With other erudite Tibetans we exchanged views on various occasion about the origins of their people and their place in the history of India.

"We were known to the Vedic peoples of India as *kiratas,* or mountain dwellers, one of the teachers of the Sarnath institute said and the equestrian warriors amongst us were called kinnaras by analogy with horse-headed mythical beings but the tribes living to the North of India in the Zhangzhung kingdom were originally designated as Turvashas, from where the names Tukhari-tokhara and Turk are derived.

Some traditions say we are related to the Moon god through his son Mercury or Budha which Hindu scholars connect with the Buddha who became our supreme master much later. We are closely linked with Mongols and our present Dalai Lama is from a Mongolian family like the spiritual mentors of the Chinese emperors, including the fourth Dalai Lama, the grandson of Altan Khan, used to be. However, historically speaking, I believe that Central Asians in general were called Angas, which the Chinese pronounced Hsiung, the Mongols Hunnu and the Europeans Huns. In some Indian works, Tibet is known as Angadesh. Our ancestors possibly gave their name to the kingdom of Anga in the eastern Ganges valley, the land now known as Bihar, Bengal and Assam which they invaded and ruled on various occasions. That helps explain the powerful and lasting presence of Buddhism in those regions as well as in Nepal and Tibet since Sakya Muni was from that area and reflected in his teachings the local tradition. The Brahmanical Vedic culture from the West was perhaps not as deeply rooted there as in its Punjabi cradle."

That explanation sounded plausible. It is well known that it is in the Eastern Himalayan foothills and along the lower course of the Ganges-Brahmaputra system that Buddhism originated and retained its centre of gravity although it had been gradually displaced by the Hindu revival and then uprooted by the Islamic tidal wave. The patron saint of Buddhism in Tibet, Padmasambhava or Guru Rimpoche is also called *Sakya Senge*, the lion of the Sakyas or Sakas.

We did ask our Tibetan hosts at Sarnath whether the Angas had played a role in the expansion of Buddhism to South East Asia and China because of their ethnic affinities with the indigenous populations there.

"Very probably," the Venerable Samdhong Rimpoche said in his usual soft, thoughtful tone of voice.

"The great East Indian dynasties which patronized Buddhism in the Middle Age must at least have had some Himalayan blood and one of them is still known as the Pala-Kamboja. One of the greatest Tantric masters, Srijnana Dipankara Atisa was from Bengal. Kambojas are also Central Asian Mongoloid peoples and they played a role in the spread of the Dharma to Burma, Cambodia, the Cham of Vietnam and later Siam. The Ahom people of today's Assam and the Thais are closely related."

We recalled that one of the objectives of German racial theorists, which had become an obsession for some, was to confirm that Tibetans were descended from the original Aryans of Central Asia or "Hyperborea" as General Haushoffer believed. There are many traces of a very ancient "Indo-European" linguistic and cultural presence in

Central Asia, including the many manuscripts on bark and silk, written mostly in kharosti script discovered by Aurel Stein and Sven Hedin in the course of their expeditions. The city of Urga, the old capital of Mongolia is built on the river Tuul, which seems to be named after the mythical polar "Thule." It is therefore quite logical to assume that the Tokhari, the people of Uttara Kurus who are described as vedic by the Puranas mingled with the Tibeto-Mongol and Turkic ethnic groups and were gradually assimilated by them. A similar mixture took place in Russia and Siberia but Tibetans and Mongols have kept a close relationship with India through Mahayana Buddhism which retains a strong Hindu mythological legacy.

"They thought that we were descended from a mixture of Aryans with Mongols," one of the scholars replied laconically, as if to indicate that the theories of the Nazi ideologues had not been forgotten.

According to their ancient lore, the Mongols and kindred tribes are one day to rule the world or at least all of Asia but in esoteric terms, the Kalkin of Shambhala is the hidden universal king in a very long line of succession that goes back to the Buddha himself.

Very few Tibetan scholars wanted to say much about *Dejung* (Shambhala in Tibetan) or its monarch. One of the lamas of Sarnath alluded briefly to Nagakpo, the present *rigden jampo*, twenty-first in the mystical dynasty, whose Sanskrit name is Aniruddha. While all Dalai Lamas are held to be reincarnations of Pundarika, the second Kalki, the Jampo's *Sakyong* (protector or regent) belongs to the Trungpa line of the monastic kingdom of Surmang in western Tibet, whose present heir, Chogyam the eleventh Trungpa emigrated to Colorado in the United States.

There is a story that the famous adventurer and esoteric teacher Gurjieff, who wandered for many years across inner Asia studied under spiritual masters at Surmang according to his own allegations and some even suspect that he may have used the alias of Dorjieff when, in a lama's garb, he went to Saint Petersburg as an officious envoy of the Dalai Lama.

We could not get any clarification from our Tibetan mentors about the source of the name Agartha or Agarthi which one finds only in the account of western writers about Shambhala. The root word may be Sanskrit *agar*, the name of a perfume producing tree that grows in the Eastern Himalayan ranges and the capital city of the small kingdom of Tripura in North Eastern India is called Agartala after that tree but there is no phonetic Tibetan equivalent. However German maps of the "inner Earth," drawn under SS supervision, allegedly copied from secret Indo-Tibetan charts, display the continent of Äsgard which belongs to Norse mythology. Agartha may thus be an oriental version of Äsgard, a name which Colonel Tod assimilated with Asirgarh, the citadel of the Asii in Rajputana, suggesting a common legendary origin.

THE HIDDEN KEYS TO THE DIVINE REALM

Tripa Zong Rimpoche told us years later, when he visited the United States and came to Aspen on our invitation about the intrinsic relation between the revelation of Shambhala and the retrieval of *terma*, the mystical treasures that were hidden in various parts of the earth and also in the sky by the superhuman vidyadharas or *rigzins*, the "keepers of wisdom." Those treasures generally but not always have a material form and appear as stones covered with inscriptions, often in the marchen-kinnauri script of the old Zhangzhung pre-Buddhist era or as symbolically auspicious objects. Others are invisible and manifest as mantras that are revealed to their discoverers, the tertons, while in a state of meditation. The physical terma are hidden in caverns (*mdsod phug* or drepug) and are guarded by the nagas, the reptilian beings who dwell in the inner earth and may be regarded as the elder relatives of humans. When on the earth's surface, they show themselves either as cobra snakes or in a human form since they are hybrid creatures. I am always tempted to think that the nagas are what certain dinosaurs may have become if they survived the great extinction of their kind and evolved, both physically and mentally, during the last many million years.

The celestial terma are in the custody of the *dakinis,* fierce female beings who live in the sky and manifest when they are invoked according to specific tantric practices. The *dakinis* are the yoginis of the Tantric cult of ancient India. In Hindu texts, they are described as vampiric creatures who ride on hyenas and are often seen on funeral grounds because they haunt the threshold of the afterlife worlds. Like all beings who live in the parallel hidden dimensions they shift shapes and take many appearances, beautiful or terrifying, contingent upon the state of mind and degree of enlightenment of the beholder. In the *vajradhatu* or "thunderbolt realm," the Buddha Sakya Muni assumes the wrathful crimson-coloured form of Vajradhara or *Dorje Sempa* performing the cosmic dance in a ring of fire, as a counterpoise to his serene and motionless pose in our world of substance and desires, the *kamadhatu*.

Some terma, such as the chintamani that had become so central to the Roerichs's mission, are visible signs of Shambhala and convey messages which open the secret kingdom to those who know how to interpret those esoteric-coded indices. They may be chiseled on thunderstones or meteorites by natural forces or unknown engravers and the tertons are in a perpetual supra-conscious quest for such messages like the knights who sought the Grail in the medieval legends.

The fact that the *terma* are held to be relics from very ancient ages, well before the carnal birth or descent of the historic Buddha leads to the conclusion that the notion or knowledge of Shambhala predates Buddhism as we know it and harks back to the Bon cosmology of Tibet, possibly contemporary with the proto-vedic civilization of India, which also has a tradition of mystical jewels hidden in caves such as the Dharmyakota of Amaravati in a *khadira vana* (acacia forest) of the Deccan where the first Dharmaraja Suchandra was initiated to the gnosis of the *kalachakra* by Buddha himself and where the *vajrashekhara sutra* (the diamond-crescent) was revealed to the great sage Nagarjuna centuries later by the tantric Buddha Manjushri.

In some of the legends the cave opens up magically when sesame seeds are thrown on the rock face or burnt on an altar as part of an incantation and that detail links the esoteric gnosis of India with the Ali Baba tale in the Arabian Nights where the password to open the treasure cave is "sesame open."

I find today as I did then that the contemplation of the splendidly elaborate mandalas of Shambhala painted on cloth by Tibetan monks, or of its tridimensional gilded and enamelled models, is even more thought-provoking and enlightening than those conversations when one wishes to gradually unravel the metaphysical enigma of the hidden domain of the buddhas and gods. According to the oldest literature on the subject, the city was created by Suchandra in the magical forest of Malaya—the name of several mountain ranges in India and South East Asia—in the form of an eight-petalled lotus and each successive lokeshvara holds court in its centre on a diamond throne, the *vajrasana,* surrounded by a vast retinue of liberated beings and supernatural creatures.

A very ancient statue of the blue-eyed, "saffron flower hued" lokeshvara made of pure gold is kept in the Potala and is deemed to be its most precious object. The monastic palace of the Tibetan God king is an earthly image of the realm of the chogyals (*dharmarajas*) of *cho kyi khorlo* (*kalachakra*) and is built on top of such a treasure cave. The very name is derived from *potalaka*, the hilltop paradise of Bodhisattwa Avalokitesvara.

XXV

Parting Garlands

Arabo-Persian Wisdom in the Turkic Citadel

During the year 1980, we had made Delhi our headquarters and had taken up residence at the Indian Institute of Islamic Studies at Hamdard Nagar, on the invitation of our friend S. A. Ali, its scholarly director and of its founder, the universally respected Hakim Abdul Hamid, perhaps the best known practitioner of the traditional Graeco-Arabic school of medicine inherited from Galen and Avicenna and preserved in India better than in all other parts of the Muslim world. That large sylvan campus faces the cyclopean walls of the ruined city of Tukhlaqabad; a four-mile long crenellated enclosure and a few crumbling structures half swallowed by thickets and mounds of dust are the sole remains of Ghyasuddin Tughlaq's proud capital. That Afghan grandee who had risen to the throne in 1320 of the common era took only two years to build the new city and dig a large lake just outside its walls but had little time to enjoy his creation as he died one year later, crushed under a collapsing pavilion where he was being welcomed on his way back from a military campaign. Suspicions of foul play whirled around his son and successor Muhammad, who had his father promptly buried in the beautiful Turkic mausoleum the latter had erected for himself on a fortified island in the middle of the artificial lake and eventually moved his residence to his own new fortified city of Jahanpanah.

Tughlakabad, where we took walks amidst the rubble and thorny bushes, remained a citadel where successive dynasties kept their treasure. The town was laid out on a gridline patterns with straight street and square open spaces lined by mosques, palaces and shops.

Ibn Battuta who stayed in the area gave a glowing account of the palace "whose tiles," "he wrote, he (Mohammed) had gilded so that when the Sun rose they shone with a blinding glow. He deposited in this town vast stores of wealth and it is told that he dug a lake and poured in it molten gold so that it became a single block."

If that detail seems too extravagant to be true, we can however take Ibn Battuta at his word when he describes the Diwan hall roofed with exquisitely sculpted precious timber and supported by a thousand ornate and painted wooden pillars. Even today the desolate expanse within the fort is honeycombed with deep round holes dug to keep either grain or valuable goods accumulated during the various plundering raids that the Sultan carried out all the way to Central India and Gujarat.

There were as always stories about secret underground tunnels leading out of the fort many miles away. At present only one such subterranean passage is known but it is quite likely that the suspicious monarchs had clandestine escape routes dug out in case they were besieged by enemies or threatened by assassins. The sense of mystery lurking beneath our feet added depth to the historical memories that arose every time I looked at the stern ramparts of the ghost city.

Hazrat Nizamuddin was not well disposed towards Ghyas-uddin Tughlaq, as we have pointed out in the early part of this book and he had reportedly cursed the new capital that the monarch was building by predicting that it would soon be deserted and settled by Gujjars. Indeed, in the last few centuries and right until our own days this tribe of nomadic cattle herders used to camp within the walls. The Gujjars, as nomads usually are, were not liked by the local inhabitants as they kept their rough customs and occasionally looted the settled populations. Although they claimed kinship with the proud imperial Kushan clans, they long ago fell from their glorious heyday and are now a relatively disadvantaged lot. The present-day Gujjars look like most other North Indians so that it is hard to relate them to the broad-faced Central Asian horsemen they once may have been. One must conclude that they intermingled so much with other ethnic groups that they lost most of their original physical traits although those relatives of the Tokharians and Huns must have, like the Scythians, been quite a mixed breed by the time they entered India almost two thousand years ago.

For centuries Gujjars were based in the hilly area around Mount Abu, on the confines of Rajasthan and Gujarat, the province which came to be named after them and they are closely related to the Rajputs, who form in fact a loose federation of warlike clans and tribes.

The Hakeem Abdul Hameed, the president of the Hamdard Foundation had the demeanour and reputation of the legendary physician-philosophers who brought so much renown to medieval Islamic kingdoms. He displayed an almost saintly humility and patience as well as unfailing affability to all and sundry. He was one of the most authentic Sufis I have ever met. His large fortune was used for the welfare of the poor and needy and he himself led an abstemious life and kept a punishing work schedule in spite of his advanced age and apparent frailty. He was a long time friend of the Nehru family and there was a photo of him seated next to Mrs Gandhi and holding her two young boys on his knees.

We undertook research into an aspect of Middle Eastern medieval philosophy that I called "the Islamic Cosmosophy," because of its Hellenistic, Persian and cosmopolitan roots that had given rise during more than six centuries to a blossoming scientific and metaphysical literature signed by the great names that illustrate the annals of Muslim civilization from Andalucia to Central Asia: Al Kindi, Al Farabi, Ibn Tufail, Ibn Arabi, Suhrawardi, Avicenna and Averrroes, to mention but a few. This work, which drew me for weeks on end into the Institute of Islamic Studies's vast domed library, took us two years and made me familiar with many of the brilliant and far-sighted texts that had a seminal role in the development of European civilisation in the Middle Age and the Renaissance when they got translated into Hebrew, Greek and Latin.

Our ongoing work in the realm of comparative spiritual traditions brought us in contact with the president of the World Conference of Religions for Peace, Archbishop Angelo Fernandes of Delhi, a tall and cordial man whose solar personality made him very popular. He was, in the best Indian tradition, quite devoid of parochialism and had no hesitation in praising the spiritual achievements of Hinduism and Buddhism while acknowledging the Church's shortcomings and errors. He did not necessarily embrace the experiments in full scale indigenization of Catholic rituals practiced by some Jesuits we knew such as Father Hirudayam in the South who wore saffron, said mass in Tamil while sitting cross legged on the ground and replaced the host and wine of the Eucharist with a cocoanut's flesh and water. Some Hindus objected to that mimesis of their practices, which could be used to convert even more people to Christianity by abolishing outer differences between the two cultures. For his part the archbishop preferred to retain the distinctive features of the roman liturgy. "We can enter into a dialogue better when we remain ourselves," he told us. "Otherwise, why maintain our doctrine if we copy the ways of worship of other creeds? We can find convergence at the philosophical level but we don't need to all look the same. Of course Christianity underwent local adaptations in all the countries where it gained followers but the Church has to keep its universal yet specific identity, wherever it is present."

GEOPOLITICAL RUMBLINGS

Living in Delhi we had occasions to meet Mrs Gandhi and members of her family. Sanjay had died tragically in a plane crash within city limits during the summer of 1980. His demise led the prime minister, aware of the need to reform the economy which was suffering from the structural inefficiencies of "license raj socialism," to grow closer to her remaining son Rajiv and to the latter's Italian wife Sonia who, with their two young children, provided for her the comfort of family life as a refuge from the hectic solitude of power. She also called to Delhi one of her provincial cousins Arun, whose influence went on increasing in the years that followed as we noticed when we met him.

Through our conversations in the political circles we could sense that the old rivalry between the Anglo-Saxon powers and the Soviet Union over India remained intense and that Mrs Gandhi and her government were in the middle of that muffled battle in which the USA had lost a potential ally in the late Sanjay Gandhi. Not long after his death, his widow Maneka, whom we knew for her interest in animal welfare and ecology, fell into disgrace with her mighty mother-in-law and had to leave the Prime Minister's house with her infant son.

It was rumored that the Americans and the British, closely aligned with Pakistan as they had been since 1947, fomented unrest in the state of Punjab where Sikhs were a majority. A section of the large and affluent Sikh diaspora in the United Kingdom and in North America had become violently separatist and claimed the right to form an independent state. The USSR on the other hand supported its important Indian ally and supplied intelligence on the alleged plots of the Reagan administration and of the Thatcher government, neither of which sought to hide their hostility to Indira Gandhi's "non-aligned" policies. The Indian Prime Minister could not easily determine whether the soviet sources relayed by the influential Ambassador at the time, Yuli Vorontsov and the large KGB station in Delhi were truthful or self-servingly denigrating their NATO adversaries who sought to thwart the USSR's military operations in Afghanistan. Her refusal to change sides in the midst of this cold war, which pitted a reinvigorated neo-liberal West against a declining USSR, prevented Mrs Gandhi from embracing the rapid economic development strategies adopted at the time by several East Asian countries including China.

In spite or rather because of efforts to remain equidistant from both camps, India stayed on what was then commonly seen as the losing side with other variously socialist countries of Afro-Asia and Eastern Europe.

In France, Mitterrand's widely heralded semi-marxist experiment came to an ignominious end within two years and the West retained its hegemonic unity. Mrs Gandhi herself realized she had to distance herself somewhat from her Russian mentors and to that effect in 1981 she set up the World Peace and Solidarity Organization as a rival to the Soviet-funded and hitherto highly influential World Peace

Council through which the Kremlin furthered its strategic aims and won allies all over India.

We had once a quiet conversation with Rajiv Gandhi at the prime minister's house where he received us with his customary, rather charmingly diffident courtesy. His new prominence made him visibly uncomfortable as he was not yet used to it, having been elected to Parliament only a few months earlier in the constituency formerly represented by his late brother. Not yet forty, he had reluctantly and lately been pushed into politics, against the wishes of his wife, by his mother who, estranged as she was from senior members of the Nehru family and much of the Congress's Old Guard, placed her trust in her immediate kin. Rajiv had an easy-going affable personality, which contrasted with Sonia's apparent coldness and reserve. Having been raised at the heart of power he was not awed by it but he was aware of his inexperience and keen to hear various viewpoints on public issues. We realized that unlike Indira Gandhi, an alumnus of Shantiniketan who had read Indian philosophy and history extensively and was familiar with her country's religious traditions, her son was a product of Doon school, an Indian version of English elite institutions and of Imperial College in Britain. If Mrs Gandhi had a literary temperament, Rajiv was an instinctive technocrat whose attraction to engineering had led him to become a civilian pilot. His main interest was not ideology but efficiency and modernization and by temperament he was a rationalist who viewed spirituality as an intriguing but rather mysterious and secondary concern, contrary to the vast majority of his countrymen.

We could not know at the time that fate would make him the prime minister of his country less than three years later but we still felt that he belonged to the contemporary crop of leaders who, in China and other East Asian countries, had launched ambitious modernization and economic growth policies, jumping on the bandwagon of neoliberalism driven by Reagan and Thatcher in the West.

Even though he did introduce information technology and the new telecommunication revolution to India, the age-old mindset and the political structures of India did not permit the radical transformation of society that he would have liked. In the years that followed Rajiv would be compared to John F Kennedy, another young and charismatic young leader with a privileged background and transformational ambitions . Those who drew this facile parallel found a grim vindication for the analogy in the many setbacks and tragic end that both men met.

In Mrs Gandhi's office, I once or twice had casual chats with one of her trusted aides Vincent George, who liked to talk of Hindu philosophy although he was a Christian. He was particularly intrigued by the rather unconventional teachings of Acharya Rajneesh, the controversial and famous guru who had attracted a wide and wealthy following in the West and whose doctrine transcended institutionalized religions but attracted criticism for its sexual permissiveness and apparent amorality. My father and I also met at his office Sharada Prasad, the Prime Minister's influential press secretary who was himself a gifted writer and an erudite literary critic. We appreciated the cosmopolitan culture he brought to the conversation despite the reserve he kept in view of his official position.

The Vice-President of India at that time, Mohammed Hidayatullah, was a judicial luminary who had practiced at Lincoln's Inn and had been made an Officer of the British Empire in 1946. Another peculiarity was that his elder brother became the foreign secretary of India's fraternal enemy Pakistan. Hidayatullah was a polished man of the world with a soft corner for France and he enjoyed reviving his admittedly rusty knowledge of the language with us on more than one occasion. His memoirs entitled "My Own Boswell," published about that period, stand witness to a classical upbringing and temperament nurtured under the colonial rule.

Madhavrao Scindia, the young Maharaja of Gwalior, was a parliamentarian and a rising star in the Congress Party, whose leader had imprisoned his own mother Rajmati Vijayaraje, a stalwart of the Jan Sangh opposition in which he also had begun his political career. The Scindias were adept at the subtle balancing politics between various powers which had helped them to gather and retain their once vast territorial possessions in the troubled environment of 18th century India. Madhavrao's own father had been given George as a first name in order to please the then King Emperor but had only used the second one, Jiwaji which was impeccably Hindu.

The Winchester and Oxford educated Madhavrao Scindia himself protected the family's legacy by switching to Mrs Gandhi's party in 1980 and was seen as a future member of her Cabinet. We liked his straightforward, common sense view of the problems of the country and his well-bred informality. When in Delhi, away from the monumental palaces of his family in Gwalior, he resided in the vast walled compound owned by the Scindias in the south of the city. Various villas were occupied by members of the clan and their household around a polo ground, stables and paddocks which attested a deep seated attachment to equestrian sports.

THE DIPLOMATIC CAROUSEL

Social life in Delhi revolved around a few such great families and the foreign diplomats, who were conspicuously present at all events and in the streets where their automobiles made up a large proportion of all vehicles. We had several friends in that community and occasionally participated in adventurous road trips and hunting expeditions into the countryside around Delhi and as far as Rajasthan and the Himalayan foothills. We did not shoot however as my father was firmly opposed to killing for sport even though at my young age the temptation and the thrill of cynegetic pursuits remained strong. A more peaceful activity was initiated by a young member of the French commercial mission, André Gleizes who was a talented amateur movie maker. He decided to shoot a feature film on the life and times of the famous Begum Samru (or Sombre in French), the Muslim dancing girl born in utter poverty who had married a German deserter of the East India Company troops and eventually became a ruling feudal princess in early nineteenth century Northern India and the morganatic wife of a British General. At her death she left palaces in Delhi and in her small provincial capital in Sardhana where she built a grand neo-classical basilica, complete with marble statues by the famous Tadolini as a testimony of her conversion to the Catholic faith.

A French diplomat once posted in Delhi had written a novel on her story under the pen name of Michel Larneuil. For an entire season we participated in the making of that historic epic in various picturesque locations of Delhi and Jaipur. The project which succeeded only partly perhaps of its overambitious scope provided various opportunities to visit and stay in charmingly exotic places and ride horses in quaint costumes and uniforms. An even greater advantage was the ability to act with the exquisitely beautiful Gayatri princess of Kapurthala, who was about my age and obligingly played the title role. Naturally I had a "big crush" on her and we remained friends over the years.

Despite featuring many original and interesting foreign personalities, the Indian capital no longer hosted such prestigious foreign envoys as the legendary first French ambassador Count Ostrorog or Octavio Paz, the Nobel prize writer who had married his Gallic wife some years earlier under the superb banyan tree that adumbrates the Mexican Ambassador's residence on Prithviraj Road.

Although Paz was gone, some poems he wrote about Delhi bore witness to his fascination for the city where he had spent a few years and developed an interpretation of India that appears too visibly shaped by his own cultural and ethnic prejudices to be reliable. Like many sensitive and sensual Latin souls, he grasped the picturesque aspects of the land and its people but did not fathom the underlying philosophy of its civilization.

His poems about India enshrine the verbal symbolism and the mysterious melodies that characterize Latin American Fantastic Realism in literature. Some of them are in the vein of Federigo Garcia Lorca and I found one on the Lodhi gardens, where we frequently took walks, particularly evocative in its haiku-like brevity:

En el azul unanime
Los domos de los mausoleos
-negros,reconcentrados,pensativos-
emitieron de pronto
opajaros.

(The black, pensive, dense
Domes of the mausoleums
Suddenly shot birds
Into the unanimous blue)

I realized that the spanish text is even closer to the Indian reality because the word for bird (pájaro) is related to the Sanskrit and hindi *pakshi* ("winged one" or bird). Likewise, the name of the sparrow is "gorión" in Castillan and "gauriya" in Hindi. Across the Arab-Islamic bridge the two languages restored their millenary Indo-European bond.

In another sketch in "zen" verse, Paz describes impressionistically the tomb of Humayun, another familiar site for us:

"To the debate of wasps
To the dialectic of monkeys
Twitterings of statistics
It opposes (high flame of rose
Formed out of stone and air and birds
Time in repose above the water)
Silent architecture."

(both translations are by Charles Donaldson).

Paz's successor at the time was Graciela de la Lama, one of the few female heads of mission, also an intellectual and perhaps the most eccentric member of her expatriate community, whose son was about my age. We made friends with Tomás Vazquez and his wife who headed the Chilean mission as their teen age daughter happened to be my pupil at the small French Embassy school where I taught classes whose students were only a few years younger than I. Mrs Vazquez was a prominent hostess and often gave balls and soirées as well as hosting monthly literary discussions for other diplomatic wives from Spain and Latin America. We were invited to speak to that pleasant audience in which politics was banished. As a result of that truce, the representatives of democratic states could enjoy the hospitality of General Pinochet's envoy but Far Right ideas and regimes had never prevented Chile from maintaining cordial relations with Socialist India.

Indeed an earlier Ambassador from Santiago, Miguel Serrano who spent ten years in Delhi between 1953 and 1962 was still remembered for his passion for Hindu esotericism, his commanding presence and his friendship with Pandit Nehru and his daughter, though not necessarily in that order. Serrano had been initiated in his youth into a "Vedic Aryan" gnostic order headed by a master of German origin known under the initial K.F. He went on with the Chilean navy on an expedition to Antarctica in 1947 and later wrote extensively about the mystery of Mount Kailash, which he believed to be inhabited by the extraterrestrial hyperboreans. According to the gnosis he professed, the hyperboreans had descended from outside the galaxy in fiery flying discs and settled down at what is now the North Pole long before a cataclysm reversed the polarity of the planet and wiped out their civilization to which the Brahmins of India were the heirs.

In 1978, his book *El Cordon dorado* (The Golden Braid) was published and in 1980 he brought out *Nos, Libro de la Resurreccion,* which enshrines a strange mixture of Apocalyptic gnosis, Hindu philosophy, Tibetan symbology, "Aryan" metaphysics and South American Pre-Columbian mythology as it weaves in one myth the figures of Lucifer, the Nordic god Wotan, Kom Tiki, Qutzalcoatl, the Kalki Avatar and the Buddha Maitreya with the visionary poetic talent that the author possessed.

Serrano was a friend of C. J. Jung, Ezra Pound, Ernst Junger, Julius Evola and Hermann Hesse among other intellectual luminaries and came close to the Dalai Lama. He went on a quest of a super-natural realm, the "Other Earth" located in the Himalayas where the Siddhas, the enlightened masters of wisdom, are said to hide and are visible only when one awakes to the secret light of the occult black Sun. His book "The Serpent of Paradise" narrates his investigations. When we brought up his name to Ambassador Vasquez, the latter made no comment because Serrano, held in favour by Pinochet's regime, was obviously controversial on account of his admiration for Adolf Hitler and the Third Reich.

Our own interest in his writings sprang from the many pages he had dedicated to UFOs which he described as the vehicles of the

Aryan hyperboreans since he had sighted them around the Antarctic in the course of the expedition to which he had participated, shortly after Admiral Byrd's mysterious and abruptly interrupted "Operation High Jump." The alleged secret story is that the US Navy had to abandon the aforesaid project after encountering the mysterious flying discs and probably incurring some material and human losses in that confrontation.

One of the Chilean diplomats in residence was more knowledgeable about Serrano and gave us some information on the ideological environment of his country, permeated in the upper classes by both an austere and highly conservative form of Catholicism and a nostalgia for remote Europe. "We are very far from almost everywhere else, he said, isolated between the ocean, high mountains and deserts and we almost touch Antarctica. It is a harsh country, periodically racked by earthquakes and held together by an ultra-nationalist military elite steeped in Spanish traditions and Germanic ideals. Our vision of the Old World is romantic and rooted in past centuries."

In Dharamshala, one of the Dalai Lama's aides remembered Serrano well as he had returned to visit the Tibetan pontiff a few years earlier. He told us that the Chilean author was especially interested in the ancient history of Tibet and in the records related to the lost cities of the Gobi and Tarim deserts, where he thought the old home of the Aryan civilization was located. "He believed that in their descent from the North Pole the ancestors of the Tibetans and Brahmins had colonized Mongolia and Xinjiang, where they were known as Uyghurs before reaching South Asia," the Lama told us without indicating whether he agreed with that version of events.

Chile remains a country rife with reports and rumours about "extraterrestrials," mysterious Nordic looking beings and UFOs, seen with some frequency in the country and Serrano belonged to a group that saw a connection between the hyperborean Aryan traditions, the Indian ancient records and the enigma of flying saucers. Like all modern esoterica in the west, his doctrine is influenced by theosophical teachings and his diplomatic postings in India and then in Eastern Europe gave credence to claims that he was an important agent of anti-communist forces.

When the Left Wing politician Allende came to power in Chile, he promptly dismissed the flamboyant Serrano from the service in 1970 and the latter only returned to his country after the 1973 military coup.

The unusual life and career of that aristocratic and wealthy diplomat would lead one to believe that he was privy to major secrets that many of the powers-that-be would not wish to be revealed. Serrano was convinced that the rulers of the Third Reich had discovered the knowledge once possessed by the original Aryas and still preserved in India and Tibet after their last homeland in the Gobi desert had been destroyed. His work supported the testimonies we had come across from Indian, Tibetan, Russian and European sources about the hidden realm of Shambhala, the inner earth and the role of mysterious superhuman beings in the history of the world. Is there a consensual agreement among the ruling powers of mankind today to hide and deny a transcendent reality too disturbing for them to be acknowledged?

We found that such an esoteric awareness still lingered among many distinguished friends, deeply aware of the extent and value of India's ancient wisdom because of their familiarity with the old scriptures and with the messages of Sri Aurobindo and other modern seers. On weekends we sometimes went for lunch more to the Solar Farm, a pioneering renweable energy research centre and country house owned by J.C. and Urmilla Kapur. Our conversations with Karan Singh and Lokesh Chandra on those topics were always spiritually enriching and at the house of the former we were introduced to Dr Kapila Vatsyayan, one of the inspiring and mighty women who have done so much, like Kamala Devi and Rukmini Devi, to preserve and highlight the civilization of the subcontinent in its many facets. Kapilaji as all call her, was a member of the inner advisory circle of the Prime Minister on matters of art and culture, together with Mrs Pupul Jayakar, a supporter and confidant of J. Krishnamurti and a well-known promoter of traditional knowledge and crafts. Dr Vatsyayan expressed her support for a proposal to set up an international organization that would spread worldwide the Indic message of Dharma as a cosmic ecumenical principle for global peace and ecological harmony.

We got to know in the same period one of Indira Gandhi's former ministers and confidants who, fallen from grace, joined the Janata party after the Emergency but returned to the Congress when it returned to power. Dinesh Singh belonged to a feudal family that owned a vast estate on the Ganges near Allahabad and he was a natty dresser, a suave diplomat and an eloquent, sophisticated orator. Although he looked like the epitome of a conservative of the old aristocratic order, his uncle Brajesh Singh had gained fame as a communist leader, even more so after marrying Stalin's daughter Svetlana in 1965, proving once more that ideological sympathies, politics and mutual attraction sometimes combine to make the most unexpected bed fellows. Dinesh Singh himself had inherited the style, polish, political ambition and flair for intrigue of the royal courtiers of yore and his conversation was interesting in spite of the careful formality of his demanour.

The most popular ambassador in our Delhi years was probably Hasan Ali Husain Al Ni'mah, the munificent Sheykh from Qatar who threw all night musical and gastronomic parties in his Lutyens-era mansion and in the surrounding gardens where he kept white gazelles, doves, peacocks and swans. He invited the best singers and instrumentalists from India to play for a select audience which gathered the most elegant couples and the prettiest women in the city. Bombay actresses, Hindu Ranis and Muslim Begums mingled with Delhi high society ladies, renowned dancers, models and visiting jet setters from East and West. We made several friends in that crowd and I remember among others the actors Kabir and Protima Bedi, Sanjay Khan, the cricket champion Nawab "Tiger" of Pataudi and his wife Sharmila Tagore, then perhaps the most famous star of the Indian screen who must have been slightly mortified when I innocently asked her what her activity was. However, she kept her smile and gently explained that she played roles in movies.

Hasan Ali Husain was passionate about Eastern music, Arabic, Persian and Indian and he also was a Sufi and often invited travelling mystics from various *tariqas* to stay at his house. More than once we were introduced to young and old "God's lovers" who generally displayed the effusive enthusiasm that denotes the *majnun* (those intoxicated by the divine presence). Those ageless portraits of long-haired, bearded men in flowing clothes remain in my memory also because of their piercing, fiery and yet liquid gaze.

CLOSING RECOLLECTIONS

Over time, an informal circle came into being in and around the India International Centre. Some of its members were Countess Marie Amélie de Robilant who followed an Indian spiritual master located in a town not far from Delhi, Princess Fazileh Ibrahim from Egypt, the writer Andres Boulton and his wife from the Embassy of Venezuela, his countryman and fellow diplomat, the avant garde film maker Bartolome Sanchez, Raja Aditya Katoch of Lambagraon and some long-time Indian and European friends we had made during our previous stays in the capital. We often saw in these surroundings the habitually barefoot painter M.F. Hussain, whose fame was growing at the time.

I recall Sunday lunches and swims in the pool of the estate owned by "Biki" Oberoi, the heir of the prestigious hotel chain founded by his father the Rai Bahadur Mohan Singh who had once memorably told us with his customary bluntness: "You think that India can save the world while I say that the entire world can't save India."

Delhi hosted numerous visits by foreign leaders and we had the pleasure of meeting again after several years the King and Queen of Spain at a beautiful reception given by their Ambassadors Enrique and Cathy Usias de Mahou. We talked briefly with Their Majesties about our activities in India and evoked memories of Queen Frederika with her daughter Queen Sofia. Many long time friends were present at the soiree, including Rajmata Gayatri Devi and I remember having a chat with the Maharani Yasho of Kashmir, the lovely wife of Karan

Singh who belonged to the princely dynasty of the Ranas of Nepal. Rajiv and Sonia Gandhi made their appearance and I was once again struck by Sonia's withdrawn attitude. Was it shyness or only the fear of making a mistake? Her sister Nadia was there with her husband, a Spanish diplomat who had been posted to Delhi soon after Sanjay's tragic demise, and she was naturally far more outgoing and relaxed than the Prime Minister's *bahu* (daughter-in-law).

At the end of his visit Juan Carlos, known to have a glad eye, remarked that among the people he would remember was "the Spanish man with a ponytail and his wife."

The man with the ponytail was a Spanish resident of India called Julio Peralta and his wife was the stunningly beautiful Jaya whose ravishing figure, almond-shaped velvet eyes, oval golden face and jet-black cascade of hair had not troubled the monarch alone. We knew both of them but in the following months and years we became friends and I can confess that, even though Julio is a pleasant and engaging man gifted with the peculiarly Spanish sharp and barbed wit, it was understandably Jaya's almost Indo-Chinese pulchritude that drew me to the couple.

In the following year 1983 the French President, Francois Mitterrand paid an official visit to India and we were introduced to him by the French Ambassador André Ross, an old school, intellectually proficient diplomat well liked in India. Mitterrand was true to his reputation as a sphinx-like inscrutable statesman who rarely smiled and laughed even less. He was coldly polite and gave the impression, despite his unaffected ways, of being constantly aware of the majesty of his office. I instinctively compared the democratic head of state's haughty reserve with the King of Spain's cordial bonhomie and it came to my mind that a hereditary monarch is less constrained to affirm his status than a temporarily elected leader tends to be.

Mitterrand's wife Danièle was on the contrary quite extroverted and accessible and we spoke a little longer with her. In the delegation was Mitterrand's Svengali, the Minister for Culture Jack Lang whose florid eloquence, costly designer tight-fitting suits, pink and mauve shirts and vivid ties contrasted with the President's austere appearance. Our conversation with him did not lead to a convergence of views as the notoriously "amoral" Lang had little use for ancient spiritual philosophies, being a promoter of the latest fads and fashions of the so-called "caviar left" that he represented so visibly.

Mitterrand who was from the pre-war generation and had begun his political career on the Far Right of the political spectrum, felt out of touch with the young generations and used the night-club haunting popinjay Lang as a herald and a symbol of hipness, a bit like De Gaulle, a stern military man raised in a royalist provincial setting, had recruited the avant-garde intellectual and former communist militant André Malraux as his cultural standard bearer. Yet it must be said that in terms of talent and background Malraux towered above Lang who rather embodies the opportunistic mediocrity of a particular *nouveau riche* "bobo" milieu.

Thus were spent the last two of our eight-year periplum in India, in the vast capital city that had been the seat of so many dynasties since thousands of years. We sometimes went walking within the crenellated walls of the Purana Qila, the "ancient citadel" where the Pandava brothers are said to have established their new capital of Indraprastha, according to the *Mahabharata.* There it is written that the cosmic architect Maya designed and built for them a splendid palace surrounded by "many gardens, many pools adorned with swans, karandavas and chakravakas." The flocks of migratory birds of diverse kinds that clustered the nearby pond of the national zoo reminded us of those mythological avians and I thought that beneath our feet is perhaps still hidden the "precious and miraculous jewels" that Maya had brought to the new city from Bindusara, the "original source lake" north of Mount Kailash in the occult land of Shambhala.

Does Delhi still stand guard over the *vajra*, the diamond thunderbolt of Indra forged by Tvastir the divine blacksmith? Some traditions report that the *vajra* was made with the bones of rishi Dadhichi and the dust of innumerable sages and kings indeed lies beneath India's often dead and reborn capital city.

Further Readings

For further readings, either of books that have inspired and guided me in my "discovery of India" or about topics broached in this book, the reader may wish to see, among many relevant titles published before or after the time of our travels in India, Surendranath Dasgupta's *A History of Indian Philosophy (5 vols., 1922-1955), The Rig Veda and the History of India* (2001) and other books by David Frawley, Ananda Coomaraswamy's *Hinduism and Buddhism* (1943), A.L. Basham's *The Wonder that was India* (1967), *India's Contribution to World Thought and Culture* published by Vivekananda Kendra (2003) under the direction of K.A. Nilankanta Shastri, *Sindhu-Saraswati Civilization: New Perspectives* edited by Nalini Rao (2014), *Pride of India* published by Samskriti Bharati – Bharatiya Bouddhik Sampada (2006), *The India They Saw* by Sandhya Jain, editor (2011), *Travel Diary of a Philosopher* (1919) by Hermann Keyserling, *Lives of Indian Princes* by Charles Allen and Sharada Dwivedi (1984), *Maharanis* by Lucy Moore (2004), *The Shadow of the Great Game* (2005) by Narendra Singh Sarila, *Red Shambhala* (2011) by Andrei Znamenski, *KA* by Roberto Calasso and Tim Parks (1999), *Celebrating Delhi* edited by Mala Dayal (2010), and, for those who read French, the *Dictionnaire des litteratures de l'Inde* (2001) by Pierre-Sylvain Filliozat.

About the Author

Côme Carpentier de Gourdon, born in the Canary Islands (Spain) of French parents, studied in Europe, India and the USA and has lived, traveled and taught in more than 50 countries on four continents (including several universities and academic institutions in France, India, the USA, Switzerland, Brasil, the UK, Peru, Russia, Italy, China, Belgium, Kazakhstan, Lebanon and Greece). He is since 2002 the convener of the Editorial Advisory Board of *World Affairs, the Journal of International Issues* (New Delhi, India), and a member of advisory boards of various scholarly publications.

He has authored more than 80 published papers and monographs in English, French, Spanish and Italian, and has contributed to various collective volumes on history, philosophy, ex-politics and international relations; his previous book is entitled *From India to Infinity* (2012).

He currently lives between India and Europe.

www.comecarpentier.com